Replacing France

REPLACING FRANCE

THE ORIGINS OF AMERICAN INTERVENTION IN VIETNAM

KATHRYN C. STATLER

THE UNIVERSITY PRESS OF KENTUCKY

Publication of this volume was made possible in part by
a grant from the National Endowment for the Humanities.

The University Press of Kentucky
Scholarly publisher for the Commonwealth, serving Bellarmine University, Berea
College, Centre College of Kentucky, Eastern Kentucky University, The Filson
Historical Society, Georgetown College, Kentucky Historical Society, Kentucky
State University, Morehead State University, Murray State University, Northern
Kentucky University, Transylvania University, University of Kentucky, University of
Louisville, and Western Kentucky University.

Editorial and Sales Offices: The University Press of Kentucky
663 South Limestone Street, Lexington, Kentucky 40508-4008
www.kentuckypress.com

Portions of this book were published in earlier form as articles in *The Cold War after
Stalin's Death: A Missed Opportunity for Peace?* © 2006 by Rowman & Littlefield
Publishers, Inc., and reproduced here by permission of Rowman & Littlefield
Publishers, Inc.; *Journal of American-East Asian Relations* (Special Issue, summer-fall
1997) © 1997, and reproduced here by permission of Imprint Publications; *The First
Vietnam War: Colonial Conflict and Cold War Crisis* © 2007 by Harvard University Press,
and reproduced here by permission of Harvard University Press; and *The Eisenhower
Administration, the Third World, and the Globalization of the Cold War, 1953–1961* © 2006
by Rowman & Littlefield Publishers, Inc., and reproduced here by permission of Rowman
& Littlefield Publishers, Inc.

Map by Dick Gilbreath, University of Kentucky Cartography Lab
Cataloging-in-Publication Data is available from
the Library of Congress.

ISBN 978-0-8131-9330-4 (pbk: acid-free paper)

This book is printed on acid-free recycled paper meeting
the requirements of the American National Standard
for Permanence in Paper for Printed Library Materials.

Manufactured in the United States of America.

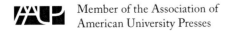

Member of the Association of
American University Presses

Seven years of war were required for our "enemies" to chase us out of North Vietnam. One and a half years of "solidarity" with our allies were sufficient for them to chase us out of South Vietnam.

—*Maurice Duverger,* Le Monde, *March 21, 1956*

CONTENTS

Acknowledgments

A number of individuals and institutions have my enduring gratitude for their help in producing this work. Many thanks to the University Press of Kentucky, and a special *merci* to Stephen Wrinn and the Editorial Board for agreeing to publish the book, to Liz Smith for her skilled copy editing, and to Anne Dean Watkins for her prompt assistance in all matters. Isabelle Nathan and the staff at the French Foreign Ministry Archives were always gracious and informative during my many trips to Paris, as were the archivists and personnel at the Dwight D. Eisenhower Presidential Library, the College Park National Archives, the Washington D.C. National Security Archive, the National Archives in Paris, the Château de Vincennes French Military Archives, the Pierre Mendès France Institute, the Center for Twentieth-Century European History, the French Overseas Archives in Aix-en-Provence, and the British Public Record Office. Anthony Edmonds, Maarten Pereboom, Michael Adamson, David Anderson, George Herring, Walter Hixson, James Matray, Mark Lawrence, Pierre Journoud, Laurent Cesari, Jason Parker, Nigel Quinney, and David Schmitz provided excellent feedback of the work-in-progress at conferences and in more informal venues. The manuscript has also benefited enormously from the constructive suggestions of its two anonymous readers. Former professors and advisers at the University of California, Santa Barbara (UCSB)—Fredrik Logevall, Kenneth Mouré, Laura Kalman, and Jeffrey Russell—gave invaluable advice over the years and have influenced this book in many ways. Particular recognition goes to my graduate adviser—Fredrik Logevall—who was the first to bring my attention to the importance of telling the story from as many vantage points as possible and continues to support me in presenting and publishing my work. I would also like to thank three former fellow graduate students and current colleagues—Andrew Johns, Kimber Quinney, and Kenneth Osgood—who have encouraged and prodded me every step of the way in my academic career. Each of you has had a profound influence on my research, writing, and way of thinking. Moreover, graduate school, trips to Abilene, and SHAFR conferences would have been a lot less fun without you. I am also incredibly grateful for the support of my colleagues in the History Department at the University of San Diego (USD). I could not ask for a more collegial environment, and special thanks go to Iris Engstrand, James Gump, Molly McClain, Yi Sun, Michael Gonzalez, and Colin Fisher. Assistance from USD has taken many forms, and I consider myself fortunate to work at an institution that invests in its faculty.

Research abroad is time-consuming and expensive. I am therefore most appreciative of the financial support provided by a number of institutions and grant programs. Funds for earlier research were provided by the Institute on Global Conflict and Cooperation fellowship program, the University of California Center for German and European Studies, the UCSB Social Sciences and History Department research grant programs, and the USD interdisciplinary research grant program. Help from USD via History Department travel money, a university professor fellowship, and a lengthy sabbatical, as well as a National Endowment for the Humanities summer stipend, allowed me to finish research and writing in France. All translations in the book are my own, as are any errors committed.

Finally, I could not have completed this study without the love, support, patience, and good humor of my family. Therefore, my greatest thanks go to my parents and sister, Joan, John, and Gretchen Statler, and to my husband and daughter, Craig and Claire Choisser. This book is dedicated to them. Mom and Dad, your constant encouragement and enthusiasm—not to mention long hours of babysitting—are priceless; and Gretchen, your sympathetic ear is deeply appreciated. Claire, as a two-year-old, you are not conducive to long hours of work, but you sure are fun. Craig, you are my most honest critic and strongest supporter, making me a better academic, and a better person. So, family, thank you for allowing me the many hours I spent attached to the keyboard; but most of all, thank you for the time away from the keyboard.

ABBREVIATIONS

AFV	American Friends of Vietnam
ARVN	Army of the Republic of Vietnam
AVA	American-Vietnamese Association
CIA	Central Intelligence Agency
CIP	Commercial Import Program
DOD	Department of Defense
DOS	Department of State
DRV	Democratic Republic of Vietnam
ECA	Economic Cooperation Administration
EDC	European Defense Community
EFEO	French School for the Far East (Ecole Française d'Extrême-Orient)
EMS	French Military Officer Training School (Ecole Militaire Supérieur Vietnamienne)
ENA	French National School of Administration (Ecole Nationale d'Administration)
FEC	French Expeditionary Corps
FOA	Foreign Operations Administration
ICA	International Cooperation Administration
ICC	International Control Commission
IRC	International Rescue Committee
JCS	Joint Chiefs of Staff
MAAG	Military Assistance and Advisory Group
MDAP	Mutual Defense Assistance Program
MSA	Mutual Security Agency
MSUG	Michigan State University Group
NATO	North Atlantic Treaty Organization
NIA	National Institute of Administration
NLF	National Front for the Liberation of South Vietnam
NSC	National Security Council
OCB	Operations Coordinating Board
PPS	Policy Planning Staff
PRC	People's Republic of China

SEATO	Southeast Asia Treaty Organization
STEM	Special Mission for Technical and Economic Aid
TERM	Temporary Equipment Recovery Mission
TRIM	Training Relations Instruction Mission
UN	United Nations
USIA	United States Information Agency
USIS	United States Information Service
USOM	United States Operations Mission
VNA	Vietnamese National Army
VOA	Voice of America

REPLACING
FRANCE

Southeast Asia after Geneva

RÉPUBLIQUE POPULAIRE DE CHINE
(PEOPLE'S REPUBLIC OF CHINA)

NORD
(NORTH)
Tonkin

Diên-Biên-Phu

Haiphong

Hanoï

Golfe du Tonkin
(Gulf of Tonkin)

BIRMANIE
(BURMA)

VIÊTNAM
(VIETNAM)

LAOS

Vientiane

Vinh

Mer de Chine
(South China Sea)

17°N

Hué
(Hue)

Tourane
(Da Nang)

Annam

THAÏLANDE
(THAILAND)

Rangoon

SUD
(SOUTH)

Nha Trang

Bangkok

Angkor

CAMBODGE
(CAMBODIA)

VIÊTNAM
(VIETNAM)

Phnom Penh

Saïgon

Golfe de Siam
(Gulf of Thailand)

Cochinchine
(Cochin China)

〜〜〜 Limit of French Indochina

〜〜〜 New borders resulting from
the Geneva Conference

0   50   100

miles

INTRODUCTION

The Franco-American Alliance and Vietnam

THE STORY OF AMERICAN INTERVENTION in Vietnam begins with an alliance—the sometimes ambivalent, often contentious, and almost always misunderstood Franco-American alliance. Paris and Washington clashed repeatedly over how to respond to the dual threat of communism and nationalism in Vietnam when the forces of the Cold War and decolonization collided there during the 1950s. When a colonial power leaves a former colony, the new state usually grapples with growing pains on its own. In this case, the South Vietnamese were never given the chance as the Dwight D. Eisenhower administration systematically replaced French control in South Vietnam with American influence. Why and how the United States did so are the core questions of this book.

In answering these questions, a transnational perspective is critical.[1] Throughout the 1950s, a significant cast of characters—including Paris, Washington, London, Saigon, Hanoi, Moscow, and Beijing—had a major impact on the denouement of events in Indochina.[2] There is a world of difference between the 1950s, when the United States played the role of puppet just as often as that of puppeteer, and the 1960s, when U.S. policy was the most important of any country's in determining the course of American intervention in Vietnam.[3] In the earlier decade, a host of great and small powers vied to pull the strings; but by the end of Eisenhower's presidency there was only one puppet master.

The story contained within these pages, featuring the Franco-American alliance as the main character, explains how—much to the consternation of the French—the United States emerged as that puppet master. The primary focus, therefore, rests on intra-alliance politics, among those who claimed to be on the same side. Decision making at the highest levels in Paris and Washington, and how these decisions played out domestically and abroad, receive the lion's share of attention.[4] Particular emphasis is placed on Franco-

American unwillingness to work together against the communist threat in Vietnam. Saigon and London had major supporting roles, as they, too, often made a united policy against their adversaries in Moscow, Beijing, and Hanoi more difficult. The Soviets, Chinese, and North Vietnamese occupy more minor, but critical, parts in the story. Ultimately, the decision to replace France came from American officials' certainty that their methods to create a viable noncommunist South Vietnamese nation had the best chance of success.

Momentous steps such as the Gulf of Tonkin Resolution, Operation Rolling Thunder, and the commitment of ground troops dramatically increased the U.S. presence in Vietnam in the 1960s; however, this book is concerned with the evolving process of American involvement—the groundwork, so to speak—that began in the 1950s. Long before decisions made in the 1960s led to the Americanization of the war in Vietnam, an entire bureaucracy was set in motion on the political, military, economic, and cultural levels that paved the way for the Americanization of Vietnam itself. The mechanism that activated this machinery and sustained it, at least until the end of the Eisenhower administration, was the Franco-American alliance. In short, Franco-American discord ensured the decline of French influence and the rise of American power in South Vietnam. For this reason, American intervention in Vietnam can be understood only within the context of the French exit from Vietnam, an exit abetted by the United States.

Even though they faced the same threat, American and French leaders proved incapable of agreeing on a common policy to stop the communists in Vietnam. The question is, Why? What explains the mutual suspicion and animosity between Paris and Washington in the 1950s and the regular flareups ever since? After all, although they differ in terms of power and tactics, France and the United States are still allies, who should, in theory, collaborate. And yet this alliance breaks down with alarming frequency. When members of an alliance fail to cooperate, as in Vietnam, the potential fallout can be serious, as each player pursues an independent, contradictory, and sometimes directionless policy. A more recent example occurred in 2003, when French and American leaders, as well as their publics, preferred to savage each other in the diplomatic arena and press instead of hammering out their differences to forge a common strategy toward Iraq. Americans expressed bafflement and anger over French president Jacques Chirac's contention that the "use of force [was] not a solution" to the Iraqi conundrum and his determination to veto a war resolution in the Security Council.[5] In turn, the French could not understand why the George W. Bush administration was unwilling to give diplomacy, economic sanctions, and international pressure more time to work. Although both countries sought to neutralize Iraqi president Saddam Hussein, Franco-American disagreements on how to do so sabotaged a united policy toward Iraq.

What many Americans—and many French, for that matter—fail to grasp is that both nations have long-held convictions that they represent the future of western civilization, that they always know best and that this gives them the right to pursue a unilateral foreign policy, and that coercive tactics can be applied in convincing smaller nations to comply with their interests. The unease that leaders and citizens from both countries felt about one another in the 1950s was not a historical aberration, as was demonstrated in 2003, when the Western alliance once more failed to deliver on its promise of cooperation. Not only did Paris and Washington fall short of finding a common resolution to the situation in Iraq, but they also began to view each other as adversaries instead of allies.

In the period leading up to the 2003 invasion of Iraq, many American officials described the Franco-American relationship as "difficult," "annoying," or "useless" and France itself as part of the "Axis of Weasels."[6] And these were the polite terms. According to one Gallup poll, only 28 percent of the American public viewed France as an ally, and many went so far as to proclaim France the enemy. Such views were not new. As French leaders struggled to resolve the First Indochina War, Eisenhower referred to the French as "hysterical" in their desire to keep their great power status and remain equal to the United States. And when it became clear that French prime minister Pierre Mendès France would settle the war at the negotiating table rather than on the battlefield, Secretary of State John Foster Dulles announced that the United States would have to either "beat the French into line" or "split" with France.[7] Publicly and privately, American officials frequently expressed reservations about the value of their alliance with France. Just as often, their French counterparts voiced similar concerns about working with the Americans.

The Indochina conflict exacerbated problems within the Western alliance, and, in turn, French and American policy makers aggravated the situation in Indochina. Officials in Paris and Washington failed to understand their counterparts' motivations, domestic political situations, goals, and perceptions. Conflict is often the result not of incompatible goals, but of misperceptions on the part of policy makers. Generally, misperception has been an issue for adversarial relationships. In this case, intra-alliance misperceptions increased tensions within the Western alliance.[8]

American views of France as an unreliable and weak ally led the Eisenhower administration to reject the lessons that the French experience in Indochina had to offer. Instead, U.S. officials made unilateral decisions, first replacing the French political, military, economic, and cultural presence in Vietnam with an American one and then escalating the conflict despite repeated warnings by French leaders that escalation would not lead to victory. Rather than appreciating French goals and interests, American leaders perceived the French as dupes of communist political warfare that raised false hopes for a relaxation of tensions and sowed dissension in the Western alliance. For the French, keeping an open dialogue—even with the enemy—was an essential component of diplomacy. But the Eisenhower administration saw French eagerness to negotiate an end to the First Indochina War as a betrayal of the Western alliance.

Part of the problem was that the two countries carried out diplomacy in very different ways. There is a strong tendency in U.S. foreign policy to view diplomacy as a zero-sum game rather than a legitimate means for nations to discuss issues in the hope of achieving positive outcomes for all. In addition, differing attitudes toward negotiating on the part of the French and the Americans frequently led the two allies to work against each other. For instance, the Eisenhower administration was inclined to view a negotiated settlement to the Indochina conflict as a form of appeasement, weakness, and defeat. French officials took the more flexible and pragmatic approach, stemming from their experience in Vietnam, that a diplomatic, rather than military, solution was required.[9]

Leaders in Paris and Washington also differed in their understandings of the postwar world, the future of colonialism, and the role each country would play in the international arena. French officials and the population as a whole continued to express deep gratitude for American efforts to liberate France during World War II and American generosity in rebuilding western Europe, but the superior attitude of U.S. officials that they possessed all the answers to Cold War problems had grown tiresome. The French saw their ally as well intentioned but naive, uneducated in world affairs, and overzealous in its anticommunist crusade and attempts to impose an American brand of democracy on the rest of the world. On the other side of the Atlantic, the Americans were flushed with success over halting communist advances in Europe but remained wary of the strong leftist presence in successive French governments. They were also disgusted with French attempts to hold on to their colonial empire. American leaders viewed the French as smart and sophisticated but equally egotistical, corrupt, and defeatist. These differences in worldviews help explain the fundamental ideological and political divisions between Paris and Washington and why they often failed to present a united front to their common enemies.

Compounding the problem was the rapidly evolving international situation. The French handover of power in Vietnam coincided with the emergence of the United States as one of the two major superpowers that would dominate the second half of the twentieth century. Financially and morally bankrupt colonial powers were out. Liberal capitalism and Eastern communism (depending on one's geographic location) were in. Replacing France in Indochina was one way for the United States to score against both communism and colonialism. Early on, French officials had recognized the possibility that the United States could take control in South Vietnam. As Richard Kuisel has noted, "the most distinctive feature of French attitudes during the early 1950s was uneasiness about American domination. More than other Europeans, the French harbored misgivings about American political, economic, and cultural ambitions . . . and at the same time welcomed the Western Alliance and U.S. aid." In the foreground were the "disappointments and quarrels" among the allies and the "intermittent explosions" of resentment over decolonization. In the background were dependence on "Yankee superpower" and the fear of war raised by the Cold War and American anticommunism.[10] These concerns would only grow stronger as Franco-American negotiations over the fate of Vietnam intensified, causing the two allies to spend more time trying to modify each other's behavior than finding a solution to the "Indochina problem."

The story commences in 1950, the year that saw the first steps toward significant American involvement in what until then had been an essentially colonial war. In 1950, the United States made a small political and monetary investment in Indochina by recognizing the French-backed State of Vietnam in southern Vietnam, granting an initial financial outlay of $15 million to the French war effort against Ho Chi Minh's Democratic Republic of Vietnam (DRV) in the North, and sending a few economic advisers to help distribute American aid. Over the succeeding decade, this modest venture grew into a nation-building operation comprising thousands of Americans, billions of dollars, and a dangerous amount of American prestige. The American presence eventually pervaded every aspect of South Vietnamese life.[11]

Central to the story is the 1954 Geneva Conference, which represented both an end to the French military fight and a beginning to the American commitment to Vietnam. The accords reached at the conference brought to a close the 1946–1954 Franco-Vietminh War that had pitted France against its former colony and temporarily divided Vietnam at the seventeenth parallel. The communist DRV assumed power in the North and the noncommunist forces retained control in the South, with the stipulation that elections to re-unify the country be held within two years. The diplomatic resolution of the First Indochina War also marked an end to American aid for the French war effort, but in the months following the conference the Eisenhower adminis-tration quickly sought to build a viable South Vietnamese state that would present a political challenge to Ho Chi Minh's government in the North. Thus, whereas the Geneva Conference should have guaranteed the end of hostilities, instead it left a door ajar for future American involvement.

Various American officials had claimed they had no desire to become "more involved" or "take France's place" in Vietnam as far back as 1950, the year the Franco-American partnership began. But American agencies in Vietnam and aid to the French war effort proliferated from 1950 to 1954, with the result that the United States insisted on an ever-increasing voice in French decision making vis-à-vis Indochina. At Geneva, differing American and French priorities sabotaged allied unity and ultimately the conference itself. After Geneva, American reassurances that the Americans had no in-tention of "replacing" the French rang hollow in the face of blatant American intervention in South Vietnam. By the end of Eisenhower's second term as president, France had been eclipsed by a United States determined to pre-serve a noncommunist South Vietnam at nearly any cost.

Scholars who have studied the origins of American involvement in Viet-nam typically focus on how the Cold War's escalation resulted in the com-munist and anticommunist blocs squaring off in Indochina.[12] The "loss" of China to the communists in 1949, the outbreak of the Korean War in 1950, and the fear that Indochina would be the next domino to fall always figure prominently in histories of early American intervention in Vietnam, as they should. The East-West conflict did indeed play out on the battlefield during the eight-year conflict. The United States and Britain supported the French war effort while the Soviet Union and People's Republic of China furnished Ho Chi Minh's Vietminh forces with aid and military supplies.

But what about the process of French decolonization? North-South ten-sions also drove the war as the Vietnamese struggled to break free of French imperialism and establish an independent nation, and as the Americans reluctantly supported a colonial ally. This study, rather than viewing decolonization as a minor player in the drama of the Cold War, places it on an equal footing. The Indochinese states of Vietnam, Cambodia, and Laos were among the last areas in South and Southeast Asia to decolonize: the Philippines, Burma, and Indonesia beat them to it. American officials were exceedingly uncomfortable with this situation, and constantly pressured their French counterparts to grant independence to Indochina. The Cold War explains why the United States intervened, but the process of French decolonization explains why this intervention increased and led to a breakdown in western unity. American officials sneered at the French failure to stand up to the communists and keep the French colony and "civilizing mission" intact. Yet they too would attempt to create an artificial edifice in Vietnam, and they too would fail.

Seemingly inexhaustible sources exist on both the French experience during the First Indochina War and the American experience in the 1964–1975 Second Indochina War. But no systematic study exists of the interwar period and the transition from the French to the Americans. The Franco-American relationship with respect to Vietnam has not gone unnoticed. Indeed, a number of historians and former government officials have mentioned that the relationship was central to understanding American intervention. However, they generally focus on 1950, when the United States made its first significant contributions to the French war effort, or on 1954 and the events leading up to the Geneva Conference, specifically the battle of Dien Bien Phu.[13] Those who do explore the post-Geneva period usually refer to it as "a truce between two wars," make passing reference to France's "displacement," or claim that the United States "assumed" responsibility from the French.[14] In the literature, at least, the United States magically became the dominant western player in Vietnam shortly after the Geneva Conference. This book seeks to modify such interpretations by detailing the deliberate American process of replacing France that began after Geneva and was completed by 1961. True, a military cease-fire was achieved at the 1954 Geneva Conference, but all the parties involved continued to wage political, diplomatic, economic, psychological, and cultural warfare in Vietnam and on the world stage. The transition from French to American control of South Vietnam occurred during a time of "war by other means."[15]

Of these means, cultural factors proved the largest thorn in the side of western solidarity. The United States and France both disseminated abroad a sense of cultural purpose that emphasized each nation's belief in its role as a preeminent force in world history, and both sought to use culture as an instrument of state policy in Vietnam. The Americans, in contrast to the French, had been relative latecomers to cultural diplomacy. The United States did not have a Department of Culture as France did, and although a Division of Cultural Relations was established in 1938, American officials failed to see the immediate value of expositions of art, music, and literature as a means of promoting their policies in foreign countries. But over time, the Eisenhower administration rallied to the idea of an aggressive cultural foreign policy in Vietnam, as the French had earlier.[16]

Were the Americans cultural imperialists in Vietnam? To a certain extent, yes. As with the French, eagerness to promote what they saw as their cultural superiority and exceptional way of life led the Americans to engage, not in cultural transfer or transmission, but in a type of imperialism. American influence was more informal but nonetheless imperialistic, if we follow the interpretation established by William Appleman Williams that the United States, as an advanced industrial nation, was attempting to play a controlling and one-sided role in the development of a weaker economy. The Eisenhower administration tried to impose American-style democracy, capitalism, ideology, values, and customs on the South Vietnamese population in a way that was far too systematic to be labeled merely cultural transfer or transmission. At the very least, this imposition of cultural values to achieve foreign policy goals could be considered cultural propaganda. Eisenhower officials would have said they were simply trying to export American exceptionalism abroad, but the French and Vietnamese took a different view. Undoubtedly, the resistance of the French to American cultural forays in Vietnam resulted from their self-image as a culturally unique people and their own colonial experience as cultural imperialists.[17] Given their recent escape from French cultural control, the South Vietnamese were reluctant to embrace American culture.

This clash among cultures was personified in South Vietnamese premier Ngo Dinh Diem, whose career straddled the transition from French to American involvement in Vietnam. To administration officials, Diem appeared westernized, in part because of his Catholicism, and he seemed to be a man with whom business could be done. In addition, his anticommunist and anticolonial credentials appealed to U.S. leaders. Diem's South Vietnam was thus the product of an American rather than a French missionary impulse.

Although American actions in South Vietnam cannot be compared to the first phase of French colonialism in the late nineteenth century, when the French engaged in a brutal and bloody conquest of Indochina, a number of similarities exist between the second phase of French colonialism and post-Geneva American nation-building.[18] Although French colonialism and American neocolonialism differed markedly in some respects—the American version was indirect, informal, and incomplete—both versions rested on similar perceptions of Indochina as a place to be constructed on a western model. Paris planned to export its belief in the universal value of its civilization, as did Washington. The French called their economic, moral, and cultural policies in Indochina *mise en valeur*, or "development," whereas the Americans preferred the term *modernization*.[19] In the aftermath of Geneva, the United States tried to project the image that it was engaged in a moral mission based on generosity and protection, just as France had prior to Geneva. And both the French and the Americans employed subtle tools of empire, including cultural and language institutions, exhibits, propaganda, military and economic assistance, and political pressure in order to spread their western values.

American officials often appeared to run from the label of colonizer. The United States had freed the Philippines in 1946—the same year the French had started the war against the Vietminh to maintain their colonial empire—and Hawaii and Alaska eventually became states under the Eisenhower administration to avoid their being perceived as colonies. But in Vietnam there was a dissonance between what the United States would have said it was trying to do and what it was actually doing.[20] The skeptical reader might disagree with the picture of the United States as a neocolonial power in Vietnam, but as the succeeding chapters will demonstrate, it is difficult to find a better term for American actions.

The book is divided into three sections that mirror the three phases of transition from the French to the Americans. Part 1 traces the inception of the Franco-American partnership in Vietnam and the ensuing search for allied unity. The first three chapters examine the actions of France as the main western player in Indochina and how American support of the French war effort became increasingly paramount from 1950 to 1954. The Eisenhower administration wanted to prevent the emergence of a communist Vietnam, but at the same time it agonized over its decision to support a colonial ally, fearing that other developing countries would view the United States as an abettor of colonialism. The French agenda was much more straightforward

—Paris intended to ensure U.S. military and economic aid and achieve a united western policy against the DRV. Despite repeated Franco-American claims of pursuing a "common strategy" toward Indochina, all attempts at coordinated diplomacy failed, with the result that French and American representatives arrived at the Geneva Conference with conflicting agendas. The Geneva Conference resolved the First Indochina War between the French and Vietminh, but it contributed to American fears that Moscow, Beijing, and Hanoi planned to conquer the world through diplomacy rather than by force, ensuring that the Eisenhower administration would take steps to prevent any further losses to communism south of the seventeenth parallel. Part 1 thus provides a historical understanding of Franco-American disagreements about Cold War strategies, the process of decolonization, and the nature of the Western alliance that were fundamental to the future of U.S. intervention in Vietnam.

Part 2 examines how Paris sought to keep Vietnam French while Washington insisted on making it American. Accordingly, chapters 4, 5, and 6 emphasize the Franco-American battle for control in Vietnam. American leaders openly doubted the French ability to sustain an independent, noncommunist South Vietnam after the Geneva Conference, and although Vietnam had become a back-burner issue for the White House this did not mean the American presence in South Vietnam stagnated. Quite the opposite. Franco-American relations underwent a major shift as the United States and Ngo Dinh Diem took the lead in South Vietnam, thwarting the scheduled 1956 Vietnamese elections and reducing the French political, military, and economic presence in an attempt to eliminate all vestiges of French colonialism. Because of Washington and Saigon's actions, Paris disengaged from its responsibilities to the 1954 Geneva Accords, leaving the United States to take unofficial control of the situation in South Vietnam. As the number of American agencies in South Vietnam increased, American influence there became more prominent. The Eisenhower administration's primary goal in South Vietnam was to strengthen Asian defense against the communist threat by supporting Diem's government. But with each additional function American agencies assumed, U.S. involvement deepened, ultimately reaching a point where disengagement would have meant a perceived American defeat to the communist bloc.

Part 3 highlights the cultural, economic, and propaganda initiatives used by France, South Vietnam, North Vietnam, and the United States from 1956 to 1961, exploring how all four nations sought to gain psychological ground through "soft power" tactics.[21] Rather than using or threatening military force, governments in Paris, Hanoi, Saigon, and Washington pointed to the strength of their values and culture to further their goals on the international stage and in Vietnam. Cultural diplomacy thus came to the fore once France had lost military, political, and economic control and was left with no option except to continue cultural initiatives in the hope of maintaining some influence in both North and South Vietnam. Ho Chi Minh and Diem used soft power tactics at home and abroad as well, attempting to depict their respective governments as the only legitimate one in Vietnam. And Washington sought to promote its political agenda in South Vietnam by replacing French culture with American. Increasing numbers of American personnel and American missions thus began to take over the "civilizing mission" previously performed by France: they moved into teaching positions at universities and secondary and primary schools; controlled training for Vietnamese administrators, military personnel, and ministers; replaced the French language with English; and disseminated American cultural propaganda throughout South Vietnam via newspapers, radio, expositions, movies, and mobile exhibits.

Ultimately, as Americans undertook these additional duties, they attempted to impose American values and culture on the Vietnamese population and to modernize and westernize South Vietnam. Washington had come to view the spreading of American values in Vietnam as a Cold War operational necessity. In replacing France, Eisenhower officials were convinced that they would construct a viable, self-governing, and economically stable South Vietnamese state that could defend itself militarily against North Vietnam. They thus engaged in a full-fledged nation-building effort in South Vietnam. But they did not create a nation there. Instead, their actions in the South prompted the North Vietnamese—who had never underestimated the danger American intervention posed to their plans for the reunification of Vietnam—to consolidate their power and to prepare for the coming fight over the South's future. To the extent that Americans aided in the forging of a nation, it was on the northern side of the seventeenth parallel.

PART 1

Neither Communism nor Colonialism, 1950–1954

There was always a Third Force to be found free from Communism and the taint of colonialism—national democracy . . . you only had to find a leader and keep him safe from the old colonial powers.

—*Alden Pyle, in Graham Greene's* The Quiet American

1

Decolonization
and Cold War

THE YEAR 1950 DENOTED not only the halfway mark of the Franco-Vietminh War but also a turning point in the French approach to winning the conflict. As the year began, the March 8, 1949, Elysée treaty, promising more independence to Vietnam, languished in the French National Assembly; the French military effort against the Vietminh remained stalled; and French officials bickered among themselves about whether or not to support Vietnamese emperor Bao Dai as a viable political alternative to Vietminh leader Ho Chi Minh. Up to this point, Paris had preferred to conduct the war without interference from its allies, but when Chinese leader Mao Zedong recognized Ho Chi Minh's government in January 1950, what had been a colonial battle suddenly became part of the globalized Cold War. Henceforth, French governments attempted to portray their engagement in Vietnam as a heroic anticommunist crusade instead of a colonial war fought to preserve the empire. By emphasizing the anticommunist nature of its war effort, Paris hoped to gain political and economic support from Washington and London. Following Mao's recognition of the Democratic Republic of Vietnam (DRV), the French National Assembly ratified the Elysée Accords, the United States guaranteed American economic aid to France's military effort, and Britain and the United States recognized Bao Dai's State of Vietnam.[1]

Washington's decisions to provide Paris with significant aid and to recognize Bao Dai's State of Vietnam represented the first important steps in the long transition from the French to the American presence in Vietnam. Such steps could not have occurred without the transformation of the Indochina conflict from a colonial to an anticommunist war. This chapter thus assesses how, from 1950 to 1953, French leaders convinced a skeptical Truman administration that Indochina was much more than an exploited colony maintained for reasons of French prestige and grandeur. Indeed, French officials cleverly portrayed Indochina as an integral outpost in the new frontier battles

15

of the Cold War. Moreover, Paris emphasized the difficulties it faced in prosecuting such a war while maintaining its contributions to European defense. These laborious efforts to change American perceptions of Indochina paid great dividends as Washington decided to commit American money, materials, political support, and personnel to the French war effort. But French efforts perhaps worked too well. As the Truman administration became convinced that Asian and European policies were inextricably linked, it began to provide economic and military aid, exactly as the French had hoped; but American officials also insisted on being involved in French decision making vis-à-vis Indochina. This insistence marked the beginning of the eventual transition from French to American influence of events in Vietnam.

Were the French sincere in painting their Indochinese war as a communist rather than colonial concern? Or, were they cynically emphasizing the communist element to acquire American aid? The answer, unsurprisingly, is a bit of both. Although the French played the communist card a little too often in their requests for materials and money in the fight against the Vietminh, they were certainly sincere in establishing a common defense policy with the Americans and British in Southeast Asia. Successive French governments worked diligently to convince their American and British partners that a coordinated defense organization in Asia would halt communist aggression, as the North Atlantic Treaty Organization (NATO) had secured western European defense. With the outbreak of the Korean War, the French successfully played on American fears of communist expansion, sparking the search for a united western policy against the communists in Indochina. Ultimately, the establishment of such a policy would prove elusive as Paris and Washington disagreed on the best way to guarantee a noncommunist Vietnam.

A COLONIAL WAR TRANSFORMED

The France that had resolutely clung to one of its few remaining indicators of world power status in 1946 appeared more willing to compromise on Vietnamese independence by 1950. Frustrated militarily, Paris commenced work on establishing a separate South Vietnamese state to oppose Ho Chi Minh's regime in the North. A series of agreements promising conditional Vietnamese independence had been signed in the late 1940s, culminating with the March 8, 1949, Elysée Agreement, signed by French president Vincent Auriol and Vietnamese emperor Bao Dai. The agreement recognized the unification of Tonkin, Annam, and Cochinchina into the State of Vietnam, and the new state was given associate status within the French Union and a certain degree of autonomy under Bao Dai's leadership.[2] But the accords, which pleased neither Right nor Left in the French National Assembly, did not provide for total independence; Bao Dai's government had authority over local affairs, but the French retained control over national defense and foreign affairs. Still, the French hoped the agreement would satisfy American calls for greater Vietnamese independence and thus lead to military and economic assistance from the United States.

A critic of French colonialism since World War II, the Truman administration provided little aid to the French war effort in Indochina during 1948 and 1949. U.S. officials advised French ambassador to the United States Henri Bonnet that the communist element in the Vietminh "would not suffice" to secure American assistance to France and remained skeptical of what had become known as "the Bao Dai solution." Secretary of State Dean Acheson thought it would be unwise to commit to Bao Dai unless Paris granted more concessions toward Vietnamese independence, and even suggested sending a formal letter to the French foreign minister criticizing the Elysée Accords for not moving fast enough in this direction. U.S. ambassador to France David Bruce persuaded Acheson that such an action would be counterproductive.[3] Infighting among the Office of Western European Affairs, the Bureau of Far Eastern Affairs, and the Office of Philippine and Southeast Asian Affairs also complicated American policy toward Indochina. It was not until the occurrence of a series of international events that increased the geopolitical importance of Indochina that the Truman administration began to change its views.

The Chinese communists' victory in 1949 and the Soviet explosion of an atomic bomb the same year led the Truman administration to consider increasing its support of the Bao Dai government. Sensing an opportunity, Paris capitalized on communist successes by renewing its plea for increased American aid to Indochina. As early as May 1949, many French military officials described the war in Indochina as an anticommunist effort and insisted that Bao Dai's establishment of a base there would stop the communist advance.[4] The British also encouraged an American commitment to Southeast Asia since they feared that if Vietnam fell, areas under British influence—such as Siam, Burma, and Malaya—would be next.

The Americans listened to French and British concerns but hesitated to become involved in what they still considered to be an essentially colonial war. On July 1, 1949, National Security Council (NSC) 51 recommended greater cooperation with the British to secure French guarantees for Indochinese independence. According to NSC 51, a successful solution to the Indochina problem—Vietnamese independence—would not only halt communism, but would also demonstrate that the West could create a partnership with indigenous nationalists. In addition, Southeast Asia would be preserved as a source of western and Japanese raw materials.[5] Still, by the end of 1949, Washington remained unsure about how to achieve greater Vietnamese independence.

The Truman administration was not the only indecisive player. Although Paris was determined to seek American support, it had a difficult time deciding how to proceed in Indochina. Officials in Paris and Saigon repeatedly failed to coordinate with each other, let alone with their American and British allies. French high commissioner to Indochina Leon Pignon attempted to bring some cohesiveness to French policy in Indochina, suggesting that France create a policy of *action commune*, or "common action," with the Americans and British in the Far East. After China recognized Ho Chi Minh's government, Pignon advocated that France "guarantee the borders of Indochina, recognize Bao Dai's government, and obtain material aid from the United States." Jean Letourneau, the French minister of overseas France, added that France should focus on moving forward as quickly as possible with Vietnamese independence. Both Pignon and Letourneau were concerned that Paris was immobilized by political infighting and would not be able to take concrete actions toward independence.[6] Their fears were soon justified as Paris hesitated between supporting Bao Dai and trying to reestablish contacts with Ho Chi Minh. New losses inflicted on the French forces by the Vietminh, and the French public's growing opposition to the war, perpetuated French difficulties in determining a course of action. After much internal debate, Paris decided to support Bao Dai rather than reconcile with Ho Chi Minh.[7]

On January 18, 1950, the People's Republic of China recognized the DRV. The Soviet Union followed suit two days later. The Chinese and Soviet recognition of Ho Chi Minh's government helped turn the war from a local anticommunist struggle into a focal point of the Cold War.[8] The French Assembly quickly ratified the stalled Elysée agreements, anticipating that the United States and Britain would recognize the Bao Dai government. As expected, London and Washington recognized the State of Vietnam within a week, and an American mission was installed in Saigon shortly thereafter. The signing of the Sino-Soviet Treaty of Friendship on February 14 further heightened the western sense of urgency and led to additional American political support for the French-backed Bao Dai.

Although the American commitment to Vietnam began with a political act—recognition of the Bao Dai government—the first material step would be economic aid to France. The Truman administration began working on the question of aid early in 1950. A problem paper, drafted by a team of representatives from the Office of Western European Affairs, the Office of Philippine and Southeast Asian Affairs, and the Mutual Defense Assistance Program (MDAP), addressed the issue of U.S. policy regarding Indochina.[9] The report weighed the difficulty of convincing Congress and the American public that the United States should support a colonial war against the possibility that the U.S. failure to assist the Bao Dai government might cause the French to work actively against American goals in Europe and abandon Vietnam and the rest of Indochina. The report concluded that aid was warranted on the basis that Indochina was important to U.S. security interests. By providing such aid, Washington hoped to gain significant leverage to compel Paris to grant independence to Bao Dai's regime, although Acheson recognized that the greatest American bargaining power vis-à-vis France existed before the United States agreed to provide aid.[10]

French officials were also busy thinking of ways to gain leverage against their Atlantic ally. When Henri Bonnet formally requested economic and military assistance from the United States on February 16, 1950, he framed the request within the context of French budgetary and Cold War concerns. French representative to the United Nations (UN) Jean Chauvel emphasized that France could not afford "to continue being drained through Indochina" if French economic recovery were ever to be achieved. Unless the United States and Britain agreed to share some of France's burden in Southeast Asia, France would be obliged "to liquidate its Indochina commitment."[11] The French Foreign Ministry, or Quai d'Orsay, also recognized the importance of portraying aid as a necessity in helping French leaders avoid having to make a difficult choice between Europe and Asia during a heightened Cold War. In particular, Bonnet reminded officials in Washington that France was on the only "hot" frontline in the Cold War. He recognized that American aid would bring "faster independence for the Associated States, new personnel, and implementation of the 8 March 1949 accords" while also drawing France "more closely into the Atlantic alliance with the United States." Bonnet recommended asking for more rather than less aid and suggested French officials present themselves as "partners, not as solicitors."[12] This French gambit was successful in convincing the State Department that aid was necessary. Thus, French demands for arms and money that had been denied in 1948 and 1949 were now approved by the Truman administration. On March 10,

Truman approved an initial grant of $15 million in military aid for Indochina out of MDAP funds.

At the heart of Franco-American deliberations over aid was the issue of Vietnamese independence. Once the United States began its financial investment in Indochina, it attempted to influence the conduct of the war and the uses of American aid.[13] Both the United States and Britain urged the French Foreign Ministry to wrest control of Indochinese affairs from the Ministry of Overseas France. According to London and Washington, this act would provide some perceived legitimacy to the fiction of Indochinese sovereignty. But Paris had its own concerns about sovereignty and sought assurances that American aid would not entail reducing the French "civilizing influence" in Indochina. Letourneau was particularly concerned about preserving French political and cultural control. In a warning to both the Americans and the British, he pronounced in April 1950 that unless French influence was preserved, France would "not allow other countries to participate in the defense of the region."[14]

Collective action in Southeast Asia appeared difficult to achieve in light of the opposing currents of the French fear of losing control and the Truman administration's insistence on complete Vietnamese independence.[15] The French believed that ratifying the 1949 Elysée Accords represented a large concession toward Vietnamese independence, but the Americans remained unconvinced. Paris suspected that insufficient, often unsatisfactory, and uniformly late American aid to Indochina was a tactic to pressure the French toward granting greater independence. Although the Pau Conference of 1950 guaranteed that Vietnam, Cambodia, Laos, and France would all have an equal voice in economic decisions, the three Indochinese states continued to insist on full independence. French concerns that the United States was encouraging this demand persisted. Although the Truman administration reiterated its support of the French war effort, an image of an anticolonial United States endured in the minds of the French.[16] President Franklin Roosevelt's calls for an international trusteeship of Indochina at the end of World War II and previous American hesitation in helping France had not been forgotten.

The issue of aid and how it was to be distributed continued to plague Franco-American relations. In March, an economic survey mission arrived in Saigon. The Griffin mission, as it came to be called, was designed to assess the need for economic and technical aid, to recommend aid programs designed to demonstrate the "genuine interest" of the United States in the people of Southeast Asia, and to help the governments there strengthen their economies and build "popular support." In a significant boon to the French, the mission recommended the first large-scale aid—$23.5 million—for the three Indochinese countries.[17] According to the Quai d'Orsay, the mission was badly informed about the political situation in Indochina, and its contacts with the Vietnamese aggravated French difficulties by giving hope to Vietnamese nationalists that they could rid themselves of French control. Quai officials insisted military aid flow to Paris, not the Bao Dai regime in Saigon, and worried that as they withdrew from internal Vietnamese affairs, the Americans would replace them.[18]

These concerns were confirmed when Bao Dai notified the French that the Americans had suggested giving aid directly to the Vietnamese.[19] A battle between the French and Vietnamese then occurred as to how aid would be dispersed, which only furthered French suspicions about U.S. intentions. The Vietnamese made the most of the situation, as evidenced by the effort of the defense minister, Phan Huy Quat, to direct American aid to the nascent national Vietnamese army, bypassing the French. Ultimately, the United States funneled aid through the French, primarily because Paris categorically refused to allow direct military aid to the Vietnamese and because the Bao Dai government had no military organization that could effectively use the equipment.

Although their suspicions of American intentions did not dissipate, French leaders nonetheless welcomed American help in Indochina. By playing on American fears of the loss of Southeast Asia to communism, as well as the possibility that France would have to withdraw from Indochina to maintain its commitments in Europe, Paris succeeded in obtaining American aid in its fight against the Vietminh. But aid was only the first step; French officials believed that a coordinated effort at the highest military and diplomatic levels was essential to guarantee Southeast Asian defense against communism in general and Vietnamese defense in particular. By creating a united front against communism, the primary French goal of defeating the Vietminh would be secured.

A Common Policy?

After achieving their first goal of securing American military and economic aid, the French began their quest for coordinated action in earnest. As of March 1950, Acheson and the State Department insisted that the Indochina problem was more a political than a military one, and that the problem could be resolved through guarantees of Vietnamese independence. Therefore, although the United States provided short-term aid, Washington had no intention of establishing a long-term strategic plan in Indochina. The limited aid that the United States supplied would be used to introduce a "psychological element" necessary to finding a political solution. British foreign minister Ernest Bevin supported the American position during a tripartite foreign ministers meeting in March, when he expressed concerns that the French were not working quickly enough toward independence, and both Washington and London remained reluctant to tie their policies to the French war effort.[20]

The French began their offensive for coordinated action in April. During meetings with Truman administration officials, Bonnet pointed out that the French effort in Indochina was part "of the greater battle against the communist bloc," and that it should be treated as such. He suggested that the Americans should do their part by "positioning additional American troops on the continent to offset French troops in Indochina." Bonnet thus effectively targeted American Cold War concerns by linking European and Indochina defense when submitting aid requests to the Truman administration. Recognizing that the top American priority was containment, the French hoped to hold continuous meetings among the *trois grands,* or "big three," on the world political situation, to keep the United States on the continent, and to develop a common policy in Southeast Asia. At this point, both the French and the Americans recognized the connection between Indochina and the continent, and both believed that Indochina was draining European defense.[21]

Paris continued to lobby for coordinated action, reiterating that there should be "complete agreement" among the three western powers and a common policy on Indochina and Southeast Asia.[22] The Quai d'Orsay also emphasized the need for American supplies to fortify the war effort, indicating that Paris still envisioned a military solution to the conflict rather than a political one, contrary to the Americans' recommendation.[23] The Joint Chiefs of Staff (JCS) thought the United States should provide more aid to Indochina because it might give a psychological boost to the war effort, but it rejected the French proposal for military talks to develop a common strategy. A compromise solution, encapsulated in a State Department report, which was adopted by the NSC and signed by the president in April, provided the initial formal guidance for future policy in Indochina. The report defined Indochina as a key area of Southeast Asia and recommended that "support on a limited basis" be provided to the French.[24]

The French saw this American action as a first step toward establishing a coordinated allied policy in Southeast Asia, but much work remained to be done. The French Defense Ministry believed that an inter-allied effort in Indochina that provided materials, armament, and financial and military support for the Vietnamese government needed to be implemented as quickly as possible. Defense officials worried about presenting the Americans and British with a precise and constructive plan to achieve a "common policy" guaranteed to safeguard shared strategic interests. They feared that Washington and London would continue to resist such a policy, leaving France to fight the war against the Vietminh without allied support.[25] French ambassador to Britain René Massigli shared such concerns, discerning two contradictory American policies. According to Massigli, on the one hand the Americans did not want to become engaged in "dangerous situations" outside Europe, but on the other hand they insisted on "giving their advice" and "engaging their European partners" in the Cold War.[26] Thus, whereas the United States refused to consider contributing to a system of collective defense in Indochina, France was expected to maintain and further its contribution to continental defense while simultaneously fighting the Vietminh. The Defense Ministry's and Massigli's assessments were correct, to a certain extent. The Truman administration had been reluctant to commit to areas outside Europe, but Truman and Acheson had become convinced of the importance of stopping communism at the southern border of China.[27]

Tripartite meetings in London in early May 1950 represented the first serious attempt on the part of the French to draw their allies into a coordinated effort in Asia, as the three western powers discussed the "Indochina problem." French foreign minister Robert Schuman noted that the worst predicament arising out of the conflict was France's inability to contribute to western defense in Europe until the war was resolved. Schuman promised that France would not abandon Indochina, but he also insisted that France could not continue its "double effort" without "revising" its policy in Europe. In addition, Schuman argued that France was defending not only its own interests but the "common interests of the western powers against communist infiltration."[28] The Americans and the British accepted French claims that France could not carry out both European defense and the war effort in Indochina, but London and Washington still insisted that a common policy would be possible only to the extent that the French agreed to guarantee Vietnamese independence. Acheson pressed these concerns throughout the tripartite meetings, pointing out that Bao Dai's regime in the South should be strengthened so that the western presence could be diminished. Schuman agreed that Vietnamese independence was important but emphasized that reestablishment of security was equally so. Already in 1950, the emphasis on security that would dominate both French and American policy in Vietnam was apparent, while political reform would remain a secondary consideration.

Acheson's primary concern at the tripartite meetings was to preserve western solidarity. It was within this context that Acheson privately informed Schuman that the United States would grant aid for use in Indochina until June 30, but after that date aid questions would go to Congress.[29] Although the United States was more committed to aiding the French in Indochina, the Truman administration drew the line at complete political support of French policy; both the British and the Americans refused Schuman's request for a joint declaration on the three western powers' resolve to stop communism in Indochina.[30]

From the French perspective, the May tripartite meeting gave a certain amount of satisfaction because of the general agreement to prioritize "reestablishing security" in Indochina. Promoting "sincere nationalism" was a lesser concern. American willingness to provide aid for both these goals, and the favorable response to this news by the American press, pleased French diplomats. But the meetings also underscored the lack of coordinated action among the big three, as U.S. leaders preferred to aid the three Indochinese states directly through the private sector rather than funneling aid through official French channels. Happily for the French, logistical difficulties in direct disbursement of aid and the increasingly tense international and U.S. domestic situations would ultimately weigh in France's favor.[31]

Throughout spring, American willingness to support the French effort against the communists grew. Internal changes in the United States undoubtedly led to a growing sense of alarm among American officials and the general public. The domestic sense of crisis—symbolized by Senator Joseph McCarthy's claims of communist spies and the replacement of George Kennan as director of the Policy Planning Staff by avid cold warrior Paul Nitze—had grown stronger. McCarthy's allegations of communist infiltration in the American government created apprehension in Washington that contributed to the Truman administration's decision to pursue a more vigorous anticommunist policy. Nitze's belief that the United States needed to "roll back" communism corresponded to the new climate more closely than Kennan's cautious approach to the communist bloc. American officials had also come to recognize the psychological dangers of a communist victory and allowed another $16 million to flow through MDAP, bringing the total aid to Indochina for 1950 to $31 million.[32] In a May 24 letter addressed to

Vietnam, Laos, Cambodia, and France, Truman declared his plan to put into place an economic aid program for the three Associated States to assist them in "refinding their stability and to further their peaceful and democratic development." Truman stated that such aid would "complement" the French effort and in no way implied "a substitution of French aid or France."[33]

Increased aid to the Associated States demonstrated American concern over communist advances, but the Indochina situation remained a secondary consideration for the Truman administration as it continued to focus on European affairs. In Paris, meanwhile, French officials strategized on how to acquire American guarantees to provide even greater aid for Indochina and to help the French in the event of a Chinese attack. These issues provoked vigorous debate in a National Defense Committee meeting as high-level French officials met to discuss options in Indochina. By the end of the talks, members of the committee had failed to find a means to achieve guaranteed American cooperation.[34] What the French could not know was that their war effort in Indochina was about to receive significant assistance from the Americans as a result of the outbreak of war on the Korean peninsula.

THE KOREAN CONNECTION

In June 1950, the French war effort became an anticommunist crusade for the Americans. A number of Cold War concerns led to this decision, but perhaps the greatest single influence in convincing the United States that the French were fighting not a colonial war but one against communism was the outbreak of hostilities in Korea. When North Korea crossed the thirty-eighth parallel and attacked South Korea on June 25, 1950, the Truman doctrine's condemnation of "subjugation by armed minorities and outside pressures" and commitment to containing such subjugation would now be applied to Asia.[35] North Korea's invasion of the South convinced many American officials that the Kremlin had orchestrated the maneuver to deflect alliance concentration from western Europe as a prologue to a Soviet attack in that region. The Korean War blurred previous distinctions between vital and peripheral interests, leading the Truman administration to view communism as an integrated and cohesive worldwide movement striving to undermine western capitalist society. Such views created the basis for a vastly accelerated rearmament program after 1950.

Not only had Europe and Asia become interconnected, but a link had been established between Korea and other Southeast Asian problems—for example, Indochina. According to French-born U.S. journalist Bernard Fall, one of the most perceptive observers of Indochina at the time, the outbreak of hostilities in Korea simplified American Far Eastern policy. Once more the situation allowed for a clear-cut division between good and bad—this time not between the Axis and Allied powers, but between communists and noncommunists. The Korean War galvanized support for the anticommunist crusade in Vietnam and accelerated American aid to the French. On June 27, 1950, Truman announced that more military assistance would be provided for Vietnam and that a military mission would be sent to provide close working relations with the French. A few days later, the first direct American military assistance arrived in Vietnam in the form of eight C-47 cargo planes. The Korean War thus brought the Truman declaration of "full support for all Asian regimes fighting communism" to the Associated States.[36]

Korea would change the Truman administration's European and Asian policies. European rearmament replaced economic recovery as the first U.S. priority, and Anglo-American planners called with increasing firmness for a German contribution to this military expansion. Although American officials did not believe a communist attack on Europe was imminent, they did read Soviet support of North Korean leader Kim Il Sung's invasion of South Korea as part of a larger Soviet strategy to probe for weaknesses in the resolve of the West to meet global challenges. The Truman administration believed it had to meet the Soviet challenge head-on by hitting hard in Korea and boosting the western military presence around the globe.[37] One result of this determination to stand up to Moscow was that the American commitment to Indochina grew stronger.

Although the Korean War ensured American support for the French war effort, Franco-American disagreement on the best approach in Indochina continued. In July, Foreign Service officer John F. Melby led a mission to Indochina to determine the state of the French military effort and to make recommendations for future American policy there. The mission decried French commander in chief Marcel Carpentier's strategy, which the Americans considered to be primarily defensive. The Melby report offered three alternatives—the United States could cut its losses, engage in a holding action, or prevent a communist victory at whatever cost on the grounds that Southeast Asia was a vital national security interest. The report advocated the third option and recommended increased aid and the establishment of a military assistance advisory group, but it also suggested placing more pressure on the French to grant Vietnamese independence and to provide an offensive strategy against the Vietminh before fully committing to the French war effort. Donald Heath, the new U.S. minister in Vietnam, argued against pressuring the French and advocated developing a national Vietnamese army as a solution to French problems, since the French army was the only defense against a communist offensive in Indochina.[38] For the time being, Washington listened to Heath's suggestions, toning down its demands for full Vietnamese independence, but still believing that independence was the only ultimate solution. The Truman administration soon found another way to exercise some influence on French decision making, sending the Military Assistance and Advisory Group (MAAG) to Saigon in September 1950 under the leadership of General Francis Brink. As Assistant Secretary of State Dean Rusk stated, the United States had "no choice" but to help France, even though this would provoke charges of "imperialism."[39]

MAAG, which comprised army, air force, and naval inspection teams, would play a critical role in creating an enduring American foothold in Vietnam, and, eventually, replacing French military advisers. MAAG's initial role was to process, monitor, and evaluate American military aid to French and Vietnamese forces, but it gradually began to establish military programs, help build a national Vietnamese army, and coordinate U.S. military aid with French operational plans.[40] The French rarely made American inspections of equipment or attempts at coordination easy. In turn, MAAG members were often frustrated by French disorganization and failure to account for materials. With the establishment of MAAG and the increasing flow of American materials under MDAP, the United States indicated the importance it attached to the French war effort as well as its realization that the French were fighting an anticommunist war not a colonial one. As aid increased, so did MAAG technicians and counselors. French commanders resented MAAG from the beginning, and with good reason. Content at first with simply supplying aid and personnel, MAAG became interested in taking over instruction of Vietnamese officers, training Vietnamese pilots, and supervising the French war effort.

American military aid pleased Paris, but increasing trips from American military personnel and the inclusion of American counselors and liaison officers in the French military forces prompted French concern over what they perceived as too many Americans attempting to control policy in Indochina. According to government officials, Americans in Saigon desired to move from simply supplying aid to giving advice, and eventually to "directing the whole affair." American intervention each day became more tangible and visible, which was unacceptable to Paris since Washington did not share in French responsibilities. Perturbation with these issues, as well as other problems within the Western alliance, was evident in a detailed letter that

Massigli sent to the Quai. Massigli worried that as France became increasingly dependent on the United States for European rearmament and aid to Indochina, French goals would be subordinated to American ones. He advocated improving Franco-British cooperation that would counterbalance American preponderant power, but he also recognized the need for more open exchanges of information and viewpoints among the three allies.[41]

Meanwhile, the French continued to push for allied unity. In a strategic move, Paris decided to send a symbolic battalion to the Korean front to show French solidarity and to offset American criticism about the lack of French participation in the war. French officials argued that this act would prove France subscribed to collective security and would guarantee allied aid in the case of new difficulties in Indochina. Paris believed that the French effort in Indochina would be better understood in the United States after the exploits of the French battalion in Korea became known. According to Quai officials, the Korean War had already influenced U.S. public opinion as Americans had renewed their interest in the Far East, recognized the importance of military preparedness, and begun to view Asia as the new battleground in the Cold War. French officials helped perpetuate this view by noting that the American effort to construct a coordinated effort in Korea underlined the need for a similar common defense in Southeast Asia.[42]

A NATIONAL VIETNAMESE ARMY

As French officials pondered how a common defense in Southeast Asia could be achieved, they continued to fight an uphill battle in Indochina. The Truman administration became convinced that a unilateral French military effort would not succeed in halting communist aggression. The development of a strong national Vietnamese army had been a priority for the United States early on in the conflict and soon became viewed as essential. Acheson thought that by providing an enlarged aid program to Vietnam to create a national army, a "psychological benefit" would occur in Indochina and the "depletion of western military potential" would halt. According to Ambassador Bruce, a Vietnamese national army would "on the one hand provide a basis for French withdrawal of their own forces, needed for European defense, and on the other serve to give outward and visible expression to Vietnamese nationalist aspirations."[43]

The idea of a Vietnamese army as the answer to France's predicament of adequate troop strength for European defense pleased the new René Pleven government.[44] Prime Minister Pleven averred that the continued financial strain of funding both the Indochina War and European rearmament could result in "galloping inflation" that would impair the French role in NATO. Therefore, a supranational approach to defense budgeting in Europe was required. French claims of imminent economic collapse appeared exaggerated to American officials, who perceived little danger of inflation in France; they suspected the Pleven government of maneuvering Washington into a position where it would have to fund the entire amount of increased French military expenditures as France created a Vietnamese national army and a common European defense.[45]

Paris certainly intended to seek additional American aid. At a tripartite foreign ministers meeting in early September, France had two predominant concerns—how much aid the Americans could give France and what the United States would do in the event of a Chinese invasion of Indochina.[46] The United States was not ready to make a commitment to the French in the event of a Chinese invasion, but promised that more aid would be forthcoming.[47] Acheson also agreed to tripartite military talks to discuss the Chinese threat. Still, according to Paris, the meeting had not produced an "ironclad" American commitment to the French effort. Despite the installation of an American embassy with three hundred personnel and multiple services and the sending of information missions, military supplies, economic aid, and American loans to the Vietnamese government, American policy toward Indochina was still one of "neither communism nor colonialism."[48]

From Washington's perspective, a Vietnamese army still seemed to be the best solution to the Asian and European defense conundrum. The American Southeast Asia Aid Policy Committee recommended to the NSC a policy of encouraging the formation of national armies in Indochina. Although the committee's main focus was on the means to improve the situation in Indochina, members also recognized that a phased French withdrawal from Indochina would strengthen Europe. A Vietnamese army, according to American officials, would "help solve defense problems in Asia and in Europe."[49]

As the western governments struggled to come to terms with the rising atmosphere of crisis in Asia, Vietminh units attacked French border posts in the mountainous area near the Chinese frontier and the town of Cao Bang. A series of disastrous French military defeats followed, and the French were forced to withdraw from the Cao Bang area. By mid-October, Heath reported that the border between China and Vietnam had "virtually ceased to exist."[50] For the first time since the Indochina War began, the French were brought to the brink of defeat by Vietminh offensives.

The deteriorating military situation disrupted American plans for a

Vietnamese army while making an improved prosecution of the war an urgent priority for the French. The Vietminh had sustained heavy casualties, but the Cao Bang offensive dealt the French a major psychological defeat. In Hanoi, rumors circulated that all French dependents would soon be evacuated. Back in Paris, Pleven came under heavy fire for the disaster, and the French National Assembly passed a motion giving the government a mandate to reinforce the war effort by any means necessary. The French defeats also ensured that the notion of phasing out French forces and building a Vietnamese army, which would release French troops to the continent for the benefit of NATO, effectively disappeared.[51] Finally, the Cao Bang debacle encouraged Paris to demand more aid from Washington to salvage its position in the region.

Given the crisis situation in Indochina, were the French and Americans of the same opinion on what actions needed to be taken there by the end of 1950? The outlook from both capitals demonstrates that they were not. French thinking could be summed up in four points. First, Paris emphasized to Washington that the Indochina burden was crushing France and that the French contribution to European defense would suffer as the French sent more troops and funneled more money from the continent to Indochina. Second, the Pleven government demanded more American economic and military aid to relieve France's burden. Third, French officials insisted that augmented aid did not authorize American officials in Saigon to take a bigger role in French policy decisions regarding political and military operations. Finally, if more aid failed to materialize, France would have to disengage either from Indochina or from a common European defense.

American thinking on Indochina by the end of 1950 followed a different path. The Truman administration's policy toward Indochina contained a number of components. Although Truman did agree to more aid in Indochina, he felt that this aid should result in a greater American voice in French political and military policy toward Vietnam. American officials in Saigon concurred, advocating the appointment of an American military adviser to the French high command and American political advisers to the French high commissioner and Bao Dai government. In addition, the Truman administration was increasingly concerned about the slow pace of progress toward Vietnamese self-government. Many American officials felt the French were delaying relinquishing a number of vital powers to the Bao Dai regime, including control of communications, foreign trade, and customs. Moreover, most American officials continued to see the solution in Vietnam as political. The JCS concluded that any military victory over the Vietminh would be temporary. A long-term solution would require France to make sweeping political and economic concessions.[52] Finally, although American officials disagreed among themselves on the amount and type of aid to be assigned to Indochina, they all agreed on two points. The Truman administration was convinced that Indochina was critical because its loss could threaten all of noncommunist Asia, and in order to avoid this loss, a Vietnamese army should be built up as quickly as possible.

At least some American officials recognized the dangers of increased involvement. The deputy director of MDAP, John Ohly, saw the demands on the United States "increasing daily." He observed that the Americans were getting themselves into a position where their responsibilities tended to "supplant rather than complement" those of the French. Worried that Americans might become scapegoats for French failures, Ohly thought that the United States was "dangerously close" to being "so deeply committed" that it might even find itself involved in "direct intervention," since such situations unfortunately had a way of "snowballing."[53] These comments in November 1950 highlighted the dilemmas Washington faced vis-à-vis the French and the Indochinese states.

Although the French were not willing to make additional political concessions, they attempted to reinvigorate their military effort. French morale in Indochina received a boost when General Jean de Lattre de Tassigny arrived as combined commander in chief of the French Expeditionary Corps (FEC) and high commissioner in Indochina. On his own volition, de Lattre, a leading proponent of a national Vietnamese army, immediately relaxed restrictions on American inspections and contacts with the Vietnamese, leading to improved Franco-American relations and better coordination on creating a viable Vietnamese army. Indeed, in 1949, some 41,500 Vietnamese were working with the French troops, but by the end of 1950, thirty battalions had been organized, and by the end of 1951, fifty battalions existed. Such progress was attributed to the combined effort of de Lattre and Bao Dai.[54] Paris also enhanced its efforts to promote Indochina as an international problem by sending Letourneau and General Alphonse Juin to Indochina to assess American views on the conflict.

The ensuing report indicated three separate American attitudes toward the French. The official diplomats had serious reservations about the French effort, insisting that the Pleven government needed to grant further concessions toward Vietnamese independence. The military officials recognized the difficulty of the French position and wanted to provide more rapid and massive assistance. Economic officials wanted to see the "French era" in

Indochina ended. Finally, the report noted that British influence had declined drastically with the American arrival and that British personnel in Vietnam had grown more anti-French.[55] The solution, according to Letourneau and Juin, was to convince American diplomats of the importance of coordinated action while warning the various American aid missions that France took exception to overt American interference in its decision making. In conclusion, the report advocated closer cooperation with both the Americans and the British.

Closer cooperation proved a difficult task. Outgoing high commissioner Pignon complained bitterly about the Americans. He recognized that France and the United States needed to establish some sort of coordinated action before the Vietnamese succeeded in playing the two sides off each other, but he saw the Bao Dai solution as a failure and believed the Vietnamese had already pitted Paris against Washington. Pignon argued that the entrance of the United States onto the scene, much more than the communist peril on the frontier, was responsible for Bao Dai's reticence toward the French. According to Pignon, "while American dollars were slow in arriving, American intervention in Vietnamese politics occurred at a much faster pace." Pignon stated that since the arrival in Saigon of an American diplomatic presence and the Griffin mission, it had been "practically impossible" for the French to "advance in any domain." The problem was not American hostility, but the State Department's belief that full independence was necessary before political progress could be made. The Vietnamese, according to Pignon, gave more weight to the American legation than to the French high command, and the Americans were playing a "double game." To the French, they claimed that they were disappointed in the Vietnamese inability to unite and work together, but to the Vietnamese, they said that the French were at fault.[56]

Although various U.S. missions in Indochina were playing a double game to a certain degree, in that some American elements encouraged the Vietnamese to insist on greater French concessions toward independence, Pignon overstated the extent of American influence in Indochina. American dealings with the Vietnamese stemmed from frustration with French officials' refusal to address the political aspects of the Indochina problem. British officials shared this frustration but preferred to speak to the French separately so they did not feel their allies were "ganging up on them." In early November, British high commissioner in Southeast Asia Malcolm MacDonald met with Pleven, advocating independence for the Associated States. Pleven announced to MacDonald that he was "preaching to the converted," and that Pleven, Schuman, and Letourneau all thought that France should be promoting greater independence, but that French president Vincent Auriol was reluctant to grant further political reform.[57] This discussion illuminated the divisions within the French government on how best to prosecute the war. In addition, while many high-ranking officials in Paris had come to embrace the necessity of political reform, those in Saigon still clung to the idea of a military victory.

This ambiguity in French policy making had not been resolved by the time high-level Franco-British discussions took place in December. Pleven and Schuman indicated that the French were trying to improve their military position in Indochina and build up indigenous forces to argue from a position of strength, but still had not succeeded in moving forward on Vietnamese independence. At the meetings, Schuman and Pleven were primarily concerned with the looming threat of a Chinese invasion and asked the British to help bring about tripartite talks at which this issue could be discussed. British leader Clement Atlee agreed that London and Paris needed to persuade Truman to agree to military meetings at the highest level to create a coordinated effort in Indochina. Shortly after the conference, the French signed a military convention with the Bao Dai government in which France took further steps toward the creation of an independent Vietnamese army. In a symbolic gesture, France agreed that French officers serving in the Vietnamese army would wear Vietnamese uniforms. More substantive was the agreement that Vietnamese officers and enlisted men serving in the French armed forces would be transferred to the Vietnamese army.[58] On December 23, France, the United States, and the three Associated States signed a military assistance agreement that provided indirect financial and material aid to Indochina and augmented MAAG's role in helping centralize aid requests. These events indicated a general willingness on the part of the French, British, and Americans to work together in Indochina, but still left the French unsure about the extent of the American and British commitment.

EUROPEAN DEFENSE AND ASIAN PROBLEMS

According to French officials, as of January 1951 the foreign missions in Indochina and the various tripartite meetings had failed to provide significant inter-allied cooperation. French concerns with western solidarity in both Asian and European defense were apparent as Paris assessed its part in the Atlantic alliance structure. French officials had become increasingly sensitive to what they saw as a lack of solidarity outside the geographical boundaries of NATO. As a result, French military leaders redefined France's three essential missions: to participate in international engagements in European defense; to ensure the internal and external security of the Metropole, North Africa, and the French Union; and to reestablish order and stability in Indochina and stop communism in Southeast Asia.[59]

Internal exchanges highlighted the difficulties France faced in carrying out its three missions. When de Lattre requested additional reinforcements for Indochina in late 1950, the French National Defense Committee realized that this demand would force France to choose between Europe and Asia. French military advisers insisted that if Paris did not send reinforcements to Indochina, Tonkin would be lost, making the defense of Saigon and the rest of Southeast Asia difficult. Pleven did not share the military opinion that holding on to Tonkin was necessary for protecting Saigon and the rest of Southeast Asia. He advocated holding off on making a decision about sending more troops to Indochina and favored concentrating on European defense. Letourneau believed that the Americans could not possibly expect France to continue the fight in Indochina and still insist that absolute priority be given to European rearmament. Letourneau thus recommended securing additional American guarantees of aid and political support in Indochina as a way of avoiding a choice between Indochina and Europe.

The key element to French policy, as both Pleven and Letourneau recognized, was American help. Paris thus attached great importance to a number of meetings that took place between high-ranking French and American officials at the end of January 1951 in Washington—in particular the Truman-Pleven talks. Before the meetings, Pleven informed the Quai that it was essential to establish a common policy with the Americans in Asia and that Korea and Indochina should be considered the "same problem." On the American side, Washington moved slowly with respect to Indochina and allied unity, in part because it was reformulating its policy.[60]

As the talks began, Acheson and other State Department officials discussed the French request for $70 million in additional aid and high-level tripartite consultations on Far Eastern economic, political, and military questions. The general consensus was to avoid tripartite consultations on general Southeast Asian problems because of difficulties with the JCS, the potential hostility of other allied states, probable accusations of imperialism, and the belief that the United States would become so involved in commitments of this type that it would no longer be in a position to take unilateral action. American officials preferred to focus solely on Indochina. In subsequent meetings with the Americans and British on Asian questions, Pleven continued to press for a consultative organization, arguing that Asia had become important in its own right. Truman disagreed with Pleven's suggestion, fearing that other nations would resent a big three organization. Acheson pointed out that numerous organizations were already in place—a system of military consultations in Indochina had been established in September, and the North Atlantic Standing Group was also in place.[61] The British also announced their opposition to an organization run by the *trois grands*.

American and British hesitance on a tripartite organization for Southeast Asia stemmed from a number of other concerns that were not voiced publicly during the meetings. There was major French political instability, and the Americans feared that the French were considering talks with the Soviets on European issues. David Bruce and other American officials suspected that French demands for regular tripartite meetings on Southeast Asia resulted from their desire to be consulted as often as their British counterparts were. The British also had doubts about French motivations. According to British consul general in Saigon Frank Gibbs, during early January the French had flirted with the idea of negotiating with the Vietminh. The British speculated that de Lattre had been appointed not because Paris intended to "hang on" but because French officials desired to have a "strong man on the spot" who could negotiate with honor. Gibbs thought that the French had even begun to consider holding elections as a pretext to withdraw, since Ho Chi Minh would undoubtedly triumph over Bao Dai. Once the Vietminh halted their military offensive, it appeared the French had given up this strategy. Although Gibbs had no concrete proof for his suspicions, the Foreign Office took his views seriously, and the British remained suspicious of French motives in calling for coordinated action. By the end of the meetings, however, despite their failure to establish a tripartite organization on Southeast Asia, the French had succeeded in convincing the Americans of the importance of viewing Korea and Indochina as part of the same fight against communism and of providing a coordinated effort in Indochina.[62]

Improvements in inter-allied cooperation, resulting in large part from French planning, were evident at the Singapore conference that took place a few months later to study the strategic situation in Southeast Asia. At the tripartite military talks, the French, Americans, and British agreed that they needed better and faster exchanges of information, that Tonkin was crucial to the defense of Southeast Asia, and that Indochina should be integrated into a common defense system for Southeast Asia. At the same time, the NSC also approved NSC 90, which recommended "collaboration with friendly governments on exchange of operations against guerrillas," indicating the increasing American commitment against the Vietminh. Although the talks at Singapore produced no formal consensus on allied policy in Indochina, the French believed they had convinced Washington of the importance of beginning tripartite talks on formulating a joint strategy for the overall defense of Southeast Asia and acknowledged that Franco-American relations were progressing more smoothly.[63] The Americans remained reluctant, however, to commit to Southeast Asian defense when a coordinated continental European defense remained out of reach.

By mid-1951, the latent, if unrecognized, contest between France-in-Indochina and France-in-NATO as priorities in U.S. planning and funding had intensified for two reasons. First, NATO force levels remained alarmingly low. Second, in June the United States finally announced its support for the European Defense Community (EDC) and set about ensuring French cooperation while at the same time insisting that the French effort in Indochina continue. The pressure of EDC negotiations intensified the conflict within France over resource allocation between continental rearmament and the Indochina War.

The EDC had become a factor in American policy toward Indochina beginning in 1950. As the Cold War became globalized, the United States realized it did not have enough forces to deploy in Europe and Asia. During a meeting among the French, American, and British foreign ministers in September 1950, Acheson announced that the United States would not significantly increase the numbers of American forces stationed in Europe unless a European defense force supplemented by German participation came into being. Britain appeared willing to accept the idea of German rearmament, but France rejected this demand. The British were annoyed that France was more concerned about Germany than about the Soviet Union, and both the United States and the United Kingdom were determined to include Germany in European defense.[64] Thus Franco-Anglo-American cooperation on German rearmament at this time was nonexistent. Following the September conference, French official Jean Monnet provided the impetus for an alternative to German rearmament. Monnet was in an influential position, as a friend of both French foreign minister Robert Schuman at the Quai and of French prime minister René Pleven. His advice resulted in the Pleven Plan—a rearmament initiative that envisioned a supra-national European army of one hundred thousand men, fielding divisional units from Belgium, France, Germany, Italy, Luxembourg, and the Netherlands. Although the initial American response to the Pleven Plan—or the EDC, as it came to be known—was unenthusiastic, the French succeeded in persuading administration officials that they were sincere.[65]

In June 1951, the so-called Eisenhower conversion and French legislative elections were critical to the EDC's progress.[66] Dwight D. Eisenhower, as supreme allied commander in Europe, had initially been skeptical of the French EDC plan, but he came to view the EDC as a means of rearming western Europe with a minimum of American involvement. In addition, June elections in France left the French Assembly with six blocs and no clear majority. The Right and the Communists increased in strength, which meant more nationalist and pro-colonial sentiment as well as less interest in a common European defense, but the Socialists, who formed the largest bloc opposed to German rearmament, no longer had a place. Given his warm support of the EDC, Georges Bidault's appointment to the Ministry of Defense was of particular significance. French opinion on the EDC spanned the spectrum. General Juin warned that France could not fight in Indochina and rearm, and he refused to support the EDC unless the army was given the means to carry out its responsibilities in Indochina and inside the EDC.[67] Other officials assumed that French Assembly members would vote in favor of the EDC once they saw the unappealing alternatives, such as German entry into NATO or American and British independent rearming of Germany.

As the Americans focused on European problems, the French faced an uphill battle in convincing Washington to commit further resources to the French war effort in Indochina. Paris decided to send one of its most dynamic generals to Washington in July 1951 to jump start American interest in the war effort. De Lattre's trip proved valuable. He lamented the State Department's lack of "valuable information" about Indochina and French policy, but he did succeed in ensuring continued financial support for the war through Economic Cooperation Administration (ECA) funds and by convincing Acheson to resist placing additional pressure on the French to grant Vietnamese independence.[68]

De Lattre's voyage to Washington was successful in that the Truman administration agreed to maintain American support, but French officials began to ponder a number of unappealing options to extricate themselves from the conflict if additional aid was not forthcoming. The French could negotiate with Ho Chi Minh directly but undoubtedly at a major disadvantage given the military situation. Paris could give independence to the Associated States and withdraw troops, but the three states would protest, probably make a deal with the North, and endanger French lives and property. French forces could relinquish control in stages starting with Tonkin, but coordination of such a plan would be difficult. According to one Quai official, it was unlikely that French forces alone would achieve decisive success, but the danger of working with the UN or allied nations was that France might still end up "exiting" Indochina. France had to be frank with its allies: either they decided to help or France would withdraw. If France fell in Indochina, it would undoubtedly cause problems for the United States in Europe because French officials would resent America's failure to help in Indochina and would refuse to cooperate on European defense.[69] The French thus viewed their position in Europe as the key to extracting American cooperation in Indochina.

Western and Eastern defense problems were now intimately linked, according to French officials, but Paris had not resolved how to move forward on either issue. In a letter to Georges Bidault about Atlantic alliance defense, Schuman complained that "we don't know how much force would be needed in Europe and the East, how we would finance it, or how we would establish a long term plan since the NATO committees do not have the necessary authority to do this." During a private meeting, Schuman and Acheson agreed they would set up a small Franco-American committee to work on this problem. Regarding aid for the war effort, the French believed it would be difficult to carry out the war for more than nine months without American aid of around $420 million in addition to material and equipment.[70]

The real turning point in Franco-American discussions over aid came during top secret talks with de Lattre in September. According to de Lattre, "if Korea and Indochina [were] part of the same war, then the United States should be willing to fund the French effort." De Lattre's visit to the United States was well timed: after the Chinese invasion of Korea, the Americans were completely convinced of the seriousness of the communist menace in the Far East. During his meetings with American officials, de Lattre succeeded in convincing Washington that Korea and Indochina were one war, but such acceptance did not lead the Americans to take practical steps toward establishing a unified Franco-American war effort in the Far East.[71] De Lattre was more successful in increasing the amount and speed of delivery of American military supplies and in wresting assurances from Acheson that the United States had "no desire to replace the French or undermine the French Union." Shortly after de Lattre's visit to the United States, British military leaders concurred with the Americans that the French battle in Indochina deserved more funding and support.[72]

The issue of funding was critical. Only by obtaining more aid from its allies would France be able to pursue European defense and the war effort in Indochina. French National Defense Committee members refused to choose between the two, leading Pleven and Schuman to try to capitalize on the apparent American and British consensus by once again seeking Washington and London's cooperation in starting a tripartite consultative body to study options for the Indochina problem and a possible Chinese attack. The Americans and British, however, remained evasive.[73] At this point, the French believed that the British feared becoming entangled in a war against China and that the Americans were focused on the Korean War, therefore neglecting events in Indochina.[74] So although de Lattre had succeeded in convincing his allies of the anticommunist nature of the fight against the Vietminh, the United States and Britain once again resisted devoting their full attention to the French effort.

AMERICAN INFLUENCE AT WORK

Although the Franco-Vietminh war did not rank as a high priority for the Truman administration, American influence in Indochina grew steadily from 1950 to 1953. American military aid was important in contributing to this growth, as evidenced in MAAG's expansion, but even more so was the proliferation of agencies and personnel that focused on economic and technical aid. Indeed, French perceptions of the official U.S. position in Washington were largely colored by the activities of local American agencies and representatives in Vietnam—the United States Information Service (USIS), the Special Mission for Technical and Economic Aid (STEM), the Central Intelligence Agency (CIA), U.S. press correspondents, and numerous American visitors representing various organizations from home. Americans arriving in Saigon quickly became skeptical of both the French war effort and French claims that they were moving forward with Vietnamese independence. These Americans welcomed the opportunity to spread American, rather than French, values in Vietnam.[75]

American influence in Indochina expanded as the agency responsible for administering U.S. aid to the Associated States, the ECA, sent STEM to Saigon in September 1950. Directed by Robert Blum, STEM focused on building up the Bao Dai regime, modernizing the infrastructure of the rural-based economy, and strengthening bilateral relations between the Vietnamese and Americans in order to promote American democratic values. Unlike American military advisers, who were required to work through French representatives, STEM officials could negotiate directly with the Vietnamese government. French officials in Saigon quickly came to resent the Blum mission. In particular, they protested efforts by STEM officials to promote Vietnamese interest in American culture, which were perceived as a gratuitous insult to the French civilizing mission.[76] The French feared that American intervention would lead to a loss of French cultural influence and political control in Indochina.

French concerns about the consequences of additional American economic aid increased over time. STEM aid was administered first through the ECA then, after 1951, through its successor organizations, the Mutual Security Agency and the Foreign Operations Administration. On September 7, 1951, the United States and the Bao Dai government reached a bilateral accord. The United States promised direct economic and technical aid through STEM—conditional on Congressional approval each year—and the South Vietnamese promised to use the aid according to American goals specified by Washington, to communicate the information necessary to carry out aid programs to U.S. officials, to hold consultations with American representatives, and to support STEM activities. Two types of economic aid existed. Commercial aid allowed dollar credits to be put at the disposition of Vietnamese importers and was administered through the Provisional Commission for the Importation of American Economic Aid—which included one member from France and each of the Associated States, as well as an American observer. The Provisional Commission received applications from prospective importers and awarded licenses.[77] The second form of economic aid—direct aid—completely bypassed French control. The French representative on the Provisional Commission ensured that American commercial aid did not eliminate French production in the Vietnamese market, although cheaper American products could still reduce the French economic presence. French officials also succeeded in sabotaging American efforts to promote local industries that could produce rudimentary military materials and thus boost the independence of the Vietnamese economy.

STEM originally had representation in Saigon, Hanoi, Phnom Penh, and Vientiane, employed about two hundred people, and possessed the statute of a diplomatic mission. Through STEM, Americans assisted Franco-Vietnamese forces in matters of technical, medical, and civil works programs, including building roads, airfields, ports, and railroads; helping with road repairs; public health and sanitation; rehabilitation of war victims and refugees; education; agricultural production; forests; fishing; public administration; and purchasing supplies and equipment. STEM recognized its role as a supporting one in cooperation with existing programs, at least in its first year. Members worked closely with French specialists who helped with technical advice, focusing on specific projects in agriculture, public health, handicrafts, relief, industry, and education. For example, in carrying out their malarial work,

STEM members relied on the documentation and experience of the French Pasteur Institute. French and Americans cooperated in distributing fertilizer to individual farmers, reconstructing the Sontay pumping station and irrigation system in the Red River delta, and airlifting emergency supplies, medicines, vitamins, and clothes to refugees gathered in Central Vietnam. Another joint effort was "The Great Village of Dong-Quan" in the delta border of the war front. The American Economic Aid Mission provided eleven million piastres, and a committee of French, Americans, and Vietnamese helped oversee the project. Top Vietnamese, French, and American officials all visited the village.

Americans made use of a number of informational tools for their aid programs. A wide variety of exhibits, posters, pamphlets, and leaflets were prepared to assist in antimalarial programs, the fight against trachoma, the promotion of the use of fertilizer, and the provision of first aid care in rural areas. STEM also launched a series of technical films, such as *Selling Produce*, *Hands across the Sea* (which emphasized the science of growing bananas and their transportation, storage, and distribution), and *Avery Community* (which showed how the people of Avery community in Cherokee County, Georgia, had established a leading farm community). Other films included *Living Rock*, which stressed the importance of minerals; *The Streamlined Pig*, for tips on pig raising; *Breeding for Eggs and Meat Quality; Celery Harvesting Methods; Gardening for a Better Living;* and *Suggestions for Bean Pickers*.[78] All of these films emphasized the ingenuity of American, not French, agricultural methods, technology, and culture.

As a result, STEM's presence continued to exasperate French officials. Although Blum recognized that the United States should avoid undermining the French position and civilizing mission, he noted that STEM officials faced constant suspicion even when they tried to cooperate with their French counterparts. American efforts such as the model low-cost housing project Cité Nguyen Tri Phuong—which included one thousand housing units, forty-four commercial buildings, schools, a dispensary, and a police station—aggravated such suspicions because they demonstrated the magnanimity of American aid to the detriment of French projects.[79] Blum and American chargé d'affaires Edmund Gullion favored direct American support of the Vietnamese, a fact they did not hide from the French. Indeed, de Lattre on numerous occasions protested STEM's efforts in Indochina, referring to Blum as "the most dangerous man in Indochina," and he was not alone in his concerns. French officials worried about the direct aid aspect of the mission, especially the frequent contacts Americans had with local administrations. In one of the more laughable moments of Franco-American discord, de Lattre, during a dinner party, launched into a tirade against the Americans, accusing them of everything from supporting the Vietminh to having a larger stand at the annual kermis in Hanoi. In fact, the Americans did have the larger stand. The point was, the French understood exactly how dangerous American aid in Vietnam could be for French interests there.[80]

Leon Pignon had warned as early as 1950 that the Vietnamese were becoming fascinated by "American civilization" and all that it could procure. According to Pignon, American transportation, radio, cinema, music, and advertising were all being diffused in Vietnam. The French tried to slow down this process, but the Americans in Vietnam insisted that the colonial appearance was still too noticeable and needed to be modified. Pignon feared that the American agencies in Vietnam were determined to "depuppetize" Bao Dai and "defrancify" Indochina. He noted that France did not have the means to combat American cultural propaganda, so French officials should make Washington more aware of the "essential nature of French cooperation in Indochina" to withstand the communist threat.[81]

The French kept a watchful eye over American cultural and propaganda activities from their inception, carefully noting exactly how many Americans were in the Saigon legation, economic, military, and religious missions, and the private sector. French officials also kept track of American journalists, the number of Vietnamese students who arrived in the United States each year, and the ways in which propaganda was distributed through information halls, libraries in Saigon and Hanoi, tracts, bulletins, and cinemas. The French remained dismissive of American tracts, brochures, and posters as mediocre and simplistic in their anticommunism, but they recognized the value of increasingly sophisticated USIS films, especially *One Year in Korea* from 1951, which emphasized the anticommunist—and anticolonialist—nature of the American effort in South Korea. As of 1951, USIS had about two hundred films in French, a few in Vietnamese, and more in Vietnamese arriving. Popular English classes were met with growing French concern, as only the "lack of professors" kept the United States from establishing more courses. About one thousand Vietnamese were learning English in the early 1950s, most of whom were located in Saigon. American officials also loaned records to Radio Vietnam to promote American music, and one of the first American books to be translated into Vietnamese was a text on American life and civilization. The U.S. federal government broadcasting service Voice of America began broadcasting in Vietnamese as well. It is worth pointing out that British cultural activities in Indochina, according to the French, were "practically nothing."[82]

Despite their concerns that American economic aid and cultural activities were "not exactly in line with French ones," some French officials argued against accusing the Americans of "systematically contravening French influence" since the Americans were in a "difficult position." As one official noted, the Americans appeared to recognize that it was in their "best interest" to work with the French, but they wanted to avoid leaving themselves open to criticism from the Vietnamese or other newly independent Asian countries that they were aiding a colonialist power. It was thus "tempting" for them to work without the French and "to follow their own ideas to achieve the best possible results."[83]

With the finest of intentions, Americans had become more involved in Vietnamese internal affairs while trying to maintain some distance from the French. Blum, who was recalled by Washington in late 1951 as a result of French objections to Blum's claims that American officials should play a larger role in Vietnamese affairs, stated that because of the "prevailing anti-French feeling, we knew that any bolstering by us of the French position would be resented by the local people," and because of the traditional French "sensitivity" at seeing any increase of American influence, "we knew they would look with suspicion" upon the development of direct American relations with local administrations and peoples. American infighting over these issues had percolated throughout 1951, with Blum and Gullion pushing for greater involvement while Heath and U.S. ambassador to France David Bruce argued that the United States was not in a position to "replace" France.

Donald Heath, in a fascinating cable, noted that when sent to Saigon he had been instructed that Americans were to "supplement but not to supplant." He added that, without the French, the State of Vietnam would "not survive six weeks." Militarily, no other power could "take over" from the FEC. Politically, no group except the Vietminh espoused the elimination of the French, and there was no place "behind which such American influence could be exerted and none is likely to be permitted." Nor could such a party or such a pro-American movement be "built overnight" out of the military and economic aid programs in existence. Economically, the ECA and MAAG budgets were "minor" compared with French expenditures; they were "sufficient if wrongly applied" to "embitter" Franco-American relations, but they were "not enough to replace" the French contribution.[84] There we have it. The cable outlined exactly what the United States would have to do, and what it eventually did, to set in motion the gradual replacement of France in Indochina.

STEM was not the only organization to grate on French nerves. CIA officers also had a number of ideas on how to improve the French campaign against the Vietminh and were not shy about sharing them. Although the French tended in public to reject CIA advice—such as forming partisan groups to fight behind rebel lines—they often quietly implemented CIA recommendations. Despite their antipathy, by the end of 1952 Paris had agreed to host more CIA personnel in Indochina.[85]

Economic and military aid had a number of political consequences. The United States was subsidizing about one third of French costs in Indochina by 1952, and in July of that year the U.S. legation in Saigon was raised to embassy status. Heath presented his ambassadorial credentials to Bao Dai and Prime Minister Nguyen Van Tam, who had replaced Tran Van Huu in June 1952, and a Vietnamese embassy was established in Washington. Meanwhile, the French National Assembly and Council had passed the Indochina budget by overwhelming majorities in January 1952, but such enthusiasm rested on the assumption that France would share even more of its burden with the United States. On the American side, Acheson assured the French that Indochina was of "extreme importance" to the United States but that "it was a very difficult problem to resolve and the Americans did not know what to do yet"; this demonstrated the Truman administration's willingness to continue its current efforts, as well as its reluctance to commit additional resources to Vietnam and its determination to maintain the status quo in Southeast Asia during an election year. A side effect of U.S. aid was the realization by many Vietnamese in Saigon that the Americans could serve as a valuable counterweight to the French, especially considering obvious Franco-American divisions over how aid should be distributed and that American aid earmarked to fight communism seemed likely to increase over time.[86]

A COORDINATED EFFORT AT LAST?

Despite an intensified political and economic commitment on the part of the United States, the French military effort in Indochina lost steam with General de Lattre's sudden retirement and subsequent death. De Lattre's death shocked and saddened the American public. American newspapers mourned him as the "French MacArthur," noting that de Lattre had been a key figure in persuading the United States to support the French war effort.[87] Without de Lattre, the Truman administration worried that France would not be able to regain the initiative in Indochina. Bitter battles along the southern fringe of the Red River delta forced further French evacuations and indicated that France might have to abandon the entire North, proving that American fears were well grounded.

European concerns also kept the Americans divided over how the United States should proceed in Asia. Acheson continued to advocate holding the line in Asia while concentrating on Europe. John Allison, assistant secretary for Far Eastern affairs, disagreed, noting that "as the struggle in Indochina continues the French will find increasingly compelling the choice between the support of the Indochinese operation and the support of French commitments to NATO." He argued that the United States should bear in mind that a reduction in the Indochina operation was a reduction in the realities of men and material in an active theater of war; reduction in NATO commitments were, in fact, "paper reductions." According to Allison, the problem was "so important and so complex as to require consideration at the highest possible level."[88] Both Allison and Ambassador Heath acknowledged the importance of the Indochina conflict in its own right rather than as an extension of the Cold War in Europe but feared that the American priority on European defense would always dominate Asian policy.

French authorities used concerns over French capabilities in Europe to push for more aid to Indochina.[89] These efforts to pressure Washington once again had a considerable effect, leading the United States to sign a Memorandum of Understanding with the French during the NATO council meetings at the end of February 1952. The United States promised to buy $200 million worth of military equipment for French use in Indochina to help France meet European defense obligations, indicating that the Truman administration was well aware Paris would not be able to carry out European and Indochina defense simultaneously. At a meeting of the NSC in early March 1952, Acheson asked senior NSC staff to conduct a major study of the priority of Indochina defense as compared to NATO defense, and what the United States was prepared to do to keep France in Indochina.[90]

American officials also began to target other problems that impeded allied unity. Soon-to-be-director of the State Department's Office of Philippine and Southeast Asian Affairs Philip Bonsal focused on the psychological factor. If the Indochina effort was to be anything more than a "holding operation," according to Bonsal, a "climate of confidence" needed to be created among Vietnamese, French, and Americans. The only way to convince the Vietnamese to shoulder their own problem lay in granting them independence. As yet, however, no one had "thought this through to the end."[91] The

United States wanted to sustain the struggle against communism in Asia, but not at the expense of defense in Europe, hence the long-standing concern for building native forces. The trouble lay in persuading France to grant the amount of independence needed to make the scheme work. The effort to bolster France in both Indochina and Europe, neat in theory, would be more difficult to put into practice.

Following the devastating French military losses in North Vietnam, in early 1952 a chiefs of staff meeting took place to discuss common strategy in Indochina. American general Omar Bradley, British field marshal Sir William Slim, and French general Alphonse Juin agreed that the threat from the Tonkin border was significant and that the Americans should send air and naval reinforcements if necessary. Recommendations on inter-allied cooperation—including a free exchange of information, acceleration of aid to Indochina, a common system of navigational control in Southeast Asia, and measures against contraband—were approved and put into practice. An ad hoc committee under French general Paul Ely's leadership, composed of French, American, British, Australian, and New Zealander officials, was also established to study the measures to be taken in the event of a Chinese attack on Indochina. For the French, American agreement to such a committee represented the long-sought U.S. commitment to Southeast Asian defense.[92] Thus, despite de Lattre's death, the French policy of urging a coordinated effort in Southeast Asia was finally paying dividends.[93]

American officials confirmed French beliefs that the United States had become more committed to Indochina's defense. Robert Hoey, chief of Indochina affairs at the State Department, noted that the chiefs of staff meeting at Washington and the formation of the ad hoc committee marked an important turning point. For the first time, an inter-allied conference at the "highest military level recognized not only the capital importance of Indochina, but also the necessity of integrating a system of common defense" against Chinese aggression. The French believed that as a result of these two meetings, France was on track to achieving "a solid Anglo-American guarantee of the Tonkin border." Further affirmations of such hopes could be seen in NSC 124/2, which called for the United States to contribute air and naval support for the defense of Indochina, to interdict Chinese lines of communication, and to blockade the Chinese coast. If those measures proved to be insufficient, NSC 124/2 further specified that the United States would take air and naval action in conjunction with France and Britain against all suitable military targets in China.[94]

Although the Truman administration had established a firm strategy regarding Chinese intervention in Indochina, the government's overall approach to Asia was less resolute. In May 1952, Republican leader John Foster Dulles demanded a more "positive" and "dynamic" U.S. foreign policy. He was particularly concerned with Asia, arguing that the United States needed to "retake the initiative" in the Cold War. Dulles had been an early critic of the French war effort, accusing the French at a 1950 Council on Foreign Relations discussion of a "Maginot Line" mentality in their dealings with Indochina. The JCS also wanted a more offensive policy and worried that French sensitivity about NATO strength might hinder efforts in Indochina. The problem for American policy was not to keep the French indefinitely in Indochina, but to facilitate the inevitable transition from colonialism to independence in such a way that there was no opportunity for communism to flow into an intervening power vacuum. During a mid-May meeting with Truman, Acheson explained that the best possibility for handling the current situation in Indochina was to reattempt the buildup of the native army. Acheson also wanted a tripartite warning issued to China that the big three would react immediately to any aggression and that it would be impossible to confine that reaction to Indochina.[95]

Regular tripartite meetings from 1950 to 1953 were designed to iron out allied difficulties regarding Southeast Asian defense; however, in practice they usually highlighted allied disagreements and hesitations in establishing unified action. The two biggest French concerns regarding Indochina remained American financial and military aid and the problem of a coordinated strategy. A common theme throughout this period was French insistence that France might not have the resources to fund defense spending in Europe and Asia. Paris maintained that if it was to enter the EDC, it needed to have the same (or higher) force levels as the Germans. In order for this to occur, the Indochina situation and its resulting resource drain must be resolved. As French official Edgar Faure claimed, "Indochina [was] at the heart of the European problem."[96] The signing of the EDC treaty on May 27 by France, West Germany, Belgium, Luxembourg, and the Netherlands marked another turning point; European defense would demand a heightened degree of political commitment in U.S. planning at precisely the moment when the Truman administration had begun to focus on Southeast Asia.[97] From this point, it became increasingly difficult to distinguish European from Southeast Asian policy in U.S. national security planning. The muddle permeated strategic planning for the rest of the Truman administration and would also plague the Eisenhower administration.

A foreign ministers meeting among Acheson, British Foreign Secretary

Anthony Eden, and Schuman at the end of May 1952 emphasized the inter-
mingling of European and Asian policy. One of the biggest French questions
at the conference was whether Indochina was to be considered an international problem. The French asserted that despite the Truman-Pleven meetings in 1951 and de Lattre's visit in September 1951, American views on the
conflict remained obscure. During the meetings, the French once again attempted to create a common Southeast Asia military organization, but allied
unity on this issue remained elusive; Acheson was opposed to a permanent
organization, preferring a tight association with existing organizations.[98]
Moreover, how to build a viable Vietnamese national army also continued to
be a top priority. Letourneau, whose duties as minister resident of Indochina
were roughly equivalent to those of high commissioner, asserted that only
through increased American aid would France be able to build Vietnamese
national armies, which would allow for a continuation of the French effort
in Europe. If American aid did not materialize, French officials threatened,
France would have to slow down its effort in both Indochina and Europe.[99]

As Henri Bonnet observed, all the effort going into integrating the French,
American, and British strategies would never pay off until the three governments agreed on the principles that would determine a common strategy in
Asia.[100] How could such an agreement be reached? According to Truman
and Acheson, Paris needed to retake the offensive in the war. Implementing
such a strategy proved difficult, as the most serious military crisis since the
1950 Cao Bang disasters occurred in the Black River area of northern Vietnam in late 1952. The largest French operation ever attempted, Operation
Lorraine, quickly became bogged down in the face of stiff Vietminh resistance. The operation taxed French resources, leading to the now ubiquitous
French demands for more American aid, which Acheson refused.[101]

The British, when looking back over the past few years, realized that
Franco-Anglo-American thinking on Indochina had been dominated by
consideration of what collective action should be taken in the event of open
Chinese aggression in Indochina. By the end of 1952, the possibility of such
aggression had become remote, according to the Foreign Office, and in the
meantime, Paris and Washington had closed their eyes to the actual danger
of the Vietminh. British officials had become convinced by Quai d'Orsay
arguments that Indochina represented the biggest obstacle to European defense and that France had to obtain more financial and material aid from the
incoming Eisenhower administration in order to secure both Europe and
Indochina.[102] London was particularly concerned that if a concrete policy
toward Indochina failed, the West would end up fatally undermining NATO

in Europe. Consequently, the Foreign Office suggested that if France could "face the facts" in Indochina and send more reinforcements, then the British, along with the Americans, could perhaps guarantee forces equal to the German forces proposed under the EDC for the next two years. The British even went so far as to suggest that they would agree to increased American military and economic aid to France for Indochina and a temporary diminution of aid to Europe, provided the French had a sound plan for "clearing up the Indochina situation."[103] In the end, London accepted the French argument that their ability to maintain European defense depended on the rise or fall of French fortunes in Indochina.

Fears of communist expansion, French skill at manipulating these fears, and periodic French claims that France might have to withdraw unilaterally from Indochina if it did not receive more aid, led to increased American support of the war effort in Vietnam during the last few years of the Truman administration. French documentation overwhelmingly points to Paris's determination to secure an American commitment to the French war effort and to use the Atlantic alliance to retain colonial possessions. But French political leaders were not simply trying to manipulate or blackmail their counterparts in Washington; they were sincere in their belief that without American help they would not be able to continue a colonial but also anticommunist fight that was unappreciated by the United States.[104] Additionally, American attempts to promote Vietnamese independence and a Vietnamese army, the search for a European defense alliance against the communist bloc, and the nature of the Western alliance itself all played a role in furthering the American commitment to France. The Truman administration constantly wavered on whether to pressure France for additional reforms in exchange for more American aid, but ultimately decided to provide the aid without the reforms, thus decreasing its leverage vis-à-vis Paris.

From 1950 to 1953, American economic, technical, and military assistance gradually increased as European and Southeast Asian defense became linked, and the United States began to view Indochina as an essential outpost in Southeast Asia. Although Washington still opposed a combined command arrangement for Southeast Asia, the French had succeeded in portraying Korea and Indochina as two separate fronts in the same war against communism. The American commitment to a noncommunist Vietnam had undoubtedly grown larger over the last years of Truman's presidency, but at the end of 1952, American officials still sought a political solution— Vietnamese independence—instead of a military one. This would change during the Eisenhower administration.

2

A Death in March

AS DWIGHT D. EISENHOWER PREPARED to assume the presidency, he and his newly appointed secretary of state John Foster Dulles discussed the "Indochina problem" on board the cruiser *Helena* in December 1952. Eisenhower and Dulles recognized that the current situation was the "most serious single problem of international relations" facing the United States because of "France's weakness and the colonial aspects involved," and the possibility that the "results of loss could not be insulated."[1] Their concern demonstrated that the situation in Vietnam had become a considerable priority to the U.S. government. But the Eisenhower administration, like its predecessor, remained uncertain of the best way to proceed. Thus the issues that had beset the last years of the Truman administration—the search for allied unity, the American desire for Vietnamese independence, and the French unwillingness to commit more resources to European defense while fighting the Vietminh—would plague Eisenhower's presidency as well.

The nascent EDC further complicated American and French policies toward Vietnam. Following the Truman administration's lead, Eisenhower and Dulles were determined to bring West Germany into the Atlantic alliance. But in France, memories of German occupation during World War II were still fresh, and many French citizens feared a revival of German military power as much as the Red Army, if not more so. To the French, European security problems were closely connected to the war in Vietnam, where the military situation was rapidly deteriorating in the face of stiff Vietminh resistance. Government officials and the public feared that withdrawing more troops from Europe would weaken French military preparedness, not only with respect to the Soviet Union, but also vis-à-vis growing German power.[2]

Joseph Stalin's death in March 1953 and the ensuing Soviet "peace offensive" compounded these problems. By raising the possibility of a relaxation of Cold War tensions, the new leadership in the Kremlin signaled that diplomatic solutions to European and Asian security problems could be found—solutions that would end the war in Indochina and obviate the need for the

EDC. Such possibilities widened existing cleavages between France and the United States as the two countries disagreed over the intentions motivating Soviet diplomacy. These diverging views led Paris and Washington to pursue conflicting agendas regarding the EDC, the First Indochina War, and relations with the Soviet Union. In addition, Soviet and American willingness to negotiate an end to the Korean War caused the French to demand a similar diplomatic solution to the Indochina conflict. French officials encouraged Washington to test Soviet intentions through negotiation, while American leaders—Dulles in particular—pressured Paris to pursue a military victory in Indochina, to accept German rearmament through the EDC, and to ignore the fact that the United States was settling the Korean War at the negotiating table. This dynamic within the Western alliance played a key role in determining how East-West and West-West relations unfolded. Rather than capitalizing on Soviet confusion and apparent moderation by presenting a united front to the Soviets, Paris and Washington pursued separate policies in Europe and Asia that obstructed western policy toward the USSR, weakened allied unity, and ultimately increased American intervention in Vietnam.

CAUGHT BETWEEN THE RHINE AND THE MEKONG

Eisenhower's Republican administration entered office in January 1953 determined to defeat the communists in Indochina and to secure French support for the EDC.[3] Stalin's death made both of these goals more difficult, since the possibility of a relaxation of tensions, and hence a diplomatic resolution to the Indochina conflict, appealed to French leaders. The American leadership feared that if France negotiated with the Soviet Union on Indochina, Paris would become less concerned with the communist threat, thereby dooming the EDC.[4] As a result, the Eisenhower administration sought to prop up the French war effort with promises of American aid in return for French cooperation in ratifying the EDC.

No one in the Eisenhower administration was more committed to a military victory in Indochina and ratification of the EDC than Dulles.[5] Throughout 1953 and 1954, the secretary of state's hard-line approach was predicated on his belief that no viable alternative to the EDC existed and that, contrary to the belief of the Truman administration, a military rather than a political solution could be found in Vietnam. Stalin's death did little to change Dulles's appraisal of the world situation. He remained determined to secure German rearmament through the EDC, and he steadfastly opposed negotiations with the new Soviet leadership on Vietnam. He insisted that negotiations would have to take place *after* the West had secured German rearmament, if at all.

As the Asian and European theaters became increasingly intertwined, intense Franco-American negotiations regarding the EDC and Indochina took place throughout 1953 and 1954. While the Americans' desire for the EDC's success resulted in an ever-increasing commitment to Vietnam, Paris exploited American enthusiasm for linking the two issues by promising, though not delivering, on the EDC in order to receive greater aid for Indochina. The link between European defense and the French war effort had become apparent during Truman's administration, but under the Eisenhower administration this link grew unmistakable. Franco-American conflict over the EDC thus became an important step in the process of the French exit from, and the American arrival in, Vietnam.

Although eager to shore up western defenses against the Soviets, French officials had assumed that the EDC's ratification would be a leisurely process, buying France time to win the war in Indochina and build up military forces on the continent to counter German rearmament. To the surprise and annoyance of French policy makers, Eisenhower and Dulles began lobbying the French to ratify the EDC treaty immediately. Dulles believed that furnishing financial and military aid to the French war effort would induce France to ratify the EDC and integrate West Germany into the Western alliance; and it would have the further desired effect of leading to a French victory in Indochina and a noncommunist Southeast Asia. French archival documents suggest that Paris labored to find independent solutions to the EDC and Indochina problems despite Washington's insistence on linking them.[6] At the same time, French officials willingly exploited Washington's refusal to pursue separate EDC and Indochina policies. With American money, French policy makers intended to buy time in both Europe (to avoid Bonn's entry into NATO) and Indochina (to avert outright defeat).

The Eisenhower administration understood the risks of connecting the two policies and attempted to avoid an explicit linkage. But Dulles and other American officials erred in drawing implicit linkages that the French exploited. Dulles's tactic of insisting that the EDC was the only solution to the problem of German rearmament allowed the French to influence American policy significantly. The Eisenhower administration had considered alternatives to the EDC—bringing Germany into NATO, or American-British independent rearming of Germany—that would have limited French influence, but it spent little time assessing the viability of these alternatives because it assumed the French National Assembly would ratify the EDC. This conscious decision kept money flowing into French coffers and created a series of events and miscalculations that increased tensions between the United States and France. The Eisenhower administration's insistence on the EDC became the Achilles' heel of Franco-American negotiations, allowing Paris to gain the upper hand over both the Indochina and EDC issues.

As the Republican administration came to power, the French pondered what changes would occur in American foreign policy toward Indochina. When Eisenhower took office, the United States had established American influence in Vietnam but had little desire to take France's place. But as American aid increased in 1953, so did the American conviction that the United States could run the war effort more effectively than France. Eisenhower and Dulles became increasingly impatient with French military delays and demands for more aid, making it much more difficult for Washington to maintain flexibility in its dealings with Paris.

Initially, the incoming Eisenhower administration had a fairly positive view of the equally new René Mayer government and wanted to work with French officials on both European defense and Indochina.[7] Eisenhower and Dulles admired French foreign minister Georges Bidault and thought he had a first-class professional team of experts at his command. They also recognized that the Quai d'Orsay was a major force in the Fourth Republic, understanding that the Quai had taken on an increasingly important role in both European and Asian policy as numerous government crises forced French prime ministers to leave office. In addition, since 1950, the Quai had begun to control decision making on Vietnam. According to Assistant Secretary of State Livingston Merchant, the instability of the French political situation was highly exaggerated in terms of its practical effect on foreign policy, since France had the best civil service in quality and tradition in the world, and, more important, power was divided in ministerial teams among a relatively small number of personalities. Although jobs at the Quai d'Orsay reshuffled frequently, the same men simply moved from one position to another.[8] Despite this stability, the Quai was divided into two factions by early 1953—those who saw Indochina as the most important issue facing France and those who insisted that European integration had priority over all other concerns.

As the Eisenhower administration attempted to keep the French fighting in Southeast Asia, many French officials and most of the public sought to escape a humiliating and resource-draining war against the Vietminh. By 1953, government and private French figures demanded an end to what they referred to as the "dirty war." Concern over the war effort had moved beyond the editorials of communist newspapers and into the mainstream press. Prominent political leader Pierre Mendès France called for negotiations with the Vietminh, as did the influential newspaper *Le Monde*. The Mayer government feared that withdrawing more troops from Europe to fight a colonial battle would place western European security at risk, and Mayer thus refused to ratify the EDC and commit troops to the European continent before France had resolved the Indochina conflict. Yet French military forces remained unable to launch a successful offensive against the Vietminh. American officials worried that French hopes of the "world situation" entering a period of détente that would benefit Indochina were not conducive to a dynamic approach.[9]

In 1953, the Franco-Vietminh war was in its seventh year. Neither the French nor the Vietminh had succeeded in breaking the military stalemate. The French-held cities were islands in Vietminh territory. Hanoi, Hue, and Saigon were all under French control, but there were no land communications between them; only by air or sea could the traveler circulate in Vietnam. Continued attacks against French strongholds in the North had ended any possibility of a reduction in size of the FEC for 1953.[10] French officials believed that only additional American aid would resolve the stalemate.

And yet, French officials feared that increasing American aid would lead Washington to attempt to control the situation in Vietnam. During a ministerial meeting in early 1953, Minister of the Associated States Jean Letourneau worried that Indochina could shift from being a French affair to a "free world affair, completely escaping French control." According to Letourneau, no one could "take France's place," and France would "not allow the Americans to direct Indochina" as they had directed the Korean War. Bidault acknowledged that the United States might attempt to take control, but concluded that the "risk was acceptable if France could obtain the aid necessary to continue the conflict." Turning to the EDC, Bidault and Mayer recognized that for many French National Assembly members, one of the biggest arguments against ratifying the EDC was that France would lose its great power status vis-à-vis the United States and Britain. The French position on the Atlantic and world levels would disappear with the EDC, as would certain French sovereignty prerogatives. Before the EDC could be passed, French sentiments would have to change. According to Bidault, "Dulles had failed to understand this point."[11]

In the French National Assembly, perspectives on Indochina and the EDC varied dramatically. Supporters of the EDC envisioned it as one step on the path to a European supranational political and military structure. Their vision did not include a divisive war in Indochina. The most nationalist elements remained eager to carry on the war in Indochina but opposed an international vision of Europe, fearing the loss of France's status as a world power. In keeping with their worldview, they argued that the effort to regain colonial control must continue in order to reestablish France's "national grandeur." These nationalists also feared Germany's resurgence as a military power too much to approve a defense arrangement involving Bonn. As it tried to sell the EDC to the National Assembly and public, the Mayer government also had to take into account increasing demands for an end to the Franco-Vietminh war, which far outweighed national support for the EDC.[12]

Because of mounting problems with the EDC and Indochina, Paris requested a substantial financial aid increase from the United States. If the United States could guarantee such aid, the Mayer government promised to bring the EDC to a vote while continuing the Indochinese fight against the communists. Mayer intended first to obtain American financial aid and second to ratify the EDC, believing that he could obtain the necessary votes in the French National Assembly. As French officials observed, assurances of American aid that would help France meet its European and Asian responsibilities made a vote on the EDC more likely; otherwise, public opinion and the National Assembly would turn against it.[13] But when Dulles asked Bidault to set a specific date for the debate over the EDC's ratification, Bidault indicated that the National Assembly would not concurrently ratify the EDC and continue the war. After their meeting, Bidault observed that Dulles was "difficult to deal with, had few original ideas, and was narrow minded," and concluded that Dulles had "an elementary and a Manichean view of the world: between the camps of good and evil there is no possibility for maneuvers or compromise." French officials also found Dulles "ignorant" of the fundamentals of French policy, and "naive."[14] Such views did not bode well for smooth relations with the new American secretary of state.

Discussions among the Americans, British, and French at the Paris Conference in early February 1953 highlighted the problems the French faced in simultaneously ratifying the EDC and continuing the war. French officials clamored for additional protocols that would tie Britain more closely to the EDC, and for a reaffirmation of Washington and London's commitment to the Atlantic alliance to quiet domestic discontent. Mayer also emphasized that the defense of Indochina signified security for the West: "the French government assumes, in Asia, the defense of Indochina—a key territory for the security of the western powers."[15] Mayer confirmed his intention to continue on both fronts, but urged the United States to recognize French difficulties, particularly with regard to public opinion.

Meanwhile, the Eisenhower administration attempted to assess the psychological implications of supplying aid to France and why this aid had not ensured French cooperation. U.S. officials concluded that when economic aid became linked to mutual defense, the French recognized that they had something to contribute and bargain with—their strategic position in France and Indochina. As the French increasingly came to feel that U.S. military aid was very much a matter of advancing American strategic interests along with European interests, they also came to doubt that it would be immediately terminated should France fail to meet American stipulations such as Vietnamese independence or ratification of the EDC. Hence the French concluded that a "reciprocal political-military dependence between France and the United States overshadowed economic relationships." In the French view, if the United States were to drastically reduce military or economic aid to the French, American overall interests would be adversely affected by such possible consequences as a slackening of the French military effort in Indochina or in Europe. Thus, if aid were cut, "both France and the United States would suffer." Insofar as Washington appeared more interested than France in building up American military bases in French territory, in enlarging the French defense contribution, in ratifying the EDC, and in maintaining or intensifying the struggle in Indochina, the French became more conscious of their strategic position in the Cold War as an "element of bargaining power."[16] This assessment went to the heart of the internal debates in the Eisenhower administration. On the one hand, mid-level American officials recognized the dangers of linking aid to mutual defense. On the other hand, their superiors, Dulles in particular, saw such a link as the best chance for guaranteeing both Asian and European security.

As Washington attempted to define its policy toward France, the deteriorating military situation in Indochina continued to amplify the French public's hostility toward the war. The military had sustained heavy losses by 1953. The willingness of the French public to sacrifice Frenchmen to a colonial war had weakened after so many years of fighting with no apparent gains. American pressure to ratify the EDC and continue the war placed an added burden on the Mayer government. Fears of a resurgent Germany, as well as the imminent loss of the colonial empire and hence France's self-conceived view as a great power, limited Paris's options.

During this period, the French dilemma received significant attention from the international press. French ambassador to the United States Henri Bonnet remarked that "many different [American] articles note that in reality, the Indochina War, which handicaps France in Europe, constitutes one of the biggest obstacles to the realization of the EDC." British newspapers also remarked on "the ties between French responsibilities in Indochina and the potential decisions on the EDC" and suggested that "the whole defense of Western Europe is imperiled by the fact that France is being bled to death by the Indo-Chinese War."[17] Clearly, news correspondents on both sides of the Atlantic understood that a dual policy of ratifying the EDC and continuing the war in Indochina would prove difficult for France, yet the Eisenhower administration persisted in this very policy.

American journalists urged the administration to either pressure French officials or find alternatives to the EDC. For example, some correspondents seconded Representative James Richards's (D-SC) suggestion of an explicit quid pro quo: American aid to France in return for the EDC's ratification.[18] Others questioned the Eisenhower administration's wisdom in refusing to consider alternatives to the EDC. Commenting on Eisenhower and Dulles's thinly veiled threats to the French to ratify the EDC or lose American aid for Vietnam, one editorial asked, "isn't it short-sighted to demand both a continuation of the Indochina War and the creation of a European army at the same time?" Another article condemned the Eisenhower administration for not having determined its line of action "in the face of the EDC's failure [and the] French refusal to continue the war long ago."[19]

For the time being, Eisenhower and Dulles decided to back away from placing explicit conditions on American aid to the French war effort. At a White House breakfast meeting in early spring 1953, Dulles recognized that the Indochina situation "probably had top priority in foreign policy, being in some ways more important than Korea because the consequences of loss there could not be localized, but would spread throughout Asia and Europe."[20] Dulles and Eisenhower agreed that the United States would have to step up aid to the French in Indochina if they provided a military plan promising real success. Congress would disperse aid to France through the Mutual Security Act for 1953–1954, then under discussion in the House Committee on Foreign Affairs and the Senate Foreign Relations Committee. On April 16, Eisenhower, in his first major foreign affairs pronouncement, called for a united defense in Southeast Asia. The administration asked for a Congressional appropriation of $400 million earmarked to assist the noncommunist forces in Indochina, and in late April, France secured a package of nearly $1 billion in aid for Indochina and French rearmament in Europe.[21]

Although Eisenhower and Dulles were willing to supply unconditional aid, Congress was not. Republican senator Barry Goldwater and Democrat John F. Kennedy introduced an amendment that would have made authorization of the $400 million in budgetary aid to the French contingent on an early promise of independence for the Associated States, which the two senators saw as key to warding off communism in Indochina. Kennedy had visited Vietnam for the first time in October 1951 and had been persuaded by American officials there that independence was the only solution. The Goldwater-Kennedy amendment represented a drastic departure from Congress's actions during the Truman administration, when members had acquiesced to Truman's requests for additional aid for Indochina. Of course, $400 million was a far larger sum than any amount previously provided to the French war effort. The amendment eventually failed because of Republican Senate leadership and Republicans and Democrats on the Foreign Relations Committee, all of whom wanted to avoid an action that would interfere with executive and diplomatic efforts to influence France on the issue of independence and prevent French withdrawal.[22] Another attempt to obtain American foreign policy goals through stipulations on aid was James Richards's introduction of an amendment to the Mutual Security Act. The amendment proposed withholding military aid from EDC signatories until they ratified the treaty, and was specifically intended to place pressure on the French to ratify the EDC, as Richards had threatened to do earlier.

Other prominent members of Congress supported Richards's amendment. Senator William Knowland (R-CA) denounced French pleas for American subsidization of the war in Indochina, arguing that Mayer had made little effort to bring the EDC to a debate in the National Assembly. He conceded that France had weakened under the weight of its military efforts in Indochina but wondered why it remained opposed to the incorporation of West Germany into the European defense system. Knowland threatened that if nothing changed by January 1954, the Senate would take the initiative and reappraise the amount of aid Washington gave Paris. Eisenhower and Dulles quickly notified the French that they did not support the Richards amendment, but it lent credence to their warning to the Mayer government that Congress might retaliate against French equivocation on the EDC.[23] Richards's addition to the Mutual Security Act threatened to establish an explicit link between the EDC and Indochina.

From the French perspective, Paris feared that if Congress approved the Richards amendment its options in prosecuting the war would be reduced, since the war effort depended largely on American financial aid. But the Mayer government also recognized that increased American aid could result in American control of French military forces in Indochina. Concerns about an unbalanced budget, continuing hostilities in Indochina, and German rearmament caused the French to worry that they would become dependent on the United States for economic aid in Europe and military support in Southeast Asia. In the long run, this dependency could lead to "France's diminished position in the Western alliance and a loss of international prestige."[24] Yet the Mayer government could not continue the war without American money.

Senior administration officials believed that substantial financial aid to the French should produce a quick vote on the EDC, but members on both the Senate Foreign Relations Committee and the House Committee on Foreign Affairs had their doubts.[25] The EDC thus once again played a crucial role in March and May Congressional discussions over the amount of financial aid France would receive for the war in Indochina. During a Senate debate over potential means to ensure the EDC's success, Senator Mike Mansfield (D-MT) proposed cutting through the "Gordian knot" that existed between the EDC and Indochina by bringing West Germany directly into the NATO alliance. In response to Mansfield's suggestion and other inquiries by Congressional members, Dulles assured them that "no good alternatives to the EDC existed," without explaining why this was the case.[26] Administration officials continued to insist that additional aid would break the deadlock in Vietnam and, at the same time, secure western European defense.

A DEATH IN MARCH

In the end, it was not American aid that broke the deadlock, but a death. Stalin's demise in March 1953 forced the Eisenhower administration to confront yet another challenge in its attempts to bolster the French war effort against the Vietminh. In the months following Stalin's death, the Soviet Union proposed a new policy of peaceful economic and political coexistence. Soviet premier Georgi Malenkov advocated a relaxation of tensions that would allow him to concentrate on domestic economic reform while encouraging western Europe to reduce its dependence on the United States.[27] This policy was excellent propaganda for the Soviets, as the Americans were aware. The Soviet peace offensive immediately raised French hopes that a negotiated solution could be found to the conflict in Vietnam.

The Soviet peace offensive placed the Eisenhower administration on the defensive, forcing it to reconsider strategies in Asia and Europe. Although

Dulles openly doubted any possibility for a serious shift in Soviet policy that could lead to negotiated settlements, there were other voices in the Eisenhower administration. C. D. Jackson, Eisenhower's psychological warfare adviser, argued for bold diplomatic initiatives to exploit the succession crisis. Believing that the post-Stalin leadership was in a vulnerable position, he advocated moving quickly to embark on a diplomatic offensive that would take advantage of Stalin's death. In early March, he urged Eisenhower to make a speech proposing a foreign ministers' conference to discuss a truce in Korea, German unification, an Austrian peace treaty, and disarmament. Jackson dismissed the State Department's concern that such a conference would raise "false hopes" of a Cold War settlement and ruin the EDC. More than any other American official, he recognized that the United States needed to *appear* willing to negotiate to win over allied leaders and public opinion. He argued that an American appeal to world leaders could create a unified sense of purpose and address European concerns, thereby hastening, rather than retarding, the creation of the EDC.[28] The Soviet peace offensive thus forced the Eisenhower administration to seriously consider the development of a psychological strategy in its European and Asian policies.

Eisenhower understood the importance of psychological warfare. Although the Soviet peace offensive had not changed Eisenhower's perceptions of the Soviet Union, he eventually forged a middle ground between Dulles's and Jackson's views by publicly announcing his willingness to negotiate with Moscow to ease world tensions. He thus countered the Soviet peace offensive with his own, while reassuring American allies of his commitment to negotiations and strengthening western resolve. Eisenhower recognized that the Soviets were engaging in a change of tactics rather than a change in overall strategy, but he, more than Dulles and other State Department officials, wanted to at least investigate the possibility that Malenkov might be sincere in resolving long-standing problems.[29] In the end, Eisenhower, along with most other administration officials, remained pessimistic toward the idea that negotiations, disarmament agreements, and other nonconfrontational means could lead to détente. Those officials advocating negotiations, like C. D. Jackson, did so from a concern for allied unity rather than a belief that East-West diplomacy would prove fruitful. The problem, for American officials, was how to convince their French and British allies that the Soviets were engaging in psychological warfare rather than sincere diplomacy.

In preparing for high-level Franco-American talks in March 1953, the Eisenhower administration took the position that alterations in the Soviet government had not transformed the basic nature of the threat facing the

West. American officials pointed out that the situation in the Kremlin was unpredictable. If the West did not build its strength, the new Soviet group might well undertake "adventures" of one kind or another. According to one CIA estimate, the new regime would probably find it more difficult to abandon positions than Stalin did and might feel itself "compelled to react more strongly" if the West confronted it with the need for major decisions. Conversely, the new leadership would probably "exercise caution" in the near future in taking action that it thought would force the West to make comparable decisions. Another intelligence report asserted that intra-leadership "intrigues" would probably occur, but that it could not be assumed that these intrigues would lead to serious "weakening" of the regime or to "significant changes" in Soviet foreign or domestic policies.[30]

American officials thus sought a way to convince the French that Soviet peace gestures were merely attempts to sabotage allied unity.[31] Recognizing that Mayer would bring up Indochina and European defense when discussing American assistance for 1953–1954, at least some American officials felt that increased aid should be offered only in the context of an overall package agreement for the purpose of securing French ratification of the EDC. Director of the Office of Philippine and Southeast Asian Affairs Philip Bonsal, a holdover from the Truman administration and familiar with the problems of connected European and Asian defense, objected to this proposal of "placing the Indochina egg firmly in the EDC basket," insisting that the two issues should be "dealt with separately."[32] By spring 1953, the Eisenhower administration was still undecided on whether aid for Indochina should be directly tied to the EDC's ratification.

As the talks approached, Washington assumed that Paris would demand significant American economic and military aid for the Indochina effort and that the Mayer government would portray France as "overextended and overcommitted" in order to secure this assistance. While acknowledging that the French government was "in a most difficult position in the face of sorely divided public opinion" on the EDC and Indochina questions, the Eisenhower administration hesitated to provide detailed commitments in Europe and Asia immediately, preferring to engage in preliminary conversations instead. As American officials acknowledged, Franco-American relations had reached an "unhappily low ebb" on these issues.[33]

The Mayer government did indeed portray itself as "overextended and overcommitted." In response to domestic turmoil and military losses in Indochina, Mayer appealed to the United States for unconditional economic and military aid. According to Quai officials, it was the Indochina War more than French rearmament in Europe that permitted France to speak to the American government as "associates in a common enterprise and not as debtors in difficulty." American aid was necessary because of the particularly hard burden the French had to carry in Indochina, but the war was "a French effort and must remain so."[34] The Mayer government thus attempted to frame its requests for aid as coming from a partner rather than a supplicant.

Ultimately, the Eisenhower-Mayer talks did not create closer allied unity on Vietnam; instead, the cracks in the Western alliance grew wider. The Psychological Strategy Board (PSB) thus attempted to put allied unity back on track by resolving the Indochina problem. According to PSB official Charles Taquey, the French and Vietnamese were more concerned with "satisfactions of prestige than satisfactions of substance." The Joint Chiefs concurred, maintaining that Paris stayed in the Indochina War "solely to uphold French prestige and the colonial empire," and that France would resist any U.S. policy that encouraged France to disengage itself from the affairs of the Associated States.[35] The United States should therefore try to convince the French that they could make symbolic concessions to Vietnamese pride while retaining the substantive factors of power. For instance, France could enhance Bao Dai's sovereignty while keeping French advisers in key positions and acting discreetly behind the scenes. The PSB recommended that Washington should also reassure the French that the United States appreciated and recognized the international value of their effort and that U.S. help in the economic, financial, and military fields would strengthen the position of the Associated States. To take advantage of psychological warfare in the field, PSB members discussed the situation in Indochina with American ambassador Donald Heath. According to Heath, an interdepartmental committee in the embassy at Saigon—useful for coordinating U.S. psychological warfare activities in French Indochina—was in existence, as was a liaison between the committee and French officials in Saigon. Heath believed that this liaison was crucial, since nothing could be accomplished in French Indochina without French permission and clearance.[36]

In mid-1953, the Eisenhower administration thus found itself weighing the possibilities for a psychological offensive in Indochina. The obvious need to coordinate American military, paramilitary, and psychological programs with similar French and British programs in the area created the possibility of exerting greatly increased U.S. influence over the French struggle against communism in Indochina.[37] The United States thus sought to achieve a new approach on the part of French military and political leaders that would favor aggressive military operations and adroit psychological, political, and

guerrilla warfare in the Indochinese peninsula. In addition, the State Department planned to work with officers in the French general staff and at all
echelons of the French army who showed the necessary drive and experience
to obtain these objectives.

Through informal and formal contacts, Washington planned to create a
change in the French attitude by appealing to French military honor, using
American instructors to teach guerrilla warfare tactics, fostering French desire for U.S. training of local forces, and assigning U.S. guerrilla warfare and
political warfare officer specialists to MAAG. MAAG's directive would also
be revised to enable its members to participate in training and maneuvers as
operational advisers, mobilize all nationalist forces in the Indochinese peninsula against foreign communist intervention to "maximize psychological
splits" among the Vietminh, and win over the "local fence sitters." Through
the Foreign Operations Administration, American officials intended to coordinate economic support with military operations, assist the national regimes in improving agricultural methods and health practices, draw French
and Vietnamese attention to the extent of Chinese communist intervention,
secure cooperation between local officials and progressive French officials to
improve actual progress toward independence and administrative efficiency,
arrange for publication of American or French scholarly articles "extolling
benefits" accrued to Britain and the Netherlands from the independence
granted to certain dependencies, and select the French target groups sus-
ceptible to play a part in this strategy. The American policy was designed to
provide for a "discrete and unobtrusive" intervention by the United States.[38]
Its success was predicated, not on a large number of U.S. personnel, but on
the careful selection of targets. Washington thus took a number of significant, albeit quiet, steps to increase American political influence in Vietnam.
Some Americans were less discreet. One official, encapsulating the general
sentiment in Washington, commented that "everywhere in Asia the age of
foreign empire has passed" but "insofar as there is to be any imperialism at
all, let it be American imperialism."[39]

The Eisenhower administration remained divided as to the importance
of psychological warfare. Advocates, such as former chargé d'affaires to Vietnam Edmund Gullion, suggested making use of "psy war" tactics not only
in Vietnam but also in France, thus influencing military officers, civilian officials, businessmen, and churches in both countries. By identifying these
targets, American officials could "devise psychological methods" of securing
their support for U.S. policies without "compromising American interests
or showing the U.S. hand."[40] But Philip Bonsal and Donald Heath opposed

creating unofficial contacts in France to pursue American objectives in Vietnam. Meanwhile, PBS officials continued to warn that the threat to Southeast Asia was more direct and imminent than it had been at any time during the past eight years. The PBS office had predicted that the first consequence of the devolution of power in the Soviet Union would be a short-term widening of existing cleavages among the nations of the free world, which had been "tragically confirmed" by recent allied disunity. Taquey calculated that America's "greatest difficulties with France in the future will not be about the EDC but about [the] French colonial posture."[41]

Members of the PBS had accurately assessed the situation. The recent Soviet peace offensive had led a large fraction of French opinion—not to mention many civilian and military leaders—to ask whether France should profit from this change in attitude to try to find a basis for solving the Indochina affair at the negotiating table.[42] As the French attempted to determine what Stalin's death signified for the international situation, two primary objectives eventually dominated French policy in Europe and Asia. First, the French saw in Stalin's death an opportunity for meaningful negotiations on Indochina. Whereas the Eisenhower administration steadfastly opposed negotiations with the new Soviet leadership and sought to capitalize on Soviet confusion to score a Cold War victory, the French were determined to pursue diplomatic solutions to existing problems. Second, French leaders refused to move forward on the EDC's ratification before the Indochina conflict had been resolved. Paris feared that if the EDC came into being while the Indochina conflict continued to drain French troops from the continent, the Germans would achieve numerical superiority in the EDC and consequently in Europe.

Paris's first goal was a resolution to the resource-draining war in Indochina. In mid-1953, French military forces remained unable to launch a successful offensive against the Vietminh, and many officials and most of the public were clamoring for an end to hostilities. French leaders had blamed Stalin for encouraging the Vietminh's war effort, and they viewed Stalin's death as an opportunity for negotiation. Subsequently, the French eagerly embraced the Soviet peace offensive as a chance to extricate themselves from Indochina in an honorable fashion. Determined to find a negotiated solution, Paris rejected the American proposal for bringing the Indochina issue to the UN and internationalizing the conflict, fearing that the United States and Great Britain would simply fight the war themselves. French leaders felt the best chance for success was not "to internationalize the conflict" but "to internationalize the solution" by holding a peace conference.[43] The French were also convinced that the Soviet Union would veto any international-ization measure and that, if such a measure went to the General Assembly, France would have difficulty securing a two-thirds majority. The Mayer gov-ernment recognized that inter-allied cooperation was essential to bring In-dochina to the negotiating table, but the Eisenhower administration refused to make such a commitment, instead continuing its pressure on the French to internationalize the conflict by taking it to the UN. In particular, Walter Robertson, assistant secretary of state for Far Eastern affairs, argued that the Vietminh invasion of Laos in April 1953 was a "splendid opportunity" to secure international status through the UN under favorable conditions.[44]

In part to appease the Eisenhower administration, but also to indicate its intention to grant Vietnamese independence, Paris planned to turn over French leadership in the Associated States to career diplomats and to declare that the Associated States could come and go in the French Union as they pleased. In keeping with this idea, French deputy prime minister Paul Reyn-aud succeeded in having Maurice DeJean, a close friend and an advocate of genuine Vietnamese independence, replace Jean Letourneau as French min-ister of the Associated States.[45] Edgar Faure, president of the Foreign Affairs Committee of the French Assembly, also championed Vietnamese indepen-dence. He claimed that to counter international perceptions that France was acting in "bad faith," the French government needed to reiterate its intention to leave Indochina after the war and to allow the Indochinese themselves to determine whether Indochina would remain in the French Union when the war was finished. Faure advocated an immediate settlement to the war as well as granting complete independence to the Bao Dai regime.[46] The government's announcement in early July that it was prepared to transfer the powers France still retained to the State of Vietnam, and French president Vincent Auriol and Vietnamese emperor Bao Dai's communiqué issued at the end of Au-gust affirming the French government's intention to complete Vietnamese independence and free adherence to the French Union, helped persuade the Vietnamese and Americans of French sincerity.

France also began to make a series of substantive gestures—giving the Norodom Palace back to Bao Dai, transferring the headquarters of the Indo-china provinces to the Vietnamese, returning to France hundreds of function-aries whose services were no longer needed, creating a judicial convention, and establishing monetary autonomy. According to a French Foreign Minis-try report, such initiatives would have a considerable psychological effect on the Indochina population and on Asian world opinion, which were crucial to a negotiated settlement. The French people would rally, as would the *at-*

tentistes, the Vietnamese fence-sitters who had yet to choose between the French and the Vietminh. The report further suggested that Paris should try to address the Indochina question at a conference on Korea or at a quadripartite conference and entice the Soviet Union and China into playing a role by putting pressure on them to work toward an international resolution of the Indochina conflict. This way, France could test communist claims of peaceful coexistence. These actions demonstrated Paris's attempt to make use of the psychological element to end the war. But American "psy war" proponents criticized French efforts at psychological warfare in Indochina, calling them "inept and useless." According to Charles Taquey, "the key to the Indochina situation [was] not in Vietnam but in Paris."[47] Washington had to convince Paris to provide even greater independence to the Associated States.

Meanwhile, the Soviets renewed their offer to talk to the West. Since emerging as a dominant figure following the death of Stalin, Malenkov had made clear his interest in improving relations with the West. In September, he proposed the convening of a five-power conference with the United States, the Soviet Union, Britain, France, and China to examine measures for the relaxation of international tensions.[48] Chinese foreign minister Zhou Enlai also indicated China's willingness to work toward peace in the Far East in October. In light of the communists' perceived good faith, France sought a means of bringing Indochina to the negotiating table. The Americans, however, were still opposed. At the very moment when the communist threat appeared to be ebbing and a genuine possibility for a resolution to Indochina had materialized, Washington insisted on continuing the fight and keeping the pressure on Moscow.[49]

This divergence became even more pronounced as Washington and Paris continued to clash over the EDC's future. The second major objective of the French was to avoid making a decision on the EDC until the Indochina conflict ended. The Mayer government had refused to ratify the EDC and commit troops to the European continent before France had resolved the Indochina conflict. On May 21, 1953, the Mayer government collapsed because of the deteriorating financial position in France. As a result, Joseph Laniel became prime minister on June 30. The new government immediately faced American pressure to ratify the EDC and continue the war in Indochina. The proposed Richards amendment, which linked aid for Indochina to the EDC's ratification, continued to cause concern among French officials, as did the Eisenhower administration's apparent conviction that the French no longer had the will to fight in Indochina and that American policy needed to be adjusted accordingly.[50] French officials thus believed that American aid for both Indochina and Europe was in danger of being reduced.

In the end, the French had little to fear despite Congressional threats. Dulles succeeded in suppressing the Richards amendment by convincing legislators that coercion would not result in the EDC's ratification. Another piece of positive information for the French was the failure of the Goldwater-Kennedy amendment—tying American aid to independence for the Associated States—by a vote of 64 to 17 in the Senate.[51] The French decision to make further concessions toward Vietnamese independence in early July had been at least partially influenced by fears that the amendment would pass. The French also succeeded in favorably impressing Senator Knowland during his visit to Indochina. In an apparent reversal of his earlier sentiments, Knowland returned to the United States convinced of the necessity of absolute cooperation between the United States and France to sustain the Associated States in their fight against communism. The good news from Knowland's visit was that American aid would not be cut; the bad news was that the Americans expected the French to continue fighting even though American officials were well aware that France wanted to negotiate. The French agreed to intensify the prosecution of the war, leading to an additional $385 million in aid for Indochina, which brought total American aid for Indochina in 1953–1954 to $785 million.

Back in Paris, Bidault continued to provide assurances to American ambassador to France Douglas Dillon that in exchange for the additional American aid of $385 million the French would perfect Vietnamese independence, develop a strategic plan against the Vietminh, and exchange information and views on a continuing basis with American military authorities. Bidault also reassured Dillon that the increased effort that France intended to make in Indochina would not entail any basic or permanent alteration of its plans and programs concerning those forces that were placed under NATO command.[52] Still, Washington remained concerned about the war's progress. During a meeting between French minister counselor Jean Daridan and Undersecretary of State Walter Bedell Smith, Smith stated that he thought the search for negotiations was premature if France was not in a situation of strength, which could take a few months to attain.[53] As the French sought to turn their military position around with the $385 million in additional aid, the Eisenhower administration assumed that the Laniel government would respond by hastening the EDC's ratification. A New York Times article entitled "Aid for France Seen Ending Deadlocks in Europe and Asia" asserted that the additional money "is expected to go a long way toward breaking the political and military deadlocks in Europe as well as in Asia."[54] The French had their money with an implicit understanding from the American government and an explicit one from the American press that the EDC would now make timely progress.

American officials were playing a dangerous game by agreeing to provide aid to the French while simultaneously threatening to decrease or terminate aid altogether if the EDC was not ratified. The Eisenhower administration's attempt to create a quid pro quo—the EDC's ratification in return for American aid for Indochina—was ineffective. Because they were already providing aid to the French, the Americans were in a much weaker position to influence French policy than a quid pro quo situation would normally provide. The more the Eisenhower administration refused to consider alternatives to the EDC, the more leverage the French enjoyed as they continued to hold the EDC hostage to attract additional support for Indochina.[55]

Dulles decided to switch gears by advocating a harsher approach. He insisted that the Laniel government should agree in writing that American economic aid to the French war effort in Indochina depended on the EDC's ratification. Dillon, a personal friend of Dulles and an important element in the Republican Party, urged him to reconsider, warning that an attempt "to inject written reference to the EDC at this late date into the projected Indochina agreement might delay completion of negotiations and would cost the U.S. a portion of the goodwill we will acquire as a result of this new assistance." Moreover, Dillon, who hoped to improve Franco-American relations, feared that "a written connection that could only be construed as forced by the U.S. would be resented by French public opinion and might very well do harm to the prospects of ratification in the French Parliament." He suggested that when the United States formally agreed to increase French aid, American leaders should make the connection verbally in a forceful manner. Dillon himself, however, specifically linked the EDC and Indochina issues by stating that "our desire to help create the necessary preconditions for ratification of EDC was one of [the] principal reasons which decided [the] U.S. to make this additional aid available to Indochina."[56] Dillon's vacillation suggests the contradictions inherent in Washington's pursuit of a dual EDC-Indochina policy.

In addition to increased pressure for the EDC's ratification, the Laniel government encountered the recurring American demand that it continue to fight the Vietminh rather than search for a political solution in Indochina. The Vietminh were in a strong negotiating position because of their continued military offensives, and the Eisenhower administration feared that negotiations would lead to total Vietminh victory. But the Laniel government refused to limit its options: whether by military or political means, the war in Indochina had to end. Bonnet hoped to convince the Eisenhower administration that the French "no longer had the will to fight in Indochina" and that American policy needed "to accept this reality."[57]

French sources demonstrate that finding a negotiated solution to the Indochina conflict had become the overwhelming French priority; the EDC remained a secondary consideration. Yet the Eisenhower administration ignored the internal political climate in Paris, making the EDC a symbol of Washington's ascendancy and Europe's decline for both the French and the Americans. American pressure on the Laniel government to ratify the EDC reinforced this view, creating a growing resentment among the French, which in turn forced Laniel to delay the debate on the EDC's ratification.[58] As Paris struggled to negotiate its way out of Indochina, Washington attempted to maintain French involvement by increasing the level of American aid in the fiscal year 1953–1954.

From the State Department's perspective, the French military effort in Indochina was motivated by the Laniel government's awareness of its political, economic, and military weakness. According to a State Department report, French leaders knew that this weakness made French aspirations for "world power" status dependent on the continued support of the United States and Britain. The report also surmised that the serious financial difficulties France faced were all traceable to the war. Continuation of such an effort would only ensure Germany eclipsing France as more French troops left the continent for Asia.[59] Thus, while the Americans seemed aware of French difficulties in Indochina, they still insisted on the EDC's ratification.

PEACE IN KOREA

Along with conflict over the EDC and the possibilities of the Soviet peace offensive, the other factor standing in the way of Franco-American unity was the relationship between Vietnam and Korea. Eisenhower had implied during his presidential campaign that he would extricate the United States from the Korean quagmire, and Stalin's death paved the way for a settlement. The new Soviet leadership appeared just as eager to end the stalemated war as the new American president. On June 27, 1953, the United States and North Korea agreed to an armistice and began the process of establishing a peace conference. The Laniel government was convinced that Stalin's death had played a significant role in achieving the armistice and planned to attain the same result in Indochina. Although Eisenhower and Dulles recognized that the truce made it more difficult to persuade both the French and Bao Dai's forces to increase their military efforts, and although they accepted the French argument that the Korean and Indochina battles were part of the same anticommunist war, they were not prepared to end the Indochina conflict at the negotiating table.

The French refused to accept the American position on negotiations, prompting the Quai d'Orsay to begin an assessment of Soviet and Chinese policy regarding an eventual negotiation. Quai officials believed that the new Soviet leadership's acceptance of a 1952 plan to achieve a Korean armistice indicated a clear break from Stalin's earlier rejection of the plan. The events since Stalin's death testified to a "clear evolution" of Soviet general policy and indicated that the Soviets were working toward "conciliation" to avoid risking a general war. And, according to the Quai, the Kremlin was the one making the decisions in Southeast Asia. Thus, it was unlikely that a Chinese intervention would occur in Indochina, although Beijing could still speed up its arms and material deliveries to the Vietminh. The Quai also believed that China would be equally receptive to a peace conference as the Soviets because Beijing wanted to move forward with its plans for industrialization, which were being held back by the Indochina hostilities. But the communist bloc's new foreign policy orientation did not mean that there had been any "doctrinal change." French options were still limited. France could insist that China pledge not to interfere in Vietnamese affairs in return for France officially recognizing the People's Republic of China (PRC), accepting China in the UN, and reestablishing normal commercial relations by ending the economic embargo against China. American opposition to such a plan, however, would be strong. The Quai also believed that the reestablishment of peace in Indochina could be "primed" by the negotiations over Korea, but thus far the Russians and Chinese resisted any linkage between the two, and the British and Americans were also reluctant.[60]

By July 1953, in direct opposition to the Eisenhower administration's wishes, French leaders openly pressed for negotiations on Indochina. The war in Indochina was just as unpopular in France as the Korean War had become in the United States—a fact American leaders failed to grasp. French public opinion and a number of leading French officials and military generals, among them General Paul Ely, recommended negotiations. Ely resented the Eisenhower administration's willingness to resolve the Korean War peacefully while it refused to consider a diplomatic solution to Indochina. Bonnet and Bidault also claimed that "if the United States could reach an agreement on Korea, France could reach one on Indochina." French officials thus believed that the biggest obstacle to a resolution on Indochina stemmed "not from Moscow, but from Washington."[61]

Bidault argued that those who worried about French losses in Indochina affecting France's world position were wrong, estimating that Indochina was not an "essential element" of French world position and that it had "never been essential." He saw three possibilities for a peaceful solution. Direct negotiations with the Vietminh could be opened, but Paris could not go this route unless it had Washington's acquiescence. The French government could negotiate directly with China, but that course would entail officially recognizing the PRC. Or, Indochina could be included in a general negotiation of Far Eastern affairs. This last option provided the only hope, since the United States and Britain would undoubtedly reject the first two.[62]

The connection between the Indochina and Korean conflicts was critical. The armistice in Korea and the accompanying general relaxation of East-West tensions generated a groundswell of public opinion in France against the continuation of the military effort in Indochina. As State Department officials acknowledged, American willingness to reach a truce in Korea undermined Washington's claim that the Indochina War was crucial to the free world struggle against communist aggression. French public opinion therefore insisted that the French government hold the United States to previous declarations on the indivisibility of the Korean and Indochina wars: "the policy of negotiating an end to the Korean War likewise must be extended to the Indochina hostilities." French officials expressed dismay at Washington's disjointed plan of continuing the war in Indochina while preparing for an international peace conference on Korea. As Bonnet stated to Dulles, "it will be difficult for French public opinion to understand that if an end to the Korean War occurred, why the Indochina war would continue, risking a Chinese invasion." Bonnet later reported to Bidault that he had convinced Dulles that an "all-out effort must be put forth" to end the war in Indochina. Urging Bidault to say nothing about Dulles's apparent acceptance of a potential political settlement, Bonnet added that he was "surprised" at the secretary of state's willingness to resolve the two conflicts at the same time. Most likely Dulles was humoring Bonnet to coax the French toward timely ratification of the EDC.[63]

Caught in the middle of Franco-American disagreements once again, the British wavered over what policy to take regarding a conference on Indochina. London preferred to hold an Asian conference where such issues as the PRC's aggressive moves toward the nationalist Chinese government territory, the economic embargo against the PRC, and its entry into the UN could be discussed. British foreign minister Lord Salisbury disclosed to René Massigli that if real progress were made on Korea, the British would not oppose consideration of Indochina at a political conference, but that was as far as they were prepared to go.[64]

The French remained internally divided on how to negotiate an end to the war. Bidault did not necessarily want to tie Indochina and Korea together at a conference, but Paul Reynaud continued to force the issue. According to Bidault, greater independence for Indochina was unnecessary and direct negotiations with the Vietminh were out of the question. Bidault believed that the July 3 declaration promising to speed up Vietnamese independence should satisfy both the Vietnamese and French allies and that Bao Dai should continue to be the only Vietnamese representative France recognized. Unlike Bidault, Reynaud desired greater independence for Indochina, direct negotiations with the Vietminh, and faster creation of a national Vietnamese army. Reynaud wanted France to leave Indochina entirely, granting complete independence to the Bao Dai government. He saw direct negotiations with the Vietminh as the easiest way of obtaining this objective. In addition, he argued for a policy of Vietnamization, in which a Vietnamese national army would replace the FEC.[65] Marc Jacquet, French undersecretary of state responsible for the Associated States, also advocated direct negotiations with the Vietminh. If the Americans were negotiating on Korea, and the British were trading with China, why then, Jacquet wondered, did French allies continue to resist a negotiated solution to the Indochina problem. Indicating how drastically French opinion had changed on these issues was Albert Sarraut's telling interview with the Swedish daily *Expressen*. Sarraut, one of France's greatest colonial promoters, stated that "if he had the Ho Chi Minh of 1946 in front of him he would have negotiated."[66] Such remarks increased the pressure on the Laniel government to find a political solution.

Paris and Washington continued to debate the merits and drawbacks of negotiations throughout the summer. When Bidault raised the issue of an Indochina armistice following the Korean one, Dulles responded that Korea was a UN conflict and that peace would be conducted under UN auspices, whereas the French had refused to bring Indochina to the UN. Dulles insisted that the French should negotiate from a position of strength. Therefore they had to achieve military victories. French leaders received more bad news during a meeting among Jean Daridan, Philip Bonsal, and Walter Bedell Smith. Smith emphasized that the United States could make "no commitment" to enlarge the agenda of the Korean political conference to make a place for Indochina or any other topic. Although, in a subsequent meeting, the Americans did not rule out the possibility that if Korea was successfully resolved, other conferences could follow.[67]

The French received some hopeful news on this issue when Dulles gave a speech in early September stating that Korea was part of a larger problem, and that "out of the Korean conference could grow an end to aggression and restoration of peace in Indochina if China wanted it." Daridan noted that this speech marked the first time a member of the American government had publicly acknowledged the possibility of a negotiated settlement in Indochina. In addition, Foreign Office official Selwyn Lloyd announced in front of the UN that there could be no peace in Asia as long as war continued against the three Associated States whom the United Kingdom had recommended for entry into the UN. Lloyd declared that "the ending of the war in Indochina is an essential step along the path of pacification and conciliation in Asia which began with the armistice in Korea."[68]

In the interim, the Soviets continued their flexible approach regarding Indochina. Soviet propaganda attacks against French colonialism became less frequent; the Soviet press favorably mentioned the idea of a negotiated settlement; and Moscow announced its intention to send a mission to Hanoi to discuss potential negotiations with the West. Moreover, in July, Soviet foreign minister Vyacheslav Molotov sent a note to the French Embassy in Moscow suggesting a Franco-Soviet discussion to resolve the Indochina problem. The French ambassador to the Soviet Union, Louis Joxe, postulated that the Soviets had perhaps decided communism could triumph in Indochina through political means as easily as military ones, since the Vietminh would have at least 60 percent of any election vote. Previously, the Soviets had thought war in Indochina useful—it weakened France and slowed the development of the Atlantic alliance in Europe. Stalin, when speaking of Korea in February 1951, had prophesied that war could finish only by crushing the western interventionists. But Joxe noted that "what [had] changed in Korea could also change in Indochina." The Soviets might now think that by helping in Indochina, they would put France in a stronger position against Germany, and France would decide that the EDC was no longer necessary. Joxe expressed a concern—shared by Washington—that if Paris negotiated directly with Moscow instead of holding an international conference on Indochina, France would have to make a deal with the Soviets: in exchange for peace in Indochina, the French would not ratify the EDC.[69]

An End to the "Dirty War"

In the meantime, the French had finally begun preparations to retake the offensive against the Vietminh. Paris had urged French general Henri Navarre to find an honorable way out of the war that would allow the government to negotiate and bring the war to an end while keeping French casualties to a minimum. A career army officer, Navarre was appointed commander of French forces in Indochina on May 8, 1953. Although he had little knowledge of the situation in Indochina, he was considered a brilliant strategist. His instructions were to study the situation in Indochina and report back to Paris. Three weeks after his arrival in Indochina, Navarre outlined his plan to his regional commanders, and shortly thereafter he presented his plan to the French government. The Navarre Plan proposed a slow buildup of French and Vietnamese military strength sufficient for large-scale action against Ho Chi Minh's Vietminh during the 1954–1955 campaign season. The French would use cautious restraint during the 1953–1954 campaign season, reconstituting the FEC. The FEC would maintain a strategically defensive position north of the eighteenth parallel, using mobile units for short engagements and avoiding a general battle. In the South, the FEC would launch an offensive, termed Operation Atlante, which would attempt to eliminate the Vietminh from that region. Once the South had been subdued, the FEC would take the offensive north of the eighteenth parallel. Navarre's goal was to create a military situation that would permit a political solution to the conflict.

In order to achieve these objectives, the Navarre Plan proposed a major strengthening of the Vietnamese National Army under the command of General Nguyen Van Hinh, the addition of ten new French battalions to the Indochinese theater, and French maneuverable divisions of a size equal to those of the Vietminh but possessing much greater firepower. Navarre would then use the 1954–1955 campaign season to consolidate the French position and develop his battle force, anticipating a full-scale French offensive in the summer of 1955. In the meantime, limited French operations would be carried out in the Red River delta. Navarre recognized that his plan could succeed only if Chinese aid to the Vietminh remained at mid-1953 levels and if he received reinforcements from France. He also noted that the best he could accomplish would be a military stalemate.

The French government approved the Navarre Plan, intending to use it to improve their military situation and either win the conflict or, more likely, attain a better negotiating position.[70] However, it did not reach a decision on what to do about Laos. The defense of northern Laos was a major problem.

In the spring of 1953, the Vietminh commander, General Vo Nguyen Giap, had sent troops into Laos from the remote village of Dien Bien Phu, located in mountainous northwestern Vietnam just a few miles from the Laotian border. Giap withdrew his forces from Laos, but the French expected that the Vietminh would attack again in 1954. For the French command, the taking of Dien Bien Phu became a critical objective in order to prevent another attack on Laos and to establish a mooring point from which an offensive could be launched to destroy a major part of the Vietminh army.

The Americans, initially skeptical of the French ability to implement all the provisions of the plan with the resources on hand, embraced the Navarre Plan in September 1953 as a means to achieve military victory in Indochina. But by October, public statements by Laniel, Edgar Faure, and Quai spokesmen had persuaded the Eisenhower administration that the recently announced additional American aid and the Navarre Plan were intended not to achieve military victory but to improve France's negotiating position with the Vietminh.[71] The Americans had it half right. Navarre was serious about the plan, thinking that he had convinced key figures in political and military circles that the solution was to maintain an "impasse" in Europe for two years while focusing all the troops in Indochina so that he could win at least a part of the war and negotiate from a position of honor. But Paris once again "decided to cut the pear in half," refusing to completely deplete French troops in Europe but sending some additional troops to Indochina. Navarre claimed that as a result, Europe was "not well protected" and there would "not be enough French troops" in Indochina.[72]

Further confirmation of the French desire to negotiate could be seen at a French Assembly debate at the end of October. The National Assembly invited the French government to "develop" the forces of the Associated States; to "reduce progressively" the French military effort; to "put everything in order" to achieve general peace in Asia by negotiation; to ensure, "on an international basis," a "just distribution of efforts and sacrifices" of the free nations in all the different parts of the globe where they must exercise their solidarity; and to "carry out the defense and independence" of the Associated States "within the framework of the French union."[73] More encouraging news was heard on November 29, when the Swedish daily *Expressen* published a statement by Ho Chi Minh that the DRV was ready to study every proposal for a cease-fire. These developments, combined with continued French hesitance over the EDC, contributed to a growing sense of uneasiness among the Americans. For Eisenhower, the EDC was still the most important objective, and nothing should be done to endanger its success.[74] French determination to negotiate over Indochina led the Eisenhower administration to become more concerned about a breakdown in allied unity. American officials thus looked forward to the scheduled Bermuda Conference in December as a means to put allied unity back on track in both Europe and Asia.

According to C. D. Jackson, the Bermuda Conference was shaping up as something of "great significance and hope." In fact, it was one of the few really "tremendous" opportunities the United States had to recapture allied unity and to negotiate with the Russians from a position of strength rather than weakness. In order to plan for the meeting, Jackson recommended that it was necessary not only to think as Americans, but also to be "very much aware of what was going on in the minds of U.S. allies." Regarding Indochina, the United States should accept the Indochina problem as of "equal status" to Korea, and, if necessary, provide a serious increase in allied military assistance to the French. In addition, the French should increase their moves toward eventual independence for the Associated States. Jackson wanted tripartite unity in order to negotiate from a position of strength, but at "the apex of the triangle there must be the U.S." And, if it was necessary to fund the Indochina effort to arrive at this position, then the United States should do so.[75] Jackson's letter to Eisenhower addressed the issues that would continue to vex Franco-American diplomacy throughout 1953 and 1954 as Washington attempted to achieve policies toward Europe and Indochina amenable to its allies.

When Eisenhower, British prime minister Winston Churchill, and Laniel finally met in Bermuda in early December, the conference disappointed everyone. Instead of providing cohesive western unity, it merely pointed out the differences among the three nations. At the end of the conference, the three powers issued a joint communiqué emphasizing western solidarity, but privately recognized that the conference had been a setback for allied unity. Regarding Indochina, Bidault made clear his plan to discuss the possibility of a five-power conference, including China, at the upcoming four-power foreign ministers meeting at Berlin. Disagreements at the conference led Eisenhower to the conclusion that the French were receiving excessive military, economic, and technical aid from the United States and that they could not possibly use it all, especially if they planned to negotiate. So whereas French officials thought they had too little assistance, Eisenhower thought they had too much.[76]

The EDC and Indochina linkage once again became more explicit in mid-December. Theodore Streibert, director of American Information Services, told French officials that the Eisenhower administration placed the utmost importance upon the EDC's ratification. He added that continuation of aid to Europe, and even continuation of aid to Indochina, would cease if France failed to ratify the EDC. This was the most explicit connection an American official had drawn between Indochina and the EDC. Both Dulles and Smith feared the consequences of making such a connection. They immediately rushed to refute Streibert's claim and to reassure the Laniel government in a formal statement that financial and military aid to Indochina did not depend on the EDC's success: "Military aid for the war in Indochina is not based on the question of the EDC's ratification but on the importance the U.S. attaches to Indochina's maintenance in the Free World."[77] Dulles eschewed an explicit quid pro quo in favor of veiled threats and implicit linkages.

There was also trouble at home. In early 1954, the Eisenhower administration scrambled to defend its unproductive Indochina policy against critics. The president set up a special committee on Indochina to formulate a coherent strategy. Dulles was also coming under fire from Republicans who felt that too many holdovers from Acheson were still involved in Far Eastern Affairs at the State Department. Dulles emphasized that the Truman and Eisenhower policies toward Asia were completely different. He pointed out that Walter Robertson and Deputy Assistant Secretary of State for Far Eastern Affairs Everett Drumright were the two people now running Far Eastern policy, and that Robertson and Drumright had always been violently opposed to the communists in China.[78] Although Dulles insisted that the Eisenhower administration's commitment to Indochina was much stronger than the one made by the Truman administration, in fact Eisenhower and Dulles were still attempting to define American policy in Vietnam.

As the Eisenhower administration struggled to maintain a coherent policy, American aid to France continued. The American aid effort to France had evolved from a haphazard affair in 1950 to a well-organized business by early 1954. American aid was divided into four categories. First, Washington supplied financial aid to France for military expenditures on behalf of the Associated States—this budgetary support to help French expenditures for NATO and Indochina allowed the simultaneous prosecution of the war and buildup of defense in Europe. Second, the United States provided military end-item assistance, mostly military equipment provided by MAAG. Third, the American military support program supplied items not necessarily military in nature but that would further the military effort and assist civilian recovery by providing, among other things, airfields, roads, and railroads. Finally, STEM provided direct economic aid and continued to help with health, agriculture, transport, industry, and education. In addition, the commercial import program begun under the Truman administration was expanded to make dollars available for importation of equipment and materials for private firms and individuals. Military aid was channeled through France, whereas economic aid went directly to the Associated States. In evaluating American aid, a special Congressional mission to Vietnam advocated that deliveries of military equipment should be accelerated and that less emphasis should be given to long-range technical assistance programs; economic assistance should be confined to producing a military victory.[79] This recommendation supported the Eisenhower administration's goal of finding a military rather than political solution to the Vietnam problem.

Although the Eisenhower administration had assumed, as the Truman administration had, that increased aid entitled the Americans to a bigger role in Indochina policy, the French were of a different opinion. The policy of American expansion had become "the most active agent in the disintegration of the French Empire," according to Paul Ely. Ely stated that if France did win the war, "it would not be a genuine victory if the Americans were the ones in control." According to French officials, if the United States wanted to direct events, then American military forces needed to participate. If this was not the case, then France "should not tolerate American intrusion in the war," and "guarantees should be secured so that France [did] not risk everything for the benefit of the Americans."[80] The French thus sought to clearly define the objectives and limits of American aid in Vietnam as they also struggled to find a way out of their colonial predicament.

A resolution to the "dirty war" finally appeared on the horizon when Dulles, Bidault, Molotov, and British foreign secretary Anthony Eden agreed to meet at a diplomatic conference in Berlin (from January 25 to February 2, 1954). The three issues that governed the discussions were the possibility of a conference held at Geneva to resolve the Korean *and* Indochina conflicts, German problems (including the EDC), and Austrian problems. The French, Americans, and British had finally agreed to talk directly to the Russians but held very different views on the upcoming conference. The Eisenhower administration was convinced that negotiations with the Russians would not produce results except perhaps on Korea. Eisenhower and Dulles went along with the conference primarily to appease their allies and present a united western front to the Soviets. Churchill, however, wanted to revive his image as a peacemaker and intended to place the British at the center of an effort to bring about an overarching Cold War settlement.[81] The Laniel government also accepted the usefulness of the Berlin Conference, especially as it repre-sented an opportunity to place the Indochina conflict on the Geneva Con-ference agenda—a key goal of the French. French leaders recognized that their best chance to resolve the Indochina crisis diplomatically was to make it part of the program at Berlin.

The conference got off to a rocky start when, after Bidault and Eden's conciliatory openings, Molotov returned to the standard Soviet line of re-criminations against the West in general and against the United States in particular. Apparently, Molotov decided to depart from his more peaceful stance of November 1953, when he had proposed a foreign ministers confer-ence to consider measures for easing international tensions. Molotov was undoubtedly trying to disrupt Atlantic unity to ensure that a five-power con-ference took place on Korea and Indochina.[82] Throughout the conference, Dulles attempted to hold the western front together while trying to stop a five-power conference on Indochina.

Bidault, on the other hand, was under intense pressure to bring about such a conference. In a meeting with Dulles, Bidault stated that he had "very few cards in his hand to play." Dulles replied that this might be true but that one of those cards was U.S. support and that one he "must not throw away." Dulles had mentioned to Eisenhower that he would attempt to play a "some-what inconspicuous role" at the Berlin Conference, allowing the French to lead so they might feel that they had concluded negotiations on their own. In this way, Dulles planned to avoid the accusation that France had been forced to support the United States or that American leaders desired the confer-ence's failure. Eisenhower, according to Dulles, "fully agreed with these tac-tics." At Berlin, Dulles tried publicly to downplay his inflexibility, allowing Bidault to lead negotiations. Privately he continued to press Bidault to stand firm against Soviet pressure to negotiate on Indochina.[83]

In the end, Berlin was a victory for the French. Most significantly, Bi-dault succeeded in placing the Indochina problem on the agenda for the forthcoming Geneva Conference—a maneuver the Quai d'Orsay had been attempting since spring 1953.[84] The final agreement at Berlin stated that a conference regarding a peaceful settlement of the Korean question would be-gin on April 26 and that the problem of restoring peace in Indochina would be discussed in May. The final clause of the agreement, which Dulles had insisted upon, was that "neither the invitation to, nor the holding of, the above-mentioned conference shall be deemed to imply diplomatic recogni-tion in any case where it has not already been accorded." Bidault surmounted Dulles's efforts to keep such a meeting on Indochina from taking place, and he even persuaded the secretary of state to go along with the Soviet demand that the PRC participate in the Geneva talks.

According to French minister of state for foreign affairs Maurice Schumann, the French had gained on a number of other fronts as well. What appeared to be irreconcilable differences were resolved because of "American concessions" and "even more important Russian ones." For example, Schumann noted that although Washington had remained wary that the Soviets might insist on diplomatic recognition of China, the Soviets had eventually dropped this demand. The Geneva Conference would include not only the five world powers, but also both North and South Korea and other countries involved in resolving the Korean and Vietnamese conflicts, and the conference would not change China's international status. For the French, Chinese participation was crucial to successful negotiations on Indochina and Korea. If the PRC was not represented at the conference, one of the major belligerents would not be a signatory to the accords reached at Geneva. Regarding Korea, the USSR was not simply an observer but would be held accountable to any decision reached. Moreover, neutralist countries would not be invited, and the question of formal invitations was avoided because the USSR would invite China and North Korea and the United States would invite South Korea. By establishing a single conference devoted to both conflicts, France had also ensured that the Indochina question would not be subordinated to a favorable progression of the Korean question, and the mode of invitation would serve as a precedent that would facilitate the convocation of the Associated States when the conference turned to Indochina. Schumann pointed out that at no moment did the Soviets try "to link European and Asian affairs" and that western solidarity "had not cracked in the slightest." The three foreign ministers presented a united front to Molotov, who eventually renounced any attempts at creating a rift among the allies.[85] Thus, on the surface, allied unity had apparently been preserved at Berlin.

A number of American observers concurred. According to former American ambassador to France David Bruce, western solidarity was much enhanced because Bidault had not made a deal with the Soviets to sabotage the EDC and because France vowed to continue the fight in Indochina. C. D. Jackson also had a positive outlook on Berlin, claiming that Berlin proved that the Eisenhower-Dulles foreign policy was not just a tougher "me too" to Truman-Acheson foreign policy, but something distinctive. According to Jackson, "virile diplomacy at Berlin under the field generalship of Dulles produced voluntary if not enthusiastic western unity such as has not been seen for one hell of a long time."[86]

Dulles disagreed. Worried that a five-power conference could be perceived as a sign of western weakness, Dulles immediately engaged in damage control at a press conference the week after Berlin, emphasizing that the negotiations at Berlin should not be construed as an "Asian Munich." He also noted that he had only conceded to a five-power conference because he assumed that the EDC would be brought to a ratification vote before the Geneva Conference began. Although Dulles had privately stated to Eisenhower that he saw Berlin as a success and that the Geneva Conference had potential, he clearly did not trust his Gallic allies to persevere against the communists at Geneva. Dulles even discussed the possibility of an Anglo-American joint position vis-à-vis the French, explaining his fears to Merchant and State Department counselor Douglas MacArthur that the French would either "sell out Indochina to the Soviet Union" and that the entire area of Southeast Asia would thereby be "greatly endangered" or that they would sabotage the EDC to obtain peace in Indochina. In the end, observing that French pressure for a political settlement of the Indochina War had increased as a result of Berlin, Dulles somewhat helplessly realized that if the United States stopped financial support or attached impossible conditions to it, "the anti-American reaction in France would be very severe and almost certainly defeat [the] European Defense Community." He also noted that the United States should, if at all possible, "seek to assure successes both in relation [to] Indochina and [the] European Defense Community." But American officials "must be on guard lest Indochina also carry [the] European Defense Community down the drain."[87] Dulles's comments exemplified his concern that events in Indochina would dictate the EDC's outcome. Yet he did not take concrete steps to break the linkage between the Eisenhower administration's European and Asian policies. Apparently, neither Eisenhower nor Dulles considered what might have happened if they had halted diplomatic pressure on the French—which might have made the French more amenable both to the EDC and to American suggestions regarding Indochina.

Following Berlin, during the 184th meeting of the NSC, Eisenhower commented on the extraordinary confusion in the reports that reached him from Indochina, stating that "there were almost as many judgments as there were authors of messages." There were, nevertheless, only two critical factors in the situation. The first was to "win over the Vietnamese population; the other to instill some spirit into the French." Chairman of the JCS Arthur Radford claimed that the differences in the reports resulted from the different situations of their authors: there were those that came from the service attachés and other semipermanent personnel, and those from visitors such as General John O'Daniel. According to Radford, attachés tended to become frustrated as a result of continuously being on the scene. Eisenhower then stated that he had just about reached the conclusion that it was time for a change of ambassadors in Vietnam and that Heath, although a "good man, well-liked, and doing a capable job," had stayed too long at his post. Eisenhower felt somebody "a little on the Machiavellian side" was needed.[88]

This policy of downplaying reports by experienced officials in the field and relying on newcomers' assessments was a structural flaw in the Eisenhower administration—the incoming top American official would always be more optimistic than the outgoing, which ensured that the United States would always stay in Vietnam just a little longer. For example, after his visit to Vietnam, O'Daniel recommended that the United States organize a small joint staff, assign two officers for psychological warfare attached to the appropriate U.S. organization in Saigon, provide additional funds for STEM to assist in rehabilitation of war-ravaged areas, and employ liaison officers. Such seemingly small and logical recommendations gradually increased the American investment in securing a noncommunist Vietnam.

Throughout 1953 and into 1954, the Eisenhower administration struggled to find the best course of action in Vietnam. The United States committed more aid to the French war effort while continuing to fear that the Soviets' acceptance of a peaceful settlement of the Indochina conflict would divide the West. The soft line coming from Moscow suggested to the French that a positive approach to negotiations with the Soviet Union might make German rearmament unnecessary while providing a diplomatic solution to the debilitating war in Indochina. But where Paris saw a chance for peace and an opportunity for relaxing Cold War tensions, Washington saw a menacing strategy to weaken the West by preventing German rearmament through the EDC and facilitating a communist victory in Indochina. Officials in the Eisenhower administration concluded that the Soviet call for peaceful coexistence was merely a calculated ploy to win the Cold War through propaganda and psychological warfare rather than through military action by easing western, and especially French, concerns about European and Asian defense.

According to Dulles and others in the administration, continuing political and economic support of the French war effort was the only way to ensure that both the EDC and Indochina were preserved. Despite its recognition of problems in the Western alliance, the Eisenhower administration consistently failed to understand French motivations. The Laniel government's attempts to cling to its empire, its difficulties in rolling back communist influence in Indochina, its willingness to negotiate with the communist bloc, and its hesitation over ratifying the EDC perplexed American officials, who became increasingly disillusioned with their ally. Increasing Franco-American tensions seemed to prove correct earlier predictions that "the first consequence of the devolution of power in the Soviet Union would be a short term widening of existing fissures among the nations of the free world."[89] The Soviet peace offensive would continue to reverberate as Paris and Washington prepared for negotiations at the forthcoming Geneva Conference and as the Eisenhower administration became more vested in ensuring a noncommunist Vietnam.

3

Negotiating
toward Geneva

AS A RESULT OF THE BERLIN CONFERENCE, France now had a political end in sight to more than seven years of conflict in Vietnam. However, its American ally was still focused on a military victory. Intra-alliance politics played an important role in dictating how France and the United States proceeded in the months leading up to the Geneva Conference and at the conference itself, demonstrating the fragility of allied solidarity. Designed to settle the Korean and Indochina conflicts, Geneva would be the first major test not only of East-West but also of West-West negotiations on Asian issues since Stalin's death. Ultimately, allied solidarity failed at Geneva as the accords left the door wide open for the United States and France to pursue separate policies in Vietnam.[1]

Shortly after Berlin, the Vietminh launched a major offensive against the French outpost at Dien Bien Phu. In keeping with Chinese foreign minister Zhou Enlai's advice that "in order to achieve a victory in the diplomatic field" they should emulate the Chinese success on the eve of the Korean armistice by winning several battles in Vietnam, the Vietminh planned to strengthen their negotiating position at Geneva through a major military victory.[2] Paris asked Washington to intervene unilaterally to lift the siege at Dien Bien Phu, but the Americans preferred to intervene multilaterally and suggested that a number of anticommunist countries join together against the Vietminh. The British wanted no part in a multilateral military intervention. They feared that such a move would provoke a Chinese invasion of Vietnam and escalate the conflict into a major war before negotiations could begin at Geneva. These differing goals prevented the French, Americans, and British from developing a coordinated policy to save the French military effort at Dien Bien Phu, resulting in the fall of Dien Bien Phu on May 7—the day before the Indochina phase of the Geneva Conference began.

The Geneva conferees had a number of agendas. The Soviets undoubtedly hoped to enhance international communist prestige through their support of China, the Vietminh, and peaceful coexistence while sowing seeds of discord among the Western allies. At the same time, Moscow also wanted to avoid further escalation of the Korean and Indochina conflicts that could lead to full-scale world war.[3] China planned to make the most of its first official international conference, whereas the exhausted Vietminh wanted a cease-fire. The noncommunist nationalists in South Vietnam were skeptical of the conference, expecting that the French would yield to DRV demands. The French, British, and Americans all had different goals for the conference. The French were determined to settle the Indochina conflict at the negotiating table and were prepared to go to great lengths to achieve peace; the Americans wanted the French to keep fighting and avoid a settlement that gave away too much to the communists; and the British intended to resume their role as a world leader through their co-chairmanship of the conference with the Soviets and create a relaxation of tensions between East and West. From the beginning of the conference, western interests diverged widely, leaving the United States feeling increasingly isolated from its allies. Ultimately, the British and French agendas prevailed at Geneva, leading the United States to the fateful decision that it could secure a noncommunist Vietnam without France.

UNITED ACTION

In early 1954, negotiations remained front and center as the Laniel government focused all of its attention on Geneva. A January visit to Vietnam by French minister for the Associated States Marc Jacquet, and one in February by the minister of defense, René Pleven, confirmed the overwhelming problems France faced in trying to continue the war. Their conclusion? Negotiate. The Laniel government recognized that France could not negotiate directly with the Vietminh because France needed to tie the Soviet Union and China to the accords as well. According to French deputy prime minister Paul Reynaud, China wanted peace in order to proceed with its domestic consolidation and hoped to receive concessions from the West for helping solve Asian problems. The Soviets also advocated peace because they feared the expansion of Chinese influence in Southeast Asia. In addition, China and the USSR were worried about American intervention.[4] Reynaud thus believed that the Chinese and Soviets would not hinder a peaceful resolution to the Indochina conflict. French foreign minister Georges Bidault was not so sure. He worried that the communists would drive a hard bargain at the negotiating table. Other top officials, including Pleven, believed that at the base of any French policy had to be the guarantee for Vietnamese independence. Pleven also advocated "Vietnamizing" the armed forces, and insisted that if the South Vietnamese did not make an effort to combat the North, France should consider itself free of obligations.[5]

While the Laniel government continued to debate the French approach to Geneva, American officials also scrambled to develop a policy, but one that involved military, not political, action. The Operations Coordinating Board (OCB) played a key role in formulating Indochina policy. According to the board, the key to the success of military operations continued to be well-trained, properly led indigenous forces effectively employed in combat operations against the communist forces. The eventual goal should be homogenous indigenous units with a native officer corps. One OCB report noted that the French had "insufficient success" in this area.[6] According to another assessment of the situation by a special committee comprised of defense, state, CIA, and JCS members, the American and French "investment in dollars, casualties, and moral and political involvement would be fruitless" if the communists won. Therefore, the committee recommended that the United States, Britain, and France reach an agreement with respect to Indochina rejecting any compromise that would "cede all or part of Indochina to the communists." The committee proceeded on the assumption that the status quo could be altered to result in military victory prior to discussions at Geneva. Failing this, Washington "should not entertain discussion of Indochina at Geneva or having entertained it, should ensure that no agreements were reached." If France accepted a negotiated settlement, the Eisenhower administration should "decline to associate itself with such an agreement and find a means of continuing the struggle without the French."[7]

Meanwhile, French military victory remained elusive. By the end of 1953 it had become clear to General Henri Navarre that his central objective of recovering the initiative in Tonkin's Red River delta was failing. Consequently, he decided to draw the Vietminh into battle where superior firepower and control of the skies would ensure success. He took the calculated risk of garrisoning Dien Bien Phu with the best units and reserves from the Tonkin delta. According to Navarre, Vietminh leader Vo Nguyen Giap lacked the logistic capacity to concentrate enough troops to overwhelm the garrison. The French artillery and airpower would pulverize any artillery the Vietminh attempted to place on the heights overlooking the valley. Navarre was certain that these weapons, in combination with his tanks and machine guns, would decimate the Vietminh infantry battalions as they descended into the valley.

He planned to keep the two airfields in the valley open during the battle to supply and reinforce the garrison. Dien Bien Phu thus ended the search for the classic, set-piece battle in which the French hoped to bring the destructive power of modern technology to bear on the elusive communist enemy. A battle at Dien Bien Phu, according to Navarre, would inflict a stunning defeat on the Vietminh and was the final element in the Navarre Plan.[8]

Navarre's decision to give battle at Dien Bien Phu had the support of the French and American governments, although some of his subordinates remained unconvinced that Navarre's strategy was sound. The battle of Dien Bien Phu began on March 13, 1954, and it soon became apparent that Navarre had completely miscalculated Giap's intentions and capabilities. In the first five days of battle, the Vietminh overran the fortress's three northern artillery bases, which rendered the airfield useless. The Vietminh had the superior numbers, guns, and strategy at Dien Bien Phu.

The worsening situation at Dien Bien Phu made a coordinated Franco-American policy toward Geneva even more difficult. The Eisenhower administration expected that Paris would ask the United States to intervene militarily, which the French did. In March, the Laniel government formally requested American military intervention to relieve the pressure on Dien Bien Phu. By shoring up Dien Bien Phu against Vietminh attacks, French leaders hoped to strengthen the French bargaining position at the Geneva Conference. The French demand provoked enormous debate within the United States and among the Western allies. President Eisenhower and John Foster Dulles had already begun to explore the possibility of military intervention but exhibited a reluctance to proceed without Congressional and international support. They formulated a new American policy that contemplated military intervention under the mantle of "united action," whereby Western allies, namely the United States, Britain, France, Australia, and New Zealand, would intervene multilaterally at Dien Bien Phu.[9]

As conditions at Dien Bien Phu grew increasingly ominous, the Laniel government sent General Paul Ely to Washington in a last-ditch effort to secure American military assistance. Ely would soon replace Commissioner General Maurice DeJean and Commander in Chief Henri Navarre by taking over both their jobs to become French high commissioner in Indochina. He was familiar with the situation in Vietnam because he had attended numerous tripartite talks in the early 1950s on the issue of a common Southeast Asian defense. Although Ely did receive guarantees for aircraft and aircraft technicians, help with the formation of the Vietnamese National Army, and fresh warnings to Beijing not to intervene, it was not until a private meeting at the end of Ely's visit between Ely and Admiral Arthur Radford that the possibility of direct American intervention was dangled in front of the French general. At the meeting, Ely and Radford apparently discussed what would become known as Operation Vulture, an American B-29 bombing raid against Dien Bien Phu.[10] Ely later claimed that Radford had promised the United States would intervene unilaterally, whereas Radford denied it. The meeting became more a series of complaints than a policy discussion. Ely accused the Americans of comporting themselves as though they wanted "to replace the French politically and economically in Indochina." Radford retorted that France was moving "too slowly in these areas," that the French were not keeping their engagements to keep the Americans informed, and that the French were "too sensitive about being replaced."[11]

Eisenhower remained reluctant to involve the United States in the fighting and cautioned Dulles not to say anything to the French that the Eisenhower administration could not guarantee, but he did suggest that he would not "wholly exclude the possibility of a single strike, if it were almost certain this would produce decisive results."[12] Plans for Operation Vulture were discussed during a March NSC meeting. Two objectives for the immediate future emerged from the meeting: to create a framework for "possible united action to assist or possibly replace the French in Indochina," and to consider possible courses of action "in case the French decided to withdraw from the area." Complaining that France was incapable of making the hard decisions required of a great power, Dulles feared French weakness "would leave a vacuum in Asia, which the Soviets would fill if the United States did not act."[13]

On March 29, 1954, in a speech entitled "The Threat of Red Asia" given at the Overseas Press Club of America, Dulles announced the need for united action in Indochina. This speech represented the Eisenhower administration's first public announcement of an American plan for a coalition of western powers and their Asian allies against any further communist advance in Southeast Asia. Dulles's speech was intended to warn the Soviet Union, China, and the Vietminh of the possibility of some form of multilateral action in Indochina.[14] Although the French desired American military intervention to lift the siege at Dien Bien Phu, they had been counting on a unilateral effort, not a multilateral one. The Laniel government opposed internationalization of the forces fighting in Indochina, fearing that the Americans would take over the military decision making. The French thus approached the concept of united action cautiously.[15] What the French did want was immediate relief for Dien Bien Phu in the form of an American bombing attack.

Throughout March and April, the Eisenhower administration never defined united action except in the broadest terms indicating some sort of military action. At his weekly press conference on March 31, Eisenhower failed to further clarify united action and left wide open the question of whether he would use U.S. force in Indochina. In the meantime, the concept of united action slowly evolved from a straightforward effort to arrange favorable conditions for an air strike to a longer-term effort to create a Southeast Asian alliance structure. The United States began to follow a two-track approach, enlisting support for intervention to be followed by an alliance. The Americans made it clear to the French that they would not intervene militarily in Indochina unless both France and Britain agreed to united action.

On April 10, Dulles went to Europe to secure western support for united action. Dulles had received a certain amount of encouragement from Thailand, the Philippines, Australia, and New Zealand, but the French and British worried that united action would torpedo the discussions on Indochina that were to begin on May 8 at Geneva. The British resisted being committed to a common defense of Southeast Asia that could drag them into the Indochina War, and Paris did not want to internationalize the war through united action, fearing that Washington would gain control of the war effort. Worried about a breakdown in allied unity, Dulles sent a letter to Prime Minister Churchill outlining his concern that the possibility of the communists driving a wedge between the allies, given the state of mind in France, would be "infinitely greater" at Geneva than at Berlin.[16]

United action also faced problems at home, as Congress wanted an understanding with American allies before moving forward. Building on Congress's hesitance, and in order to give his administration some time to explore all options, Eisenhower set forth three conditions to be met before he would approve American intervention: Congressional approval; international cooperation with active participation from Britain, Australia, and New Zealand, including troops and, if possible, participating units from Thailand, the Philippines, and other states in the region; and a full political understanding with France that it would remain in the war to the end and that it would guarantee independence for the Associated States.[17] After a controversial discussion, American officials during an April NSC meeting agreed to postpone for the time being any military action on Indochina until the United States determined how negotiations at Geneva were proceeding.[18]

Although still unsure about multilateral action, Eisenhower categorically opposed unilateral American intervention, which he believed would result in world condemnation of the United States as an imperialist power. In order to ensure victory, according to Eisenhower, the Associated States had to be granted complete independence and the United States should intervene only in concert with other western and Asian powers. In an interesting assessment of the French, Eisenhower wrote that the French government lacked the capability to make up its mind what to do in any given set of circumstances and that, since 1945, France had not been able to decide who it feared most—the Russians or the Germans. As a consequence, France's policies in Europe had been nothing but "confusion, starts and stops; advances and retreats." According to Eisenhower, France still wanted to be considered a world power but was entirely unready to make the sacrifices necessary to sustain such a position and was bound to be shown up, as in Indochina, as incapable of doing anything important by itself. Eisenhower also stated that the only hope for France was to produce a new and inspirational leader—by this he did "*not* mean one that is 6 feet 5 and who considers himself to be, by some miraculous biological and transmigrative process, the offspring of Clemenceau and Jeanne d'Arc." Clearly Eisenhower did not see General Charles de Gaulle as the solution to current French problems.[19] Supreme Allied Commander in Europe Alfred Gruenther, on whom Eisenhower depended as his most reliable link to the French leadership, agreed that French defeatism was "very bad," especially Pleven's attitude, and that Bidault was also "very wobbly."[20]

Further undermining both unilateral and united action was Matthew B. Ridgway, who had become the army chief of staff in mid-1953. According to Ridgway, only a decisive defeat of China in a general war would accomplish American objectives of defeating the Vietminh. Ridgway considered the costs of achieving such a victory too high. If the United States did invade, it would leave the American army in a very bad position vis-à-vis Russia. Even intervention limited to Vietnam would constitute a dangerous diversion of limited U.S. military capabilities and would commit armed forces in a "non-decisive theater" to the attainment of "non-decisive local objectives." In a memorandum to Eisenhower, Ridgway claimed that a war limited to Indochina would at best result in stalemate as in Korea. Other American military officials, in particular General James Gavin, also expressed misgivings early on about united action and whether France would find U.S. requirements politically acceptable.[21]

Although Eisenhower and Dulles appeared to alternately embrace and reject united action in a series of speeches and pronouncements throughout the spring, in the end, British and Congressional opposition prevented such action. British concerns about public support of a multilateral force in Indochina, as well as London's determination to await the outcome of Geneva, resulted in London's refusal to condone united action. Dulles and Eisenhower castigated Britain, with Eisenhower at one point going so far as to suggest sending a note to Churchill positing that "the Churchill Government was really promoting a second Munich." London feared harming the Anglo-American relationship but was more concerned about becoming involved in a military action that could turn into a world war. Foreign Secretary Eden's statements had been deliberately vague, but by mid-April the British had clarified their position. They would not support united action.[22]

Congress also played a vital role in ensuring the rejection of military intervention. When, in early April, Dulles and Radford met with members of Congress, they decided against Congressional action until U.S. allies were on board. An extended debate took place in the Senate a few days later, and members again expressed their opposition to unilateral U.S. involvement, leading Eisenhower to reassure members that American combat troops would not be introduced except as part of a coalition. Senator William Knowland, in particular, opposed any Congressional resolution giving the president more power.

Eisenhower and Dulles had agreed to proceed with military intervention without British cooperation if Congress would provide a resolution granting the president "discretionary authority" in Indochina.[23] Although there were a number of drafts of the resolution, the final draft read as follows: "The President is authorized to employ Naval and Air forces of the United States to assist friendly governments of Asia to maintain their authority as against subversive and revolutionary efforts fomented by Communist regimes, provided such aid is requested by the governments concerned. This shall not be deemed to be a declaration of war and the authority hereby given shall be terminated on June 30, 1955, unless extended."[24] The resolution was a daring move on Eisenhower and Dulles's part as it would have opened the door for unlimited naval and air intervention in Vietnam. In addition, six divisions of marines, each twenty thousand strong, could have been used in such an operation.

Knowland informed Dulles and Eisenhower that the draft of potential discretionary authority they had in mind would not be endorsed by Congress and that both the Democratic and the Republican leadership in Congress felt that the United States should not intervene unilaterally but should only intervene in the event that U.S. allies would as well. Knowland also insisted that the French guarantee immediate independence for Indochina. American allies were not prepared to accede to the first Congressional requirement and the French were not willing to compromise on the other.[25] Congress thus remained the biggest domestic obstacle against united action. Most Congressional members were willing to increase American participation in Indochina providing the executive branch did not gain predominant control, but they drew the line at military intervention under presidential discretionary authority. Both Dulles and Eisenhower complained that Congress had "hamstrung" them by refusing to give the president discretionary authority.[26]

Other forms of military intervention were also on the table. In mid-April, Dulles and Bidault met to discuss options. Bidault came away from the meeting convinced that Dulles had offered him two nuclear bombs to use at Dien Bien Phu. French officials stated that Bidault had been almost incoherent at the time, and Dulles denied making the offer.[27]

Despite British and Congressional stonewalling, as well as increasing French incoherence, the Eisenhower administration considered united action well after the Geneva Conference was underway. Dulles kept Ambassador Douglas Dillon and Undersecretary of State Walter Bedell Smith informed about the possible internationalization of the war, stating that France had only two choices: American intervention or capitulation. He asserted that "intervention might involve consequences of utmost gravity." The reactions of the communist bloc could not be predicted. Also, if it became necessary to proceed without active United Kingdom participation, the implications would be "extremely serious and far-reaching."[28] Dulles thus kept united action alive; he urged Dillon and Smith to discuss military plans orally with Laniel, but cautioned them against leaving anything in writing. In the meantime, the French clearly wanted to end the conflict at a diplomatic conference rather than on the battlefield. French ambassador Henri Bonnet recognized that American willingness to work toward a negotiated settlement at Geneva was absolutely vital to French success but doubted the Americans would cooperate since they believed "Geneva could only result in communist advances." According to Bonnet, the French should "endorse" united action only if the communists intensified the conflict as the conference proceeded. Bonnet thought it unlikely that the communists would jeopardize their chances at Geneva by starting an offensive. Thus, on the eve of the Indochina talks at Geneva, the Americans and French continued to discuss the possibilities for direct American military intervention, but the American refusal to intervene unilaterally and Congressional and allied opposition to united action precluded a military solution to the French dilemma.[29]

In assessing American policy toward united action, it seems likely that

Eisenhower declined military intervention because of France's refusal to meet conditions rather than any particular aversion to the use of force against the Vietminh. According to Eisenhower, he "had been unable to obtain the conditions under which the United States could properly intervene to protect its own interests."[30] Eisenhower viewed the French as frantic in their desire to be thought of as a great power, to the extent that it was "beneath their dignity" to accept help in the conflict. Eisenhower claimed that he had tried to create a political climate among the interested powers that would make it politically feasible for the United States to intervene.[31] In addition, Eisenhower did attempt to coax Congress to pass a resolution giving the president discretionary authority in Indochina even after the British had declined to participate in united action. He sought a blank check from Congress for united action, urged the French to continue the struggle, asked Churchill and Eden to reconsider their stance against united action, and, finally, was willing to move ahead without British participation.[32] Thus, the evidence suggests that Eisenhower did not use united action as a tactical ploy to bring about greater communist concessions at Geneva. The French, rather than the Americans, were more interested in using the possibility of American intervention as a trump card in their negotiations at Geneva, and complained bitterly whenever high-ranking American officials suggested that such intervention was no longer an option. Dulles, more so than Eisenhower, was committed to united action and willing to escalate the conflict, but in the end British and Congressional pressure forced him to set aside united action as a strategy to keep the war going.[33] Dulles, on June 8, and Eisenhower, two days later, announced that they would not ask Congress for additional authority for U.S. direct intervention in Vietnam.

French morale crumbled with the major military and psychological defeat at Dien Bien Phu on May 7, 1954, the day before the Indochina phase of the Geneva Conference began. French military leaders had been convinced that they would crush the Vietminh at Dien Bien Phu, thereby establishing a strong negotiating position at Geneva. Their plan backfired when the Vietminh launched their devastating attack, eventually forcing a French surrender. Bidault was "much discouraged" as he did not see any way to avoid an outright French military defeat. When looking at the Vietminh decision to take the offensive at Dien Bien Phu, French officials concluded that the Vietminh were well aware the Soviet Union and China might use the upcoming Geneva conference for their own ends. The Vietminh had thus tried to reach a direct accord with the French before April 26. But after Franco-American collaboration increased with Ely's trip to the United States and the provision of more American supplies, the Vietminh realized they would not be able to negotiate directly and were worried that South Vietnamese leader Pham Buu Loc might conclude a favorable treaty in Paris that would grant Bao Dai's State of Vietnam complete independence. For that reason, the Vietminh recognized that a victory at Dien Bien Phu was a necessity.[34]

What can we conclude from the failed allied effort at Dien Bien Phu? For the French government, military leaders, and public, Dien Bien Phu epitomized the hopelessness of the war. The Americans, on the other hand, wanted to continue plans for an international military effort to salvage Dien Bien Phu as the conference opened. Both Paris and London stood firm in their refusal to consider such an effort until prospects for peace had been fully explored. Ultimately, Dien Bien Phu represented an enormous symbolic victory for the Vietminh; it took what remained of the fight out of the French and consequently dashed American hopes for a continued French war effort in Indochina, convincing the Eisenhower administration that the United States would have to halt the communist advance in Indochina on its own. Washington chose to keep its distance from the proceedings, replacing Dulles with Smith as the Indochina phase began.[35] Although the Eisenhower administration exercised some restraint against a complete rupture with France, recognizing that an openly divided western presence at Geneva would only strengthen the communist position, American officials at all levels were beginning to conclude that the best way to achieve a noncommunist Vietnam was to remove the colonial element—that is to say France—and start over.

THE GENEVA CONFERENCE

The Americans were worried. As the Indochina phase of the Geneva Conference began, collective action among the Western allies at this point looked difficult indeed. Dulles hoped that the French delegation would not agree at Geneva to terms that the Eisenhower administration felt involved "virtual abandonment of [the] area to communist forces." "Certainly," according to Dulles, American officials "should have full opportunity to know what was going on and have timely opportunity to express our views, and if they are ignored, publicly to disassociate ourselves." Dulles also continued to keep the idea of united action alive, but downplayed his interest in it by insisting that the Eisenhower administration refused "to intervene purely as part of a white western coalition which is shunned by all Asian states."[36] As he watched from Washington, Dulles feared the worst at Geneva.

Dulles's concerns were well warranted as the French committed themselves wholeheartedly to a political solution. Paris had developed two tactics for pursuing negotiations. Laniel and the Quai favored negotiating with the Soviets and Chinese, while Pleven advocated negotiating directly with the Vietminh. Eventually, French negotiators would pursue both options. In assessing their Russian and Chinese adversaries, the French adopted the position that Moscow did not want war, did not control China, and feared that China, by engaging in imprudent actions, could launch a world conflict. Soviet foreign minister Vyacheslav Molotov's earlier concessions at Berlin to bring about the Geneva Conference, and Moscow's abandonment of a conference dedicated to resolving all Asian problems, led the French to believe that the Soviets would cooperate on a peaceful settlement to the Indochina conflict. With respect to Chinese policy, the French assumed that China feared the substitution of the United States for France in Indochina and needed material and equipment on a long-term scale to modernize its economy and consolidate its regime. Therefore, China would also cooperate at Geneva.[37]

Regarding French policy toward the Vietminh, there were three possibilities according to Bidault. Paris could withdraw completely, which would be unacceptable to the South Vietnamese. Tonkin could become an independent state in Vietminh hands, but such a solution would need to be negotiated with the Chinese and imposed on the Vietminh. Or, the country could be partitioned. This last solution was the best compromise, Bidault felt, even though the Americans would be annoyed—Bidault had given them formal assurances that France would not accept a division of Vietnamese territory.[38] Other Quai officials concurred, noting that any classic political solution, such as a coalition government between Bao Dai and Ho Chi Minh or popular consultations, would be advantageous for the Vietminh. Dividing the country in two would be the least hurtful to French interests; but it was essential that such a solution appeared to come about "not as a result of a French initiative, but as a consequence of the armistice imposed by the circumstances."[39] Although France had publicly denied that it advocated partition, in private circles French officials recognized that partition might be the best compromise that Paris could expect. The British also viewed a division of Vietnam as the best solution.

British and French actions at Geneva demonstrated the limits of American influence in a region where Europeans held substantial interests. Paris and London's determination to negotiate had prevented the United States from organizing a coalition to intervene militarily in Vietnam, thus denying the Eisenhower administration the internationalization of the war it had long sought. The British and French were much more interested than the Americans in reaching a modus vivendi with the Soviets and Chinese, and they planned to work for an implicit spheres of influence agreement. Paris and London were determined to prevent the outbreak of a regional war that would divert resources into a secondary theater of combat.[40]

The United States had other plans, and embarked on a series of actions that could be construed as attempts to sabotage the conference. The French were incensed by Dulles's May 11 speech in which he stated that Southeast Asia could be held "without Indochina." According to Ely, who was shocked by the speech, "rarely did a great power change its tune so quickly, from insisting on united action to preserve Indochina, to announcing that Indochina was not indispensable to Southeast Asia." Ely believed that France had been "deceived" by the United States and would subsequently have to rethink its negotiating position at Geneva.[41] It is difficult to arrive at any other conclusion but that Dulles was deliberately trying to undermine the French position at Geneva by taking away the threat of American intervention in case communist demands were unacceptable. Dulles later rectified his comments, but this did little to calm French suspicions.

Following the May 11 speech, other American actions indicated to the French that the United States was reconsidering its agreement to the Geneva Conference. Many American officials who visited the Far East did not stop in Indochina at that time, and American declarations on Geneva were uncertain, contradictory, and conditional, giving the French the impression that the United States was willing to accept the loss of Indochina. Moreover, the Americans once again wanted to bring Indochina before the UN, which French officials vehemently opposed, fearing such action would "wreck the Geneva negotiations." The British also rejected this stratagem, seeing it as a cover for future American intervention in Indochina. Paris and London worried that an appeal to the UN would cause the Soviets to become more difficult, just when they had eased up slightly in Geneva.[42] Dulles noted at an NSC meeting that an appeal for UN observers made by the Thai government (at the behest of the United States) had made some progress, "despite obstacles placed in its way by the British and French," to whom it had been necessary to present a virtual ultimatum. At least there had been first steps toward "getting the UN involved in Southeast Asia," according to Dulles.[43] These American actions indicate that the United States at least tested the waters to see how easy it would be to sabotage Geneva.

From the French viewpoint, the Americans appeared to be trying to torpedo the conference. Paris believed that if Geneva failed, the United States would make plans to intervene militarily. Maurice DeJean, commissioner general for the Associated States, had become suspicious that the Americans were using their recent declarations about the unimportance of Indochina as a tactic to ensure American control of Indochina when Geneva failed.[44]

French suspicions were at least partially justified. In an attempt to bring back a modified form of united action, Dulles indicated that the United States would internationalize the war or ask for UN intervention if an acceptable solution at Geneva was not reached. In a clear example of contingency planning, Dillon notified the Laniel government in mid-May of seven conditions the United States would require before Eisenhower asked Congress for authority to use American armed forces in the war. High-level Franco-American talks followed, at which Laniel informed Dillon that the French had agreed to most of the conditions. Washington and Paris thus proceeded with extensive contingency planning in the event of Geneva's failure. According to Bonnet, if the Soviets and Chinese did not settle, there was a real possibility that there would be an unleashing of war in Asia and that the Americans would provide military support.[45]

French officials were becoming increasingly convinced that *any* American intervention would be disastrous and that France should reach a peaceful resolution as quickly as possible. But if Geneva failed, according to DeJean, it was preferable to have American intervention than to have a direct accord with the Vietminh with no international guarantee. Indochina represented "the future of the French Union, France's world position, and American friendship with all that it signified, particularly with regard to France's position in Europe," since France was incapable of defending itself against Russian imperialism. DeJean was worried that the loss of Indochina would result in a complete revision of American policy that would then favor Germany. The result would be German rather than Soviet hegemony in Europe. Bidault also thought France needed to indicate that it would continue the fight if necessary. Franco-American collaboration, notably American training of the Vietnamese armed forces, would result in an increase of American materials and aid in establishing an infrastructure in the South, according to Bidault.[46] Bidault thus returned to Paris from Geneva at the end of May for one purpose—"to get mad and raise hell." This tactic apparently worked, as the French government decided to stand fast at Geneva and send reinforcements to Indochina.[47]

Although by late May it looked as though the conference had stalled, with neither side appearing willing to compromise, secret talks between

French military representatives and the Vietminh leadership had already begun. These talks were a result of Eden and Zhou Enlai's encouragement and French internal debates on how to proceed with the conference. Bidault and Laniel had planned on a cease-fire with pockets of regroupment—the so-called leopard skin strategy—instead of vast territorial zones. Vietminh representative Pham Van Dong brought up the idea of a readjustment of zones, which left the door open to a division of the country. But Bidault, De-Jean, and Navarre all insisted on the leopard skin strategy. Thus chief French representative Brigadier General Henri Delteil and chief DRV representative Vice Minister of Defense Ta Quang Buu, along with their seconds, Colonels Michel de Brébisson and Ha Van Lau, met secretly to discuss cease-fire arrangements, as directed by Chauvel but bypassing Bidault. Brébisson and Lau had already been working together since mid-May to settle the evacuation of the wounded at Dien Bien Phu. It was at a June 10 secret meeting that the Vietminh agreed for the first time to divide Vietnam temporarily, but with no indication as to how or when elections to reunify the country would be held.

Undoubtedly, part of the reason for this concession came from the DRV's fear of the consequences of two treaties signed between the French and the State of Vietnam on June 4. The two treaties, initialed by Laniel and Prime Minister Buu Loc, but not signed by Bao Dai or French president René Coty, recognized the State of Vietnam as a "fully independent and sovereign state invested with all the competence recognized by international law." Moreover, the treaties stated that the French and Vietnamese would associate freely within the French Union and mutually agree to the establishment of defense and foreign relations conventions on the basis of complete equality. Not only did the treaties finally grant Vietnamese independence, but they also paved the way for the Americans to provide direct aid to the State of Vietnam.[48] Although Dulles had publicly insisted on Vietnamese independence, privately he was not so sure, commenting to Eisenhower that Vietnam, Cambodia, and Laos were not ready for complete independence. It would be, in his words, "like putting a baby in a cage of hungry lions. The baby would be rapidly devoured."[49]

As a result of the June treaties, both combatants began to explore the idea of a temporary partition of Vietnam. Despite promises to Bao Dai, Buu Loc, and the Americans about not partitioning the country, that is precisely what the French began to do. In mid-June, during the secret negotiations—which excluded representatives from the State of Vietnam—the Vietminh indicated that they wanted an end to the war, two zones, elections in six months, and negotiations directly with the French, not with the Vietnamese State. In addition, Tonkin was non-negotiable. Delteil and Brébisson both noted in talks with Bidault in mid-June that the division was a temporary military partitioning to separate combatants and allow peace to return, not a political one à la Korea. The French also learned from Buu Loc that the Vietminh were most concerned with American intervention and increasing Chinese influence over DRV affairs. The Vietminh thus were willing to compromise, even allowing Bao Dai to come back as chief of state. The priority was to avoid U.S. intervention.[50] French diplomat Jean Sainteny confirmed these views, claiming that the decision to send Pham Van Dong to Geneva was an indication of Hanoi's seriousness in ending the war, and that the Vietminh's "greatest fear" was U.S. intervention and "greatest impetus" was Chinese pressure. The French were correct—the DRV representatives were sincere. The Americans, however, had gotten many things wrong, not least of which was communist earnestness in negotiating an end to the conflict in Indochina.[51]

Or had they? Since the Americans were kept apprised of the secret talks and allowed them to go forward, it is worth speculating why they made no effort to ensure the State of Vietnam's representation. If one subscribes to conspiracy theories, it is possible to conclude that the Eisenhower administration did nothing to stop negotiations at the time to preserve greater liberty of action later. In other words, if Bao Dai's government did not take part in the eventual Franco-Vietminh agreement, even though the State of Vietnam had been recognized as an independent country by the French, then Saigon and Washington would be on somewhat tenable legal ground in claiming that they were not bound by the agreements. But this possibility must rest in the speculative realm until further evidence surfaces that the Americans were already pursuing a post-Geneva policy that would not include Franco-American cooperation.

As negotiations at Geneva still appeared stalled, American officials asked themselves how they had gotten into such a position. The answer, for many, centered on the EDC-Indochina connection established so many months ago. U.S. officials were well aware that the American obsession with the EDC had delayed or inhibited its Indochina policy. American insistence on the EDC gave the French an additional argument for a policy of liquidating the war in Indochina—namely that they must save their limited military strength in order to outweigh the expected German forces in the EDC. Moreover, this EDC factor appeared to have had an important effect in precipitating the conference at a time when the weak French position in Indochina would reduce the bargaining power of the anticommunist side. Since at least 1952, the "failure to implement U.S. policy in Indochina" with respect to the Associated States' independence could in large part be attributed to the "desire to secure French ratification of the EDC" and to the consequent hesitancy to irritate French "sensibilities" by pressuring the French to make significant concessions to the national inspirations of the peoples of Indochina.[52] State Department officials eventually recognized the dangers of letting one policy dominate all others, and saw that the EDC had obstructed American policy in Indochina. But as the EDC had become Eisenhower and Dulles's personal priority, State Department officials could not speak out against it, and U.S. policy remained unaltered.

According to Dillon, Indochina had, by spring 1954, replaced the EDC as the biggest French concern; French hopes centered on the Geneva Conference as a means to achieve a political solution to the Indochina War, but Dulles continued to urge Dillon to keep the pressure on the French to ratify the EDC. A frustrated Dillon sent a message to Dulles indicating his concern. He noted that, although pro-EDC members of the French government originally saw "no connection between EDC and Geneva," the fall of Dien Bien Phu and the present military crisis in Indochina had "drastically changed" the situation. The EDC was, for the most part, "inextricably intertwined with both Geneva and Franco-U.S. negotiations regarding united action in Indochina." Although there was no "direct logical connection" between the two, the way in which "we handle present Indochina negotiations with France is bound to have great effect on our friends in French Government who are supporting EDC."[53]

No "direct logical connection" existed between the EDC and Indochina issues; the Americans had invented one for themselves. Dillon recognized that only the conclusion of Franco-American negotiations on Indochina would push the EDC to a vote with a reasonable chance of success. A spirit of alliance between the two countries could then be renewed. Dillon argued against exerting more pressure on the French, which he feared would greatly strengthen the position of those deputies in the French National Assembly who favored peace in Indochina at any price. Dillon did convince Dulles to delay sending an official letter to the Laniel government warning that unless France ratified the EDC treaty immediately, the United States and Britain would consider practical steps needed to integrate West Germany without France.[54] Still, Dillon's efforts to salvage the situation ultimately proved unsuccessful. In the Cold War climate, few American officials challenged the secretary of state's conception of the EDC as the best solution to the German problem as well as the best line of defense against the Soviet bloc. Thus,

Dulles's insistence on the EDC led to a series of events that American officials had tried to avoid.

The first of these was the collapse of the Laniel government on June 12. According to Laniel, his government fell because of American pressure to ratify the EDC. American attempts to keep a distance between the United States and the results of the Geneva Conference probably further weakened Laniel's position. Laniel later wrote in his memoirs that it would be his "policy toward Europe rather than Indochina" that would topple his government. Laniel knew that in their desire to avoid ratification of the EDC treaty, elements of his majority coalition, although supporters of his policies in Asia, were going to "abandon" him and would not hesitate to use the tragic events in Indochina to overturn his government, "whatever the cost." The fall of Dien Bien Phu had been the occasion, but not the true cause, of his removal. "Harassed on Indochina," he was "really overthrown on the European issue."[55] Attempting to force the Laniel government to deal with the EDC and Indochina at the same time had backfired, as Radical Socialist deputy Pierre Mendès France took over the government. Mendès France had been a vocal opponent of the war for months, and Eisenhower and Dulles distrusted him because of his supposed stance against the EDC and his determination to find a political solution to the Indochina conflict. Upon taking office, Mendès France swore that he would resolve the Indochina conflict within thirty days, or resign.[56]

Despite the secret Franco-Vietminh talks, deadlock on almost all major issues led Eden to leave the conference in mid-June, and Smith left for Washington a few days later. Parliamentary Secretary of State for Foreign Affairs Lord Reading and Foreign Service officer U. Alexis Johnson took their places. Before his departure, Smith notified chief French delegates Jean Chauvel and Marc Jacquet that the option of American intervention no longer existed, since it seemed the French had wanted it primarily as a negotiating point.[57] The British and Americans thus reduced their presence at the conference, and French policy making appeared to be falling apart as Quai officials squabbled amongst themselves.[58]

The already harassed French leadership became exasperated with a new Anglo-American initiative. In an attempt to repair Anglo-American relations that had been damaged over the united action fiasco, the British and Americans agreed to an Anglo-American study group, which would coordinate the two countries' responses to the outcome of the conference and lay down minimum conditions for a settlement. The United States and Britain came up with a seven-point communiqué necessary for their agreement to respect the settlement: (1) preservation of the integrity and national independence of and removal of Vietminh troops from Laos and Cambodia; (2) preservation of at least half of Vietnam and, if possible, an enclave in the Red River delta; (3) no restrictions on the maintenance of stable and secure noncommunist regimes (including the right to import foreign advisers and weapons and to maintain adequate forces for internal security) in all three countries; (4) no political provisions that would risk the loss of the retained area to communist control; (5) no exclusion of the possibility of reunification by peaceful means; (6) peaceful transfer of refugees; and (7) an effective control mechanism. Mendès France eventually accepted the conditions. Although Washington had hoped to produce a definite agreement with London, Churchill and Eden had merely stated a hope that the French would not settle for anything less than the Anglo-American conditions.[59]

As of July 1, State Department officials were still advocating sending American troops to Indochina, arguing that its loss would be a terrible blow to U.S. prestige throughout the world. Dulles at this point remained unconvinced, believing that world opinion would condemn such a move.[60] Despite his disgust with Mendès France's promise of peace in Indochina, Dulles recognized that it would be "better for Franco-American relations if [we] don't have to disassociate ourselves from the French under spectacular conditions."[61] The Americans continued to follow the conference proceedings without intervening directly. Paris was less than thrilled with the American claim to "respect the accords [at Geneva] if the terms were not too far from American conditions." The French were convinced that the United States did not want success at Geneva and that if the conference failed, the Eisenhower administration would intervene militarily.[62]

The Americans also doubted their ally's intentions. During the Geneva negotiations, American leaders, and Dulles in particular, concluded that Mendès France had negotiated a secret deal with Moscow. Dulles believed that Mendès France had promised to sabotage the EDC in exchange for Soviet pressure on the Vietminh at the Geneva Conference. Refusing to accept assurances that the French had not made this deal with the devil, Dulles believed that they had actually reached a point where they would rather abandon Indochina altogether than save it through American intervention. He mused that the United States would have to either force the French "into line" or else accept a division with France. Both courses of action involved the "gravest difficulty," particularly in relation to the EDC.[63]

In numerous internal documents, Mendès France clearly stated that he did not meet with Molotov to discuss the German problem until after the end of the Geneva Conference. The Soviets did not have any acceptable propositions, according to the French prime minister, who found Molotov's solutions "rather deceptive." Mendès France added that "as I have already stated many times there was no deal at Geneva." He did remark that "maybe it would be okay to let them [the Soviets] think [he] had agreed," as there was no chance that a majority in the National Assembly would ratify the EDC.[64] Smith also reassured Dulles that no under-the-table deals between Molotov and Mendès France existed, but Dulles remained skeptical long after the EDC's eventual defeat.

Misperception played a key role in how the western powers negotiated at Geneva. Looking back, Mendès France indicated he had no idea how suspicious Eisenhower and Dulles were of him, especially since he had agreed to the seven Anglo-American conditions for a peaceful resolution and had assured the Americans that he would not discuss the EDC with Molotov until after the conference. Of course, when he also refused to discuss the EDC with Dulles during the conference, Dulles assumed the worst. Dulles and a number of other high-ranking American officials were already disposed to dislike Mendès France, in part because of all the anti–Mendès France letters that the Eisenhower administration had been receiving from more right-leaning figures in France.[65]

Dulles should have been more concerned about Franco-Sino negotiations as France had hoped to negotiate with China at Geneva, promising French "good offices" with respect to UN representation if China pressured the Vietminh to reach an honorable accord. The possibility of a Sino-Franco deal—UN representation of the PRC for peace in Indochina—rather than a Soviet-Franco agreement—the EDC's demise for peace in Indochina—did not figure in American concerns.

Throughout the conference, Henri Bonnet played a key role in smoothing tensions between Dulles and Mendès France, constantly reassuring Dulles that the French government would uphold the Franco-American alliance.[66] In turn, Paris expected Washington to respect the Geneva results. Dulles realized that any impression that the United States had intentionally blocked an Indochina settlement might damage the EDC, but he remained incapable of separating Asian from European policy. According to the Eisenhower administration, the United States had to go along with the Geneva Conference or face a complete loss of American influence in France, in relation both to the EDC and to Indochina. American interests would thus be best served, not by burying the Geneva Conference and beginning immediate military intervention, but by helping the French negotiate.[67]

As negotiations over the fate of Indochina intensified, Smith and Dillon attempted to soften Dulles's alternately belligerent and conciliatory stance toward the French. They differed from Dulles in that they did not see the EDC as the only option regarding West Germany's rearmament; nor did they believe the French could continue the fight in Indochina. This contrast in approach to European integration and to Indochina became apparent when Smith reassured French officials that the United States would give certain guarantees to the settlement reached at Geneva and confirmed that the United States would continue to aid France once negotiations concluded. He also stated that the outcome of the EDC would not affect the "collaboration" of the two governments in Indochina.[68] Bonnet remarked that he had never "found an influential member of the American government more willing to help preserve the French Union."[69] Despite Dillon and Smith's attempts to modify Dulles's decisions, in the end Dulles was the one responsible for linking the EDC and Indochina and must bear the brunt of responsibility for the outcome at Geneva that he despised.

Once it became clear that the French and Vietminh were close to reaching a final agreement, Mendès France successfully coaxed Dulles into sending Smith back to the conference table for the last phase of talks. After his return, Smith and Molotov appeared to achieve an acceptable armistice for both sides, but Dulles forbade Smith to sign any declaration in concert with the Soviets. Consequently, the accords were signed by all the participants except the Americans and the State of Vietnam and went into effect on July 22. The main clauses of the Geneva Agreement on the Cessation of Hostilities for Vietnam included provisional partitioning of the country at the seventeenth parallel, regrouping of French forces to the south and Vietminh forces to the north of the seventeenth parallel within three hundred days, and a ban on increasing any military material in either part of the country (although equipment that became obsolete could be replaced—a clause that would become increasingly important to the Americans). The three other key points were the creation of an international control commission composed of Indian, Canadian, and Polish delegates; the organization of elections to ensure unification of the country before July 20, 1956; and the prohibition of international military alliances for both sides.[70] The agreement included six chapters, forty-seven articles, and an annex that delineated the boundaries of provisional assembly areas and the location of the temporary military demarcation line and demilitarized zone. The accords demonstrated the undersecretary of state's point that "diplomacy has never been able to gain at the conference table what cannot be held on the battlefield."[71] Militarily, the

French were incapable of winning the war, which meant they had to make major concessions during the Geneva negotiations, no matter how urgently the Americans insisted they should not.

In the end, Smith signed a separate American agreement not to obstruct the resolutions of the Geneva Conference as long as they did not interfere with American national security, which, by this point, had come to be defined very broadly. Thus, the United States was not bound to uphold the decisions made at Geneva the way other signatories were. Smith's unilateral declaration at Geneva stated that the United States "will refrain from the threat or the use of force to disturb" the Geneva agreements, that it would "view any renewal of the aggression in violation of the aforesaid agreements with grave concern and as seriously threatening international peace and security," and that the United States should "continue to seek to achieve unity through free elections, supervised by the UN to insure that they are conducted fairly."[72] And yet, the United States consistently undermined these points during the following years as it created an international military alliance (the Southeast Asia Treaty Organization [SEATO]), brought in military personnel, and helped sabotage the 1956 elections.

As for Bao Dai and his representatives, they had remained adamantly opposed to partition, and this position did not change when Ngo Dinh Diem replaced Buu Loc as prime minister in June 1954. In fact, Diem's independent nature manifested early on when he almost resigned after learning the terms of the cease-fire. Washington worried that Bao Dai and Diem would declare unilateral independence from the French Union or even come to a negotiated settlement with the DRV.[73] The former action would have severely tested Franco-American relations, which were already on difficult footing. Instead, the chief negotiator for the South Vietnamese, Tran Van Do, under orders from Diem and Bao Dai, abstained from signing the final Geneva Accords and registered his protest against the Geneva Conference agreements. Bao Dai had suspected all along that France would betray him at Geneva. French actions, including a refusal to include his representatives in the secret Franco-Vietminh military talks, failure to keep Tran Van Do apprised of the evolving negotiations, and willingness to partition the country, confirmed Bao Dai's suspicions.

After agonizing debates among the French, British, and Americans, what did the Geneva Conference actually achieve? Ultimately, the Geneva Accords did establish peace in Indochina, at least temporarily. Both China and the USSR exerted pressure on the North Vietnamese to compromise, with the result that the North did not capitalize on its military victories, settling for partition at the seventeenth parallel. This partition temporarily created the two political entities of South and North Vietnam. The Soviet Union had only limited interests in Southeast Asia and appeared to have pursued a conciliatory line toward France at the conference to encourage French rejection of the EDC. China sought to enhance its international prestige and avoid American intervention. Bao Dai and Diem decried the accords, protesting that they had not signed them and would not adhere to them. The major issue of reunification was left deliberately vague, and the accords themselves were so ambiguous that they could be interpreted in a number of ways. The French were relieved because peace in Indochina meant that France could finally turn its attention to other issues, such as European defense. The Americans were decidedly less enthusiastic but now had time to build up noncommunist forces in South Vietnam. The British congratulated themselves that a full-scale war over Indochina had been prevented. The French and British saw the accords as an imperfect but acceptable solution to a difficult problem, but for the Eisenhower administration, "the net effect of the Geneva Conference and of subsequent developments had been to advance the communist position in Asia."[74] In arriving at a truce in Indochina, allied pressure had been critical: it led the Eisenhower administration to acquiesce in negotiations that it did not desire or think prudent. The allies therefore deserve most of the credit for opening the door to negotiations and bringing about a solution in Indochina in spite of Washington's wishes.

In examining the Geneva Conference, one point becomes clear: the western leaders spent more time negotiating among themselves than with their communist rivals. This phenomenon had become the order of the day. By the time the West arrived at a compromise policy, events had usually overtaken Paris, London, and Washington's decisions. In addition, the West spent much time and effort in trying to smooth over internal disagreements. After the conference, both French and American leaders proclaimed their commitment to a common policy in Indochina, but the end result of conflict within the alliance was that the West had difficulty in presenting a united front to the communist bloc.

AFTERSHOCKS

The end of the Geneva Conference on July 21, 1954, brought a political settlement of the First Indochina War and relief for the French. Publicly the Eisenhower administration stated that it was satisfied with Geneva, but privately American officials worried that U.S. prestige had "suffered greatly" and that to regain it the United States would have to "disassociate itself" from France in Indochina.[75] As for the EDC, Bonnet and Mendès France consistently reiterated throughout the summer that the French National Assembly would refuse to ratify it. Mendès France made it clear that he did not have a majority in the National Assembly even with his stature enhanced by the peaceful resolution of the Indochina conflict. Bonnet insisted that the United States, and Dulles in particular, accept this fact.[76] Despite numerous warnings, the Eisenhower administration was shocked by the French National Assembly's defeat of the EDC on August 30, 1954, by a vote of 319 to 264. French fears of German resurgence, aversion to American strong-arm tactics, and belief that the communist threat on the European continent had diminished combined to precipitate the EDC's defeat. And yet Washington saw this vote as a French betrayal of allied unity.

Significant fallout from Geneva occurred on many fronts, from the petty to the critical. Mendès France was annoyed when Dulles bypassed Paris on his trip to London and Bonn at the end of September, viewing Dulles's act as a deliberate weakening of his influence when he needed all the strength he could muster. The French press was also critical; *Aurore* regretted that "American diplomacy has once more shown a remarkable lack of psychology" in its dealings with other nations.[77] More significantly, Washington continued to criticize Paris's failure to ratify the EDC and moved quickly to admit Germany into NATO. The French had little choice but to accept this move because of the Eisenhower administration's fury over the EDC's demise, its refusal to wait any longer for West Germany's integration into the Western alliance, and its threat to cut off all aid to Indochina.[78] If the United States had insisted on West Germany's integration into NATO or established a bilateral agreement with West Germany before Geneva, would the reduced tensions over western European security have allowed for a political solution in Asia acceptable to the Americans? Although there is no conclusive answer, the evidence suggests that perhaps subsequent American intervention in Indochina would have taken a different path.

Now that the EDC-Indochina link had been broken, what did this severing mean for future American involvement in Vietnam? Dulles's linkage of the EDC and Indochina from 1953 to 1954 had already increased Washington's financial and political commitment to a noncommunist South Vietnam. American insistence and French delays on the EDC's ratification had created immense frustration on both sides of the Atlantic that would reverberate in later years. Franco-American mutual distrust increased, with the result that both sides were less willing to work together in Vietnam after

Geneva. The EDC's failure also prompted the United States to disassociate itself from French policy in Europe, leading a number of Americans to think they could just as easily pursue their own course in Vietnam. The French were well aware that the EDC's failure had jeopardized their liberty of action in Asia, recognizing that in order to stay a great power, France had to remain in the Far East and Indochina and thus had to create a policy that the Americans would support.[79]

The U.S. diplomatic setback at Geneva also accelerated momentum toward greater American involvement in Vietnam.[80] By the end of the Geneva Conference, Eisenhower and Dulles seriously considered pushing France out of Indochina completely so the United States could rebuild from the foundations. They realized that the French presence was still needed, but the balance of power between the French and Americans was changing rapidly and would soon weigh in the Americans' favor. According to a post-Geneva NSC briefing, the main French effort was to maintain a "presence" in the South to the "detriment of a more effective and popular Vietnamese government" that would be able to "rally nationwide support."[81] Eisenhower and Dulles thus had three options: pull out of Indochina, increase American involvement, or maintain the status quo. They chose to increase American involvement by demanding a larger U.S. role in training troops and overall strategic planning. These efforts were meant to substitute French control in Vietnam with greater Vietnamese independence and American informal influence. Washington wanted to maintain a French military presence, but as France withdrew politically the United States would take France's place as the major western power in Southeast Asia.

In a precursor of moves to come, in late May Dulles sent a cable to Dillon urging contingency planning. Dulles wanted the Associated States to play a role in the programming of American aid and to receive military aid directly. Americans in Saigon, while also recommending more direct intervention, recognized the importance of working with the French. The French military and STEM had begun to coordinate more effectively on public works projects in 1953 and 1954, and economic aid, health, sanitation, and agricultural practices would suffer if Franco-American collaboration broke down. Counselor Minister Robert McClintock in Saigon advocated cooperation with the French but argued that French commanders should be subordinated to American strategy. McClintock believed development of the Vietnamese National Army should be the number one American military objective. The United States should directly train troops, the chief of MAAG should have authority to organize such training, and MAAG should be increased to accommodate its new role. The United States also needed to abrogate the existing pentalateral agreement between the Associated States, France, and the United States by which aid was funneled through the French. In late June, ninety additional personnel were assigned to MAAG and American officials began work on a system to provide direct aid to South Vietnam.[82]

The French were also thinking ahead. Mendès France sent a letter to the head of the French delegation at Geneva emphasizing the importance of providing an aid program to the South Vietnamese. Attempting to deflect the Eisenhower administration's unilateral move toward direct aid, he suggested the three western powers should make a public announcement about their intention to help Diem's government and then bring research groups together to figure out how to implement such a plan. He suggested they could work something out either through a tripartite agreement or through the UN. He also indicated his willingness to work on a multilateral program of assistance to Dillon a few days later.[83] The French were also considering how to avoid increased American involvement. French and South Vietnamese representatives agreed in a secret annex at Geneva that the State of Vietnam would not place any facilities at the disposal of foreign armed forces without the acceptance of the French government; nor would they allow increased personnel and materials for the training of Vietnamese forces without first consulting the French. Clearly, French officials were preparing for an American attempt to bypass them in the South.[84]

Both Paris and Washington made at least some attempts to analyze what had gone wrong in Vietnam. Perhaps C. D. Jackson said it best when he summed up the last few years of American involvement in Indochina as the "U.S.-Indochina Mess." According to Jackson, U.S. decisions could be attributed to "wishful thinking, rosy intelligence, oversimplified geopolitical decisions, deliberate French bending of the facts, and unwillingness to retreat from previously taken policy decisions." Jackson saw the "big black mark" against Eisenhower as his failure to give Indochina the continuity of thought that it rated. It kept reappearing before his mind as an endless series of irritating incidents, when either Robert Cutler or Arthur Radford or Walter Bedell Smith or Allen Dulles or John Foster Dulles came "rushing in with the latest bulletin and asking for a decision on a Navarre Plan or another $500 million, or the dispatch of six flying boxcars, or what have you." The line to Eisenhower was always, "Well, things don't look too hot right now, but I think if you will do just this one more thing everything will be all right," followed by an invocation of the domino theory. But Jackson did believe that Eisenhower saw earlier, more clearly, consistently, and forcefully than

anyone else the fatal weakness of the whole French situation, namely the political weakness, which was inevitably reflected in the fighting qualities of the
Vietnamese soldiers. He worked harder than anyone to try to get the French
to agree to U.S. training of Vietnamese troops. The Eisenhower administration was also frequently torn between conflicting intelligence reports from the
embassy, MAAG, STEM, and special emissaries. John Foster Dulles realized
the gravity of the situation and the importance of the area from the beginning.
In fact, according to Jackson, he more even than the military kept stating that
if Indochina went, all of Southeast Asia was gone. But Dulles also encountered
strong State Department pressure to "play along with the French."[85]

As for the French, Jackson believed "they were just being very French."
They guessed that if the United States had appropriated $800 million for In-
dochina aid in one year, if the United States felt "as strongly" about Southeast
Asia as it apparently did, and if the United States was going to be as "diplomatically correct" as it always had been in the case of France, the policy to be
pursued was to "siphon" as much out of America as possible, in the forlorn
hope that the sheer weight of dollars and hardware would bring about the
"needed miracle." Jackson's comments are yet another demonstration that
American officials recognized the Franco-American relationship had dominated U.S. policy toward Indochina, but Jackson tended to blame State Department officials for urging the Eisenhower administration to continue "the
American commitment to France." What Jackson failed to understand was
that, by refusing to break the link between the EDC and Indochina, Dulles
was the real culprit in creating the "U.S.-Indochina Mess."[86]

After Geneva, the blame game also began in France. According to Navarre in his bitter autobiography of the war, "it was Geneva and not Dien
Bien Phu that signaled the defeat of France." Navarre blamed Mendès France
for selling out to the communists. National Assembly deputy Edouard
Frédéric-Dupont claimed that if Laniel had still been in power, a Korea-type
settlement would have occurred and elections would never have been agreed
to. Frédéric-Dupont had served as minister for the Associated States (after Bidault had forced Marc Jacquet to resign from the position) and had
attempted to alert officials in Paris of the secret Franco-Vietminh negotiations regarding the partitioning of Vietnam to try to save the Laniel government. Frédéric-Dupont was forced to resign after his attempt failed. Mendès
France, in response to Navarre and Frédéric-Dupont's attacks, noted that he
had not given away any more than Laniel, and that the Vietminh had always
insisted that any division of the country would be temporary.[87] Neither the
Vietminh nor the French could have suspected the fatal consequences of

partitioning Vietnam, as the United States now had a pro-American South Vietnamese government, two years, and half a country to work with. Intensification of the war and the broadening of the conflict had only been averted at Geneva.[88]

The Eisenhower administration learned a number of lessons from what it considered the triple failures of united action, the Geneva Conference, and the EDC. Perhaps the most important was the need for a preexisting network of regional alliances to support U.S. activities in any given area of operations. Dulles consequently proceeded with discussions of a regional coalition that had begun during the crisis atmosphere of Dien Bien Phu. Indeed, according to NSC 5429, the "damage done" to the United States because of French "reverses" would have to be fixed through a Southeast Asia treaty organization (what came to be known as SEATO). Attendees at the Manila conference of September 1954 completed work on the organization, creating a regional multilateral defense system composed of the United States, France, Britain, Australia, New Zealand, Thailand, the Philippines, and Pakistan. SEATO, which had strong Congressional support, was officially implemented on February 19, 1955, to deter communist aggression in Southeast Asia. Cambodia, Laos, and Vietnam would be covered under the SEATO umbrella, despite French attempts to keep SEATO discussions separate from tripartite talks on Indochina.[89]

SEATO was thus, in many respects, a response to the perceived loss at Geneva. It was not as strong as NATO as it only obligated member states to "consult" with one another in the event of aggression, but it did serve as an American warning to Hanoi and Beijing that the United States was prepared to act if hostilities resumed. It appeared that the continual French plea from 1950 to 1953 for an allied Southeast Asia military organization had been answered. The only catch was that the Americans were running the show. The French had given SEATO a cool reception in the wake of what they considered American and British betrayal at Dien Bien Phu. Moreover, they had resisted moving forward with SEATO too quickly so as to avoid jeopardizing negotiations at Geneva and for fear of having to commit yet more French troops to another supranational organization they would not be able to control. The EDC debacle was, of course, still fresh in their memories, but it was also fresh for the Americans, who insisted on SEATO. Thus, not only had the Geneva Conference diminished the power of French colonialism, but it also accelerated the American transition toward closer alignment with the South Vietnamese. SEATO would become another weapon in the American arsenal for replacing French influence with an American one in Vietnam.

Until 1953, France and the United States had been drawn together by their mutual concerns in Europe and in Indochina, cemented by France's dependence on American foreign aid. From early 1953 until the summer of 1954, Washington and Paris pursued different objectives, both in Indochina and in European defense policy. The Eisenhower administration sought a continuation of the French war effort and ratification of the EDC but obtained neither, seeming to have seriously misjudged the political prospects for both in France. French ratification of the EDC was highly unlikely by 1954 even without the French defeat at Dien Bien Phu. As the Gaullists asked: Were the French to countenance a retreat from Southeast Asia *and* give up maintaining a national army in Europe? The disparity between French and American aims during this period raises serious doubts about the Eisenhower administration's de facto policy of linking the EDC's ratification to American aid for France. Although the Eisenhower administration never formally linked the two issues, both Paris and Washington recognized that a connection existed and successive French governments did not hesitate to exploit American insistence on the EDC.

The timing of increasing Franco-American disagreements is intriguing. As one American national intelligence estimate noted, "since the death of Stalin and the calling of the Geneva conference, the chief new element of Soviet policy was a heightened effort to convince non-Communist countries that Moscow and Beijing desired peaceful coexistence, and that U.S. policy was the only obstacle to a new era of peace in Asia." According to the report, this new element conformed to the present worldwide communist tactics of "minimizing tensions and of exploiting methods" to divide the free world, and particularly to detach the United States from its allies.[90] Indeed, throughout 1953 and 1954 the western powers spent at least as much time second-guessing each other's intentions as they did Soviet plans. Paris and Washington pursued divergent policies after Stalin's death, exactly as U.S. analysts had predicted. Stalin's death, it seemed, had a profound influence on West-West relations.

With the death of Stalin in early March 1953, both Washington and Paris saw new opportunities for reducing East-West tensions. The Americans were slower to act, in part because the Eisenhower administration saw no reason to soften U.S. policy in the event of a change in Soviet leadership. In responding to the Soviet peace offensive, Eisenhower and Dulles intended to place pressure on the Soviet Union and exploit the succession struggle to gain concessions at the bargaining table. From the French perspective, Soviet concessions at Geneva represented concrete evidence that Moscow truly desired détente with the West. Thus, at the moment when American fears of the EDC's failure and a negotiated peace detrimental to western interests in Indochina peaked, the French decided that European defense and the EDC had become less pressing, and that the Soviets were equally interested in establishing peace in Asia. Mendès France insisted that he had made no deals with Molotov to exchange peace in Indochina for the non-ratification of the EDC, but the EDC's defeat poisoned Franco-American relations and furthered Washington's perception that Soviet claims of "peaceful coexistence" were a ploy to undermine western solidarity. In the end, American predictions of allied disunity became a self-fulfilling prophecy, as Washington failed to test the validity of Soviet claims while Paris attempted to verify Soviet peace offerings.

The Soviet peace offensive was at least partially successful. The First Indochina War ended with the July 21, 1954, Geneva Accords, and the French National Assembly defeated the EDC on August 30, 1954. The Soviet Union thus avoided becoming further embroiled in a war that was not vital to Soviet security and it escaped facing a united European defense community. But the Soviets had perhaps scored a bigger victory than they realized. Franco-American relations would become even more difficult as the two countries competed for influence in South Vietnam after Geneva. Until Geneva, the Americans maintained a careful balance between urging the French to pursue the war aggressively and not pressing them so hard that they retreated completely from Vietnam or the EDC. But with the EDC-Indochina connection finally broken, the Eisenhower administration was free to pursue its own course of action in Vietnam, which is precisely what it would do. The European shadow that had dominated Asian policy since 1950 was gone.

France achieved remarkable success in acquiring American aid, linking Korea and Indochina, and internationalizing a solution to the Indochina conflict at the Geneva Conference. After Geneva, this success would come back to haunt them, as it appeared that they had done too good a job of interesting the United States in Vietnam. Franco-American competition would increase as the two western powers turned to the task of finding a capable South Vietnamese leader who could inspire confidence, maintain a noncommunist South Vietnam, and win the 1956 elections.

PART 2

After Geneva, 1954–1956

There is nothing as durable as the temporary.
—*French aphorism*

4

The Diem Experiment

THE DIEM EXPERIMENT BEGAN on July 7, 1954, when Ngo Dinh Diem took control of the South Vietnamese government. Initially, Diem inspired little confidence in the French, Americans, and South Vietnamese. Despite its misgivings, the Eisenhower administration welcomed Diem's rise to power; the Mendès France government did not. The Franco-American relationship had become increasingly fragile during the Dien Bien Phu crisis and the Geneva Conference as leaders from the two countries vehemently disagreed about how to preserve a noncommunist South Vietnam. Both France and the United States desired the establishment of an independent and pro-western South Vietnamese government, but they had other, conflicting aims as well. The Mendès France government's primary goal after Geneva was to avoid a resurgence of war. Paris also planned on maintaining an economic and cultural presence in both South and North Vietnam and ensuring that the 1956 Vietnamese elections, stipulated by Geneva, took place. Emperor Bao Dai's appointment of Diem as prime minister presented an immediate problem to this plan given Diem's antipathy toward France and unwillingness to uphold the Geneva Accords. Compounding the problem was the Franco-American relationship in Vietnam. The Americans, still scarred from France's determination to negotiate with the communists at Geneva and the EDC fiasco, placed a priority on strengthening the noncommunist South Vietnamese state, isolating North Vietnam, and avoiding the 1956 elections if it looked like the DRV would win.

Although France and the United States had agreed to a policy of "joint action" in South Vietnam after Geneva, their disagreement on goals and the means to achieve these goals led to conflict instead of cooperation between the two western powers. Nowhere was this battle for control more evident than in the debate over the viability of the Diem government. The French saw Diem as a risky experiment at best, while the Americans believed they had found a steadfast, if flawed, South Vietnamese leader. Franco-American negotiations over Diem culminated in May 1955, accelerating America's replacement of France as the dominant western power in South Vietnam.

DIEM'S APPOINTMENT

Diem had gained national attention when he resigned as minister of interior from Emperor Bao Dai's restructured cabinet in 1933. Bao Dai tried to interest Diem in the premiership in 1945, but Diem, determined to avoid being associated with the taint of French colonialism that enveloped Bao Dai, refused, and remained removed from politics until his appointment as prime minister in 1954. During the First Indochina War, Diem became known for his anti-French as well as his anticommunist sentiments. He left Vietnam in 1950 and lived a secluded life in a Roman Catholic seminary in New Jersey for two years. During his stay in the United States he made frequent trips to Washington and managed to establish some contacts with Catholic leaders such as New York archbishop Francis Cardinal Spellman, officials in the State Department, and members of Congress such as Senator Mike Mansfield (D-MT). The French were also well aware of Ngo Dinh Diem. As early as 1950, French officials in Saigon had recognized Vietnamese Catholics' disgust for Bao Dai and their hope that Diem could be "imposed on France by the Americans." Already, in February 1953, Diem was being discussed in French circles as a "card France will have to play one day." A number of Quai officials accepted the fact that Diem might be the only one who could provide a "psychological boost" in Vietnam because of his appeal to South Vietnamese nationalists and his integrity.[1]

In early 1954, Diem began to announce his views on Indochina more loudly. During a speech at Cornell University, Ithaca, N.Y., in February, Diem denounced French colonialism and, seconding many American officials, suggested that the Vietnamese National Army (VNA) be trained directly by the Americans and South Vietnam and integrated into a Southeast Asian security system. Because of Diem's anticommunist and anticolonial appeal, by spring 1954 it appeared likely Bao Dai would appoint Diem as prime minister. Not all French officials opposed Diem, as Eisenhower administration officials tended to assume. In fact, there was considerable internal debate in Paris and Saigon, and Diem had a number of influential high-level supporters—Deputy Prime Minister Paul Reynaud and French Undersecretary for the Associated States Marc Jacquet among them. Several thought Diem was South Vietnam's only chance. Of course, Diem also had his detractors, the most vocal being former French commissioner general to Indochina Maurice DeJean, who maintained a grim outlook on Diem's abilities and advocated Bao Dai's immediate return to Vietnam to assume the premiership.[2]

In mid-May 1954, Bao Dai sent Ngo Dinh Luyen (Diem's brother) to meet with Undersecretary of State Walter Bedell Smith and Director of the Office of Philippine and Southeast Asian Affairs Philip Bonsal to assess U.S. intentions in Vietnam. Bonsal reported that Bao Dai was contemplating the dismissal of Pham Buu Loc as prime minister and might play the "Ngo Dinh Diem card" if he could be assured of American support. Bao Dai's concern was that the French would oppose such a move and that he would be unable to overcome this opposition.[3] This conversation revealed that Bao Dai was carefully weighing his options as he became more suspicious of French intentions at Geneva and recognized Diem's growing influence in the United States and in Vietnamese Catholic circles. When Bao Dai ultimately appointed Diem in the middle of the Geneva Conference, much speculation arose over the role the United States had played in his appointment.[4] The available French and American documentation indicates that Bao Dai made a calculated decision to appoint Diem on his own, after listening to the French and the Americans, and that the French did not attempt to block the appointment. Regardless of the murkiness surrounding his ascent, when he assumed power in July 1954 Diem certainly did not view himself as a "creature of the Americans," but as the only alternative to a French-backed puppet or a communist stooge.[5]

French and British officials and, to a lesser extent, American officials in Saigon were not so sure; they remained skeptical of Diem's ability to become an effective South Vietnamese leader. In contrast, American officials in Washington, in particular Secretary of State Dulles and Department of Defense officials, as well as MAAG officers in Saigon, were committed to Diem and his anticommunist and anticolonial credentials. Dulles, the Defense Department, and MAAG believed that the crux of the South Vietnamese problem was national security, arguing that this problem could be resolved by building up the VNA and Diem's government. But many civilian officers in the State Department and in the U.S. Embassy in Saigon felt the underlying problem was Diem's inability to govern effectively.[6] Thus, while the French, British, and American officials in Saigon viewed the Diem government as an experiment, Washington perceived Diem's leadership of South Vietnam as more of a fait accompli.

Extensive scholarship has focused on how the United States began its effort to build South Vietnam into a nation after Geneva.[7] Less well studied is the conflict between France and the United States that occurred once Diem took power. This fight transcended the Diem experiment while the French and Americans each struggled to realize their particular visions of South Vietnam. London attempted to mediate between the other two western powers in an attempt to uphold the Geneva agreements, but the conflict was not resolved until Diem consolidated control in May 1955.

Soon after Diem's appointment, some French officials began a campaign against him. Paris was determined not to associate itself with any action that might lead to a renewal of the Vietnamese war, and the Mendès France government, according to American officials, viewed Diem as a threat to maintaining peace because of his "rabid Francophobia."[8] In mid-August, French officials reported to American ambassador to France Douglas Dillon that the "ineffectiveness of Ngo Dinh Diem has exceeded [their] worst fears," urging that Diem be replaced with a more dynamic South Vietnamese leader since he could not match Ho Chi Minh's "leadership qualities, personality, and mystique." Moreover, French officials pointed out, Diem "lacked support in the South, had no political finesse, and faced resistance from various politico-religious sects, parts of the army, and some Catholics."[9]

The Eisenhower administration differed with the Mendès France government on Diem's chances for success. In the aftermath of Geneva, American officials in Washington, in contrast to those in Saigon, saw Diem as the best chance for a noncommunist South Vietnam and believed his government should be strengthened to maximize its chances of survival.[10] As early as mid-August, Dulles communicated to French leaders that although the United States was not irrevocably committed to Diem, the "kind of thing Diem stands for is a necessary ingredient to success and we do not see it elsewhere."[11] The British government occupied a middle position. London shared Paris's fears that if the West repudiated the Geneva agreements, North Vietnam would resume hostilities. Moreover, British officials tended to discount the American assertion that if South Vietnam fell to communism, the rest of Southeast Asia would follow. But London agreed with Washington's assessment that finding an alternative to Diem would prove difficult.[12]

Wrangling over Diem and South Vietnam's fate dominated Franco-American discussions for the next ten months. After the initial disorder following Geneva, four distinct periods can be perceived that demonstrate how Franco-American conflict over the Diem experiment evolved. First, from September to December 1954, Washington struggled to develop a coherent policy toward Vietnam. American officials wanted the French out of Vietnam but were unsure whether Diem could survive without the FEC. In this period, the Americans hesitated to provide unconditional support to Diem and at least listened to French suggestions that alternatives to Diem be considered. Second, after Franco-American talks in December, French and American officials agreed, at least in theory, to support Diem as his government appeared to stabilize. The third and most critical period was from March to May 1955, when Diem faced an internal crisis as the three principal political sects in South Vietnam (the Binh Xuyen, Cao Dai, and Hoa Hao) united in opposition to his government.[13] At this point, it seemed that the French would succeed in replacing Diem. Once Diem defeated the sects, a fourth period began in which Diem consolidated his power. Although the American viewpoint on Diem prevailed in the end, U.S. officials erred in refusing to consider French and British suggestions. This refusal ultimately resulted in an early loss of international support as the United States proceeded essentially alone in its crusade to preserve a western bastion in South Vietnam.

THE DIEM EXPERIMENT BEGINS

After the frantic activity during the Dien Bien Phu crisis and Geneva Conference, South Vietnam looked relatively quiet. In the United States, Indochina no longer dominated NSC meetings, and most communications about South Vietnamese affairs were cables between Saigon, Paris, and the Department of State. Behind the scenes, however, the Eisenhower administration scrambled to uphold American credibility by strengthening South Vietnam even as the Mendès France government began the process of withdrawal from Indochina in accordance with the Geneva agreements. Thus, a declining French presence and an increasing American influence in the political life of South Vietnam were already evident in the weeks immediately following Geneva. Meanwhile, Diem tried to set the tone for his government early on; the *Vietnam Press* in late June had stated that Diem's program would include neutrality under the slogan "Neither valet of Russians, nor servant of Americans, Vietnam must be Asiatic Switzerland."[14] Of course, such a goal would prove difficult as Diem needed American support.

Exactly what type of support should be provided was the subject of a "U.S. Policy for Post-Armistice Indochina" study. Counselor Minister Robert McClintock noted that the American policy of winning the war in Indochina by operating through "a French keyhole and subject to a French veto" had failed. Therefore, a new policy for U.S. direct aid to Vietnam should be established. The United States had no desire to "usurp France's place in the economy of Indochina or in its cultural hegemony," but McClintock recommended increasing MAAG's functions and instituting a program to teach the rising generation English so that South Vietnam could have contact with the rest of "free Asia." Most important, he concluded that "fundamentally U.S. policy toward Indochina should be determined by what is in our national interest in Southeast Asia. U.S. policy toward France should be determined by what is in our national interest in Europe. Our policies thus far have failed because we tried to hit two birds with one stone and missed both."[15] For the first time since 1950, an American official was suggesting that Washington formulate policy regarding Indochina without considering European factors. Smith also recognized the importance of establishing a policy specifically for Indochina and tried to ensure that the OCB Special Working Group on Indochina (established by Eisenhower and Dulles in August), the JCS, and the Department of Defense would coordinate with one another to establish U.S. policy.[16]

As the Americans attempted to separate their European and Asian policies, the French strategized on how to work closely with the United States and maintain their presence in Indochina. French officials recognized that the EDC's failure had already weakened the alliance as well as their liberty of action in Asia. Government officials did not want to put the alliance further at risk and feared jeopardizing their place among the *trois grands* by pursuing a unilateral policy in Indochina. According to High Commissioner Paul Ely, for France to remain a great power, it had to maintain a presence in the Far East and in Indochina. Therefore, France should do nothing to raise American suspicions as experience had shown that the Americans remained "wedded to the ideas of anticommunism and anticolonialism." Ely advocated "speaking the same language" as the Americans (anticommunist rhetoric) in order to convince them that Diem was not the best solution for South Vietnam.[17]

Despite Ely's plea, tensions escalated as French officials increasingly viewed American support of Diem as a concerted effort to undermine their interests and prestige in South Vietnam, while many Americans in Saigon became convinced that certain French elements were scheming to overthrow Diem. For example, according to a CIA report in mid-August, the French would "not trust any Vietnamese government" that was not headed by individuals under French control. The report asserted that the French were "actively undermining" Diem but had limited their actions to demonstrating that Diem was "incompetent" and "lacked public support." A letter from Eisenhower to Diem that addressed him personally rather than the head of the South Vietnamese government served as further proof that the Americans were already "committed" to Diem.[18] The divergence of French and American goals added to these tensions. The French wanted to prepare for the 1956 elections, to preserve their political, economic, and cultural presence in both South and North Vietnam, and to withdraw their military forces.[19] Washington required Paris to provide strong support to a regime that was adamantly anti-French, to accept the progressive relinquishment of French political, economic, and cultural influence, and to maintain a large French military presence.

Until the Geneva Conference, Washington was desperate to keep France in Vietnam. Thereafter, the Eisenhower administration began to consider how to get them out. On August 20, Eisenhower approved an NSC document that entailed working with the French in Indochina "only to the extent necessary," reflecting the American consensus that the French presence was at best a transitional reality.[20] Dulles agreed, having sent a personal message to Mendès France two days earlier emphasizing U.S. backing of Diem. Dulles recognized that the Geneva Conference had created a political vacuum in the South and desired a complete French withdrawal that would permit the United States to work directly with Diem. His views corresponded with Diem's goal to remove the French from South Vietnam; Diem viewed the French and the French-backed Vietnamese as a greater immediate threat to his consolidation of power than the communists.[21] Yet Dulles was reluctant to hasten the FEC's withdrawal as it was the only military force capable of guaranteeing South Vietnamese stability.

Eisenhower and Dulles hoped to use the OCB Special Working Group on Indochina to resolve this dilemma. Under the chairmanship of the State Department, the group's mission was "to assist" the Associated States in "strengthening their position" against the Vietminh. The group was designed to make "rapid decisions" on a day-to-day basis with respect to necessary readjustments of existing programs and redeployment of resources occasioned by or resulting from the termination of hostilities. Among other matters, members would be responsible for the "movement and resettlement" of North Vietnamese refugees, the evacuation of military equipment, and the provision of military and other types of assistance to the Associated States.[22] Recognizing that Diem's chances of remaining in power depended on the whim of Bao Dai and the demands of French policy, an American army assessment recommended the elimination of the French as a "controlling political factor, the building of a government under leaders acceptable to the people and a psychological and information campaign pushed with vigor."[23]

The French also debated how to handle the situation in Vietnam immediately after Geneva. Of utmost concern was whether to keep Diem in power and how France could maintain control of the situation.[24] Ely, French deputy high commissioner in Indochina Jean Daridan, and other French officials held a high-level meeting to discuss options. After ruling out Bao Dai's return, a coup d'état, and a new, more pliable South Vietnamese government, the French decided they would try to persuade Diem to enlarge his regime while "guiding" Bao Dai to replace Diem at a later date. This discussion demonstrated that the French still considered themselves masters of the game in Saigon, but Ely recognized the importance of securing American cooperation in supporting a South Vietnamese government. If the government proved untenable, it would be a "shared failure" and hence less serious for Franco-American relations. Ely also realized that the French Foreign Ministry might pose an obstacle to his plans in Indochina, since many officials predicted that the DRV would take over all of Vietnam in the 1956 elections, and this communist victory would in turn necessitate the speedy withdrawal of the FEC and cooperation with the North. Ely feared Paris would advocate replacing Diem with someone who would deal with Ho Chi Minh. To avoid American accusations of unilateral abandonment of Diem, Ely and others advocated integrating French and American policy toward South Vietnam "as closely as possible."[25]

Eisenhower and Dulles remained skeptical about the compatibility of French and American policies in South Vietnam. American officials believed that Guy La Chambre, the French minister in charge of relations with the Associated States, sought to oust Diem or at least force him to work with the Cao Dai, Hoa Hao, and Binh Xuyen. Ambassador Donald Heath's reports to the Department of State confirmed that French officials, including Ely and Daridan, were convinced Diem must go.[26] A series of meetings and conversations between South Vietnamese and French officials, in particular Maurice DeJean's repeated attempts to convince Bao Dai to replace Diem, indicated that France still had significant power in internal Vietnamese affairs, and that the American suspicions of French intriguing against Diem were at least partially justified.[27]

Tensions between American and French officials over how to proceed in South Vietnam increased to the point that La Chambre and Ely came to Washington in September to discuss the situation. By the end of the meetings, in an attempt to follow a policy of joint action, French and American representatives agreed to support Diem in the "establishment and maintenance of a strong, anti-Communist and nationalist government." To this end, France and the United States would urge all anticommunist elements in Vietnam to "cooperate fully with Government of Ngo Dinh Diem" in order to "counter vigorously" the DRV and "build a strong, free Vietnam."[28] La Chambre declared that "from now on there will be no place for the slightest misunderstanding, the least divergence of views between France and the United States, on Southeast Asian questions . . . those who try to play the United States against France or vice versa will be thwarted." However, events over the next eight months would prove the inaccuracy of La Chambre's claim. Instead of promoting closer cooperation, the September entente paved the way for further Franco-American conflict over the Diem government as Paris and Washington accused each other of violating the spirit of the agreement.

While Washington assumed that the French had agreed to provide support to the Diem government, pointing to Mendès France's promise to give Diem a "good try," Paris evidently believed that the Americans had acquiesced to French demands to consider alternatives if Diem faltered. La Chambre noted that the political situation in South Vietnam was very bad, as Diem had "squandered" months after Geneva; however, La Chambre did not want to "ruin" the Atlantic alliance by pursuing a unilateral policy.[29] The French continued to press for alternatives such as former Vietnamese members of government Buu Loc, Phan Huy Quat, or Nguyen Van Tam, who would be more flexible and sympathetic to French interests and work with the army and Binh Xuyen. NSC estimates noted that Ely favored Tam whereas a number of officials close to Mendès France liked Prince Buu Hoi, in part because of his neutralist views and past association with the DRV. Tam, VNA chief of staff General Nguyen Van Hinh, and other French favorites (notably Tran Van Huu and General Nguyen Van Xuan) were all French citizens by naturalization. According to Kenneth Young, the State Department's officer in charge of Southeast Asian affairs, the only logical explanation for French maneuvers was that Paris preferred a new setup in Saigon that could lead to either "coexistence or coalescence" with the North before or after the 1956 elections.[30]

To counter French equivocal support of Diem, Senator Mike Mansfield stated to the Senate Foreign Relations Committee in mid-October that the United States "would suspend all aid if Diem was removed."[31] The Mansfield report undercut the Franco-American agreement in September that both countries would support a successor government if Diem lost power.[32] Indeed, Mansfield and a majority of Congressional members wanted to supplement American aid but recognized the limits of a "colonialist situation" and "anxiously waited" for the French withdrawal. The French understood Diem's appeal for Washington—he was a nationalist, an anticolonialist, and against corruption. They also recognized that Mansfield's support of Diem tended to preclude a search for alternatives as Mansfield probably held enough sway in Congress to succeed in withdrawing American aid from South Vietnam.[33] The Quai d'Orsay thus feared that Paris was being pushed aside by Washington.

Eisenhower validated French fears on October 22 when he told the NSC that it was time to "get rough and lay down the law" to the French. A few days later, Eisenhower sent a letter to Diem indicating that American aid would go directly to Diem's government if he made progress in military, economic, and political reforms in South Vietnam. Mendès France felt the letter went far beyond his understanding of the agreed Franco-American policy about Diem, contending that Diem now had guaranteed American support without providing a strong and stable government in return. French officials saw the letter as a rupture of the September agreements.[34] But Eisenhower and the NSC believed the situation in South Vietnam was unsatisfactory because of French unwillingness "to actively work to consolidate" the Diem government. At the NSC meeting the day after Diem received the letter, Eisenhower suggested trying to remove the French completely from South Vietnam. Such efforts to diminish French influence were well received by Congress. Representative James Richards unambiguously declared that "Vietnam will fall under communist control, unless the French abandon it totally, one hundred percent, militarily, economically, and politically." Also working against the French was Bao Dai's reluctance to move against Diem once it became clear that the Americans supported him. Although Bao Dai had been more willing to consider alternatives to Diem in early September, he was much less amenable two months later.[35]

By late October, the United States had taken significant steps to extend American influence in Vietnam by introducing three MAAG officers into the headquarters of the VNA, one in the Defense Ministry, and one in each of the three Vietnamese regional military headquarters. MAAG officials promised to keep Ely informed of program activities and solicit his advice, cooperation, and support. Although American officials had confidence in Ely, they felt that he needed to police his subordinates more effectively. Continued tacit encouragement of opposition to Diem on the part of French officials should be grounds for U.S. requests to the French government for their removal, according to the American Embassy.[36] Despite warnings from Secretary of Defense Charles Wilson, who felt that "further expenditures in

South Vietnam [were] a waste of money since it [was] hopeless to try to save it," Dulles pointed out that, whereas a $500 million dollar program for South Vietnam "was silly," some lesser amount for the purpose of building up a sufficient local force to ensure internal stability and counteract subversion was "reasonable and wise." Dulles thought that such an effort would not cost more than $100 million, and thus pressed forward with increasing American influence.[37]

Paris was well aware of the Eisenhower administration's attempts to usurp French authority in South Vietnam. During high-level tripartite conversations among the French, British, and Americans in October, the French insisted they were willing to help Diem but believed some contingency planning was in order. During the meeting, Dulles recognized the different goals of the French and the Americans: the French wanted to maintain contact with South and North Vietnam because of their history there, whereas the main American goal was to keep South Vietnam out of communist control. The French were concerned that Eisenhower did not recognize the extent to which Paris had supported Diem, even though French officials were not sure the Diem experiment would work. As French ambassador Henri Bonnet commented to Dulles in a meeting, "despite the best will in the world to make the Diem experiment work, the outlook seemed to be deteriorating rapidly." In response, American officials insisted that the Diem experiment could work, with French support. For Dulles, there was "no alternative" to Diem.[38]

Recriminations persisted on both sides of the Atlantic. Dulles commented in an NSC meeting that "the reason the French [were] so upset about being put on the spot [was] because they had made some sort of secret deal with the Vietminh in the course of the Geneva Conference." In turn, during his visit to Washington in November, Mendès France accused the United States of "replacing" France in South Vietnam and refusing to consider alternatives to Diem. Jean Daridan seconded this complaint, accusing the United States of "totally ignoring French input and trying to take away French influence and prestige." The French were also resentful of American complaints that they were actively working to undermine Diem. According to the Quai, French officials had persuaded Bao Dai to pressure Bay Vien (leader of the Binh Xuyen) and General Hinh to cooperate with Diem. And both the Mendès France and newly formed Anthony Eden governments were annoyed that the Eisenhower administration refused to set up tripartite committees to study the problem in South Vietnam.[39]

In Saigon, at least one American official appeared to be wavering over

Diem's viability. In early November, Ambassador Heath sent a letter to Washington arguing that trying to bolster Diem's government was useless. A few days later, Heath sent a more optimistic telegram stating that he believed the United States could obtain French support for the Diem experiment in spite of the prevailing belief that "Diem is a political dodo."[40] Still, Heath's questioning of the official American position precipitated his recall from Saigon. Eisenhower and Dulles decided Heath's hesitancy was detrimental to American interests in South Vietnam and that a stronger presence was required. This presence would be General J. Lawton Collins. Eisenhower believed that Collins would provide an accurate assessment of the situation in Vietnam because Collins, like his counterpart Ely, was familiar with the Indochina situation, having been involved in earlier tripartite meetings on Southeast Asian defense.[41] Collins arrived on November 8 as the special representative of the president with the rank of ambassador. He had two initial objectives: to achieve an agreement with Ely on U.S. support and training of the Vietnamese armed forces, and to initiate a series of steps by which Diem's government could be strengthened and stabilized. Along with Collins's arrival, the Eisenhower administration augmented the small numbers of American military, economic and technical assistance, and foreign personnel. Washington thus increased its commitment to the Diem government at a moment when British and French officials seriously questioned Diem's capabilities.[42]

Franco-American conflict increased toward the end of 1954. Although Collins and Ely had maintained a good rapport, American officials in Saigon were sharply critical of other French officials, accusing them of obstructionism and of having moved from a position of "acquiescence" to American demands in September to one of "opposition" by November. In turn, the French contended that the Americans were trying to supplant them in spite of their loyal support of the "Diem solution."[43] The incongruence between French and American policy toward South Vietnam could no longer be hidden.

Meanwhile, the Diem government's fragility had become equally difficult to conceal when, in the fall of 1954, General Hinh threatened to topple the government. Beginning in late August, Hinh had periodically boasted that he could take control of South Vietnam. The United States blamed France for the immobilization of the Diem government in the face of Hinh's aggression. Dulles believed the French could have exerted more pressure on Hinh, concluding that he probably had their secret backing. Hinh was a French citizen with a French wife; he was also an officer in the French air force and thus supposedly under French military discipline. In fact, according to a CIA report, Diem stayed in power only because Hinh and the Binh Xuyen were unwilling to take the chance of throwing him out physically, as the "prereq-uisite for any coup attempt was assurance of French non-interference." As the Hinh crisis played out, NSC planners also believed that the French "still hold the key to the situation," as they controlled the city of Saigon and could keep Hinh "under wraps" through control of troop pay and supply.[44]

On the French side, Diem's inability to stabilize the government con-firmed Paris's suspicions that he was not worthy of support. Daridan reminded the Americans that French willingness to view Diem as a "per-manent solution" was conditional on the premier making peace with the army. Meanwhile, La Chambre repudiated the charge that the French had not given all-out support to Diem as a "slur on French honor," and criticized the U.S. decision to give direct aid to South Vietnam before the crisis was resolved as a violation of the September accords. Such unilateral U.S. action risked "breaking Franco-American teamwork," but in the end, La Cham-bre conceded that "we prefer to lose in Vietnam with [the] U.S. than to win without them."[45] The Eisenhower administration notified Hinh that Ameri-can aid to South Vietnam would cease if Diem was ousted, and the CIA tried to persuade Hinh and his cohorts to leave the country, but it was not until Bao Dai finally ordered Hinh to France in November that the crisis ended.[46] The crisis proved that the French, not the Americans, were still in control of the situation on the ground in South Vietnam, but it also demonstrated how anxious the French were to avoid unilateral action as they deferred to American pressure to support Diem.

Not only did the Eisenhower administration have to contend with the French, it also had to deal with Congress. Mansfield insisted that Collins give Diem more time to improve the situation and suggested sending Dr. Wesley Fishel, a political scientist at Michigan State University and a close friend of Diem's, to South Vietnam. Mansfield also refused to even consider British and French pleas for Diem's replacement.[47] Eisenhower and Dulles recog-nized that Mansfield could withhold funds to South Vietnam if he chose and thus had to consider his advice, confirming their inclination to stay the course with Diem.

Despite Congressional pressure to keep Diem, in mid-December the French were still exploring alternatives. Earlier in the month, Guy La Cham-bre had notified Dillon that by mid-January the French government would have to reach a decision on the future role of France in Vietnam. La Cham-bre indicated the French were so discouraged that serious consideration was being given to a full evacuation of civilians, starting in a few weeks, to allow for a subsequent large withdrawal of French forces. With this not-so-subtle threat, La Chambre was undoubtedly trying to prompt Washington to consider alternatives to Diem.[48]

American officials attempted to decipher their counterparts' motives. U.S. official Turner Cameron viewed French policy as rather "Machiavellian," arguing that the French, during the Ely–La Chambre talks and Mendès France talks, agreed to support the U.S. position with respect to Diem because they were confident that this policy would fail. In addition, the French, in view of the U.S. fixation on Diem, felt that this failure had to be a "demonstrable" one. Therefore, Cameron recommended that when the French suggested an alternative, the United States should consider acquiescing and providing qualified support. The French undoubtedly wanted to organize a government under "strong French influence" that would protect French interests and cultural and economic prestige so that Paris could reach an advantageous accommodation with the DRV when it took over the country.

The United States, according to Cameron, should acknowledge that the effect ultimately might be a gradual American withdrawal from Vietnam, but that the Eisenhower administration would gain time to build up the rest of Southeast Asia. Thus, the United States should "back away" from Vietnam and let France take charge, accepting a "minor loss of prestige now rather than a major defeat later on." Washington could use this decision in Indochina as a lever on French policy in Europe and place responsibility for the ultimate failure in Vietnam "squarely on French shoulders." If "Free Vietnam" were lost to the DRV under a U.S.-selected and -supported successor to Diem, the unfortunate effects on U.S. prestige in this area "would be incalculable."[49] Cameron displayed a clear understanding of the situation in Vietnam and the pitfalls the United States would face whether it continued to support Diem or chose a successor. Collins and his second-in-command Randolph Kidder paid close attention to Cameron's report, but were not quite ready to endorse Cameron's conclusions.

In the interim, Eisenhower and Dulles strengthened their commitment to the Diem regime, believing that the Hinh crisis had fortified the government and that Diem had a chance to establish a stable South Vietnamese government if the French let him. By December, then, the United States was no longer asking for French support of Diem, but demanding it. The hardening of the American position resulted in part from what American officials perceived as a schizophrenic French policy of professing support for Diem while acting to undermine him—a policy that explained, in large part, Vietnamese difficulties, according to American officials. Matters came to a head when

Dulles, Mendès France, and British prime minister Anthony Eden met in Paris in mid-December. Dulles's single-minded support of Diem disturbed Mendès France, but, by the end of the meetings, Mendès France believed that he had convinced Dulles to consider replacing Diem if the situation did not improve within a month. Dulles appeared willing to allow Mendès France to leave with this assumption, knowing that it would undoubtedly result in at least short-term French cooperation.[50] The problem, according to Douglas Dillon, was that the French saw Diem as an American protégé, whom they supported to ensure continuing American aid to the French in South Vietnam. Dillon believed that the French would eventually demand either clear proof that Diem had "changed his spots" or an agreement that he should be replaced.[51]

In light of diminishing French patience, Kenneth Young suggested that perhaps Diem should act as spokesman for the government and the running of the government should devolve to a vice president in charge of key ministries such as defense, interior, and national economy. Still, Young wanted the United States to resist British and French calls for formal tripartite meetings and working groups on Vietnam, which might compromise American decision making.[52] During this time, Collins and British commissioner general for Southeast Asia Malcolm MacDonald discussed the situation in South Vietnam. MacDonald agreed that Diem should be supported and that Diem's ability to take the army in hand, strengthen his cabinet, and produce such reforms as a national assembly should be the criteria for judging his success. If Diem failed, MacDonald and Collins thought that the best alternative would be Bao Dai's return as a constitutional monarch to preside over a government headed by Phan Huy Quat.[53]

In a secret letter to Eden, MacDonald noted that although Diem was a "bad" prime minister, "the vital need to cooperate with our allies compels us to pursue a policy loyally whilst there is any reasonable chance of its developing in a way to produce success." But MacDonald argued that if there was no improvement over the next few weeks, London should urge Paris and Washington to consider alternatives. MacDonald, British ambassador to Saigon Sir Hugh Stephenson, and Ely had already thought through the options—Quat should be prime minister, Nguyen Van Tam should have an important post, probably minister of interior, and Bao Dai should be encouraged to return to South Vietnam. MacDonald believed that before moving forward on this idea, all three western governments should agree to it. Ely and MacDonald concurred that they would not tell Collins about their agreement on an alternative plan to the Diem experiment, wanting the idea to appear to evolve from the Americans themselves. MacDonald concluded, "I dislike intensely this lack of candor with our American colleagues but in view of their strong and proprietary feeling about Diem, I believe that any other line for the present would risk a serious breach of Franco-Anglo-American cooperation in Indochina."[54] Because of their unwillingness to do further damage to the Western alliance after the problems at Geneva, the French and British did not insist—as strongly as they could have—that their American counterparts consider alternatives to Diem, but instead met secretly to circumvent American support of him.

At the same time, although American officials continued to promote Diem during conversations with their Western allies, internal assessments demonstrate that the United States was much less sure of its course of action. In a very pessimistic account of the current situation in late December 1954, at a time when South Vietnam appeared more stable, an NSC briefing stated that Diem's chances for success appeared "dimmer than ever." Diem had barred Quat from a cabinet post, the sects gave him only lukewarm support, and the rift with the army had not really healed. Collins deferred judgment on Diem until early January but argued if there was no development by then there were three alternatives: "a government under Quat, a government under Bao Dai, including Diem and Quat, or U.S. withdrawal from Vietnam."[55] The tragedy here is that the Americans, French, and British appeared relatively close in their assessment of Vietnam, but the ambivalence of their alliance stopped them from dealing honestly with one another.

THE DIEM EXPERIMENT IN ACTION

Beginning in January, the Diem government stabilized and the American policy to support Diem appeared set. This calm was due in very large part to the Collins-Ely team and their willingness to work together to create a secure situation. Although Ely had resented Collins's appointment at first, construing it as evidence of the U.S. intent to "take over," he quickly grew to respect Collins and the two established a close working relationship.[56] Throughout December 1954 and early 1955, Ely and Collins tried to form a plan that could salvage the Diem government and the South Vietnamese nation, agreeing to U.S. support for refugee resettlement, land reform, creation of a national assembly, economic development aid, and a program to train interested Vietnamese in public administration. The two men resolved a number of points of contention for the time being: the United States would not replace France in Vietnam; Ely and Collins would work together to present Diem with a plan of action; and the Americans would not protest against another government if Diem failed.[57] During this period, no overt challenges to the government arose, but French and British lack of faith in Diem's chances for success grew stronger. In particular, Paris and London again attempted to establish regular tripartite meetings to discuss alternatives to Diem, but once again the United States refused, wanting to preserve its freedom of action.

Leaders from the three western countries did not meet again until February to discuss Indochina, as the Eisenhower administration intended. Both the French and British wanted an earlier meeting but the Eisenhower administration purposely delayed while it attempted to shore up Diem's government. The general consensus among British officials was that the United States did "not have a clear-cut long-term policy for Indochina." The Americans had little tolerance for British suggestions that implied anything other than full support of Diem or that questioned American decision making. On the French side, Ely recognized the value of British contributions. He was convinced that the British wanted to pursue a policy of joint action that would require the three western countries to work together. Ely saw only advantages in the solidarity of the three NATO powers in South Vietnam; such cooperation, he believed, would be one of the best guarantees against the communist advance in the region and for the maintenance of peace. Ely was also tired of being seen as "America's man" in many French circles and wanted to establish a closer working relationship with the British.[58]

The Americans, on the other hand, wanted to break free from the French. In a study on what to do next in Indochina, the State Department suggested that true independence from France, an autonomous American-trained national army, a national assembly, a more broadly based government, and genuine land reform—those things that had been frustrated mainly by the subordination of Asian policy to the French alliance—might now finally become real thanks to the work of the Collins mission. According to the report, Diem owed his tenure and many of his achievements to the Collins-Ely team. This collaboration had been managed by the United States, "in spite of difficulties with the French, in the best interests of the Vietnamese, and probably, if they only knew it, of the French themselves." In the report, Edmund Gullion wrote that France "in due course *should* be supplanted, not by Washington, but by the people of Indochina." The Eisenhower administration should thus "tactfully encourage the withdrawal of French forces" except minimal base and staff components prior to the elections scheduled for July 1956.[59]

Ely recognized that the French were losing ground to the Americans in South Vietnam for a number of reasons. Reduced French economic aid, Diem's refusal to send more military trainees to France, French policy toward the North that remained ambiguous in both American and South Vietnamese eyes, and the French dislike for Diem all contributed to growing Francophobia. Ely conceded that Diem had achieved some genuine successes and that the Americans appeared resolved not "to change the horse in the middle of the torrent." But what the Americans saw as major policy triumphs for the Diem government—successful resolution of the Hinh conflict, integration of the Hoa Hao army into national forces, no renewal of Binh Xuyen gaming houses—the French and British viewed as superficial improvements. British officials saw themselves as mediators between the French and Americans, but their desire to avoid antagonizing either side did little to resolve Franco-American differences.[60] The timidity of the British stemmed, in part, from their unwillingness to risk diplomatic capital on Diem when it could be expended more fruitfully on ensuring the 1956 elections. In addition, by allowing the United States some leeway in South Vietnam, London undoubtedly hoped to gain American support on other world issues. This position, along with American refusals to consider British suggestions, left the British out of the decision-making process. Ambassador Stephenson correctly assessed the American position: "The American flag is now nailed so firmly to the Diem mast that I believe there is a serious risk that American aid would be withdrawn if a successful attempt was made to oust Diem without their concurrence."[61]

At the end of February, after a three-week ministerial crisis, Edgar Faure replaced Pierre Mendès France as prime minister. Faure assured American officials that it was the policy of the French government "to work 100%" with the United States in Indochina, and that the "closest Franco-American cooperation" was not only important to Indochina states but "essential to the Free World."[62] American officials in Saigon remained unconvinced and accused Jean-Pierre Dannaud, head of the French Information Service, of conspiring to oust Diem. The Americans were also annoyed because Radio France Asie was directly controlled by Paris, and a number of broadcasts contained anti-Diem sentiment.[63] These reports persuaded Dulles that the French were still actively pursuing alternatives to Diem. According to Dulles, Diem was the answer not only because he was "untainted by colonialism and remained adamantly anti-French," but also because "no alternative existed."[64] Apparently Dulles had not learned his lesson from the EDC fiasco; he once again persisted in a single-minded policy, and Franco-

American bickering over Diem continued throughout the winter and into early spring.

THE END OF THE DIEM EXPERIMENT?

With significant help from the Americans, Diem was still in control by March 1955. Both Diem and the Eisenhower administration were taken by surprise, however, as a major crisis rocked the government at the end of March and throughout April. In response to increasing government repression, the Binh Xuyen, Cao Dai, and Hoa Hao sects formed a "united front" against the Diem government and demanded either reforms or Diem's ouster.[65] A joint Franco-American team had been formed to study the sect problem but had not reached any conclusions by the time open warfare broke out on March 29–30. The "sect crisis" had begun. Given their skepticism about Diem, France and Britain were more prepared than the United States for such a challenge. Major differences developed among the three countries as they responded to the crisis. Washington clearly wanted to retain Diem. Paris and London, on the other hand, placed a higher priority on containing the fighting, avoiding a civil war, and finding a more reasonable South Vietnamese leader.

French armored units quickly blocked the streets to prevent more bloodshed, but, according to American officials, French forces also barred the national government from wiping out the Binh Xuyen in the initial fighting of late March by withholding fuel and other necessary military supplies. Moreover, certain French elements, probably without official sanction, aided the Binh Xuyen during the later fighting. The Eisenhower administration received reports that French officers sympathetic to the Binh Xuyen fed its officers with intelligence reports and erected road barriers against Diem's troops. Undoubtedly, some French obstructionism occurred, since many French officers were sympathetic to the Binh Xuyen and had little respect for Diem. Because of such accounts, both Eisenhower and Dulles believed that the French had purposely hindered Diem in his fight against the Binh Xuyen.[66]

Dulles was annoyed by the actions of the French. He argued that France should not restrict Diem in reestablishing his authority, whereas the Faure government feared that allowing Diem free rein might lead to a widened conflict. Dulles maintained that if the French assured Diem "moral and logistic" support, the challenge from the Binh Xuyen would "evaporate or be contained."[67] American and French officials also disagreed over who had caused the crisis. Washington contended that the Binh Xuyen had deliberately attacked Diem. Paris countered this view, suggesting that Diem had provoked the clash. The British had a more impartial stance, holding Diem partially responsible but also recognizing that matters would probably not have reached the present stage without French sympathy for the sects and lack of strong support for Diem. Stephenson concluded that, "so long as the present crisis continues and until we reach some equilibrium, I see no alternative course to continuing to back Diem. Any change now would be a risk to Franco-American cooperation which is held together at the top."[68] London concurred, maintaining a wait-and-see approach.

As the crisis deepened, the Faure government repeatedly urged the Eisenhower administration to set up meetings between France and the United States so that some sort of joint action could be established. The Quai instructed Ely to be extremely careful not to put himself in the position of being held accountable for Diem's failure and that he should use the FEC only to protect French lives and property. The Quai also asked Ely to think of possible replacements for Diem.[69] Ely blamed Diem completely for the mess in South Vietnam. In a telegram to the Quai, he argued that France had saved the day by stopping the fighting and avoiding a civil war. Still, Ely argued against Diem's replacement for the time being for a number of reasons: the American 1955–1956 budget (which would determine aid for France) had not yet been decided in Congress; Diem's defeat would lead to dangerous internal movements; and if Diem did fall he was likely to begin an exile government and denounce the French. Ely proposed that Diem broaden his government immediately and that Bao Dai be brought in to help resolve the crisis. Paris agreed that Diem should either enlarge his government or be replaced.[70]

Collins corroborated the French view in a top secret telegram to Dulles on March 31, stating the United States must face the fact that "Diem [was] operating a one man government" and was "entirely isolated." Collins doubted that Diem would be able to change his nature, noting that the French had not only ceased to obstruct Diem but, under Ely's guidance, had been making "positive efforts" to assist him. The major portion of responsibility for the "critical situation" in which Diem found himself must, in all fairness, "be laid squarely at Diem's door." Just as Donald Heath had decided six months earlier that Diem should be replaced, Collins had now arrived at the same conclusion. The French had been trying to persuade Collins to this point of view for months, but both American and French documentation indicates that Collins reached his own decision.[71]

Paris maintained that Diem could not defeat the Binh Xuyen militarily. The Quai pointed out that Diem had never been a national figure, that he had no roots in South Vietnam, and that he had managed to alienate just about everyone—Catholics, sects, police, army, administration, politicians, and intellectuals.[72] A political solution was therefore required. The French argued that Bao Dai should be approached and that he should call a meeting in Europe with Diem and sect leaders to broaden the government.

Dulles was shocked by this plan. His opposition, according to the French, stemmed in part from his "puritan disgust" for the Binh Xuyen and Bao Dai. Dulles believed that the French were closely connected to the Binh Xuyen and that they were only paying lip service to Diem. In a conversation with French ambassador to the United States Maurice Couve de Murville, who had replaced Henri Bonnet in February 1955, Dulles made it perfectly clear that if Diem left, the United States would withdraw from South Vietnam as well.[73] Collins thought the French plan might work, but Washington preferred to see whether Diem could triumph over the Binh Xuyen before making any deals with the French.[74]

The British were not surprised by Dulles's position; they assumed that the Eisenhower administration would maintain its blind faith in Diem and refuse to listen to any proposals likely to impair his prestige. Since American money was running South Vietnam, the British surmised, the United States would presumably "continue to call the tune."[75] British officials recognized, however, that events in Saigon showed "the Diem experiment [was] very near failure now."[76] Still, the British did not budge from their position of waiting to see what future events would bring.

Back in Saigon, Ely explained his concerns about worsening Franco-American relations to the Quai. He believed the principal obstacles to Franco-American cooperation were not rooted in Vietnam, but within American "incomprehension" of colonial affairs. Ely particularly resented continued American accusations that the French had prevented Diem's victory against the sects. Ely saw a lack of Franco-American understanding on colonial affairs since September 1954 as the "biggest obstacle" to success in South Vietnam.[77]

In mid-April, Couve de Murville and Dulles met to discuss the differing perspectives of the two countries. Whereas Washington saw the development of the crisis as a result of Diem's failure to take the necessary action against the Binh Xuyen, Paris believed that the crisis had arisen because of Diem's general inadequacies. Dulles expressed his doubts that the French had ever fully supported Diem, stating that the French press continually referred to Diem as "U.S.-supported." "Presumably if he fell," Dulles added, "French skirts would be clean and the loss of prestige would be the U.S.'s." Dulles insisted that the French had failed to respect the September and December accords. Couve de Murville pointed out to Dulles that Ely had valid reasons for stopping Diem: no guarantee of support by the VNA, no guaranteed chance of success even if he was supported by the VNA, and no guarantee that the Binh Xuyen would go quietly. In response, Dulles emphasized that Congress still viewed Diem as the only alternative.[78]

In a telegram to Collins, Dulles persisted in his recriminations against the French. "The French Government and press have made no secret of their desire to find a replacement," he wrote. They have "uniformly put the United States label on Diem. To them he is always 'American-backed Diem' or 'the Diem Experiment.' Never have they suggested that he is 'French-backed' or looked upon as other than an 'experiment.'" Toward the end of April, Dulles sent a top secret telegram to Dillon conceding that "some reorganization" in Saigon may be necessary but blaming the French for not supporting Diem fully. He further noted that ambiguities in French policy vis-à-vis the North and South had "impeded effective political development in Free Vietnam." The key difference between the French and Americans was Paris's belief that the French had done their best to support Diem, as agreed during the 1954 September and December meetings, but that even such support was insufficient to salvage him.[79] In contrast, Washington maintained that French obstructionism, not Diem's general ineptitude, was to blame for current South Vietnamese difficulties.

Despite Dulles's insistence on Diem, Paris maintained some hope that the situation in South Vietnam was about to change. A flurry of telegrams between the State Department and Quai d'Orsay in mid-April indicated to the French that the Americans were at last serious about replacing Diem. The Eisenhower administration sent a list of questions to the Faure government, asking them to specify alternatives to Diem. The questions addressed such issues as who had the best prospects of carrying out government programs and strengthening South Vietnam and would succeed Diem; when such a change would take place; which actions would be taken to ensure government control of the national police under the Binh Xuyen; what procedure would be followed in any proposed change; how the French would ensure the sects' support of a new government; and what support a new government could count on from French forces.[80] Dillon specified that the United States wanted a French response, not agreed Franco-American recommendations from Saigon.

Paris recognized that Washington was forcing the French government to make a decision so that if something went wrong, the Faure government would be blamed. French officials were concerned about putting forth unilateral decisions because they wanted to avoid later accusations about what could be considered solely "French" proposals for Diem's replacement. In particular, Couve de Murville feared that when the Diem government fell, the common belief would be that the "American solution" had failed and now a "French formula" would be tried. He urged his superiors to avoid making Diem's departure look like a "French victory" and "American defeat." Officials at the Quai also wanted to avoid this scenario, assuming Washington would decide to withdraw completely from South Vietnam.[81]

Despite such hesitations, the Quai d'Orsay concluded the moment for action was at hand and within days produced a fairly detailed outline of how Diem could be replaced. The Quai argued that both the French and Americans must agree on a successor to Diem. Once the decision had been made, "regime change" should be carried out as soon as possible. The Quai felt that a new government should be established in three phases: first a Franco-American decision; then a Franco-American-Vietnamese discussion in which French and American officials would approach Bao Dai secretly; then a Vietnamese declaration by Bao Dai. Only the Vietnamese phase would be made public. The French believed that the sects would support a new government if they were included in it, and the Quai claimed that the Binh Xuyen had already promised to behave. Finally, Paris would maintain a position of "non-intervention but sympathetic neutrality," while the presence of the FEC would guarantee order.[82] If the Americans refused to replace Diem, many at the Quai advocated a complete French withdrawal from South Vietnam.

The French answers to the list of American questions were telling. Clearly the French were exerting some sort of control over the Binh Xuyen. In addition, Paris did not plan on consulting South Vietnamese officials about Diem's replacement but insisted that an alternative to Diem should be decided by Washington and Paris and then announced by Bao Dai. Specifically, the Quai recommended well-known South Vietnamese leaders Phan Huy Quat or Tran Van Do as possible successors.

The Eisenhower administration's willingness to finally think about discarding Diem was also revealing. Even as the American presence in Saigon became more noticeable, the United States had created a back door out of Vietnam by agreeing to consider alternatives. If Diem's government did fall and a French alternative took over South Vietnam, Paris would be accountable for either the triumph or the defeat of the successor. That Washington considered alternatives at all stemmed, in part, from Collins's efforts. During a number of meetings in Washington in late April, Collins continued to press for Diem's removal, insisting, despite Eisenhower, Dulles, Young, and Assistant Secretary of State for Far Eastern Affairs Walter Robertson's doubts, that the French had made a bona fide effort to support Diem. Collins also urged that Phan Huy Quat take over the government through the intervention of Bao Dai. In response to skepticism about Bao Dai, Collins replied he was a man of "more substance" than the press gave him credit but that Diem was an "impossible fellow."[83]

French officials in Washington confirmed that Quat was aware of the situation and had reacted favorably to assuming control. In addition, Bao Dai was willing to stake his prestige that Diem would go to France without protesting and that in his absence the sects would desist from any act that would increase the present crisis. The cabinet would be headed by Quat and would include approximately twelve ministers. Bao Dai also urged that if the present plan was to be put into operation and succeed, it was absolutely essential that the United States take no visible role in the matter.[84]

As Washington prepared to move on Diem's replacement, French officials in Washington were convinced that Collins had succeeded and that Dulles was willing to sacrifice Diem to keep close Franco-American cooperation.[85] The moment for joint action had finally arrived. On April 27, the American Embassies in Paris and Saigon received instructions to initiate a change in the government. On that same day, fighting broke out again and the instructions to replace Diem were blocked by Dulles. For the next few days it was not clear whether Diem would triumph, and French and American officials continued to meet to discuss options.[86]

Ultimately, American officials could not overcome their deep suspicions of French motives and actions in the crisis. State Department officials reacted poorly to the prominent role Bao Dai would play, assuming that the French were behind the move and would reestablish control through Bao Dai once Diem left South Vietnam. Moreover, press reports that Ely had recognized Bao Dai's choice to head the South Vietnamese army—Binh Xuyen sympathizer General Nguyen Van Vy—further enflamed American sentiment that the French were acting directly against Diem. Prime Minister Faure's poorly timed claim that Diem "was not up to the difficulties of his task" caused the Eisenhower administration to publicly proclaim its support of Diem and to send Ambassador Dillon to lodge a formal protest against French actions. All of these incidents led Dulles and other American officials to cling to Diem.

As Ambassador Couve de Murville noted, the crisis in Saigon led to one in the Franco-American alliance itself.[87]

By May 2, when Collins returned to Saigon, Diem had vanquished the sects and was still in control of the government. The French felt betrayed by the breaking of what they considered American promises to replace Diem. Paris had devoted substantial time to formulating a plan for a new government, coordinated with Ely and the sects, and worked with the United States in a number of Franco-American meetings. Ely commented that the French had insisted the Vietnamese should determine their own government but that "it was along the Potomac that Diem's fate had been decided and where future South Vietnamese governments would be decided."[88]

Americans in Saigon were also attempting to decide South Vietnam's fate. There is little doubt that Diem started the fighting and was aided by the CIA. The French certainly believed that the CIA, and intelligence officer Edward Lansdale in particular, had been instrumental in the resumption of hostilities. Lansdale had first become involved in Vietnam in late 1953 when he accompanied a military survey mission. Lansdale saw psychological and unconventional warfare as the keys to success in Vietnam, and he was eventually stationed there, along with other CIA and U.S. military specialists, to work with partisan elements.[89] Lansdale's methods, a constant irritant to French sensibilities, resulted in mutual hostility as the sect crisis evolved.

USIS Saigon was also planning South Vietnam's future. During the sect crisis, USIS officials concluded that the successful accomplishment of U.S. programs for South Vietnam could not be ensured through French implementation because France would accept the concept of these programs only insofar as they contributed to its efforts to maintain a presence in the Far East. Further, the French were capable of negating U.S. programs, as demonstrated by their attempts to bring about the downfall of the Diem government through an internal coup and to influence Bao Dai to dismiss Diem. The French could also refuse to cooperate in the training of the Vietnamese army, withdraw completely from Indochina (thus forcing the United States to increase substantially its political, financial, and military commitments in the area), or unilaterally reach a rapprochement with the DRV and insist on executing their obligations under the Geneva agreement by working toward holding the elections scheduled for July 1956.[90] All of these factors led American organizations in South Vietnam to disassociate themselves from the French.

Back in Washington, Eisenhower's role remained unclear throughout the sect crisis.[91] He was willing to support an authentic and nationalist government, as indicated in his October letter to Diem stating American support. But Eisenhower had remained behind the scenes for the most part, allowing Dulles to increase the American commitment to Diem. In the end, Eisenhower sanctioned Dulles's delay in making a decision on Diem's removal, permitting Diem to renew the fighting to secure his position. The final result was a clear commitment to Diem by the United States.

Although Diem had won the battle, Franco-American conflict over South Vietnam's future continued. The French complained about American intervention, in particular Lansdale's role in Diem's victory over the sects. In turn, the Americans pointed out that the Binh Xuyen strongholds left in Saigon were in areas controlled by the French and that French personnel had been found in them. General Fernand Gambiez's decision to try to stop the fighting also furthered American suspicions that France was protecting the Binh Xuyen. Joint action was too difficult to achieve, according to both sides. Ely recommended that France should still try to work with the Americans to keep South Vietnam anticommunist, to establish South Vietnamese independence, and to respect the Geneva Accords. But Ely saw little chance of future Franco-American coordination given the Eisenhower administration's pursuit of a unilateral policy and its anticolonial attitude. Ely believed that the United States had two options: Washington could "persist in its unilateralism," in which case the FEC should withdraw, or Washington could "realize the FEC [was] necessary" and should stop considering its presence as an expression of colonialism. Ultimately, the sect crisis destroyed what remained of Franco-American political collaboration in South Vietnam. After it became clear Diem would defeat the sects, Randolph Kidder told Diem that he had Washington's full support and notified Ely that "joint action" no longer existed.[92]

The Eisenhower administration was disinclined to continue working with the French now that American officials believed that Diem might actually fill the political void left by the Geneva Conference. A National Intelligence Estimate stated that although the French would find it difficult to accept Diem's success, the fear of large-scale violence and of adverse domestic and world reactions would cause them to refrain from overt action in Saigon to remove Diem, unless the situation should threaten serious loss of French lives. The British hoped to buy some time and bring "moderating elements" into the government, but following the State Department's support of Diem, and Diem's success against the sects, the British were left with "no alternative" to supporting Diem. Still, Foreign Office official James Cable noted "one cannot help feeling that the Americans are as confused and uncertain as we are, but that, whereas we are remaining aloof until the dust settles, the Americans are plunging blindly in several directions at once."[93] In fact, the Americans were moving in a very specific direction. Once Diem proved his mettle in dealing with the sects, Eisenhower and Dulles decided they no longer needed French support or Bao Dai's blessings as they had during previous South Vietnamese crises. Indeed, much of the U.S. leadership advocated taking over completely. General Charles Bonesteel of the NSC encapsulated the crossroads the United States had reached, suggesting that getting the French to leave would "disengage us from the taint of colonialism." Although this might result in "substantial commitment," Bonesteel argued that it was "by no means certain" and that there was a "real likelihood" that training, technical assistance, and moderate aid would "be all that is required."[94]

The Diem Solution

Ten months after his assumption of power, Diem defeated the Binh Xuyen, secured American economic and military aid, and expedited the French withdrawal from South Vietnam—the Diem Experiment had become the Diem solution. The consolidation of Diem's regime in late 1954 and early 1955 gradually shifted the balance of power between the Western allies in Vietnam, with the United States supplanting France politically. This process culminated in Paris in May 1955 in a series of talks among American, French, and British representatives in which the Americans underscored the fact that they were taking charge in Vietnam. The "gentlemen's agreement" reached during the meetings effectively ended the allies' entente in Indochina.[95]

American officials during the May tripartite meetings convinced Edgar Faure to repledge support to the Diem regime. The meetings had begun badly when the French premier threatened to remove the FEC immediately. Dulles retaliated by suggesting instead that the Americans withdraw completely.[96] Both sides eventually retreated from their initial threats. During the meetings, Dulles made it clear to the French that "Diem must not be looked upon as an experiment to be ended when desired," arguing that it was far from sure he could be removed even if that was the American wish. According to Dulles, the real problem was to convince Diem that no one was working against him. "Like most orientals," Dulles said, "he was very suspicious and would not accept advice, however friendly, from anyone whom he thought might be working against him." Faure replied that he did not know how to work with the United States unless some political concessions were granted because he could not face the cabinet and parliament on a program of having "sold out 100%" to the Americans in South Vietnam. Faure was quite specific that the French government was not in accord with U.S. views, concluding that, "Diem is a bad choice, impossible solution, with no chance to succeed and no chance to improve the situation. Without him some solution might be possible, but with him there is none."[97] But by the end of the talks, although Faure had not received any concessions, he and British foreign minister Harold Macmillan agreed to support Diem. They could have refused, but chose instead to accede to American pressure, reasoning that opposition to Diem was not worth further weakening the Atlantic alliance, and preferring to focus on ensuring the 1956 Vietnamese elections. These talks marked the end of Franco-American collaboration in Vietnam, shifted the political balance from the French to the Americans, and accelerated American intolerance for the French presence there.[98]

Nine months of uneasy and superficial partnership regarding Diem were over. In May, Ngo Dinh Nhu, Diem's brother and adviser, asked Eisenhower and Dulles whether they would support Diem's plan to oust Bao Dai as chief of state. They agreed. Collins departed in mid-May, convinced that Diem's regime had little chance for success because his suppression of the Binh Xuyen did "not change his basic incapacity to manage the affairs of government." According to Collins, the Eisenhower administration was making a serious mistake.[99] Ely left two weeks later, claiming that he could not continue to carry out a policy in which he did not believe. Ely was particularly annoyed that he had spent so much time persuading "two American Ambassadors to his way of thought and to what he considered a sane policy only to find them overruled on each occasion by Washington officials who refused to listen to their advice and who only thought in terms of Congress' reactions and American public opinion." Ely had no reason to believe that if he stayed on he would not suffer the same experience again and had no inclination to try. According to Ely, a "common policy" between France and the United States "was now impossible."[100] Collins's successor, G. Frederick Reinhardt, arrived in Saigon to express unequivocal American confidence in the regime, just as Collins had six months earlier when he replaced Donald Heath.

Diem moved swiftly to consolidate his control, eliminating what remained of his domestic competition. By September, the remnants of the Binh Xuyen had been destroyed. In late October 1955, Diem carried out a national referendum between Bao Dai and Diem in which Diem garnered an impossible 98 percent of the vote. He also renewed his calls for the elimination of the Ministry of Associated States, which he viewed as a "colonial anachronism." As a consequence, Vietnamese representation in the Assembly of the French Union ended, France dissolved the Ministry of Associated States, and the French Foreign Ministry took over relations with the former Indochinese colonies. All these actions reinforced Diem's independence from French control. Then, on October 26, when the promulgation of the South Vietnamese constitution occurred, not a single reference to the French Union could be found. The referendum and constitution represented the coup de grâce to Franco-Vietnamese relations as they infuriated French officials in Paris and Saigon. By early 1956, South Vietnamese government forces occupied the Caodaist Saint Siege in Tay Ninh to break up the organized Cao Dai insurgency, and Cao Dai pope Ho Phap Pham Con Tac fled to Cambodia. An agreement with the remaining Cao Dai leaders legalized Cao Dai religious practices but forbade its political activities. General Tran Van Soai, commander of the Hoa Hao, surrendered to Diem; and in mid-April, the chief Hoa Hao dissident, Ba Cut, was arrested (and later executed), ending the Hoa Hao insurgency.

The bigger concern, of course, was the communists. The French noted that although Diem had managed to consolidate his power, nothing from the events of the past few months had proven that he would be able to rally the South Vietnamese against the challenge from the North.[101] In particular, Quai officials recognized that just as the French had tried vainly to create a noncommunist Vietnamese nationalism with Bao Dai, the Americans were making the same mistake with Diem. The French analysis would prove prophetic as the Eisenhower administration moved deeper into Vietnam.

THE REFUGEE CRISIS

As the French and Americans wrestled over Diem's fate during 1954–1955, one other development was central to Diem's continued viability—the refugee crisis. This exodus of primarily Catholic North Vietnamese refugees who fled to South Vietnam from August 1954 to May 1955 captured the free world's imagination and had major repercussions for domestic politics in South Vietnam and in the United States. Both a major humanitarian effort and a powerful propaganda tool, the handling of the refugee crisis was one area where planned Franco-American cooperation actually worked, remaining the only bright spot in post-Geneva Franco-American relations with respect to Vietnam. At first, it looked as though the French and Americans would fail to coordinate on this issue as well when, despite French claims that they were hard at work helping the refugees, Cardinal Spellman accused the French of "abandoning and betraying" Catholics fleeing the North.[102]

Article 14(d) of the Geneva agreements had specified that "any civilians residing in a district controlled by one party who wish to go and live in the zone assigned to the other party shall be permitted and helped to do so by the authorities in that district" within a ten month period.[103] The final declaration at the Geneva Conference reinforced this position in paragraph 8: "The provisions of the agreements on the cessation of hostilities intended to ensure the protection of individuals and property must be strictly applied and must, in particular, allow everyone in Vietnam to decide freely in which zone he wishes to live."[104] In the months following Geneva, a number of Vietnamese Catholics and those who had served as French functionaries or in the French army began preparations to leave the North. French leaders were determined to aid the refugees, no doubt bothered by recent memories of Vietnamese clamoring to be taken along as French ships, filled to the brim with French civilians and military personnel, fled North Vietnam immediately after July 21, 1954.

More problematic for the French was the issue of those refugees who wanted to leave Vietnam completely. In preparation for a Ho Chi Minh victory in the 1956 elections and a subsequent flood of Vietnamese trying to leave the country, the Quai recommended Madagascar or New Caledonia as resettlement areas, not France proper, as those fleeing would be "without resources." The climate in other colonial possessions was "similar" to Vietnam, and refugees would be able to "acclimate easily."[105] Thus the French were happy to assist in the refugee movement but wanted to ensure that those refugees did not actually arrive in France.

In response to the large numbers of refugees attempting to flee the North, Diem appointed Nguyen Van Thoai as high commissioner for evacuation to oversee transportation of the refugees, and created the Refugee Commission (COMIGAL) to focus on resettlement in the South. General Gambiez served as the head of the French Military Mission for Refugee Affairs. Fears that the French and South Vietnamese did not have the transportation or the organizational capabilities to handle the refugee situation prompted Diem on August 7 to officially ask the United States for help in transporting the refugees. The United States agreed to provide resources to move an additional hundred thousand refugees. The next week, Thoai, Gambiez, and a number of other high-ranking Vietnamese, French, and American officials met to discuss the situation.

The major issues were coordinating arrival times, supplying tents and food, and ensuring proper sanitation. As a result, a Franco-American working committee for Vietnamese evacuation—the Refugee Coordinating Committee—was set up, with MAAG director General John O'Daniel directing the American component from his headquarters on 461 rue Gallieni, and Gambiez leading the French one. The French air force and U.S. Navy task force 90 would be the most important instruments in transporting the refugees. At a Refugee Coordinating Committee meeting on August 27, Gambiez promised all-out French army cooperation in assuming responsibility to set up tent villages.[106] Ely and Admiral Robert Carney, chief of naval operations, who was in charge of U.S. Navy task force 90, met in late September to discuss additional needs for transport of the refugees by sea.

Franco-American–South Vietnamese planning soon paid off, and Operation Passage to Freedom, originally dubbed "Operation Exodus" by the Diem government, began quickly. Haiphong became the main staging area as 28 ships, including 15 attack transports and 5 attack cargo ships, began embarking refugees on August 16. From there, refugees were placed on American ships for the two-day, three-night journey to Saigon. The first ship to depart, the USS *Menard*, left Haiphong on August 17 with 2,000 refugees. By the end of the month, 50,000 people, 133 vehicles, and 117 tons of military equipment had been transported south.[107] Haiphong was an obvious choice as the French and Americans had already collaborated on building a port there in 1953.

The world had never seen the like of Operation Passage to Freedom. The distance from Haiphong to Saigon stretched over a thousand miles and could be traversed only by air or sea. The quantity and rate of arrivals at Haiphong required the establishment of facilities for registration, housing, feeding, water, sanitation, and medical care. The needs were met largely through the joint efforts of French, U.S., and Vietnamese military and civilian agencies. According to General O'Daniel, meetings in Haiphong with the French and Vietnamese resulted in "complete cooperation" on the part of the French military and Vietnamese civilians. An embarkation camp was set up to take care of refugees, and STEM tents could house seven thousand people.[108] In a status report on the situation, American officials noted that in the North, the French military and civilian authorities whole-heartedly assisted in the setting up of a staging area, camp erection and supervision, land transportation, provision of small craft for transporting refugees to U.S. ships, and maintaining an exceedingly comprehensive air lift from Hanoi to Saigon for both military and civilian evacuees.[109] Ultimately, French air and sea transport moved about two thirds of the refugees, while U.S. vessels accounted for the other third.

With daily arrivals in Saigon exceeding ten thousand persons at the peak of the operation, U.S., French, and Vietnamese agencies successfully coordinated their efforts to provide shelter, food, internal transportation, potable water, and medical care.[110] French military personnel assisted in erecting tents and in providing transportation for refugees to reception centers and resettlement areas. The French noted that from the very beginning, the Diem government was completely overwhelmed by the refugee problem, and that the entire operation would have gone very badly without French and American help. Although South Vietnamese officials greeted the refugees, all medical and social services were directed by the French—France provided thousands of tent shelters, medicine, cargo trucks, wells, and engines. The French also constructed a village for ten thousand refugees in the province of Bien Hoa, spent millions of dollars on operations, and worked closely with local authorities to help establish the refugees.[111]

French and American representatives met on December 14, 1954, to discuss action on the five main points agreed upon by Ely and Collins for the improvement of the refugee situation in Vietnam. The five points included developing a national unified plan; decongesting certain reception and relocation centers; decision making on the productive use of all available land in rehabilitation of refugees, displaced persons, and discharged military personnel; reviewing initial needs for subsistence and rehabilitation; and streamlining coordination among the Vietnamese, American, and French efforts. As of January 15, 1955, more than six hundred thousand refugees, military personnel, and civilians had been evacuated from the North, comprising perhaps the greatest successful migration in human history.

Although transportation and settlement of the refugees was successful because of joint Franco-American efforts, both western powers tended to emphasize their own deeds. American newspapers underscored American aid and French newspapers heralded French, with the result that both sides were convinced the other had played a minimal role. For example, during the annual meeting of Catholic Bishops of the United States in November, the two hundred Cardinals, Archbishops, and Bishops who attended agreed to produce an official report, or "white book," detailing violations of the Geneva Accords and emphasized U.S. naval efforts in aiding the refugees. That December, Bonnet criticized the National Catholic Welfare Council's publication *Terror in Vietnam*, the white book that stemmed from the November conference, for ignoring the French role. In turn, the United States Operations Mission (USOM) censured persistent French use of the airlift for the evacuation of refugees as "costly and undesirable."[112]

The saga drew the attention of the American and French Catholic communities, witnessed by the outpouring of articles in the *New York Times, Le Figaro, Le Monde, Look, Reader's Digest,* newsreel series, the American Catholic press, and diocesan newspapers. Leading the crusade was the ubiquitous Tom Dooley, a navy doctor who provided medical services to refugee assembly camps in North Vietnam during 1954 and 1955, and whose horrific descriptions of North Vietnamese atrocities first captured the American public's attention in *Reader's Digest* and then later in his best-selling book *Deliver Us from Evil,* published in 1956. Dooley's sensationalist accounts of the munificence of American aid and dismissal of French efforts led the American public to believe that France played a bit part in the operation. In fact, the French played the major role in the evacuation, guaranteeing security in Haiphong until mid-May 1955, and even Dooley recognized that the French navy did a great deal to help the refugees.[113] Newspapers, nongovernmental groups, and religious charities on both sides of the Atlantic worked hard to draw attention and money to the refugees' plight.[114] For example, the French newspaper *Le Figaro* raised 34 million francs for relief efforts, and in early February 1955, Cardinal Spellman traveled to South Vietnam to visit with the refugees.

Who should settle the refugees, and how, was a major issue. The French created a Society of Rural Establishment, which had two governmental commissaries, one Vietnamese and one French. The FEC also provided equipment and technical advisers. However, STEM and USOM officials felt they were being excluded and wanted to "reexamine the policy involving the active and increasing participation of the French army in resettlement."[115] Internal squabbling also existed among American agencies. USOM officials worried that MAAG had taken over operational responsibility and overall supervision for all evacuation tasks in the North, as well as sea transport and reception areas, which implied the American military's assumption of the Diem government's responsibilities as well as those of other elements of the United States. USOM officials wanted MAAG's approach modified from one of control to one of cooperation and assistance and argued that MAAG's responsibilities should stop with the accommodation of refugees in reception areas and extend in no way to resettlement. USOM personnel accused MAAG officials of being "completely uninformed" with respect to the complex social, political, and economic problems involved in resettlement and satisfactory integration of refugees into a new economy, and asserted that MAAG's sole interest was one of "getting rid of the refugees in the Saigon area."[116] This disagreement among American agencies would continue as the armed services focused on resolving immediate crises and guaranteeing security while USOM focused on long-term planning.

Numerous American and international volunteer agencies were active during this period, including CARE, the International Rescue Committee (IRC), the American Women's Association, the American Red Cross, the United Nations International Children's Emergency Fund, and the National Catholic Welfare Council (NCWC). The NCWC and CARE were the largest, with the NCWC eventually spending $35 million in Vietnam.[117] The IRC, led by Leo Cherne, sent Joseph Buttinger to Vietnam to organize a relief program. Their efforts would have far-reaching consequences as Cherne and Buttinger helped found the American Friends of Vietnam (AFV) in late 1955, which would prove to be an influential lobby group for South Vietnam in the United States. On September 15, 1954, a meeting of mostly American voluntary agency representatives was held to develop coordinated plans for supplementary assistance to refugees. The agencies agreed to create a coordinating committee known as the Voluntary Agencies' Coordinating Committee for Vietnam, and this was chaired by Mrs. Frank O. Blake, head of the American Women's Association of Saigon. The committee worked closely with both COMIGAL and USOM, thus bolstering the American presence in South Vietnam.

As the crisis unfolded, propagandists in the North and South attempted to take advantage of the situation. North Vietnamese propagandists were busy printing leaflets with such statements as "The aid program of American imperialism is an invader's trick," "Why does America give aid to Vietnam? America wants to kick out the French and interfere directly in an invading war, with the hope of making our country a colony," and "The French are tricky and truthless, but American colonialism is even more truthless and wicked. The Americans plot to supply the French with arms in order to reoccupy our land and cause many deaths and painful destruction." South Vietnamese and American propagandists were just as busy as their counterparts, claiming that the "Virgin Mary had left North Vietnam" and that the Vietnamese would have to go South to receive her benediction, that in a few months there would be no priests left to hear sacraments, and that if Catholics stayed they would "lose God, religion, their soul and be excommunicated." Rumors also circulated in the North that those who stayed would become victims of an American atomic bomb.[118] In the end, the South Vietnamese regime scored the biggest propaganda victory, as those fleeing the

North far outnumbered those who left the South during the 1954–1955 period. Although many refugees would have fled anyway, more came south as
a result of American and South Vietnamese propaganda.

In spring 1955, as the three-hundred-day deadline stipulated by article 14(d) approached, the number of Vietnamese trying to flee the North
increased dramatically, as did North Vietnamese efforts to hamper them.
North Vietnamese authorities made arbitrary arrests of Catholics and refused permits for transportation, especially in the two predominantly Catholic provinces of Phat Diem and Bui Chuu. Incidents were reported all over
North Vietnam as refugees attempted to escape without authorization or
sought immunity with International Control Commission officials. Documented episodes included refugees trying to escape from Ba Lang, the Ninh-
Bing province, and Van Ly. French and American ships coordinated in one
rescue effort three miles off the coast from the village of Van Ly, where they
waited as thousands of Vietnamese quietly headed out to the western ships.
French ships also rescued thousands of refugees in danger of drowning close
to shore despite Hanoi's warning that it would fire upon any ship in North
Vietnamese waters. France argued that its actions were permissible under
the International Convention of Saving Lives, signed in London in 1948.
However, the North Vietnamese were not signatories and did not recognize
the convention. The French were particularly worried about the situation as
they prepared to evacuate Haiphong before the May deadline and seriously
debated requesting an extension.[119] In May 1955, France asked the U.S. Navy
to engage in a last-ditch effort to transport as many refugees as possible, with
the result that the two western countries helped transport thousands more
before the deadline. Meanwhile, the Saigon regime appealed to the United
Nations and to the nine powers who had signed the Geneva agreements to
extend the deadline.

The question of what to do with the refugees once they had arrived south
of the seventeenth parallel would place enormous strains on the Franco-
American–South Vietnamese partnership. Dulles had noted that absorbing
and adapting the refugees was "one of *the* major problems facing Diem."[120] In
the end, the three governments proved equal to the task. The French played
a role in the immediate crisis of settling refugees. The Americans, however,
had more ambitious plans. Officials in Washington and Saigon carefully considered long-range projects of material assistance in housing, resettlement,
professional rehabilitation, and education—all of which indicated American determination to play a major, and indefinite, role in South Vietnam.
American officials understood the consequences of increased American

intervention, noting that if Diem's plan to settle refugees in approximately two hundred thousand acres of abandoned rice land in the Rach Gia-long Xuyen region failed, then his government could become unstable and make the United States, which had backed the project financially and technically, a scapegoat.

Almost the entire amount needed for refugee resettlement in South Vietnam came from the United States. For both 1955 and 1956, resettlement made up the largest component of U.S. economic and technical assistance. The Foreign Operations Administration in Saigon, headed by Leland Barrows and Paul Everett, spent approximately $45 million in 1954–1955 and $35 million in 1955–1956. In many respects, the flood of refugees turned into an economic, political, and moral commitment on the part of the United States. Actively encouraging North Vietnamese to flee saddled the United States with at least some moral responsibility in seeing that the refugees were properly settled in the South. Moreover, this accountability now extended to ensuring that the North did not take over the South, thus limiting U.S. options. These obligations would continue to concern Eisenhower-administration officials, but they did not slow their decision to support Diem's efforts at home and abroad while at the same time trying to ensure that he listened to American advice as he tried to build a viable South Vietnamese state.[121]

The ultimate results of the Diem experiment raise questions. First, did the Eisenhower administration analyze what it would gain through its support of Diem? It appears that Washington committed to Diem because, as Dulles put it, "there were no alternatives." But did Dulles take the time to assess what this support would mean for future American policy makers in Vietnam? Both French and British officials at the highest levels were convinced that U.S. policy in Vietnam could not succeed. Without American aid and political support, it is highly unlikely that Ngo Dinh Diem could have kept himself in power. Second, were there alternatives to Diem, as the French suggested? A number of South Vietnamese officials, who would have worked with both the French and the Americans, were willing to take over if the Diem government fell. In addition, Bao Dai could have been brought in to strengthen any successor government. But would any alternative have stood a better chance than Diem in strengthening South Vietnam? We will never know, but French, British, and some American officials had all concluded that Diem should be replaced and that a number of Vietnamese leaders existed who could create a more representative South Vietnamese government. Finally, what if, during the frantic days of the sect crisis, the Eisenhower administration had moved a little faster in agreeing to replace Diem? The French and British, not to mention Diem himself, came close to convincing the United States that the Diem experiment could not succeed. In the end, Diem solved the Franco-American debate himself, with a little help from the Lansdale cohort, and France lost not only Franco-American cooperation in Indochina, but also French influence on Vietnamese political affairs.[122]

In short, throughout 1954 and 1955, Paris and Washington agreed that a noncommunist South Vietnam should be preserved. But they disagreed and continued to disagree on the means to achieve this goal. Their two different approaches resulted in continuing conflict that did not subside until the Diem experiment became a fait accompli. The French had consistently reiterated the danger of supporting one individual rather than a particular policy in South Vietnam, but the Americans chose to support Diem. Despite the prevailing view that by May 1955 France's role in Vietnam was finished, the French still had a few cards left to play.[123] Diem's consolidation of power was a significant factor in reducing the French presence in Vietnam, but, having lost the battle over Diem, the French turned to other domains in the struggle for supremacy against the Americans in the South. Paris would seek to ensure that the 1956 elections took place, and focused on preserving its economic and cultural presence in Vietnam.

5

The Non-elections
of 1956

THE SPECTER OF THE 1956 ELECTIONS posed the next challenge to French influence. Back in mid-July 1954, the weary conferees at Geneva had reached an agreement on all major issues except for the difficult problem of national elections.[1] The DRV refused to end hostilities until a specific date for all-Vietnamese reunification elections had been identified. As a result, point 14(a) of the cease-fire agreement between the French and DRV representatives (the Agreement on the Cessation of Hostilities in Vietnam) recognized a two-year interval before general elections "which will bring about the unification of Vietnam." The only other mention of the elections existed in the deliberately vague final declaration. According to point 7, "General elections shall be held in July 1956, under the supervision of an international commission composed of representatives of the Member States of the International Supervisory Commission, referred to in the agreement on the cessation of hostilities. Consultations will be held on this subject between the competent representative authorities of the two zones from 20 July 1955 onwards."[2] Thus, the Geneva Accords stipulated that elections would take place in 1956 to reunify the country but left out the details of how such an election would be achieved. Understanding why these elections failed is central to explaining the increased American presence in Vietnam.

The period immediately after the Geneva Conference, and, in particular, the problem of how to bring about, or not bring about, the 1956 elections, was a critical juncture for the Vietnamese, French, and Americans. Much current scholarship dismisses the 1956 elections as a non-event resulting from firm American backing of Prime Minister Ngo Dinh Diem's refusal to consult with the North.[3] The situation, however, was more complex. In examining the changing international landscape, the differing concerns of the Geneva participants, and Diem's 1954–1956 diplomacy, a more nuanced view of who, and what, derailed the 1956 elections emerges.

Despite the vague wording of the cease-fire agreement and final declaration at the Geneva Conference, it appears unlikely that the provisions
for national elections were simply a cosmetic means of obtaining North
Vietnamese consent to end the war. Most of the governments represented at
Geneva took the election provisions seriously and expected the elections to
be held.[4] However, the international situation evolved quickly after the conference in ways none of the participants had foreseen. The elections failed
because the primary conferees involved, with the exception of Hanoi, had
other concerns that took precedence. In addition, Diem's refusal to work
with the French and the subsequent French withdrawal from Indochina created a change in the players on the field and hence in the scenario for the
1956 elections. What follows is a perspective of the changing international
scene from each of the major players involved in the elections issue.

WASHINGTON

The prospect of the 1956 elections posed a serious challenge to U.S. policy
in South Vietnam. At the final session of the Geneva Conference, Undersecretary of State Walter Bedell Smith gave a "unilateral declaration" of U.S.
policy toward free elections in Vietnam in which he claimed to "make clear"
the American position. He failed, but for good reason—during and following the conference, American officials were scrambling to develop a coherent policy toward the 1956 elections. In the first part of Smith's declaration,
he upheld Washington's traditional stand in favor of free elections. In the
second part, Smith indicated a loophole for the South Vietnamese government by recognizing South Vietnam's right to determine its own policy.[5] The
declaration pointed to the Eisenhower administration's difficulties in recon-
ciling the traditional American ideal of free elections with the reality that if
an election took place, North Vietnamese leader Ho Chi Minh would deliver
a crushing defeat to Diem. The United States had continually advocated free
elections in Germany, Korea, Austria, and Greece and would be in an awk-
ward position vis-à-vis world opinion if it did not do the same in Vietnam.
And yet, a communist triumph in elections could also cost the United States
dearly in terms of world opinion. What to do? Secretary of State John Foster
Dulles suggested that by affirming they would participate in genuinely free
elections, Washington and Saigon would be "taking the high ground." Such
a position was "unassailable in intent," Dulles argued, and it held out little
danger since communist nations "never permitted a free and open political
process."[6]

According to Kenneth Young, director of the Office of Philippine and Southeast Asian Affairs, the dilemma facing the Americans was that American policy goals were at odds with long-held values. The United States could not press France to oppose elections without running grave risks on disclosure, which would seriously damage the French government and the U.S. position in Asia at this time. On the other hand, uncertainty regarding the elections weakened U.S. efforts to build up strength in Vietnam.[7] As early as mid-November 1954, French high commissioner for South Vietnam Paul Ely raised the issue of elections with U.S. special representative to Vietnam J. Lawton Collins. In turn, Collins requested guidance from the State Department. Not until the end of January 1955 did the NSC request that the State Department devise a position paper. The American position paper, which was not completed until early May, recommended that consultations be held providing North and South Vietnam were the only parties involved.[8]

By late January 1955, the Eisenhower administration recognized it had to establish a specific policy toward the elections.[9] In February, the Division of Research for the Far East prepared an intelligence report with the assumption that elections would take place, but, given the ambiguous nature of the Geneva Accords and subsequent statements by the parties involved, Washington had almost no guidance on how to proceed. In addition, DRV statements regarding the elections had not advanced beyond vague generalities. The most interesting aspect of the report was that none of the Geneva participants had taken a stand on the elections issue yet—everyone was waiting for someone else to make the first move.

Following Geneva, the French and Americans first discussed the elections issue formally during the November 1954 talks between Dulles and Prime Minister Pierre Mendès France. Mendès France suggested breaking the elections into small local units rather than holding national elections. The Americans countered with the idea that the North and South should elect an equal number of delegates to a single assembly and that the assembly's power should be confined to drafting a constitution subject to ratification by both governments prior to its adoption. Eisenhower officials also believed it was conceivable that the requirement for elections in Vietnam might be satisfied by a simple referendum on the question of reunification or by holding elections for a constituent assembly—in which membership from the North and South might be roughly equal.[10] Either way, Washington hoped to present the appearance of cooperating while indefinitely prolonging the partition of Vietnam.

In early March 1955, Dulles met with South Vietnamese foreign minister Tran Van Do, after being alerted by Collins that the Diem regime apparently had no firm policy on elections and wished to discuss the issue. Dulles urged Diem to accept the principle of holding elections and then to insist on procedures that would guarantee that they would be carried out fairly. Dulles pointed out that in the case of Germany, the West and East had been discussing elections for ten years without being able to come to an agreement on what constituted free elections.[11] Diem remained noncommittal, and Dulles returned to the United States convinced that South Vietnam was too inexperienced in free electoral processes to negotiate effectively with the DRV on the issue of nationwide elections.[12]

By the end of March, a draft on American policy toward the elections had been prepared. The administration recognized that if the United States urged South Vietnam to avoid elections, it would forfeit any possibility that it might eventually be able to secure British or French support for its policies in Vietnam. American officials thus argued that the only reasonable course of action was to give South Vietnam general support and encouragement to open discussions with the North on the elections issue. This policy would allow Diem to pose as a "champion" of national unification.[13]

In a follow-up memorandum, Assistant Secretary of State Walter Robertson pointed out that when the French learned of the U.S. position to encourage, but not command, Diem to begin consultations with the North, French suspicions would be confirmed that the United States was attempting to "scuttle" the elections. They might then try to bring to power someone less amenable to U.S. influence. American officials feared the prospect that Paris and London would reject Washington's stringent conditions for elections, especially if the DRV resumed hostilities. American officials also considered how to discourage the International Control Commission (ICC)—which had been set up at the Geneva Conference to ensure that South and North Vietnam upheld the Geneva provisions—from playing too prominent a role in the electoral discussions. The Eisenhower administration hoped that South and North Vietnam would be the only principal parties in the negotiations.[14] In deliberating over acceptable and unacceptable conditions for the elections, one American official noted that "this whole question of the elections in Vietnam may be the key issue on which we hold or lose Vietnam." U.S. policy was to encourage South Vietnam to proceed with consultations for the elections, while urging Diem to stress the need for free expression of the national will. Washington wanted Diem to agree to consultations because the North Vietnamese already had the political advantage of claiming that they were fighting a nationalist war of liberation.[15]

A critical obstacle to formulating U.S. policy toward the 1956 elections at this time was the uncertainty surrounding Diem's position. Throughout April 1955, as Diem battled against the Cao Dai, Hoa Hao, and Binh Xuyen, it remained unclear whether Diem would survive the crisis. Washington also recognized that it might find itself alone if it urged South Vietnam to insist on terms unacceptable to the communists while Britain and France advised the South to capitulate to communist terms rather than run the risk of a resumption of hostilities. The NSC was concerned that if South Vietnam tried to avoid elections, the communists would be able "to pose as the sole champions of national unification." The overall U.S. position in the world "would be harmed by American identification with a policy which appeared to be directed towards avoidance of elections." The NSC also acknowledged that the British and French believed themselves "committed," as signatories of the Geneva agreements, to a program of "encouraging" elections.[16] Thus Diem's triumph over the Cao Dai, Hoa Hao, and Binh Xuyen did not bolster the Eisenhower administration's confidence in opposing elections. Indeed, American officials feared that the ICC and co-presidents would intervene, and the international situation as well as American public opinion would slip if Diem continued to stall. Kenneth Young suggested that the United States might have to strongly suggest to Diem that he should not count on Washington's assistance if South Vietnam were responsible for "election breakdown and Vietminh action."[17] And yet, at the same time, the State Department worried that Diem would think the western powers were "ganging up on him" if Washington agreed to the French and British proposals to put more pressure on South Vietnam to begin consultations.

During a June NSC meeting, when the issue of the State Department's recommendations (NSC 5519) on pre-electoral consultations and the elections came up, Eisenhower and Dulles postponed discussion because the situation was "not sufficiently clear to warrant Council action at this time," and because the British, French, and South Vietnamese had not made their positions clear. The general consensus remained that the United States should try to persuade Diem to agree to consultations and to notify him that if he refused, he would face great difficulties with the French and British. Young recommended that the United States go along with Diem's refusal to consult, recognizing that the main problem would be persuading the French and British to agree to this idea. Eventually, the State Department produced a policy statement that said the United States "should leave the issue to the Vietnamese themselves."[18]

American officials in Saigon also recommended postponing NSC consideration of the 1956 elections. With Diem's position still shaky, American ambassador to Saigon G. Frederick Reinhardt thought that the United States could run into trouble if it developed a firm and rigid government policy while several elements involved were "subject to change." American policy at the time assumed there was a possibility that South Vietnam would be able to "deter or defeat" North Vietnamese insurrection, "sustain order" in the South, and become "strong enough" to win a free election confined to the South. Should this not be the case, it would be necessary to review not only U.S. policy on elections but also basic U.S. policy toward Vietnam. American officials acknowledged that Washington could not take the position of opposing the principle of unifying Vietnam through free elections, but they also believed that the Geneva agreements were ambiguous and unspecific regarding the type of elections to be held, the specific purposes of the elections, and the procedures to be followed, all of which would provide some leeway for American actions.[19]

Throughout spring 1955, internal discussion centered on how best to proceed. American officials seesawed on whether to support or discourage elections, suggesting that the UN should be asked to step in but worrying that U.S. allies would react unfavorably. By early July, most American officials began to fear a crisis was looming. With the Geneva summit scheduled to begin on July 18, Dulles urged the Saigon Embassy to convince Diem to issue a statement acknowledging Hanoi's willingness to begin consultations. This way, Dulles hoped to head off Soviet claims at the summit that the South had repudiated the Geneva Accords.[20]

The more important reason for urging Diem to agree to consultations was that American officials recognized U.S. credibility would be harmed by identification with a policy that appeared to be directed toward avoiding the elections. An NSC report stated that "world public opinion and, for that matter, domestic opinion would have difficulty in understanding why the United States should oppose in Vietnam the democratic procedures which it advocated for Korea, Austria, and Germany." The United States also acknowledged that France and Britain wanted the elections to take place and that the French, in particular, feared that failure to hold the elections would provoke a resumption of hostilities by the DRV in which France would be "directly and involuntarily involved" due to the presence of large numbers of the FEC through 1955 and the first half of 1956.[21] All of these factors made it difficult for Washington to arrive at a coherent policy toward the elections.

During the second half of 1954 and much of 1955, the Eisenhower administration was in a quandary as to how to deal with the elections issue, hoping the elections would not take place but anxious to avoid the charge of having sabotaged them. The best option, for Washington, was indefinite postponement. Diem made the choice for the United States by refusing to cooperate and ignoring the July 1955 deadline to begin consultations with the North. The Eisenhower administration considered using the threat of cutting American aid in order to force Diem to consider consultations, but in the end chose not to. Against its better political instincts, but fearful above all of the collapse of the anticommunist government in the South, the Eisenhower administration decided to support Diem.[22] Throughout these developments, one theme can be clearly seen—the United States operated on an ad hoc basis when dealing with the 1956 elections.

Scholars have argued that because of U.S. backing, Diem assumed a bold and confident posture in opposition to the national elections that were so central to the Geneva agreements.[23] In fact, senior American officials tried to coax Diem to participate in preliminary consultations—albeit primarily for propaganda purposes—but even before he was sure of U.S. backing, Diem refused to agree to such consultations. Perhaps one American official summed it up best when he wrote, "Although our ability [to] exert pressure is apparently great because of government's dependence on U.S. support, in actual fact, if we wish our efforts to be effective we can do little more than use ardent persuasion, basing our arguments exclusively on Vietnam's self-interest."[24]

PARIS

While American policy was more ambivalent toward the 1956 elections than scholars have acknowledged, French officials at the time were convinced that the United States would not go through with the elections. American officials continually pointed out to the French that "neither France nor Britain nor any other power made any specific pledge to these elections. No government signed any document, no assembly discussed it, it was ratified by no Parliament. It is therefore really binding on no one." Paris thus assumed that Washington would do nothing to help promote the 1956 elections, concluding as early as November 1954 that the United States "would stop the elections and refuse to consider alternatives to Diem." Still, in the period immediately following the Geneva Conference, French officials felt the elections should be held. The official position in Paris was that a failure to hold elections would violate the spirit, if not the letter, of Geneva. More importantly, French leaders feared that if the elections did not take place, North Vietnam would have a pretext to renew the war.[25] At the same time, French officials wanted to avoid promoting the elections too forcefully for fear of creating a diplomatic rift with the United States. For Paris, an election would essentially terminate French responsibilities, but so too would an overt U.S. or South Vietnamese assumption of blame for the consequences of what might follow if elections failed to take place.

The French Foreign Ministry also recognized that some kind of entente between North and South Vietnam could result in smoother Franco-Vietnamese relations and avoid a resumption of hostilities. Mendès France thus advocated a flexible policy in dealing with the elections. During a tripartite meeting in May 1955, French officials tried to decide who should take the initiative to bring South and North Vietnam together. The French saw two possibilities: an approach could be made to the co-presidents or to the ICC. Paris preferred the second option since the ICC was officially in charge of supervising the elections. French officials also suggested that senior American, British, and French representatives should meet in one of the western capitals to discuss views on objectives and conditions of the elections rather than relegating such discussions to local officials in Saigon. This way, Paris planned to hammer out a common policy to be presented jointly at a four-power conference with Diem. The United States quickly put the brakes on American participation, fearing that France wanted to place responsibility for upholding the Geneva Accords on the United States. Washington thus declined French suggestions for a tripartite working group on the elections. After the July 20 deadline to begin consultations passed with little notice, France became less concerned about a renewal of hostilities on the part of the Vietminh and the 1956 elections became a less pressing matter. The loss of momentum was apparent; ICC members noted that all sides were at an impasse. New Delhi notified French officials in Saigon that perhaps the ICC's presence in South Vietnam was "no longer necessary" since the elections were stalled, implying that Paris "could and should place greater pressure on Diem" to begin consultations.[26]

In fact, New Delhi had it wrong—French officials could not place greater pressure on Diem. Rather, Saigon's policies posed an immense obstacle to moving forward with the elections. The FEC continued to be the biggest issue plaguing Franco-Vietnamese relations. According to South Vietnamese officials, Franco-Vietnamese relations "would improve" and the elections is-sue "could be resolved" once military issues were settled, in particular the withdrawal of the FEC. The French, for their part, insisted that if the Diem government became the sole power in the South, it had to agree to respect the clauses of the Geneva Accords or else the French would have to notify the other members of the Geneva Conference. During a February 1956 meeting between French foreign minister Christian Pineau and South Vietnamese representative in Paris Pham Duy Khiem, Khiem urged Pineau to publish a declaration that the elections issue should be solved by the North and South themselves. Pineau accepted in principle as long as such a declaration did not violate the Geneva Accords. Still, the South Vietnamese continued to stall on the elections issue, insisting on further French concessions on mili-tary matters, and the French quickly had to decide what their policy toward elections should be.[27]

Pineau decided on gradual disengagement from the accords, evidenced in his February 8 announcement that, with respect to the political clauses of the Geneva Accords (i.e., elections), France was "no more accountable than any other country and had no further obligations than any other signatory." Paris's agreement to the South Vietnamese request that France withdraw its troops also indicated French determination to withdraw, as did the deci-sion to have the ICC work with the South Vietnamese leadership rather than French officials in Saigon. The South Vietnamese Liaison Mission to the ICC was established and all French Liaison Mission functions were transferred to the South Vietnamese. France also refused to continue its ICC payments, questioning why, if it was being relieved of its responsibilities in South Viet-nam, it should continue to pay a quarter of ICC costs and half its local costs. And, in a May 14 note to the co-presidents of the Geneva Conference, France stated that it had "relinquished all responsibility to the Geneva Agreements." Finally, on August 15, Pineau officially notified North Vietnamese foreign minister Pham Van Dong that France had no further responsibilities with respect to the Geneva Accords.[28]

French officials had a number of comments on both their speedy with-drawal and the elections issue. French representative to South Vietnam Henri Hoppenot sent Pineau a long and detailed letter on failed Franco-American cooperation in Vietnam. Regarding the elections, Hoppenot contended that "no effort whatsoever was made to begin consultations, and exchanges of view on topics of mutual interest only occurred when the French ambassa-dor instigated them."[29] Pineau concurred that the non-elections were key to Diem's survival, and that after the election date passed, South Vietnam was determined to maintain its independence, evidenced in the non-renewal of France's commercial status, the withdrawal of the FEC, and the turning of high commissariats into embassies. Regarding the Americans, Dulles and the State Department had assured France on numerous occasions of their willingness to establish Franco-American cooperation in Vietnam, but Pineau noted that "the facts showed otherwise."[30]

By the end of November 1956, French officials recognized that Vietnam no longer had need of French aid—military, financial, political, or otherwise—and that France inspired "neither hatred nor envy." One historian has claimed that France had little leverage in South Vietnam and was too dependent on American economic support and political backing of French interests elsewhere in the world, particularly North Africa, to challenge the repudiation of the elections. Others have asserted that France simply "abandoned" South Vietnam.[31] French documentation demonstrates that neither of these explanations satisfies. Rather, Diem's unwillingness to work with the French, the withdrawal of the FEC, and the dissolution of the French high command led France to reevaluate the nature and extent of its responsibilities to the Geneva Accords and hence the 1956 elections. Once it was clear that Diem would remain in control of South Vietnam, that the FEC would be withdrawn, and that the DRV would not renew hostilities after South Vietnam's refusal to begin consultations by July 20, 1955, France chose to focus on preserving its economic and cultural presence in Vietnam. After all, its attempts to maintain a political and military presence had been thwarted by Diem and the Americans. In the end, France had little choice in its gradual decline from guarantor of the Geneva Accords to minor player.

LONDON

As co-chair to the Geneva Conference, Britain considered itself responsible for ensuring that the Geneva agreements were fulfilled and for keeping the peace in Vietnam.[32] In the end, however, London failed both in persuading Diem to begin consultations and in convincing the United States to adopt a stronger stance against Diem's intransigence. British attempts to bring about the elections were stymied by Saigon and Washington's machinations. The British were also less willing, after Geneva, to challenge the Americans directly on Vietnamese issues, as they had expended significant diplomatic capital in spring 1954 by refusing to go along with united action and by insisting on a negotiated settlement.

By early February 1955, the British had become convinced that the Americans would not promote Vietnamese elections and that it was therefore up to London to take an active role in ensuring that the elections took place. Frank Tomlinson, head of the Southeast Asia Department of the British Foreign Office, in a letter to the Foreign Office noted that, "while the British proceed on the basis that elections will be held unless good reason is shown to the contrary, the Americans are certain *now* that there will be good reason to the contrary and that elections will therefore not be held." Scrawled on top of the letter was a note from senior Foreign Office official Denis Allen stating, "we have been relying, apparently quite vainly, on the fact that Dulles spoke in Paris of the importance of abiding by the provisions of Geneva." In addition, by April it was clear that Saigon refused to begin preliminary talks with Hanoi. Therefore, British officials urged the Diem government to respect the framework of the Geneva agreements. If, for example, the South insisted on elections under UN supervision, it would open itself to the charge of failure to comply with the Geneva agreement. The British recommended that the elections should aim at setting up a "joint constituent assembly" that would then draft a constitution for the entire country, a suggestion that both the Americans and French had also considered.[33]

All that the British wanted was for Diem to initiate "preliminary contact" with the DRV on the subject of the elections no later than July 20. If the South Vietnamese did not, and fighting broke out, London emphasized that it would not support South Vietnam. When informed of continued South Vietnamese intransigence, Prime Minister Anthony Eden commented that "American support of Diem has been obstinate and unhappily successful. Does it have to continue whatever the price?" But Eden recognized how difficult it would be to convince Diem to begin consultations if the Americans failed to pressure the South Vietnamese leader as well.[34]

In mid-April 1955, the British Embassy in Washington notified the State Department that provisions for consultations and elections were fundamental to both the spirit and letter of the Geneva settlement and that the British would not welcome a SEATO attack should South Vietnam's refusal to begin consultations precipitate a North Vietnamese invasion of the South. Accordingly, the British urged Diem to respond to the North Vietnamese note in which Hanoi expressed its willingness to begin consultations on schedule. London asserted that it would approach Diem unilaterally, without American support, if necessary.[35] Although Washington did agree to ask Diem to contact the North, neither British nor American officials succeeded in convincing Diem to begin consultations. The British were particularly concerned because of the fast-approaching Geneva summit. London feared that the Soviets would make an issue of the 1956 elections during the summit, which began on July 18, 1955. Surprisingly, the Soviets appeared content with British promises that they were doing their best to bring Diem to begin consultations with Hanoi. Much like the French, the British breathed a sigh of relief after the July 20 deadline had passed.

The process was repeated in mid-September when the British proposed a joint démarche to convince the South Vietnamese to respond to Hanoi's overtures. After American officials suggested that the British make the attempt alone, British ambassador in Saigon Sir Hugh Stephenson urged Diem to cooperate, and, in return, London would defend the South Vietnamese position at the forthcoming four-power foreign ministers meeting in Geneva at the end of October. When Soviet foreign minister Vyacheslav Molotov brought up the issue of the 1956 elections at a co-chair meeting in late September, British foreign minister Harold Macmillan stated that Diem still insisted he did not have the authority to speak for South Vietnam until the National Assembly elections were held, and that once they were held, Diem would be less opposed to consultations.[36]

In an attempt to exert more pressure on Diem, the Foreign Office looked to the Quai d'Orsay. British officials recognized their failure to consult Paris and French officials in Saigon because of waning French influence in Vietnam. London had come to consider the French a liability rather than an asset in dealing with South Vietnam. But after listening to French complaints about being ignored, the Foreign Office decided to work with them, despite the "great sensitiveness in Paris about any indication, however groundless, that the French government was no longer regarded as playing a leading role in matters related to Indochina."[37]

Regarding the Americans, Eden believed that Dulles moved further from his promise to respect the Geneva Accords every time he spoke. Eden wanted to address Washington on this issue in the near future. According to Eden, if the Americans were going "to advise a wrecking of the Geneva agreement—for that is what it amounts to—we should make it clear it is their sole responsibility." Eden urged the Foreign Office to remind Dulles that his recent public statements about Diem were not consistent with the American position at Geneva. London assumed that persuading Diem to do anything depended on the amount of pressure the United States was willing to place on him. Stephenson recommended trying to avoid linking British policy "with the fate of one man who might not always be strong enough to carry through what he himself wishes and undertakes to do."[38]

As the communist bloc continued to protest South Vietnamese intransigence, the British adroitly sidestepped the issue. In one case, British officials went so far as to suggest that Diem's public statement of October 7 (which simply reiterated past statements that free elections were impossible in the North) constituted a form of consultation and that it was up to Hanoi to provide a concrete response. But London understood the communists might shortly become annoyed with western stalling tactics. During a Molotov-Macmillan meeting on November 9, Molotov mentioned the fourth interim report of the ICC, which was severely critical of South Vietnam and called for action by the co-chairs. Molotov therefore recommended a formal co-chair meeting. Macmillan wanted to avoid such a meeting, which would put London in the difficult spot of explaining Diem's behavior. Molotov decided to back away from his recommendation when Macmillan threatened to bring up communist interference in Laos at the meeting. Both Macmillan and Molotov acknowledged that they had to address the August 17 letter from North Vietnamese foreign minister Pham Van Dong protesting South Vietnam's conduct; the September 12 letter from Indian prime minister Jawaharlal Nehru to Eden asking the co-presidents to intervene; the October 7 letter from South Vietnamese foreign minister Vu Van Mau, in which Mau reiterated the South Vietnamese position as stated in the July 16 and August 9 declarations; the letters of October 31 and November 7 from Chinese foreign minister Zhou Enlai, in which the Chinese called for a reconvening of the Geneva Conference; and the fourth report of the ICC. On December 21, the co-presidents (after much stalling) sent a vague letter to Geneva participants stating that the Geneva Accords were not being respected and that something needed to be done.[39] The essential point here is that the co-presidents were unwilling to take a decisive stand on the elections issue.

In late January 1956, the British received another Chinese note demanding the reconvening of Geneva. In response, British foreign minister Selwyn Lloyd made a half-hearted attempt to persuade Dulles that the way to maintain peace in Indochina was to pressure Diem to "consider" elections. He also wanted Diem to "adopt a more conciliatory attitude" toward the ICC. The Foreign Office opposed holding another conference, which would take up time and money, and which the Americans would probably boycott. The British decided their best option was to stall as long as possible by pretending to consider the Chinese proposal. Given the South Vietnamese and American repugnance for such a conference, this tactic might cause them to make more concessions to British views. In addition, the Foreign Office did not feel that the French had much to contribute toward a constructive policy because of their wounded pride at being forced to withdraw the FEC. British policy was thus to keep everyone in suspense, even though London had decided that another conference would not be advisable.[40] In some respects, British officials appeared to spend more time confusing their allies than their adversaries.

Rather than a reconvening of the Geneva Conference, London succeeded in convincing Moscow that a co-president meeting would be more useful. The results of a co-chair meeting in April 1956 between British representative Lord Reading and Soviet foreign minister Andrei Gromyko were again vague. The co-chairs urged both North and South Vietnam to "transmit to the Co-Chairmen as soon as possible, jointly or separately, their views on the time required for the opening of electoral consultations and the holding of elections." They also stressed the importance of maintaining the cease-fire. In addition, the Soviets agreed that the two co-chairs would request that the ICC stay on to continue its normal activities.[41] The result of this meeting was that the 1956 elections were delayed indefinitely and the ICC agreed to the Saigon government's offer to ensure the safety of ICC members after the French left.

Following the meeting, British officials closely observed American actions toward the elections, ultimately concluding that American support of Diem would cause Diem to become even more opposed to consultations with Hanoi. In particular, British minister to Saigon Sir Hubert Graves noted that Walter Robertson's recent speech at an American Friends of Vietnam (AFV) meeting had stiffened Diem's resistance to elections. The British interpreted Robertson's appearance as State Department support against the elections, which made Stephenson's efforts of persuading Diem toward a conciliatory attitude more difficult. The AFV meeting did not represent a clear American policy on the elections, but it did further Franco-American discord for a number of reasons: the French ambassador received an invitation only at the last minute; Senator John F. Kennedy referred to the South Vietnamese as having suffered through "centuries of colonial exploitation" and "deliberate policies of illiteracy"; and renowned American foreign policy professor Hans Morgenthau declared that the French war "was essentially a colonial war waged for retention of French control under whatever constitutional guise."[42] Such rhetoric convinced the British that the Americans and South

Vietnamese would continue to avoid any actions that would bring North and South Vietnam closer to an election.

The main British concern during the period of negotiations over the 1956 elections was to ensure that the South Vietnamese government respected the conditions of the cease-fire so that the British could claim the Geneva agreements were being upheld. London needed South Vietnamese cooperation to maintain "the fiction" that negotiations within the framework of the Geneva agreements continued. That way, the British could avoid being forced into a position where they would have to admit that the South Vietnamese were in breach of the agreements. The best tactic to obtain this result, according to the Foreign Office, was to work with the Americans to urge Diem to enter into consultations that "would lead to deadlock and the status quo." It was felt that the ultimate objective was to "arrive at a stalemate resulting in acquiescence in indefinite partition, but that this hope should not be made public and that in any event communist reactions may prevent the realization of British policy."[43] In other words, London should continue to procrastinate.

Foreign Office official F. S. Tomlinson agreed, noting that, "we have been procrastinating for over a year now and much of the heat and venom has disappeared from communist propaganda . . . there accordingly seems a chance that, if we go on dilly-dallying without ever confronting the communist powers with what they could plausibly represent to be a repudiation of the Geneva agreement, they may be content to let matters slide indefinitely." The British thus planned to maintain the cease-fire in a divided Vietnam while allowing the idea of nationwide elections to slip gradually into oblivion. The Foreign Office hoped that the temporary partition of Vietnam would become as much a fait accompli as those of Korea and Germany, and was convinced that the British policy of seeking to postpone a crisis had already done much to remove the danger of one.[44]

The critical tactic in London's greater strategy of procrastination was jump-starting consultations between North and South. The British thus remained engaged in South Vietnam, trying to smooth over matters with the ICC and making sure that the Geneva agreements were not destroyed. Still, Diem's intransigence, doubts about American support of British attempts to convince Diem to begin consultations, and lack of Soviet insistence on elections all led Britain to press the issue of the 1956 elections less forcefully than it could have. When few comments or protests arose from the co-presidents' decision in April 1956 to postpone the elections indefinitely, the British breathed a sigh of relief, and continued to work quietly toward preventing an outbreak of hostilities between North and South Vietnam.

MOSCOW AND BEIJING

A key factor in the western decision to avoid pressing Diem on election issues was Moscow and Beijing's amazing lack of concern about the subject.
Although the Soviet Union and China should not be treated as a single entity, in the case of the proposed 1956 Vietnamese elections, both countries had
similar aims. Neither wanted to risk war with the United States over Vietnam
and both were in the middle of pursuing a new peace offensive of international communism. The Soviet Union was not eager to risk a confrontation
with Washington or broader western counteraction in South Vietnam in the
event of an attack from the North. In addition, Moscow was well aware that
by indefinitely postponing elections, it had the advantage of avoiding a precedent that, if followed in Germany and Korea, would be to the detriment
of the communist bloc. The Chinese made periodic attempts to hold South
Vietnam to the 1956 elections, in particular by claiming that France was
responsible for upholding Geneva, but these attempts were never followed
by concrete action toward elections. China also feared war with the United
States as it was still recovering from Korea. The West correctly assumed that
neither the Soviet Union nor China wanted to engage in any actions in Vietnam that might risk a world conflict.[45]

The first Soviet statement regarding the 1956 elections appeared in mid-
August 1954. The Soviet position was that the elections would be entrusted to
an all-Vietnamese consultative body composed of representatives from the
DRV and Diem camps. The consultations, to begin in July 1955, appeared to
be the device by which the communists hoped to create a coalition government even prior to the holding of elections.[46] Despite public declarations
promoting the elections, the Soviets made a number of conciliatory gestures
regarding Vietnam. One of the most interesting occurred during the summit
conference at Geneva during July 1955. The western powers had been urging
Diem to make a statement on the 1956 elections in order to avoid Soviet accusations that the West was not upholding the Geneva Accords. During the
conference, Molotov raised the issue of the 1956 elections but did not press
it. Perhaps, as Dulles noted, the Soviets were more focused on promoting
their peace offensive and wanted to avoid dealing with Vietnam at the conference. Soviet hopes of raising their reputation in the international arena,
their concern with getting the Americans to talk to them as equals, and their
focus on resolving European security problems must have influenced their
thinking. They also could not have missed the implications for Germany if
free elections were in fact held in Vietnam.[47]

Then, at a foreign ministers meeting in early fall, Harold Macmillan notified Molotov that Diem would not cooperate until a South Vietnamese National Assembly was elected. Molotov replied that "the prior establishment of an Assembly [was] a legitimate pre-consultation step."[48] In addition, the Soviets agreed to a co-president meeting instead of a reconvening of the Geneva Conference in April 1956. The Americans had been fearful that the Soviets would insist on resolving the elections issue. Why the Soviets did not is still something of a mystery. Almost certainly the internal power struggle between Soviet leader Nikita Khrushchev and Molotov played a role, as Khrushchev had advocated a buildup of Soviet strength rather than an exploitation of divisions in the West as the best means to secure Soviet foreign interests. In addition, as Eden remarked, food struggles and peasant uprisings against collectivism led to "relatively modest pressure" from communist sources for the 1956 elections.[49] The outcome of Soviet reasoning was Moscow's decision to avoid pressuring the West on the 1956 elections issue and instead content itself with publishing periodic communiqués, such as the joint Khrushchev-Nehru declaration of December 13, 1955, calling for all parties to cooperate.

The Chinese put forth more, but not much more, effort than the Soviets to see that consultations for the 1956 elections took place. China periodically appealed to the ICC and co-chairmen to force Diem to comply with the Geneva Accords. For example, in August 1955, Zhou Enlai addressed Macmillan and Molotov, giving his "total support" to the DRV's position and demanding that the co-presidents take all actions "necessary" to uphold Geneva.[50] Eventually, in January 1956, the Chinese proposed to the British that a new conference on Indochina be convened at Geneva because of South Vietnamese noncompliance. To derail this idea, London suggested a co-chair meeting, which the Soviets agreed to, effectively ending the debate.

During a bilateral Anglo-American meeting at the end of January 1956, British and U.S. officials indicated their belief that the communists had become resigned to the postponement of elections. The North Vietnamese now wanted at least two to three years to undermine the South. Although the communist bloc desired another Geneva Conference, it was not necessarily to promote the 1956 elections. The Americans and British believed that the communists hoped to bring Zhou Enlai into contact with the West and to allow Molotov and Zhou Enlai to promote proposals for regional pacts and neutralization. Reconvening the Geneva Conference would give the two communist powers contact with the neutrals and a "propaganda forum," which would probably be their primary purpose in any conference. Moreover, western officials believed that the Chinese requests for reconvening Geneva meant that the communists favored political and diplomatic means rather than large-scale violence.[51] It appeared that the Soviets and Chinese had more important issues to consider than the 1956 elections.

A key international event that confirmed western beliefs that the communists would not insist on the 1956 elections was the April–May 1956 meetings between representatives of Britain and the Soviet Union in their capacity as ongoing co-chairmen of the conference. Gromyko and Macmillan agreed that maintaining the cease-fire was paramount and that the deadline for holding elections could be extended past July 1956. Although at first Gromyko insisted on a new conference and the legal obligation of the French to the Geneva Accords, he eventually dropped both issues. Following the talks, the Soviet Union and China did little to press for a political settlement. So the deadline, July 1956, passed without any action to fulfill the most important clause in the Geneva agreement, and it looked as though Vietnam would become another truncated nation, like Germany and Korea. According to American officials, the leisurely pace the communists followed regarding the consultations issue indicated that they would not place unbearable pressure on reunification.[52] Indeed, the Soviet Union appeared to accept South Vietnam as an independent nation. When South Vietnam requested to join the UN in 1957, the Soviet Union even went so far as to suggest that both South and North Vietnam be allowed in—without consulting Hanoi—which might have resulted in a de facto permanent division between North and South Vietnam.

The British contended that the Soviets did not want to engage in any risky policies toward Indochina because more time for consolidation in North Vietnam was required. London also theorized that the Soviets accepted that communist unification of Vietnam in the near future was unlikely and were content to settle for the propaganda advantage of claiming they supported free elections. The Foreign Office concluded from Soviet actions that the Russians did not have a direct interest in Indochina and that they therefore did not want to gamble on dubious policies that might lead to a crisis with the West.[53] With respect to the Chinese, London noted that Beijing was still recovering from the unfinished revolution at home and the effects of the Korean War, and would therefore seek to avoid another direct confrontation with the United States.

Communist reasoning for not insisting on the 1956 elections remains unclear. Bernard Fall has noted that perhaps the ambiguity of the final declaration of the Geneva Conference explains why the communist powers, after South Vietnam's refusal to hold the nationwide elections referred to in the declaration, did not raise more than a perfunctory outcry about "treaty violations" and did not attempt to submit the agreement or the final declaration to the International Court of Justice for an advisory opinion.[54] Still, additional factors must have played a role. Perhaps China and the USSR did not press the elections because they wanted to promote their adherence to the principles of "peaceful coexistence" to the West as well as to neutralist countries. Or perhaps China and the USSR were more concerned with stabilizing North Vietnam economically rather than achieving immediate national reunification. It appears that both the Soviet Union and China tried to promote international communism through peaceful means and that neither was willing to risk a war with the West over the 1956 elections. As Ilya Gaiduk has noted, the Soviets undoubtedly wanted to prevent Vietnam from becoming a major issue among the great powers.[55] Moreover, the nascent Sino-Soviet split became apparent in 1956, thus hampering a coordinated communist policy toward elections and leaving Hanoi precariously balanced between its two allies.

HANOI

The North Vietnamese public position on the 1956 elections was less of a mystery than the Soviet and Chinese positions—Hanoi wanted the elections to occur. Ho Chi Minh certainly realized that the elections would greatly benefit the North and thus made every political effort to see that the elections took place. The North Vietnamese repeatedly attempted to ensure that the Geneva co-chairmen, as well as the ICC, China, and France, pressured the United States and Saigon to cooperate. Still, Hanoi realized early on that Diem and the United States would attempt to sabotage the elections and that internal problems would also prevent the North from making as strong a case as possible. French diplomat Jean Sainteny was one of the first observers to recognize the importance of the elections to the North Vietnamese, noting that "it is indeed undeniable that any policy tending to confirm the partition of Vietnam by opposing free elections carries within it the seeds of a new conflict."[56]

In adopting a diplomatic strategy, the North Vietnamese focused on France. The DRV welcomed Sainteny as delegate general of France in North Vietnam and stated its willingness to preserve cultural contacts with France. These moves were undoubtedly made with an eye toward the elections, since the North assumed France would maintain control in the South. The North

Vietnamese gambled that the French would continue to support unification in order to maintain their presence in Vietnam. Hanoi could not possibly have anticipated how quickly France would lose control in South Vietnam to Diem and the Americans.

The Soviet Union and China's lack of support for North Vietnam's position was a huge disappointment to North Vietnamese officials. Much has been made of this point. Ho Chi Minh realized he could not have defeated the French without Soviet and Chinese assistance and thus could not afford to resist their pressure to downplay the elections issue after Geneva. However, he and many others in the North Vietnamese leadership remained convinced that political struggle was the only option in achieving unification and were thus determined that, in two years, all of Vietnam would belong to them.[57] Despite the current focus on Soviet and Chinese influence on Hanoi, perhaps the most significant mistake Hanoi made was its miscalculation in assuming that France would maintain control of South Vietnam until at least July 1956. North Vietnamese officials, along with most of the rest of the international community, counted on Diem's inability to maintain control as well as continued French command of decision making in South Vietnam. Thus, French influence, or lack thereof, rather than Soviet and Chinese influence, was the determining factor in why Hanoi was not able to force the elections issue.

The DRV seized the initiative regarding the 1956 elections in a June 6, 1955, declaration in which they stated that they were ready to consult. A month later, Foreign Minister Pham Van Dong addressed a letter to Bao Dai and Diem, again expressing Hanoi's willingness to begin consultations and asking Diem to name his representatives. Shortly thereafter, Ho Chi Minh visited Beijing and Moscow to rally their political support (and material aid). When it became clear that the South Vietnamese would not begin consultations and the July 20 deadline passed without action, Pham Van Dong protested to the co-chairs: on August 17, he asked them to enforce the application of the accords. Hanoi continued to protest periodically well beyond July 1956, yet its protests were universally ignored or sidestepped by the other Geneva signatories. How much of North Vietnamese protest was real and how much was used for propaganda purposes remains in debate.[58] But American officials were concerned that their earlier assumptions that North Vietnam would never agree to free elections might have to be reconsidered. The DRV was undoubtedly holding off beginning a prolonged subversive movement in the South until the international situation evolved to a point where such a move would have more legitimacy—which would be the case if the 1956 elections did not take place without a new international agreement being negotiated.[59]

In early February 1956, French officials recognized that Hanoi's new willingness to speak with the French, after attempting for a certain amount of time to work with the South Vietnamese, indicated that the North no longer had any hope of beginning consultative conferences with Saigon and had instead decided to bypass the Diem government entirely. To this end, the DRV demanded a new conference be held with the same signatories and the three members of the ICC. Moscow and Beijing concurred. Ho Chi Minh, Vo Nguyen Giap, and Pham Van Dong also reiterated that the South Vietnamese, as the successors of the French, had the same obligations to the Geneva Accords. Hanoi's unrelenting propaganda on this subject was understandable, according to the French, since the North Vietnamese feared that Saigon would succeed in reinforcing its anti-Geneva stance on the international level. This, French officials claimed, was undoubtedly the real reason behind Beijing and Hanoi's diplomatic offensive to commence consultations.[60]

According to French reports, the DRV grossly underestimated the Diem regime, believing it would "fall like a ripe fruit either during the general elections or from internal subversion." Hoppenot suggested that since the elections would not take place and internal subversion had not proved successful, the North Vietnamese had become paralyzed by their policy of waiting. They now realized that their chances of reunifying the country were quickly diminishing. Thus their propaganda became more violently directed against the Americans and Diem, who were "sabotaging the Geneva Accords," and against the French, who had "shirked their obligations." Understandably, the DRV now sought to address the elections question on an international level and applauded the Chinese and Indian propositions for reconvening a new Geneva Conference.[61] Paris concluded that the situation would remain unchanged unless the North attacked the South or the South revised its stance regarding the elections.

Clearly, of all the signatories of the Geneva Accords, the DRV was the most insistent that the 1956 elections take place, but their protests against South Vietnamese violations of the accords yielded few results. The United States accurately estimated that, at least until July 1956, the DRV government would concentrate primarily on a political struggle for reunification, witnessed in Ho and Giap's emphasis on "peaceful reunification." But, as the French recognized, the question to be addressed was what the Vietminh would do next.[62] On May 11, 1956, Pham Van Dong had addressed one last conciliatory letter to Diem calling for general elections, the result of which would be a coalition government and restoration of normal relations. After July 1956, Pham Van Dong continued to press for consultations, but preparations were underway in the North to confront South Vietnam and the United States with a different type of challenge. And this time, Hanoi would not allow Soviet and Chinese influence to derail North Vietnamese plans for the South.

SAIGON

The final point to develop is the South Vietnamese perspective, and in particular, Diem's role in preventing the 1956 elections. Following Diem's appointment as prime minister, the French, British, and Americans all thought of him as a very honest, rigid, and moral person but one who was not very adept politically. The West consistently underrated him, but Diem turned out to be savvier than anyone could have anticipated. Diem's success in subverting the 1956 elections, and thus ensuring his continued regime, warrants a closer look.

By mid-May 1955, Diem had succeeded in eliminating most of his internal opposition—in particular the Cao Dai, Hoa Hao, and Binh Xuyen sects. He was now ready to tackle the 1956 elections issue. South Vietnamese officials reiterated to American Embassy officials in Saigon that they could not go along with the Geneva Accords since they had not signed them.[63] Diem was on somewhat solid legal ground here because of the June 4, 1954, treaties signed by French and South Vietnamese officials recognizing the State of Vietnam as a fully independent and sovereign state. When the elections issue became more urgent, Diem and Vu Van Mau were able to deflect pressure to consult by reminding the Geneva conferees that South Vietnam was not obligated by the accords since it had been excluded from negotiations and thus never signed the final agreements.

Indeed, the South Vietnamese position was crystal clear. South Vietnamese foreign minister Tran Van Do protested the armistice and announced that South Vietnam would reserve "its full freedom of action in order to safeguard the sacred right of the Vietnamese people to its territorial unity, national independence, and freedom." Then, as early as June 1955, Diem began to claim that the status of the FEC must be resolved before the elections could be discussed.[64] Diem also insisted that the National Assembly elections take place before he would take part in consultations.

At this point, NSC policy still operated under the assumption that consultations would occur, and Washington realized that it had to decide whether it should "compel" Diem to begin consultations. Washington also had to worry about France and Britain allowing conditions for free elections to be watered down, and that if the United States continued to support Diem, and the DRV attacked, the Eisenhower administration would have to proceed without its allies. One American official stated that if the United States was willing to intervene militarily in the case of a Vietminh attack, then it "could back Diem." If the United States was not willing to intervene, it "should not back him."[65]

In the interim, the three western powers, primarily the United States and Britain, tried separately to convince Diem to make some sort of response to the North Vietnamese letter that stated Hanoi was prepared to begin consultations on time. What eventually resulted was Diem's July 16 radio broadcast in which he declared South Vietnam was not bound by Geneva since it had not signed the accords and would not hold elections until the North renounced its "totalitarian methods of terror" and placed national interests above those of international communism. Diem claimed that he did not oppose elections but insisted such elections are "effective only with freedom," making no mention of consultations. The American Embassy in Saigon concluded that communist provocations and disturbances in South Vietnam were now "imminent possibilities" as a result of Diem's speech, which had "barely left the door open" for negotiations with the North. The embassy also noted that Diem's actions could isolate Saigon and Washington from their allies just as the threat from the North was rising.[66]

In the face of Diem's intransigence, the British, French, and Americans agreed that South and North Vietnam should have some sort of contact and decided, in a rare concerted allied effort, to impress upon Diem the necessity of providing a better response to North Vietnamese demands for consultations. These efforts proved unsuccessful. Diem managed to further western exasperation when the South Vietnamese foreign minister released a partial text of the joint French, British, and American aide memoir. After some creative editing, the released portion indicated that, although the three western powers had put pressure on Saigon to hasten the elections, they were actually in complete agreement with Diem's position on them.[67] Then, even before Diem had received Pham Van Dong's September 20 message calling once again for talks, Diem categorically declared that there would be no consultations or negotiations, undoubtedly to forestall further interference on the part of the western powers. Both Ambassador Stephenson of Britain and Ambassador Reinhardt of the United States tried to moderate Diem's response to the North, and throughout the rest of 1955 and into early 1956, the West continued to urge Diem to begin consultations and to make contact with Hanoi, to little avail.[68]

Diem had already offended American sensibilities regarding democratic procedures when he staged a referendum in October 1955 on the question: "Do the people wish to depose Bao Dai and recognize Ngo Dinh Diem as the Chief of State of Vietnam with the mission to install a democratic regime?" Diem garnered an impressive and impossible 98 percent of the vote as a result of propaganda, intimidation tactics, and tampering with votes. Diem's autocratic style was repeated in the March 4, 1956, South Vietnamese elections for a National Assembly, whose task was to produce a constitution for South Vietnam. During the elections, one of the seats created for the so-called refugee constituencies went to Diem's sister-in-law, Madame Nhu, who ran as an "independent" to ensure government control of the assembly. The results of the elections gave pro-government forces a solid majority. Hoppenot noted that the various American organizations in place in South Vietnam wanted Diem to provide at least a semblance of democratic elections, but Diem refused to allow any opposition party to develop; he disqualified all candidates with any organized support outside the government—ranging from the conservative Dai Viet to the radical Vietminh. Kenneth Young had advocated delaying the elections out of fear that they might result in a splintered assembly, but he need not have worried. Diem ensured that he would remain in complete control. Other Americans, both official and unofficial, were less comfortable with Diem's actions. As David Anderson has noted, Washington finally had the "trappings if not the substance of substantive government."[69] Diem's flagrant disregard for democratic principles did not bode well for the American officials encouraging him to begin consultations for the 1956 elections. In fact, South Vietnamese ambassador to the United States Tran Van Chuong notified the Eisenhower administration at the end of 1955 that his government would not participate in elections.

In a typical encounter, Dulles met with Diem in mid-March 1956 to suggest that the time would come when it would be useful for Diem to take a positive stance on the principle of free elections. This would entail no danger to Vietnam, since free elections could never take place in communist-dominated territory, but such a declaration would be helpful to Vietnam and its friends. Diem appeared receptive, but a few days later, in a meeting with Young, he countered that such a statement in support of free elections "might confuse and upset the people in Vietnam and perhaps lead them to believe the Vietminh were playing [the] predominant role here." As the French wryly noted, South Vietnam's refusal to consult with the North obliged its partners—France, the United States, and Britain—to resort to all kinds of machinations to avoid being condemned for undermining the Geneva Accords.[70]

For Diem, proof that his policy of firmness and independence had succeeded could be seen in the co-presidents meeting during April 1956. According to Saigon, the results of this meeting meant that the country would not be reunified through elections and that no consultations or contacts would occur between South and North Vietnam.[71] By making consultations with Hanoi contingent on National Assembly elections, French withdrawal of the FEC, and the dissolution of the French high command, Diem, much more so than the United States, succeeded in sabotaging the 1956 elections.

Even before the July 1956 deadline, Diem had begun to look to the future, and he sought to consolidate his rule by promulgating the South Vietnamese constitution, reorganizing the government, and working on economic reform. Hoppenot claimed that "the seriousness with which Diem envisages these tasks will not allow, no matter how warmly he smiles through his refusals to his French and American partners, any economic, military, and above all political concessions."[72] Diem was determined to follow an independent policy.

THE 1956 NON-ELECTIONS

As a result of the April 1956 meetings between the co-chairs, the status quo in Vietnam moved beyond the July 1956 date given in the Final Declaration at Geneva for reunification through elections. In May 1956, South Vietnam agreed to take over French responsibilities for maintaining the cease-fire, the ICC agreed to continue its supervisory functions, and the French agreed to exercise their good offices in Saigon for the preservation of the armistice arrangements. Thus, the issue of the 1956 elections was indefinitely postponed. Thereafter, Hanoi continued to bring up the issue periodically, but for all intents and purposes, the 1956 elections became the 1956 non-elections and were quickly forgotten. The West viewed this fact as a communist failure, while the communists decided to retrench and increase their internal subversion in South Vietnam.

So what, if any, conclusions can be reached about the 1956 non-elections? Perhaps, the first is that the approach taken by the signatories of the Geneva Accords was one of confusion. The western approach to the elections was one of disorganization and mistrust, in which events tended to overtake policy. French officials placed a high priority on moving forward with the 1956 elections but were convinced that Washington would not allow the elections to proceed. American officials were more concerned with building up the Diem government, hoping to prolong consultations for the 1956 elections to buy time to either stop the elections completely or to ensure that the South Vietnamese candidate won.[73]

When Diem insisted that the United States take over training of the Vietnamese army on January 1, 1955, and the French withdrew the last of the FEC from South Vietnam on April 28, 1956, Paris became more politically disengaged from the Geneva Accords and hence the 1956 elections. The French were more concerned about the preservation of their air and navy missions left in Indochina, the dissolution of the French high command, their loss of cultural influence, and their accountability to the Geneva Accords when they no longer had any political or military control in South Vietnam. Ultimately, then, the failure of the 1956 elections was not a foregone conclusion, nor was it a result of a coherent American policy of abetting Diem in his refusal to begin consultations. Rather, the elections failed because the major players involved focused on other concerns and because France had lost military and political control in South Vietnam by 1956. If Saigon and Washington had not succeeded in reducing the French military presence, the French would probably have insisted on holding elections. Thus, although it is undoubtedly true that the Geneva agreements regarding elections were vague, that the final declaration was not signed by the United States and South Vietnam, and that no concrete system had been put in place for implementing the elections, the most important factor leading to their failure was the French military withdrawal.

As for Diem, no one in July 1954 predicted the staying power he would demonstrate. Diem played a much larger role in undermining the 1956 elections than he has been given credit for. Diem continued to pursue an independent policy after he ensured that the 1956 elections would not take place by distancing himself from U.S. policy and trying to create a better working relationship with other Asian nations. In a rather shrewd diplomatic move, Diem attempted to style himself as both a noncommunist and a nationalist Asian leader. In this way, Diem calculated that he could avoid being too closely associated with the United States, thus escaping Bao Dai's fate of being considered a puppet.[74]

With respect to the supposed puppeteer, most scholars have assumed that the United States was responsible for ensuring that the 1956 elections did not occur, and, to a large degree, the United States must be held accountable. Certainly the United States had a hard time accepting the diplomatic solution reached at Geneva and exerted its influence in preventing the 1956 elections. But for the two-year period following Geneva, the United States proceeded on the assumption that consultations for the 1956 elections would have to take place, if only for propaganda purposes. It was only after Diem's continued intransigence that American policy evolved toward opposing the elections. Furthermore, the United States continued to equivocate on the elections issue until it became convinced that France and Britain would offer only token resistance to Diem's refusal to consult with the Vietminh. This acquiescence was due in large part to French disengagement from Vietnam. Moreover, the Americans, French, and British correctly concluded that the Soviet Union and China were not willing to risk a war with the United States in order to ensure the elections took place. Thus, American policy was not the only factor involved. When examining the failed 1956 elections from an international perspective, the fluid nature of the world situation and Diem's agency emerge as the more important reasons for this failure.

The non-elections of 1956 were critical to future American intervention in Vietnam. With the French out of Vietnam, the British acquiescing to Diem's refusal to negotiate with the DRV, and Soviet and Chinese acceptance of the indefinite postponement of the 1956 elections, the United States had an open field to continue and increase its already significant nation-building system in South Vietnam. Washington still had to contend with Diem's continued resistance to American policies, but the biggest challenge to preserving a noncommunist South Vietnam had already begun. Modifying Walter Bedell Smith's claim that "diplomacy has never been able to gain at the conference table what cannot be held on the battlefield," Hanoi had decided that what could not be gained diplomatically (reunification of Vietnam) would now be tried on the battlefield.[75] Preparations had commenced to increase North Vietnamese activity in the South. Thus, the failure to carry out the 1956 elections limited the possibilities for peace between South and North Vietnam, intensified problems in the Western alliance, and helped ensure that the United States would continue to operate in Vietnam without much international support. In the end, the non-elections ensured the continued reduction of the French presence and paved the way for an increased American presence in Vietnam.

6

From the French to the Americans

WRITING SHORTLY AFTER THE Geneva Conference, French official Jean Chauvel optimistically averred that France would be able to "rein in American impulses" in trying to replace France in Vietnam since the Geneva Accords "did not allow new personnel or materials." Chauvel proclaimed, "we are in Vietnam and the Americans aren't. American financial and material assistance passes through France. Any change in this reality would certainly be considered an infraction to the accords. All American initiatives must pass French inspection and approval no matter if the Vietnamese government appeals directly to the Americans."[1] How quickly it all changed. Perhaps the single greatest factor leading to the American commitment in South Vietnam was the Eisenhower and Diem administrations' determination to end the French presence there in the two years following Geneva. Politically, the French had already faced major setbacks as Diem became ensconced as prime minister and refused to begin consultations for the 1956 elections. These political setbacks led France to question its remaining military, economic, and cultural presence in Vietnam. In addition, fearing that continued French resistance to South Vietnamese and American pressure to leave would create a rupture in the Atlantic alliance, French officials decided they had no choice but to relinquish control in South Vietnam to the Americans.

This loss of control was a long, drawn-out process. It had looked possible, even likely, that the French would not have to withdraw at all as American and French officials tried to cooperate in late 1954. Searching for a united Franco-American policy in South Vietnam—as they had done so many times in the past—Paris and Washington sent instructions to French general Paul Ely and U.S. special representative to Vietnam J. Lawton Collins underlining that competition between the two countries should be avoided and that the United States did not seek to replace France. In this new period of collaboration, mixed committees were created to solve problems in the areas of public order, information and propaganda, refugees, agricultural reform, establishment of a national assembly, economic and financial measures, education and formation of administrative personnel, and military training. This period represented the high point of Franco-American cooperation in South Vietnam and coincided with the French plan to keep the FEC in place and maintain military and political control. France also had major economic plans such as agrarian reform and agricultural and technical aid.[2]

But the increasing American presence in South Vietnam would lead to Franco-American conflict rather than cooperation. As Washington strove to secure Diem's government and delay the 1956 elections in the political arena, it also engaged in a planned operation to replace the French militarily, economically, bureaucratically, and culturally. Militarily, the U.S. ended the Franco-American Training Relations Instruction Mission (TRIM), helped diminish the French military training school for Vietnamese officers (Ecole Militaire Supérieur Vietnamienne, or EMS), set up the Temporary Equipment Recovery Mission (TERM), and took over the training of the South Vietnamese army. At the same time, South Vietnamese and American pressure led Paris to withdraw the French high command and FEC. Economically, the United States replaced France as the leading exporter to South Vietnam and sent increasing amounts of economic aid through the Commercial Import Program (CIP), the Food for Peace program or PL 480, and the International Cooperation Administration. American officials advised Diem, helped train his administration, and began building up both an official and an unofficial bureaucratic and cultural presence in South Vietnam through organizations such as the United States Operations Mission (USOM), the United States Information Agency's Vietnam center (USIS Saigon), the Michigan State University Group (MSUG), the American Friends of Vietnam (AFV), and the American-Vietnamese Association (AVA). The United States also sought to replace the French language with English and French customs with American ones.

MILITARY MATTERS

France itself had left the door open to French military withdrawal at the Geneva Conference. Paragraph 10 of the Final Declaration took note of the French statement that expressed French readiness to withdraw forces from Vietnam at the request of the government concerned. But of course, France had anticipated that it would be in control of any South Vietnamese government and would be able to choose its own departure time. Indeed, under article 14(a) of the armistice agreement, civil administration in the South was to remain under the control of French Union forces, and article 27 stated that the North Vietnamese and French commanders "shall take all steps and make all arrangements necessary to ensure full compliance with all the provisions of the present Agreement by all elements and military personnel under their command," thus implying continued French military control in the South.[3] Diem and many American officials had other ideas, viewing the French military presence as an obstacle to building a viable South Vietnamese nation.

As the Eisenhower administration began to displace the French militarily in the years following Geneva, the first target was the FEC. Kenneth Young, director of the Office of Philippine and Southeast Asian Affairs, had advocated the gradual and steady reduction of the FEC down to a division or corps level to be stationed near the seventeenth parallel or pulled out completely, with air and naval units possibly remaining on, as he did not see the "value of the FEC as a deterrent to a North Vietnamese invasion."[4] Immediately after Geneva, however, the United States appeared to support the FEC's continuation. In August 1954, Undersecretary of State Walter Bedell Smith promised French ambassador Henri Bonnet all the aid France would need for the FEC, as both men recognized the importance of establishing a strong South Vietnamese army before the FEC was withdrawn. At the end of the month, MAAG leaders were also trying to coordinate with the FEC, indicating that, at least early on, the United States had no intention of pressing the French to withdraw the FEC.[5] But the evolution of the political situation in South Vietnam—Diem's consolidation of power in particular—created a different outcome. The FEC consisted of 271,000 men at the end of the Geneva Conference, but that number would drop dramatically in the next eighteen months. By June 1955, the FEC had been reduced to 75,000; by October, 60,000; by November, 30,000; by January 1956, 15,000; and by April, 9,700.

After Geneva, the French sought to preserve the FEC, as evidenced by the talks between Secretary of State John Foster Dulles and Prime Minister Pierre Mendès France in November 1954, when the two men met to resolve a number of lingering Franco-American differences about western policy toward South Vietnam. Mendès France had urged Dulles to recognize that France and the United States needed to work together "in the long term as well as the short term." At the heart of the problem was "whether the French presence would be maintained or there would be a progressive transfer of responsibilities to the U.S." Mendès France stated that he was ready to acknowledge American leadership in Asia but thought it would be "dangerous" to diminish the French military presence in Indochina. Dulles replied that he understood the need for close collaboration and that the two governments at all levels needed to consult and avoid a "battle for influence" in a vain attempt at prestige. He added that competition between the two western countries and their representatives interfered with progress in Vietnam, and reiterated numerous times that "it is not the intention of the United States to replace France."

In trying to implement Franco-American agreements reached at the end of September, Mendès France and Dulles eventually agreed that both countries would work with the South Vietnamese to respect the Geneva Accords, and that directions would be given to representatives in Vietnam to be in constant consultation. In the end, joint instructions to Ely and Collins stipulated "cooperation at all levels with some autonomy of action," periodic bilateral discussions in Washington at a "high level," "no competition," and no U.S. attempt to "replace France." Most importantly, the two countries agreed that representatives would exchange official views before all decisions. Thus, by December 1954 the French had forestalled further reductions in the FEC and their removal from South Vietnamese officer training—Collins's suggestion of putting instruction under American command had been rejected— while ensuring Franco-American cooperation and a continued French role in officer schools, or so they thought.[6]

Although the Americans had agreed in a series of political agreements to keep the French presence, their actions in the military and economic realms undermined these accords. Prior to Geneva, the FEC had received aid from the United States in two ways—the Mutual Defense Assistance Program (MDAP) sent aid to Indochina and offshore aid to France for the FEC. After Geneva, MDAP aid was transferred to Cambodia, Vietnam, and Laos, and the Americans made clear that they would be reducing aid for the FEC's continued maintenance. The French had requested $330 million for 1955 FEC support and were disappointed when they only received $100 million, especially since Washington had promised much greater aid during the September 1954 meetings. Mendès France considered American aid for 1955 "totally insufficient," and felt that France would be forced to revise its entire military budget in Indochina. In particular, the French resented American attempts to take control of military assistance to South Vietnam, bypassing the French, while still expecting France to bolster the country militarily.[7]

French officials thus struggled to redefine the FEC's mission and decide how many FEC troops could be supported without continued American aid.

French officials even toyed with the idea of threatening Diem and the Eisenhower administration with the total withdrawal of the FEC, but recognized such a bluff could be dangerous. In a December 1954 ministerial meeting, Mendès France and Finance Minister Edgar Faure, among others, set forth four goals for the FEC. The FEC's first priority was the protection of French representatives in Vietnam. The FEC would also need to organize strongholds around Saigon and Cap St. Jacques (which was located sixty miles from Saigon). The other two aims were maintaining order in the region of regrouped FEC units and aiding the South Vietnamese in the reorganization of their armed forces. But shortly thereafter, as the French learned about drastically reduced American aid, they were forced to withdraw about eleven thousand men per month, with the result that French forces could not maintain order in designated regions, French representatives' safety could not be guaranteed, and strongholds around Saigon and Cap St. Jacques faced an uncertain future. With the absence of sufficient American financial aid, incertitude about the length of the FEC's continued presence, difficulties in Franco-American cooperation on training Vietnamese forces, and South Vietnamese and American hostility to the French, the French were forced to reconsider whether they wanted to continue the FEC's presence at all.[8]

During a series of meetings from March to May 1955, French leaders debated the FEC's future. Part of the problem was the delay in Franco–South Vietnamese negotiations regarding the FEC, the French commander in chicf's role vis-à-vis the South Vietnamese army, the reestablishment of order in South Vietnam, and the French responsibility to the Geneva Accords. French officials feared they would be held accountable for the application of the military clauses of the Geneva Accords, especially those that dealt with the seventeenth parallel and non-augmentation of the two Vietnamese armies, just as they were losing political power in South Vietnam to Diem and the Americans. By May, Diem had established control after routing the sects, but France succeeded in stressing the importance of the FEC to the Americans as a contributing factor to the security of South Vietnam. As a result, the United States did not push for the FEC's complete withdrawal. In fact, American general John O'Daniel urged Diem to slow the FEC's withdrawal; South Vietnam could not hope to fill the military vacuum created by the FEC's departure until 1956 and would be in serious trouble in the event of a North Vietnamese attack. O'Daniel went so far as to suggest that the FEC remain under the auspices of SEATO. But Diem argued that the FEC would be more of a hindrance than a help during battle and would result in DRV propaganda about the colonial nature of the Saigon regime.[9]

By mid-October 1955, the two highest ranking French officials in South Vietnam—Henri Hoppenot and General Pierre Jacquot—saw only two options: either withdraw completely or maintain twenty thousand troops around St. Jacques and the port of Saigon and wait and see. Jacquot preferred the second solution but was critical of Diem, accusing him of "throwing away his mask" and being a "philosophically hostile" and "irreducible adversary" of France. Of pressing concern was the realization that any further reductions in the FEC without French policy being clearly set would put the FEC in a position of "inferiority." France would find it difficult to have "any leverage in negotiations with the Diem government on economic and cultural matters," and the Diem government would undoubtedly be seriously tempted to achieve its goals through intimidation. Jacquot insisted on the importance of keeping a "French flag in the Far East." Even though he recognized militarily France might be forced to depart, he thought that the future for the French economic and cultural presence looked "auspicious."[10]

According to Hoppenot, if France wanted to keep a "preponderant voice in Far Eastern affairs—and its position as a great power requires this—France should do everything possible to keep a military presence in Indochina." The disappearance of its forces in Indochina would lead to its departure from SEATO, the abandonment of exercising its responsibilities to the Geneva Accords, and the "effective erasure of France" in Southeast Asia. Furthermore, in North Africa, such a departure could have "profound repercussions" and serve as an example of how to "eliminate" France. "French influence is thus threatened and will disappear completely to the benefit of the Americans if French missions in Indochina are withdrawn." The abandonment of French military influence would also have heavy consequences on the economic and cultural domains, which were "tied in great part to France's military presence." The Americans "would profit from our abdication and would insinuate themselves into these domains, which they haven't succeeded in doing until now." According to Hoppenot, if the FEC stayed on, France would be able "to maintain a presence which is not so against the secret desires of the Vietnamese or our SEATO partners." Therefore, France should continue its withdrawal as already established until November 15, try to obtain from South Vietnam an agreement where France could maintain a greatly reduced base, and "see what comes" of negotiations. The Mendès France government knew how difficult it might be to achieve these goals given its suspicions that Washington was trying to supplant the French military presence despite U.S. claims to the contrary.[11]

After accepting a series of reductions in the FEC's size, the French once again reassessed the situation in December. Hoppenot and Jacquot agreed that a minimum of twenty thousand FEC troops at Cap St. Jacques was required to guarantee the political stability of the country and ensure the security of French representatives and interests. Any future reduction before a military convention with South Vietnam would "leave a hole France would be unable to fill" and would have "deep political, military and diplomatic repercussions." Hoppenot argued that Diem had never indicated how quickly the FEC should leave; if France withdrew the entire FEC without contractual provisions, such an action would result in "the loss of the privileged statute" that France was trying to hold onto, the "lack of means for France to exercise its responsibilities to Geneva," and the "weakening of French positions in SEATO and in Southeast Asia." But by the end of December the "20,000 plan" had been rejected by the Vietnamese, who insisted on a fifteen-thousand limit to the FEC, and the French began to strategize on how to keep their base at Cap St. Jacques, which would allow them to evacuate Saigon and regroup in a place that was easy to defend.[12] Hoppenot and Jacquot reiterated their concerns in January that any reduction below fifteen thousand men would mean the high command would not be able to ensure the ICC's protection, or that of Saigon and Cap St. Jacques.

The catch for France regarding the Geneva Accords and the FEC was that article 27 stated France could not dissolve the position of commander in chief unless a successor agreed to uphold all the Geneva Accords or France notified the other conferees about the situation. France had to make sure that the Diem government agreed to accept all its responsibilities as successor. If Diem refused or was evasive, the only other option for France was to go to the co-presidents.[13] Of paramount concern, then, was whether, once France withdrew its forces, South Vietnam would become the "successor" to French responsibilities. Although Diem denied being a successor he did promise to protect the ICC. But Diem continued to pressure the French to reduce the FEC as quickly as possible, claiming that he could not possibly begin consultations with the North regarding the 1956 elections and that he would be equally unprepared to begin negotiations on transfers of buildings and other economic and cultural issues until the FEC was gone.

It was clear by early 1956 that all the French could hope for was to keep a toehold at Cap St. Jacques with fifteen thousand troops. Even that seemed unlikely, as the Eisenhower administration announced it would not use MDAP funds to support France in Vietnam after June 30 and the South Vietnamese government demanded a full withdrawal of the FEC. Nguyen Huu Chau, delegate minister to the Council of the Vietnam Presidency, insisted that any further French military presence would be called a "mission of military, technical and other assistance." Diem wanted France to continue its training missions in all three branches of the military, since the Geneva Accords did not allow the Americans to increase their missions, and he recognized that the French would need certain logistical and administrative support to continue these missions, but they could not be stationed in Saigon. All air and naval military presence had to be withdrawn immediately and recentered at Cap St. Jacques, which meant the abandonment of the French air mission at Tan Son Nhut and all naval installations at the port of Saigon. According to South Vietnamese officials, "Franco-Vietnamese relations would improve" once the French high command and its forces had withdrawn.[14] French counselor Jean Jacques de Bresson and General Tran Van Don led the Franco-Vietnamese talks on this subject from the end of February to the end of March, culminating with the March 30 accords that established a timetable for the withdrawal of the FEC. Despite Hoppenot's warning that France could not fulfill its Geneva obligations if the FEC dropped below fifteen thousand men, plans proceeded for complete withdrawal.

Reflecting on the situation, Mendès France noted that France had moved from a primarily political and military influence to an exclusively economic and cultural one that "necessitates a difficult reconversion," for which the men on the ground in Vietnam were ill prepared. He also realized that France "risks a contradictory policy as it tries to safeguard its interest in the North and South." Mendès France accepted that "the Americans must be consulted before any decisions are made," recognizing that Washington now held the upper hand.[15] Hoppenot bitterly remarked that "neither Dulles nor any of his colleagues showed the slightest interest, even as a common courtesy, to achieve a better collaboration between our two countries in Vietnam," and that the Americans, British, and South Vietnamese were all "trying to avoid taking a position on the judicial consequences of the dissolution of the High Command" by delaying Franco-Vietnamese talks that should have taken place before France defined its attitude toward Vietnam.[16]

The FEC was officially dissolved on April 28, 1956, as was the French high command. The quick evolution of the situation in favor of Diem was behind this feat, but Diem had willing accomplices in Washington. Other factors were also at work. Just as bureaucratic infighting plagued Americans in D.C. and Vietnam, the French Foreign Ministry, Defense Ministry, and officials on the ground in Saigon disagreed on what to do in Vietnam, in particular whether or not to reduce the FEC. It appears that one of the reasons France decided to withdraw the FEC was to ensure that FEC troops would not be used in SEATO. France feared that it would be forced to accept responsibilities that went beyond its partners, and that if it refused to engage its forces, it would face "severe recriminations," notably from the United States.[17] Another factor contributing to the withdrawal of the FEC was the worsening situation in Algeria as yet another French colony demanded full independence. Some French officials in Paris did not protest the FEC's disappearance too loudly because troops were needed in North Africa.

What is clear from both French and American documentation is that the withdrawal of the FEC had perhaps the biggest impact on the reversal of French fortunes in Indochina. The French no longer had any leverage in negotiating economic and cultural accords with the Vietnamese and could not fulfill their obligations to the Geneva Accords—a circumstance that French officials made known to their American counterparts.[18] The situation was made glaringly apparent when Paris sent a note to Eden and Molotov in mid-May stating that it had "ceased to have any further responsibility with regard to the execution of the Geneva agreements" but was willing to use its good offices providing South Vietnam would accept them. French good offices would depend on "effective cooperation with South Vietnam" and with the Americans. During a meeting between Dulles and French foreign minister Christian Pineau in mid-June, Pineau wanted to know how Dulles envisioned France's role in Indochina after the FEC's withdrawal and whether France should continue to uphold its Geneva agreements or denounce them.[19] Dulles did not have any concrete answers.

The second area of Franco–South Vietnamese–American conflict in military matters concerned TRIM, which had been established through the December 13, 1954, accords between Ely and Collins. TRIM was a Franco-American training program for the South Vietnamese armed forces and it served as a replacement for the French Mission of Military Assistance, which had been created in December 1953 and would eventually become the French Military Mission. The mission had 3,068 personnel in January 1955 but only 415 by August. Despite its reduction, and even though France had just a few advisers in the army and not many more in the navy and air force, both the Vietnamese and Americans complained frequently about the mission. When General O'Daniel began command of TRIM under the "general authority" of French general Paul Ely, the French directed four offices—air, navy, organization and general studies, and plans—and a French colonel was designated as chief of staff. The Americans, primarily MAAG personnel, directed the other three offices—logistics, instruction, and pacification. At its inception, French officers in TRIM far outnumbered American ones, but this would change.[20]

Dulles had agreed that U.S. and French personnel would continue to work together in TRIM, and he had allegedly indicated to the French through American ambassador G. Frederick Reinhardt that he wanted the French to remain involved at the "highest levels." However, when speaking with Diem, Dulles apparently gave the impression that he had no opinion on the problem of French maintenance of military training missions. Given the South Vietnamese attitude toward France and the hostility of the American missions toward the French ones, Dulles's uncharacteristic silence on this subject represented clear encouragement to push the French out of TRIM. Moreover, once the South Vietnamese insisted on the dissolution of the French high command in South Vietnam, the Americans moved quickly to place French forces in TRIM under U.S. command.[21]

In addition, Franco-American relations in TRIM remained difficult, according to French officials, because of CIA operative Edward Lansdale's efforts at creating anti-French propaganda. Ely saw "no possibility" of coming to an agreement regarding TRIM as long as Lansdale remained in South Vietnam. In turn, Lansdale was a vocal critic of the French, complaining that Franco-American teamwork had grown into a "secret understanding." He felt that American officials had incorporated a substantial amount of French thinking in plans and advice, rather than following the working arrangement originally described by Collins wherein the United States would "inform" the French of American intentions and then take up the matter with the Vietnamese. This collaboration could be a "prime target" for the communists, according to Lansdale. He also deplored the continued French presence, which he deemed "evident and heavy."[22] Lansdale was eventually transferred out of TRIM to MAAG, but remained active in Vietnam.

According to Hoppenot, "the Americans were taking over." TRIM commander Lieutenant General Samuel T. Williams, who had replaced O'Daniel, notified Paris that French officers who left TRIM would not be replaced until Franco-Vietnamese military negotiations had ended, and that thirty American officers would be included in the French air training mission. The Americans also ended funding for six hundred South Vietnamese army officers who were still training at various French military schools. These actions greatly diminished the French missions of instruction.[23] Adding insult to injury, Chau informed Hoppenot that South Vietnam would subordinate all three branches of the French mission under an American general. The coup de grâce to the French presence came at the end of April when Williams notified the remaining French officers that due to the dissolution of the French high command, French officers in TRIM would cease their functions as of April 28, 1956. TRIM subsequently disappeared and its successor became the American-run Combined Arms Training Organization.

TRIM's reorganization left the French completely out of the loop. A Vietnamese leader and a powerful American presence in the organization would henceforth exclude French input.[24] Although the French were allowed to keep their air and naval training missions in TRIM, the two together only made up 4 percent of the Vietnamese forces and were subject to American authority. Americans had a mixed reaction at the rapid reduction of the size of the French mission after Geneva. Some officials wanted to increase American military influence but thought that the Vietnamese were "ill-prepared to assume full responsibility at the higher command and staff levels and in technical areas" and that there were not enough MAAG personnel to replace all of the departing French advisers. Washington did not want the French air and naval missions to leave since MAAG ceiling limits prohibited the United States from replacing them, but Dulles stated that "it might be the lesser of two evils just to get the French out."[25]

The Americans evidently chose the lesser of two evils as Diem subsequently requested the withdrawal of French navy and air force training missions. According to American ambassador Elbridge Durbrow, although the French departure would add to the MAAG burden and require "limited increased personnel," he expected "no difficulty assuming present French responsibilities" and believed the United States would achieve a "decided advantage having one doctrine and one set [of] standards."[26] American ambassador to France Amory Houghton disagreed, noting that the French "are suspicious and alert for any move on our part to fill [the] gap caused by their departure. They will be quick to react sharply and bitterly to such a development at this time, regarding it as 'proof' [of] U.S. duplicity and intention [to] replace" the French in Indochina. Despite Houghton's concerns, the Diem regime, with American approval, insisted the French leave, and American advisers soon arrived to replace the departing French.[27] The final blow came in June 1957, when the French naval and air force training missions were withdrawn.

The Americans also sought to replace the French in the French-controlled officer training school or EMS, which had been created in June 1952 and employed French and Vietnamese instructors. American officials suggested to the South Vietnamese that they integrate the school into TRIM and move it to the Philippines so that the United States would have more direct control. The Vietnamese ignored this American initiative, but the number of Vietnamese to be trained in France declined rapidly from 1955 to 1956, while the number to be trained in the United States quickly grew. Of the Vietnamese trained abroad in 1955, there were 729 sent to France and 166 to the United States; in 1956, there were 450 sent to France and 881 to the United States. And in June 1956, Diem suspended training of all Vietnamese officers in France. By 1957, the EMS was almost nonexistent. For the French, it was difficult to imagine that these initiatives did not have an American origin when at the same time Vietnamese officers were being sent to the United States for training. Although the Americans insisted that Diem's decisions were not a result of concerted action between Washington and Saigon, the facts suggested otherwise.[28]

One of the areas of starkest disagreement concerned the South Vietnamese armed forces. French influence within the Vietnamese National Army (VNA) remained strong as the officer corps was French educated and appointed, more French than Vietnamese in culture and habits, often of French citizenship, and had fought for the French against the DRV. Duong Van Minh, commander of the Saigon-Cholon garrison, Tran Van Don, chief of staff, and Le Van Kim, assistant to the chief of staff, all fit this mold. Thus to reduce French influence within the VNA would take some doing. The Americans were up to the task.

By the end of the Geneva Conference, the French and the Americans had two different conceptions of the VNA. The French sought to create a sovereign, independent, and fairly large army of 160,000 men that could maintain order and contribute to keeping the delicate equilibrium between South and North, which was the French government's most pressing goal. Paris feared that as Washington brought in additional advisers, the North Vietnamese would respond with increasing aggression against the South, and thus a large South Vietnamese army was required. The Americans had a long-term plan to create a smaller (90,000-man), more effective army that would ensure internal security. The way to achieve such a force would be through American instruction, methods, and training. During the November 1954 Mendès France–Dulles talks regarding the VNA, Dulles had claimed that he did not want to "eliminate France" but rather to "install the United States in Vietnam," but Mendès France disagreed. If, as the Americans wanted, the army was reduced, "who would defend South Vietnam?" he queried. Dulles replied that defending South Vietnam was not "the army's purpose," but rather "what SEATO was for." According to Dulles, the South Vietnamese army was for "maintaining order and repressing subversion; only SEATO could provide an actual deterrent to the Viet Minh."[29]

A *U.S. News and World Report* headline provided one perspective on the Mendès France–Dulles conversations: "U.S. Inherits Another Headache: France Turns Over Indochina Job to America." The article clearly stated that the United States was "replacing" France, evidenced by the reduction of French forces and U.S. training of the VNA. "U.S. dollars instead of troops" were the "key to this project": economic aid to South Vietnam would increase from $25 million to $100 million, and U.S. training of South Vietnamese forces meant that the Americans were "taking over from France the primary responsibility for Indochina policy." High policy decisions heretofore made in Paris or by the French military commander in Indochina would "from now on" be made by the United States. The article stated that U.S. assumption of training terminated "the conflict" between the United States and France over what to do with South Vietnam, and it expressed shock over the degree to which the French have "abdicated in Indochina." The evidence of this abdication was the surprise American move to reduce the VNA from 270,000 to 90,000, which Mendès France did not protest. The remaining army would be used for internal security, at an estimated cost to the United States of $200 million per year. The article concluded that, all in all, the United States was getting itself "more and more deeply enmeshed" in Indochina, while the French, who were "on the way out," predicted an American takeover would find the United States bearing the "brunt of the criticism" in Indochina instead of themselves.[30]

At least some of these observations became fact with the December 13, 1954, Ely-Collins accords that were so critical to the VNA's future. The accords restructured the advising system so that MAAG would take over training of the VNA as of January 1, 1955. The Americans were limited as MAAG needed to ensure that the number of American military personnel (350) did not increase. The Defense and State Departments were therefore divided over how quickly the United States could phase the French out. The Defense Department wanted to move quickly in taking over training activities, whereas many officials in the State Department recommended moving more slowly. Assistant Secretary of State for Far Eastern Affairs Walter Robertson noted some of the pitfalls of swift action, notably that U.S. prestige would be "considerably more committed in Vietnam and the American ability to disengage made more difficult," but Kenneth Young pointed out that assuming training of the VNA would "benefit the United States as it would have more leverage in Vietnamese affairs."[31] Dulles ultimately made the decision that the United States should "take the plunge" and proceed as scheduled. January 1, 1955, marked a major step for the U.S. military presence in South

Vietnam as the VNA became the Army of the Republic of Vietnam (ARVN) and France relinquished command authority. General O'Daniel took over the organization and training of South Vietnamese troops in February 1955, and a few months later ARVN abruptly adopted American-style uniforms and the American salute, and engaged in a ceremonial burning of French-style insignia of rank.[32]

These actions did not please the French, despite the American assumption that they had preserved French goodwill and cooperation. Paris continued to protest Washington's decision to provide American military aid directly to Saigon and to take control of ARVN's training. Mendès France disdained the December 1954 Ely-Collins agreements reached with respect to the training of the Vietnamese army because they "violated the Geneva Accords." According to the French, the Americans conceived ARVN almost entirely in the "overall strategy in Southeast Asia rather than with respect to actual conditions in the country, which explained why 96% of ARVN forces were in the army and 4% were for the air force and navy."[33] Even in these areas, France was not allowed to keep a presence, formally relinquishing command authority of the navy on July 1, 1955, and transferring the Tourane airbase to Vietnamese control on September 19, 1956.

By the end of 1956, four major American military school systems were operating in South Vietnam. The army's basic training center, Quang Trung, near Saigon, was capable of handling more than nine thousand recruits in a standard sixteen-week course. An eight-week course for reservists also existed. The school for senior officers, the Military College in Saigon, offered a staff course for junior officers and a command course for field-grade officers. Dalat Military Academy provided basic officer training for about eight hundred students, and the Thu Duc School Center, a few miles northeast of Saigon, housed the major branch schools—armor, infantry, transportation, signal, administration, engineer, ordnance, artillery, and quartermaster. All together they were capable of training about seventeen hundred officers and senior noncommissioned officers. In addition to reorganizing and expanding that major training complex, MAAG established a physical training and ranger school at the coastal town of Nha Trang for approximately one hundred students, as well as an intelligence and psychological warfare school in Saigon.[34] The swiftness with which the United States began reorganizing and retraining ARVN was remarkable, especially given the constant reassurances by American diplomats to their French counterparts that the United States did not seek to replace France in this area.

Another issue facing the French was the American determination to create a temporary equipment recovery mission (what became TERM) in South Vietnam, allegedly to retrieve American material given to the French during the First Indochina War. During the four years the United States had supported France, immense quantities of military equipment—from tanks and aircraft to small arms, ammunition, and spare parts—had poured into Vietnam. Under the terms of the pentalateral agreement signed on December 23, 1950, by France, the United States, and the three Associated States, the title to the equipment, which was valued at more than $1.2 billion, was to revert to the United States at the conclusion of hostilities.[35] France had been responsible for keeping track of the equipment during the war, but had been rather careless in its accounting of materials. The recovery mission would thus provide a convenient pretext to place more American personnel in Vietnam while at the same time helping recover at least some American equipment.

Immediately following the Geneva Conference, American officials had increased their training mission but feared violating the Geneva Accords by bringing in too many Americans. The creation of TERM was a deliberate American attempt to bypass the limitations of the Geneva Accords by importing foreign military advisers. Since TERM was only temporary, the Eisenhower administration rationalized that it was not breaking the accords. In February 1956, the Americans first broached the subjects of a recovery mission and enlisting the support of one thousand French officers to help recover American equipment still in Vietnam with French ambassador Maurice Couve de Murville. If the French did this, then the Americans would intervene with Diem for a continued French military mission. When Couve de Murville noted that such an effort went beyond the Geneva limits, American officials replied that the United States did not "recognize the limits for this kind of purpose." It appeared that the Americans were attempting a quid pro quo—French help with American priorities in exchange for the continuation of the French military presence.[36] According to Hoppenot, if the French endorsed TERM, France would continue to be "held responsible for the application of the Geneva Accords, South Vietnam would think France supported its policies unconditionally, and Paris would encounter problems with Hanoi." Hoppenot concluded that "France would find itself in the worst possible situation because it would be responsible for the application of the accords, in particular the non-augmentation of military personnel, and, at the same time, would be associated with the United States and South Vietnam in violation of this accord." Jacques Roux, director of political affairs at the French Foreign Ministry, suggested that France would keep one thousand troops in Indochina for a year if the American government renounced its idea of sending American troops and if South Vietnam agreed that such a move did not contradict the French troop withdrawal it had demanded.[37]

These discussions demonstrated the Eisenhower administration's determination to increase the American presence in Vietnam and to coerce the French into supporting American policies. Ultimately, TERM members began to arrive in 1956 without French participation. In addition to "retrieving American material," 350 TERM members converted Vietnamese armed forces to the U.S. supply system, assisted in the establishment of a functional logistical organization, arranged for technicians, spare parts, and tools to be made available so equipment could be maintained, helped open the Saigon shipyard for the Vietnamese navy, and redistributed substantial amounts of material turned over by the French to the Vietnamese.[38] TERM was eventually absorbed into MAAG in 1959.

As American responsibility for the fate of South Vietnam's military increased, French influence over Vietnamese military affairs diminished. The French were phased out, evidenced by the FEC's withdrawal, the end of the French high command, the loss of French standing in TRIM, diminishment of the EMS, relinquishment of the VNA, and the TERM mission. The Americans had quietly taken control. This fact was made crystal clear at the March 1956 Karachi Conference. The meetings between Pineau, Dulles, and British foreign minister Selwyn Lloyd at the conference were strained as all three men tried to maintain some form of allied unity on Vietnam. That the allies continued to disagree on how to handle American materials left in Vietnam and that Jacquot had almost been assassinated in Saigon by an ARVN patrol did nothing to ease the situation.

At the conference, Pineau recognized that France had not always supported Diem but was still pessimistic about Diem's chances for success. When speaking privately to Dulles, Pineau expressed regret for the "lack of coordination" between the two countries that led Diem to adopt a difficult attitude toward France, and emphasized once again that if France, Britain, and the United States did not "follow a common policy in Indochina they would lose." Pineau asked Dulles whether France should "continue the role given to it at Geneva" or "leave Vietnam entirely." Dulles responded that he wanted to maintain a "good collaboration" with Diem despite Diem's "difficult nature," and that he would have Kenneth Young look into the military situation. He added that since the United States was limited to 342 military personnel, it would be a "great favor" if France could leave 220 members of the navy and air force in place, for if all French disappeared it would be a "huge loss for South Vietnam."[39] And yet, within the year, all the French military forces were gone.

ECONOMIC EFFORTS

At the end of the Geneva Conference, France was *the* economic force in South Vietnam. But the Americans hoped to change this fact, just as they had changed who controlled the military situation in South Vietnam. In late 1954, the French handed over a number of economic powers to the South Vietnamese during negotiations. France, South Vietnam, Cambodia, and Laos signed an agreement abrogating the 1950 Pau Conventions and dissolving the quadpartite bodies established by the conventions. The Diem government took control of its financial, customs, and monetary policies as of January 1, 1955—the same date that the United States began providing economic aid directly to the Diem regime, bypassing French authorities. During his meeting with Dulles the previous October, Mendès France had attempted to dissuade the United States from its upcoming plan to supply aid directly to South Vietnam, arguing that such aid was supposed to go through the French as agreed to at the Washington Conference in September. In another round of talks in November, the French wanted a formal Franco-American committee established in Vietnam to coordinate, direct, and control aid programs. According to Washington, the French would reluctantly agree to the inclusion of representatives from the Diem government on such committees but apparently expected the United States and France to have complete control of aid programs. They interpreted "coordination" in that context and felt that during the Ely–La Chambre talks the United States had committed itself to such a procedure. During the November meetings Dulles quickly backed away from former promises, stating that "there had been no specific agreement in September on the appropriate machinery for coordination."[40] Indeed, the Eisenhower administration decided to cut aid to France for Indochina by three quarters, transferred the last civilian responsibilities to Diem, and refused to keep the French apprised of how aid was distributed.

French and American economic aid to Vietnam had been roughly equivalent by 1952, but in 1953 American aid began to surpass that of the French. Although France still provided technical and economic aid to South Vietnam in late 1954, American aid had begun to "overshadow" French efforts. According to French statistics, exports to Indochina had steadily declined since 1954. In 1953, France supplied 80 billion francs in exports to

Indochina; in 1954 it was 63 billion; in 1955 it declined to 50 billion; and in 1956 France exported around 20 billion. In contrast, from 1955 to 1960 the United States funneled nearly $1.5 billion in aid to Diem. In 1955 Diem received $326 million; in 1956, $213 million; in 1957, $281 million; in 1958, $192 million; in 1959, $207 million; and in 1960, $180 million. Put another way, U.S. economic aid from 1955 to 1960 averaged $230 million a year, or roughly 22 percent of South Vietnam's gross national product.[41]

American officials advocated using foreign aid as a "major Cold War weapon," and soon after Geneva, they determined the need for rapid economic development in South Vietnam to ward off the communist threat, especially as French financial assistance, technicians, engineers, and counselors "disappeared," or were displaced. In what would later become doctrine, one American official early on argued that "we must be entirely free to use our aid and military support in the best public and international interests as concerns America. This will not deprive us of contact or coordination with the French Technical Mission or the French Military, but it most assuredly will deprive the French of dictating how we shall best help participating countries." The Americans consolidated their circumvention of the French through the International Cooperation Administration, which began to administer aid through three programs in order to support the Diem government and raise the standard of living. From 1955 to 1960, the CIP, which was a variant of the program used in Europe during the Marshall Plan, provided about $1.1 billion to South Vietnam to finance the importation of U.S.-produced goods, including cars, trucks, motorcycles, scooters, typewriters, and clothing. The CIP was for defense support, but it also served the economic and political purpose of increasing the overall strength of South Vietnam by injecting substantial aid without destroying the economic and financial system. The Food for Peace program provided surplus U.S. agricultural commodities in the same manner as the CIP to the tune of $67 million. The Project Aid program covered noncommercial economic and social enterprises, including resettlement and infrastructure projects, under the rubric of "nation-building." About $182 million was disbursed under this program.[42] Prior to these changes, American aid to Vietnam had passed through France in the form of off-shore commands, MDAP materials, and aid credit.

American and South Vietnamese economic efforts stemmed from the rapidly disappearing French economic presence, which of course Washington and Saigon had helped ensure. One of the ramifications of the FEC's accelerated withdrawal was its economic impact, leading to a sharp reduction in the volume of business, increased unemployment, the closing of businesses, disinvestment, capital flight, and general discouragement of French businessmen. U.S. planners were hard at work compensating for these problems. With the establishment of the Supreme Monetary Council on June 24, 1955, South Vietnam tried to address economic problems and became more aggressive in its economic negotiations with the French. The United States, however, recognized that the South Vietnamese needed the French at least in the interim. Still, in planning for a 1955–1956 economic recovery, American officials recommended taking "in hand key sectors yet occupied in the economic field by certain foreign enterprises presenting a character completely monopolistic."[43]

Although some American officials in Saigon realized the problems associated with pursuing a policy designed to ensure that the French economic presence diminished, the Americans continued to reduce the French financial role in various ways. As French officials saw it, the Americans were at least partially responsible for increased South Vietnamese hostility toward the French, which had reached a fever pitch by October 1955.[44] South Vietnamese delegations that had come to Paris to negotiate military, economic, and cultural conventions were recalled, as were the South Vietnamese representatives to the Assembly of the French Union. By November 1955, the United States, not France, was the number one exporter to South Vietnam. In addition, Franco–South Vietnamese monetary and commercial conventions from the previous December were voided when Diem renounced the fixed parity of the franc and piastre and quit the "zone franc" beginning January 1, 1956. Subsequently, the piastre was officially pegged to the dollar and American officials helped found new companies and reform Vietnamese banks on an American model. And in February 1956, when South Vietnam was supposed to sign a Franco-Vietnamese commercial accord, it refused to grant France preferential trade status. The preferential tariff for French companies ended on March 1, 1956, their privileged status in trade matters was revoked, and French products were unable to compete in the race for imports financed by U.S. aid programs. As a result, the French share of Vietnamese imports fell from 66.7 percent to 27.4 percent from July 1955 to July 1956, French exports diminished by more than one half, and twenty thousand French bureaucrats headed back to the metropole.[45]

In one French official's estimation, the Americans had "destroyed French markets for personal gain" as "Ford replaced Renault," and as their "insolence and interference" in all domestic affairs proved that even under the cover of Catholicism, "American colonialism was simply replacing the French system." Such claims were somewhat exaggerated as France did not simply disappear from the economic scene—French enterprises continued to command a considerable share of Vietnamese industrial and business activity, and a substantial amount of capital remained in Vietnam—but France's economic presence had diminished.[46] Notwithstanding their increasing economic activity, the Americans had failed to fill the enormous gap left by the French withdrawal because of a continuing lack of private American investment in South Vietnam.

The economic task the Americans in Saigon faced after Geneva was daunting. According to USOM officials, all economic activity had been held by a small number of firmly entrenched French companies that had prospered under the colonial administration. For example, French colonialism was responsible for a monetary supply limited almost solely to the function of issuing banknotes. Three French banks—Banque d'Indochine, Banque France-Chinoise, and Banque Nationale Pour le Commerce et l'Industrie—conducted 80 percent of the business. Even with the newly established National Bank of Vietnam's supposed control of these banks, no oversight actually existed. Banking outside of Saigon and Hanoi was handled almost entirely by branches of French banks that contracted their operations after independence. French banks refused to grant credit to importers, which helped explain the paralysis of American aid. In order to remedy the situation, Saigon created a national investment fund—Fonds National d'Investissement—and a commercial department in the Banque Nationale to halt the French monopoly.

In addition, French dominance in transportation, communications, and industry was unquestionable. Boat- and barge-building yards were operated by the French. All electric power and water companies were French. For ocean, coast, serial, and international communications, South Vietnam was completely dependent on French companies such as Messageries Maritime, Chargeurs Réunis, Compagnie Denis Frères, Air France, and Transports Aeriens Intercontinentaux. USOM thus recommended that the Vietnamese create a merchant marine and air fleet. In the industrial sector, the leading French companies were Brassaries et Glacières d'Indochine, Manufactures de Cigarettes, Société des Allumettes, Compagnie des Eaux et d'Electricité, and Forets et Soieries. The danger here was that these companies wanted to disinvest because they had no confidence in South Vietnam's future.

Equally problematic for American organizations was French dominance in agriculture. The French owned 96 percent of rubber plantations and 80 percent of tea plantations, and all of the sugar mills were French.[47] The French rubber plantations were practicing bleeding the rubber trees to excess because they wanted to get the maximum profit before the country collapsed. And in the trade sector, all South Vietnamese trade was monopolized by the French firms Diethebm, Optorg, Poinsard et Veyret, and Descours et Cabaud. These firms refused to work with the Foreign Operations Administration and paralyzed South Vietnamese trade. The French also emphasized trade over local production, and cultivation was oriented toward foreign markets rather than expansion of local demand. USOM thus recommended increasing exports such as rice and salt and blocking detrimental imports. The irony here was that at the time Americans in Saigon pointed out that France exported many items harmful to the South Vietnamese economy because of considerations of commercial profit, and yet the United States encouraged the same sort of practices in the 1960s.

Unemployment, which had soared as a result of the influx of refugees, withdrawal of the FEC, and disinvestments of French enterprises, was another pressing problem. USOM advocated a New Deal program for South Vietnam, where large construction programs—highways, bridges, railroads, airports, and canals—would put people to work. USOM also recommended concluding commercial agreements with other countries and attracting foreign capital. The French, of course, did not want to go "quietly into the night," resenting the potential end to their privileges and the paucity of French foreign exchange with South Vietnam. According to the American Embassy in Saigon, they also "displayed a tendency toward sulkiness, sabotage and refusal to adapt themselves to a new situation," although they did agree to end the currency activities of the Banque d'Indochine and hand over the administration of the port of Saigon.[48]

The Americans were also trying desperately to woo private investors, but these attempts proved unsuccessful, no doubt due to fears of renewed hostilities and because of the South Vietnamese regime's instability and ambiguous financial policies. Diem tended to pursue a somewhat contradictory policy of promising assistance to U.S. and European firms and then imposing bureaucratic controls that frustrated those businesses. And he relied very heavily on the CIP, which generated revenues through the sale of import licenses and the imposition of customs duties. The Diem regime thus did not have much incentive to work with private firms, and the CIP stifled locally manufactured goods because of cheaper U.S. imports.[49] So although the Americans had once again succeeded in disrupting the French presence in Vietnam, this time economically, Eisenhower officials would struggle to find a way to ensure aid actually went toward building a viable noncommunist South Vietnam.

THE CULTURAL CARD

In addition to supplying economic aid, the Eisenhower administration also recognized the importance of establishing a bureaucratic and cultural presence in South Vietnam. The French sought to maintain cultural influence through their educational institutions, foreign exchanges, aid programs, commercial trade, and French language classes. The Americans worked to teach the South Vietnamese what they considered more relevant technical training, American education, and the English language. The French viewed American forays into these areas as a "cultural offensive." National Assembly leader Michel Debré warned that no matter "the alliance with the United States," if France "allows the English language and culture to develop in Vietnam, French cultural influence will cease to exist in the Far East." France could not "protest that American aid, professors, and grants to American universities exist in Vietnam," but should ensure that such programs were "in tangent with French goals and the general program of western culture in South Vietnam."[50]

Such views encountered a hostile reception in Washington and Saigon. American officials perceived French cultural efforts as a pathetic attempt to maintain washed-up colonial control. Washington believed that increasing the number of U.S. cultural missions in Southeast Asia would help stem perceived Soviet successes in this area, and began building up official and unofficial agencies in South Vietnam immediately after Geneva. According to Hoppenot, these American agencies had two primary cultural goals: teaching English everywhere while relegating French to second place, and forming technical personnel to fill the economic and social vacuum—the legacy of the colonial era—that had opened the way toward communism. For both American and British officials, teaching English had become a Cold War tactic in order to bring Southeast Asia closer to the West. These officials argued that language had "gone beyond the cultural level to become almost a Cold War operational necessity."[51] Thus, setting up cultural missions would help achieve the political goal of an independent, noncommunist South Vietnam.

On the official level, the Education Divisions of USOM and USIS Saigon were in charge of cultural affairs. With an annual budget of $1 million, USOM concentrated primarily on providing technical assistance and employed sixty American experts, who were divided into the fields of pedagogical studies, professional teaching, books and libraries, translations, construction, and grants. Its Bureau of Pedagogical Studies was oriented toward technical teaching in industry, electricity and radio navigation, and commerce. In primary and secondary teaching the major obstacle was a lack of English, resulting in a $100,000 monthly budget for the libraries and books section of the Education Division.[52] Other USOM duties included pumping money into the Vietnamese economy, providing food for refugee relief, and beginning land reform. According to some USOM officials, because of the war, governmental crises, and the "third party influence of the French in interpersonal professional relations," the efforts of the division had been kept on an "emergency basis." Now the United States could "expand training, build administrative strength, reorganize the Ministry of Health, and create a medical school."[53]

USIS Saigon, which was directly attached to the American Embassy, also had significant cultural activities. According to USIS, its mission was to explain to foreigners the "objectives and policy of the American government," to emphasize the "correlation between American policy and the legitimate aspirations of other peoples," to counter "hostile attempts to discredit American policy," and to teach about the "life and culture" of the United States to facilitate understanding of the policies and objectives of the American government. Comprising about thirty agents by 1955, USIS was an integral part of the embassy, and the activities of the heads of the missions were coordinated with the ambassador. USIS Saigon maintained an information, propaganda, and psychological warfare program for implementation by the South Vietnamese Ministry of Information. Libraries, research rooms, press, publications, conferences, films, music, records, and radio were all vehicles for the anticommunist output of USIS Saigon. USIS officials also intended to establish eighteen centers for dissemination of news and information throughout South Vietnam and cooperated with the Diem regime in the production of anticommunist, pro-government textbooks for use by secondary school teachers.

Expansion and reorganization of USIS included a mass propaganda campaign aimed at instilling basic ideas about democracy in Vietnam. USIS began developing, in cooperation with the Ministry of Education, a civics or political science course for the entire Vietnamese school system, which had as its basic aim the "animation of the local population through education." The United States also engaged in a mass indoctrination program, sponsored by one of South Vietnam's largest labor unions. In early January 1955, exhibits began to expand with the recent assignment of a USIS exhibits officer, and an enlarged USIS English-teaching program had also begun.[54] Representatives of American agencies in Vietnam were enthusiastic because the USIS plan represented an organized and comprehensive approach to the problem of instilling within the native peoples of Vietnam basic ideas concerning democracy and their responsibilities to it, a theme which was inherent in all American propaganda work being done there. The 1955 budget for USIS was $1.3 million, a 66 percent increase over fiscal year 1954, and the request for fiscal year 1956 was $2 million.[55]

After July 1956, USIS entered a new phase—media program activities, radio and TV, press, publications, increased distribution, exhibits, still photographs, motion pictures, cultural activities, library and information centers, subposts at Hue and Nha Trang, and information subposts in twenty-one of thirty-six provincial capitals—which helped bring about the countrywide impact of the USIS program. Through field operations, USIS endeavored to blanket the rural and provincial areas of Vietnam with film showings, publications, and radio news bulletins. As in other Southeast Asian countries, informational activities took precedence over cultural in all fields, with the possible exception of English teaching. The USIS public affairs officer participated in embassy staff meetings, where he was considered one of the principal officers, along with the political officer and the USOM and MAAG chiefs. One problem USIS faced was that, because of South Vietnam's French orientation as of 1956, study in the United States did not have the prestige that it did elsewhere. The cultural affairs officer had great difficulty filling the annual student quota.[56]

In addition to the official American presence, a number of semiofficial and unofficial organizations existed. The AFV was formed in December 1955 in the United States to educate the American public about Vietnam and to rally support for Diem's government.[57] The AFV's roots could be traced to 1950 when some of its members had met Diem. Many prestigious officials belonged—notably John F. Kennedy, Mike Mansfield, General William Donovan (former ambassador to Thailand and first president of the AFV), TRIM commander General John O'Daniel (who served as chair in 1956), Justice William O. Douglas, political activist Joseph Buttinger, economist Leo Cherne, academics Wesley Fishel, Christopher Emmet, and William Henderson, *Time* and *Life* publisher Henry Luce, William Randolph Hearst Jr., Arthur M. Schlesinger Jr., and public relations executives Harold Oram, Elliot Newcomb, and Gilbert Jonas.[58] Also listed in 1956 were thirty-two members of the House of Representatives, including several members of the Foreign Affairs Committee, and five senators. The roster of the AFV read as a Who's Who list of American political and military leaders and other public figures.

The AFV organized many cultural activities, asking Eisenhower to be the honorary president and Tran Van Chuong (South Vietnamese ambassador to the United States) to be an honorary member. AFV members certainly lent support to the Eisenhower administration's policies and were persuasive supporters of Diem and of economic investment in South Vietnam. AFV members also tended to be critics of the French.[59] For example, the principal speaker at a June 1956 AFV symposium was John F. Kennedy, who saw the United States as the guardian of promising offspring. He proclaimed that if "we are not the parents of little Vietnam, then surely we are godparents. We presided at its birth, we gave assistance to its life, we have helped to shape its future." As French influence in the political, economic, and military spheres "has declined" in Vietnam, American influence has "steadily grown," he stated. "This is our offspring—we cannot abandon it, we cannot ignore its needs." Kennedy added that the United States was obligated to supply capital to "replace that drained by centuries of colonial exploitation; technicians to train those handicapped by deliberate policies of illiteracy, [and] guidance to assist a nation taking those first feeble steps toward the complexities of a republican form of government."[60] These kinds of remarks, redolent of the type of colonialist condescension the French were so good at, demonstrated that many Americans, like the French, saw South Vietnam as an infant country that needed to be molded and guided.

The AVA, another semiofficial organization, which was inaugurated on July 23, 1955, resided in Saigon to develop cultural relations between America and Vietnam. The AVA's primary function, and the function of many other unofficial organizations, was to teach English. One of the biggest challenges facing Americans operating in Vietnam was language. Most translators and interpreters had learned English from the French, with the result that their English was of poor quality. When the translation had to be made from Vietnamese to French to English or vice versa, most of the true meanings became lost in the process. The AVA was the most active unofficial organization teaching English in Vietnam, with more than one hundred professors— mostly the wives of the members of other American missions—working to spread the English language. The USIS English-teaching officer served as acting director, which guaranteed that the association was directly linked to official U.S. policy.[61] In fact, it was largely funded by the cultural section of the embassy. Its Board of Directors had an equal number of Vietnamese and Americans. The AVA organized lectures, recitals, concerts, art exhibits, and tours to museums, temples, and historical sites, and held orientation classes for newly arrived Americans.

Numerous Presbyterian, Catholic, and Methodist missionaries also taught English in South Vietnam. The International Rescue Committee (IRC), the American Women's Association, and the powerful National Catholic Welfare Council (NCWC) all set up English learning programs. IRC president Leo Cherne and his colleague Joseph Buttinger, both AFV members, worked closely with the U.S. government. In addition, many organizations provided grants, with the AVA providing one hundred and the NCWC furnishing another hundred annual grants to Vietnamese students who wanted to learn English.

The technical assistance group from Michigan State University (MSUG) was the most significant unofficial American organization in Vietnam, although it did have contacts with other American missions as well as some CIA officials. The MSUG functioned in Vietnam from May 1955 to June 1962. Diem's personal relationship with Wesley Fishel, a Michigan State University political scientist, led to the project's creation. The MSUG had already been interested in Vietnam as early as March 1954, before Diem's rise to power, and Eisenhower administration officials actively encouraged the program's increasing role. Diem had invited Fishel to bring the MSUG to South Vietnam to train Vietnamese administrators, police, and researchers, and MSUG officials often received preferential treatment, much to the chagrin of their counterparts in other American organizations. Embassy, USIS, and USOM officials all resented Fishel and the MSUG's prominence at one point or another, leading to difficulties in presenting a united American front to both the South Vietnamese and the French.[62] U.S. officials recognized that official and unofficial American agencies operating in Vietnam had little, if any, accountability to each other.[63] Still, the MSUG, along with the other American organizations in Vietnam, sought to fill the gaps left by the French Cultural Mission.

The gaps were significant. At the end of the Geneva Conference, the French maintained control of the prestigious Ecole Française d'Extrême Orient (EFEO), which was moved from Hanoi to Saigon, the Alliance Française, the Society of Indochinese Studies, and cultural centers in Saigon, Dalat, Nha Trang, Da Nang, and Hue. Including primary, secondary, and higher education, about 350 French teachers and 10,000 students comprised the French cultural mission in Indochina. These numbers did not include French doctors and scientists working at the Grall Hospital, the Pasteur Institutes of Dalat, Nha Trang, and Saigon, and the Cancer Institute at Saigon.

The Americans were hard at work correcting this cultural imbalance. For example, USOM and the IRC wanted to coordinate support for a "popular university" in Saigon by increasing course offerings and training leaders for youth groups and sports clubs. They hoped to make the development of a Vietnamese university that was "adapted to the needs of the country" a priority over all other proposals. American officials thought they could "go outside the existing university setup of the Franco-Vietnamese University of Hanoi" and establish university faculties, which the existing Franco-Vietnamese one did not include. Such actions would be "advisable for political as well as other reasons and to do this through a private agency strengthens the political reasons in favor of this approach." If U.S. efforts constituted "no interference with the major cultural interests of the French," then "Franco-American cultural rivalry, of such great concern to the French," would be "minimized." The French insisted on keeping their influence over the existing faculties of law and arts and letters, but had not done much, and were not planning to do much, to extend their educational influence through the creation of higher schools for technical training. Claiming that it was not in the interest of the Vietnamese people to stop the French from teaching them "poetry, French and the Code Napoleon," the IRC wanted to do something about the "need and strong desire" among young Vietnamese for other studies. These needs could only be met by colleges or faculties for the study of agriculture, engineering, forestry, nutrition, sanitation, and social welfare. Whatever schools existed for such studies were "mostly French, of a secondary level and totally inadequate."[64]

Given the differing French and American views on Vietnamese needs, one of the biggest Franco-American battles for cultural control in South Vietnam occurred over education. The first skirmish began when American officials replaced the French Ecole Nationale d'Administration (ENA) with the U.S.-led National Institute of Administration (NIA). Installed at Dalat, the ENA was created in January 1953 by Jean-Jacques de Bresson to train administrative officials and was placed under a Vietnamese director assisted by a French counselor. Courses were taught half in French, half in Vietnamese. Diem had continued to use the French-trained bureaucracy but wanted to counterbalance it with American-trained graduates. The French were particularly annoyed because the advent of the NIA went against the November 18 Dulles–Mendès France agreements as well as the December 1954 Franco-Vietnamese cultural agreements and Franco-American accords, in which the United States agreed that the existing programs at the school were satisfactory and that the French should have predominant control over the training of Vietnamese officials.[65]

In December 1954, the French and South Vietnamese had reached a

number of cultural agreements that formed the basis for the French preservation of influence in South Vietnam. In a second series of meetings, this
time between the French and the Americans, French officials tried to "sell"
the French presence to their American counterparts. During the December
1954 meetings, Ely, Collins, and their subordinates defined Franco-American
policy on a number of issues, including public order, information and propaganda, education, and formation of administrative personnel. According
to Ely, the French and Americans should work together to ensure that South
Vietnam did not slip into isolation and neutralism, or worse, drift toward
communism. Ely, clearly playing to American myopia on the subject of communism, indicated that the French wanted to keep Vietnam turned toward
the West and urged American officials to remember that French was "*the*
language in Vietnam, that all the books were written in French, and that
Vietnamese teachers, priests, and many parents all spoke French."[66] During
the meetings, Collins affirmed that Washington respected France's cultural
influence and did not seek to replace France in Vietnam.

The Americans had thus tried to reassure the French on the issue of
training South Vietnamese officials during the negotiations. The Franco-
American working group charged with examining cultural questions arrived
at a number of agreements regarding the ENA, including the adaptation of
teaching to South Vietnam's character and needs but remaining open to external influence as it would be dangerous for Vietnam to focus only on its
own culture. The French and Americans also agreed that foreign languages should be studied, particularly English, but that French would remain
predominant; that technical and material aid from France and the United
States must go to existing structures to avoid an upending of the established
system; that the ENA would be moved from Dalat to Saigon; and that five
American instructors would be established at the school. The agreements
represented a Franco-American attempt to determine a common cultural
policy in Vietnam.

Despite these agreements, the December accords were ignored: the NIA
replaced the ENA in August 1955; the MSUG brought in thirty-five instead
of the contractual five professors; the NIA was moved to Saigon without any
discussion with the French; the chief adviser of the MSUG, Edward Weidner,
took control of the NIA even though the Vietnamese were theoretically in
charge; English was given an equal standing with French; and the center of
research and documentation at the NIA was directed entirely by MSUG professors, who would be giving advice to the principal Vietnamese ministers
in public functions. In the end, the majority of chairs at the NIA were given

to Americans, the courses were taught in English or Vietnamese, American professors ran the school, and the best Vietnamese students were sent to the United States for future training.[67] Although the NIA claimed it was simply providing services—such as improving the training of government officials and employees; helping organize the presidency, police, field administration, and local government; and offering instruction in public administration at a university level—the French were outraged. The inauguration of a new American university in Hue in November 1957 and plans for three more at Dalat, Nha Trang, and Can Tho that would be heavily influenced by the United States furthered French irritation.

The closing of the ENA convinced many French officials that the Americans wanted to take exclusive control of the training for future high functionaries. Americans in Saigon, who viewed the ENA as just another training school, and one with outdated programming at that, failed to understand why the French were so upset. But for the French, the ENA was the pinnacle of administrative training, which the best Vietnamese students attended. This time, Hoppenot and Secretary of State for the Associated States Robert Laforest urged Couve de Murville to lodge a formal protest to the State Department, which occurred in mid-October 1955 when Couve de Murville confronted Kenneth Young about the NIA and lack of cooperation between American and French services. Young claimed ignorance about the situation at first, but later defended American decisions such as assigning an importance to learning English and teaching the Vietnamese American-style administration—which of course undermined the ENA.[68] In December, Jacques Roux submitted a list of complaints to the U.S. ambassador to France. Not until late January 1956 did the State Department respond to the French Embassy in Washington with a memorandum and a note. In the memorandum, Edward Weidner, counselor of the MSUG, tried to avoid responsibility, claiming that the MSUG did not seek "to eliminate French influence or replace [the] French administrative system with an American one"; rather such decisions came from the Vietnamese themselves. Young made similar arguments in his note, stating that American teachers were not up to the task in secondary and superior teaching and they often had to use (French) interpreters to explain concepts to the Vietnamese. By this, the French were supposed to be appeased.[69]

Although American officials reassured the French that the United States had "no desire to take over" and that the MSUG "was not attempting to replace French culture" or "substitute the American administrative system for the French" but was simply acting "on the request of the South Vietnamese,"

American actions did not quite correspond with these declarations. The Quai d'Orsay continued to receive reports that contradicted American claims. According to French officials in South Vietnam, American professors continuously urged their students to complete their studies in the United States and emphasized the importance of "escaping the last of colonial influence." Early American successes in establishing the NIA, replacing French with English, and ensuring pro-American Vietnamese officials in the universities paved the way for further opportunities to imprint American culture and values on South Vietnam.[70]

And what of the South Vietnamese? For many, the West, whether the sun set in Paris or Washington, meant, in theory, an enlightened civilization that had much to offer. Thus the Vietnamese agreed to American modernization programs to rise into the ranks of the civilized. Vietnamese students in the United States studied liberal capitalism, or what the Americans referred to as modernization, as an answer to the country's problems.

American and South Vietnamese views were unacceptable to the French. According to the ever-raucous Hoppenot, France should "fight against the regression of spoken French, improve the formation of technical personnel, engineers, doctors, and professors, provide more French grants to South Vietnamese students, and increase Franco-Vietnamese contacts." Evident in Hoppenot's remarks was the concern that the French language was losing ground to English as France withdrew, leaving the Vietnamese with less opportunity to speak French. According to the director of the French Cultural Mission, Jean-Pierre Dannaud, the French language was dying out not because of a "nationalist, anticommunist, anticolonialist, clerical, Americanophile spirit," but because of "Vietnamese timidity and loss of speaking French habitually." The answer, Dannaud suggested, was to "organize more discussions, movie nights, and sports events to recapture the French language."[71]

Attempts by the French to maintain a cultural presence faced stiff resistance in the American and South Vietnamese press. Articles in newspapers and popular news magazines in the United States reinforced both American and South Vietnamese hostility to the French presence in Vietnam. A series of *Newsweek* essays in June 1955 stated that any American "sincerely devoted to the survival of South Vietnam as a free nation must be critical of French behavior here." What was needed was a "large scale cleaning out of the French—all of those who put the preservation of French influence ahead of building a solid anti-Communist independent state." The essay claimed that some French in Saigon gave the impression that "unless French influence remains dominant they do not care whether or not South Vietnam is swallowed by the reds," and that some went so far as to suggest that they had a better chance of "preserving their influence under the reds than under Diem."[72]

Despite such vitriol, the Americans attempted to work with the French in some cultural matters, and even made a few efforts to understand Vietnamese culture. For example, in 1954, two members of the EFEO published an encyclopedic work titled *Connaissance du Vietnam*. In October 1955, American officials began to organize an exposition of Indochinese arts in the Natural History Museum in D.C. to show the recent contributions of Vietnam in the domain of fine arts, applied arts, history, and archaeology. The organizers worked with the EFEO to borrow certain works. USOM had also tried to introduce Americans in Vietnam to Vietnamese culture through films, Vietnamese artists, nights of Vietnamese music, publications in the AVA's journal, and promotion of Vietnamese literature.[73] And, considering that everything was in French—textbooks, training manuals, public announcements, newspapers—the Americans were forced for most of the 1950s to find French translators to help with the monumental task of switching from French to English. But by and large, American cooperation with and recognition of the importance of other cultures was scarce.

Although French officials in Saigon desperately tried to continue their cultural mission, from 1954 to 1956 France witnessed a steady decline in the number of French books, journals, and newspapers imported by Vietnam; by 1956 these imports had been cut in half. Subsequently, French books and journals disappeared from the shop windows in Saigon, and France also lost control of the last French newspaper in Vietnam, *Le Journal d'Extrême Orient*. As English broadcasts became commonplace, France was also forced to sell its radio station, Radio France Asie, to South Vietnam in February 1956, and the French news service, Agence France-Presse, began to lose its edge as Anglo-Saxon agencies challenged its hegemony. Dannaud's belief that if France simply continued to "export professors and import peanuts, then South Vietnam would remain in the French orbit" did not seem to be bearing fruit.[74] In the cultural field, too, the United States had at least partially displaced France.

LOOKING BACK

Reflecting on the 1954–1956 period, it is clear that the French had originally sought American involvement in Vietnam after Geneva. By cooperating politically and establishing a common responsibility for Vietnam, France would avoid American criticism if a common policy in Vietnam failed and, at the same time, secure aid to the FEC. Urged by the French to become more involved, and faced with an increasingly powerful North Vietnam reinforced by the Soviets and Chinese, the United States increased its aid to South Vietnam. But eventually, the United States reconciled its anticommunism and anticolonialism to form a third force capable of escaping both French and communist control—this third force was Diem. Most French officials assumed Diem would be a transitional figure, contrary to what the Americans and Diem had planned. As more Americans began to arrive in Vietnam and Diem consolidated his power, France began to lose its military, political, and administrative presence.

With the evolution of the political situation in 1955, the French grip on Vietnam became ever-more tenuous. The primary cause of this disengagement was the South Vietnamese call for the complete withdrawal of the FEC by April 1956. Paris was aware that the Americans did not want to be associated with French policy in South Vietnam and speculated whether the Americans had suggested this course of action. French officials recognized that with the scheduled withdrawal of the FEC on April 26 and the disappearance of the high command, Paris needed to reevaluate the nature and extent of its responsibilities to the Geneva Accords. Accordingly, French officials agonized over whether to work with the United States or to achieve an independent policy. Paris recognized that Washington was attempting to push France aside in Vietnamese issues and wanted to either halt this tendency or try to restore some sort of Franco-Vietnamese working relationship. But the French had little leverage on the South Vietnamese, who stonewalled on negotiating unresolved Franco-Vietnamese issues. The Diem regime was confident because it could rely on the Americans. France was clearly hesitating between continuing its commitment to Vietnam and washing its hands of the whole affair. In the end, the French chose for the most part to disassociate themselves from South Vietnam, although they continued to fight to maintain their cultural presence.[75] Most important, both the South Vietnamese and American edging out of the French in political, military, and economic matters led the French to renounce their responsibility to the Geneva agreements as well as the 1956 elections.

In March 1956, French foreign minister Christian Pineau commented that "if Franco-American collaboration in Indochina existed, France and the United States would not be in the situation they now found themselves." The situation was not good. The Americans were determined to push ahead in South Vietnam without French advice or collaboration. According to the

French, the Americans would "noisily install themselves in others' buildings and import a very stereotypical American lifestyle." Imbued with superiority about their way of life, they "shock[ed]" the local populations, who tended to hide their own intense pride of Vietnamese culture under a "mask of affability and modesty." The "simple anticolonialism" of these Americans led them to try to "dismantle" all French positions. Moreover, all their directions came from Washington with little regard for local conditions.[76] As numerous French observers were fond of pointing out, there were a large number of people who knew something about Vietnam, but they happened to be French, which automatically disqualified them due to their "colonial contamination." According to one French observer who was on hand as the Americans were "taking over," what he found most shocking was the "total ignorance" of the Americans as well as their "marvelous self-confidence" in being able to guide the country, combined with a "total unwillingness" to speak to any of the departing French because they were "tainted." So, the Americans could not plead "universal ignorance" when it came to future snags in Vietnam; rather, the one source of knowledge that existed went unheeded.[77]

Hoppenot, whose mission in South Vietnam ended in December 1955, sent a remarkable document to the Quai d'Orsay detailing how the United States had "evicted" France in Indochina. Looking back, Hoppenot traced the evolution, from the French perspective, of how the Americans came to replace the French. Since 1945 he saw the United States gradually supplanting the French, "first through economic aid, followed by military control, and finally through a preponderant political influence in all councils and organizations of the Vietnamese government." According to Hoppenot, even though the State Department promised collaboration, "the policy of replacing the French was pursued by those in Saigon who had little responsibility to the Embassy." These groups did not hesitate to use anti-French propaganda to eliminate the French. The Pentagon, special services, and technical assistance groups were not content to replace the French at the posts circumstances forced them to abandon, but "tried to eliminate them from all areas." Hoppenot asserted that Ambassador Reinhardt had made little effort to work with the French, and that they were only indirectly informed of American actions, "never consulted or forewarned" about those that affected the French directly. Hoppenot believed that it was "the combination of American anticolonialism and anticommunism" that had led to France's displacement: France had seen NATO allies act as though the French presence in Vietnam "belonged to a closed era" and "any surviving remnants would not be tolerated except where the United States did not seek to replace

France." Thus, Hoppenot concluded that in Asia, after "paying the price of a hot war," France had become "one of the victims of the Cold War."[78]

The Americans had a different view. Dulles concluded that with respect to being caught between the old colonialism and the "new nationalism" in South Vietnam, "we have a clean base there now without the taint of colonialism. Dienbienphu was a blessing in disguise."[79] By the time Vice President Richard Nixon visited South Vietnam in early July 1956, signs of the ever-increasing American presence abounded. What the United States would do with this presence remained to be seen, but American success in replacing France in Vietnam led many French political leaders, especially the Gaullists, to reconsider the Franco-American alliance. Jacques Soustelle, a leading Gaullist and critic of the United States, wrote in an October 1956 *Foreign Affairs* article that it should not be a surprise that many Frenchmen were more hostile to South Vietnam and the United States than to North Vietnam and the USSR when "hostile acts" toward France by the South Vietnamese occurred at the instigation of the Americans. France, according to Soustelle, derived no benefit from the fact that it was an ally of Britain and the United States, and found itself "ousted even from the south of Indochina under conditions that lead an important part of French public opinion to suspect that the United States actively contributed to this result."[80] This "ousting" would set the Americans on an increasingly treacherous path in Vietnam.

PART 3

War by Other Means, 1956–1960

We're going to spend this war to death, deep-sea ports for ships and airfields for the biggest jets. And add to that the bridges and roads and so forth, and technical assistance for the government ministries so that taxes can be collected and budgets balanced, little Vietnam will be the most modern country in Asia. It'll have the infrastructure, you see. It'll go from the Middle Ages to the twentieth century in five years. It'll look like California.

—*Sydney Parade, in Ward Just's* A Dangerous Friend

7

Maintaining
a Presence

AS THEY WERE BEING "EVICTED" by the Americans in South Vietnam, the French struggled to redefine their relationship with Saigon and, at the same time, maintain a separate presence in North Vietnam. Paris found itself constantly trying to balance between Hanoi, Saigon, and Washington as it clung fiercely to one last bastion—a cultural presence in Vietnam. French officials faced major obstacles in this endeavor as the North Vietnamese, South Vietnamese, and Americans sought to replace the French at every level. Although by 1960 the French had disappeared from North Vietnam, they had made a surprising comeback in the South, and not just in the cultural domain. But this comeback had high costs. As they tried to maintain institutions in both the North and South, the French faced accusations on all sides of conspiring with the enemy.

DEALING WITH HANOI

Although South Vietnam occupied the primary place of importance in Franco-American relations, post-Geneva difficulties in the Western alliance also stemmed from questions of how to deal, or not deal, with Hanoi. The Pierre Mendès France–Pham Van Dong agreements between the French prime minister and North Vietnamese foreign minister of July 21, 1954, which guaranteed the exercise of private rights of the ten thousand French nationals still residing in the North and the continuance of French cultural establishments, ran into enormous obstacles. Jean Sainteny, who had been unofficially appointed as the French delegate general to the DRV in August 1954 by Mendès France, was charged with the almost impossible task of securing safeguards for French businesses and institutions.[1] Sainteny had attempted to mediate between Paris and Ho Chi Minh before the First Indochina War, and was recognized for his sympathy toward the North. His job was made even more difficult as a result of North Vietnamese discriminatory practices and interference with personnel that led to the loss of a great number of French commercial and industrial enterprises. In addition, Sainteny had to balance his negotiations with the DRV against increasing American hostility, since Washington fundamentally disagreed with Paris's policy toward North Vietnam. American officials protested what they viewed as a contradictory French policy; the French were attempting to preserve the *présence française* in South Vietnam while at the same time appointing the supposedly pro-DRV Sainteny as a French representative in Hanoi. The Eisenhower administration was particularly concerned about a possible French rapprochement with the DRV.[2]

French officials remained reluctant to forsake their cultural and economic presence in the North, believing that France should keep separate its policies in South and North Vietnam to allow more freedom of action. General Paul Ely, despite his opposition to Sainteny's appointment, concurred with the Quai d'Orsay that it should convince Washington that American interests would be served by Sainteny's mission. Paris could then avoid being accused of contributing to the DRV's progress. The Quai and Ely knew Sainteny's appointment had spurred rumors that the French would sell out Prime Minister Diem to retain economic and cultural ties with Vietnam when the North took over completely. They also recognized that both the North and South Vietnamese would view close coordination between Ely and Sainteny with suspicion. Ely advocated harmonizing actions with both Sainteny and the Eisenhower administration so that France could bring the United States around to the possibility of coexistence "both within Europe and Asia."[3]

In French circles the general feeling was that North Vietnam was not yet "an integral part of the communist orbit," and that the opportunity existed, however small, to keep North Vietnam out of Soviet and Chinese hands. The DRV, according to Sainteny, was much closer to the Soviets than to the Chinese as the North Vietnamese feared Chinese control, and Ho Chi Minh recognized the importance of keeping an "emergency exit" toward France and the West open. Sainteny thus advocated maintaining relations with the North in the event that Chinese control became too oppressive and Hanoi decided to turn toward the West.[4] In the meantime, Sainteny disdained what he called "heavy-handed American tactics" that did not "sit well" with most observers and was convinced that the Eisenhower administration planned "to evict France from Vietnam." One French observer in South Vietnam saw the Americans maneuvering in Asia the way "elephants would in a China shop. Despite their wealth, they will finish by being detested everywhere."[5]

Economic issues in the North also weighed heavily on the French. One problem was the International Consultative Cooperation Committee, which had been created to ensure an embargo of strategic products destined for communist bloc countries. South Vietnam, Cambodia, and Laos could join the committee or could promise to uphold the embargo without joining. The bigger issue was North Vietnam. An embargo on North Vietnam would cause French products and thus French companies to suffer. The French calculated the best they could hope for from the Americans and British was that they would allow certain needed items for French enterprises through the embargo. The Quai concluded that if it were "forced" by its allies to uphold an embargo against North Vietnam, then it would not be able to continue its current policy and would renounce its presence in the North. French diplomats worked hard to persuade the State Department and Foreign Office that the conditions applied to China should not be applied to North Vietnam as this was a "totally unique situation," and that there were "advantages" to a continued presence of French industries and cultural and humanitarian agencies in the North. Still, they recognized that the North was continuing to build up its forces with Chinese help, and that they would probably have to go along with the embargo, which was one of the essential elements of American policy in the Far East.[6]

The biggest concern in Paris was that the DRV would recommence hostilities if France was perceived as violating Geneva. Hanoi worried that France was becoming increasingly tied to American policy vis-à-vis Vietnam. A different fear circulated in Washington. Despite the agreement between Mendès France and Secretary of State John Foster Dulles in November 1954 that the Sainteny mission would become an official one and that the United States would not discriminate against French who stayed in the North, the Americans viewed French attempts to stay in North Vietnam with deep suspicion. Sainteny's mission in the North became official on December 16 when he was recognized by the DRV as the French delegate general. According to high-level American officials, the mission was a major instrument of the French policy to "reach a modus vivendi" with Ho Chi Minh's government to ensure the security of French cultural and economic interests in the North, "establish a basis for a similar modus vivendi" in the South should the DRV take over, and "break ground for a general coexistence policy with [the communist] Orbit." Remarks such as former president Vincent Auriol's claim that the North Vietnamese were "sure to win the 1956 elections" and that the "only chance" for France resided in the strict application of the Geneva agreement served as further proof of French betrayal of the West.[7]

The French were undoubtedly sending mixed signals, in part because they were confused as to which mission—North or South—offered the greatest prospects for successfully maintaining a French presence. In an internal memorandum, Quai officials tried to make sense of Ely and Sainteny's respective missions. Ely wanted an end to the Sainteny mission, or at least the removal of Sainteny, and recommended "sticking with the Americans" while trying to persuade them Diem was "not the best horse." Ely believed that to safeguard France's position in Southeast Asia it was better to "run the risk of losing the game with the U.S. at our side than to run the risk of winning at the price of a policy that will bring down American reprobation." He felt that Sainteny's mission was making his own job impossible, since both the South Vietnamese and Americans thought France was playing a "double game." In contrast, Sainteny wanted a South Vietnamese government of "concurrence," neither antagonistic nor collaborationist with the North, and suggested various alternatives to Diem, who would be less antagonistic toward the North. The only point Ely and Sainteny agreed on was that France should keep a significant FEC presence. The Quai adopted a wait-and-see approach, recommending that if Ely made the most progress in safeguarding French interests he should stay, but if Sainteny did, then Ely should be recalled.[8] This document illustrates how divided France was on what policy to pursue.

The Franco-American alliance was also divided, as a February 1955 *Newsweek* article noted. France was in the throes of a government crisis, and Henri Bonnet, now retired ambassador and envoy to the United States, represented France rather than a foreign minister at a Manila Pact meeting six months after the Southeast Asia Collective Defense Treaty had been signed. The meeting was not productive. As the Manila Pact conference opened in late February the United States and France were locked in a bitter wrangle over their respective policies in Indochina. According to *Newsweek*, "the French are determined to make a deal with the Communists for the preservation of what they like to call France's 'economic and cultural presence' in North Vietnam. This 'presence' consists of important French owned industries, including coal mines and cement and textile plants in the Haiphong area."[9]

Part of the problem in negotiating with the Americans and North Vietnamese was the issue of American equipment remaining in North Vietnam. The French were once again stuck between Hanoi and Washington. U.S. officials would be angry if the material was not evacuated, thus the French needed to make such an evacuation a sine qua non of negotiations with the DRV regarding other issues. But the Americans were annoyed that, contrary to their earlier categorical assurances, the French would remove U.S.-financed equipment from Tonkin only if the evacuation "does not provoke any grave incident." USOM officials pushed for high-level pressure to be brought to bear on the French to reconcile the opposing objectives of the Sainteny mission and the French military with respect to the disposition of the Haiphong facilities. The French did begin to cautiously remove equipment, evaluating the North Vietnamese response as they went.[10]

Trying to counter American hostility, French officials notified Washington and Saigon that preserving a presence in North Vietnam would keep communications open between Hanoi and the West and would allow France to monitor North Vietnamese activities, but Washington periodically accused France of "conspiring with North Vietnam." The Americans continued to believe that the Mendès France government was hedging its bets and preparing to make a deal with Ho Chi Minh at Diem's expense to preserve French interests in the North. The British tended to share American fears. British ambassador in Saigon Sir Hugh Stephenson noted the apparent diversity of directives between those of Ely and those of Sainteny, stating that France is "speaking with two voices." Such claims were warranted. In a memorandum prepared for Edgar Faure at the moment of his investiture as premier, Mendès France again emphasized that French businesses in the North "should be maintained" but recognized the need for "close cooperation with the United States" since France "can't risk a serious dispute with the American government in bringing to South Vietnam a policy independent of the United States."[11] The French thus held the vain hope that they would be able to accommodate both sides.

But continued relations with the DRV made France's international position appear too pro-communist in Washington's eyes. French ambassador Maurice Couve de Murville reported to the Quai on State Department concerns that French plans for North Vietnam would weaken Franco-American cooperation in the South. The Americans emphasized the happy relationship between U.S. special representative to Vietnam J. Lawton Collins and Ely, and wanted such a policy of cooperation to continue "at all costs." The point for the Americans was that France was "threatening this cooperation through its negotiations with the North," something that could have "serious repercussions in Congress."[12] Indeed, French entrepreneurs in the North were concerned when American "experts" appeared at their factories asking French business owners about industrialization and capacity of production. French owners wondered whether they should worry about American reprisals for doing business in the North. In addition, the French encountered

serious opposition from the American Embassy regarding proposed Franco–
North Vietnamese businesses. According to one U.S. official, the United
States was primarily concerned with the political and psychological aspects
of this issue, seeing it as a contradiction to French policy in South Vietnam.
The DRV would get a boost in prestige if the joint businesses went ahead.
In particular, such a move, according to French ambassador to Britain René
Massigli, could create difficulties in Franco-American relations as a result
of Congressional and public opinion. In any case, Washington was insisting that any American equipment in these businesses be evacuated from the
North, and that the U.S. government would attempt to punish such businesses by denying them favorable trade agreements. The French pointed out that
in keeping with the Geneva Accords and the agreements between Mendès
France and Pham Van Dong, the DRV could have confiscated French interests and was actually choosing to be more cooperative.[13]

The biggest Franco-American fight on this issue occurred over the Société Française des Charbonnages du Tonkin, a large French-owned mining
company in the North, which the French desperately tried to keep running.
The Americans, however, were categorically opposed to any French government links with the entity because that would mean "official collaboration"
of the French government with Hanoi. Collins in particular wanted to be
sure that American aid and material, especially aid that went to Charbonnages, would not be used by the DRV. From French documentation, it appears fairly clear that the French were simply trying to maintain an economic
presence in North Vietnam. Paris hoped to apply the new communist policy
of "peaceful coexistence" to French holdings in that region.[14] Such hopes
faltered in the face of American and North Vietnamese animosity.

The parallels between Sainteny's and Ely's respective missions are most
telling. Both men were disillusioned by the end of their missions, in part
because of the contradictory nature of the Quai's policy. Both accepted that
their task was to preserve French interests, and both experienced incredible
frustration because of their untenable positions of trying to balance against
each other, the Quai, American officials in Vietnam, Washington, Hanoi,
and Saigon.

Ely accepted his government's decision that it was politically desirable
and financially necessary to work with the Americans, but he continued to
criticize Sainteny's mission and sympathy toward Hanoi. Just as Sainteny
grumbled that he was not kept informed about French policy in the South
and Ely's actions, Ely complained that he was completely "out of the loop"
with respect to French policy toward the North and Sainteny's actions and

instructions, and that he got most of his information through the press. He also noted that the risk of the Americans replacing the French in cultural and economic domains had increased, and that it was unlikely French business interests in Haiphong could be preserved because of this "dual policy" that "ruined rather than preserved" French interests.[15]

Sainteny remained unenthusiastic about his mission's chances for success, although he recognized that a continued French presence could be a very effective obstacle against communism. He wrote to the prime minister that it was entirely Faure's decision as to whether French enterprises should try to stay in the North, but warned him that the Americans were very vocal and even threatening in their efforts to dissuade France from doing so. He suggested trying to decide as quickly as possible the French attitude toward the DRV, the maintenance or departure of French persons established in North Vietnam, proper indemnization for those who left, guarantees for those who stayed, and positions to try to keep. Sainteny was particularly annoyed how the mission in the North was always referred to as the "Sainteny Mission" or the "Sainteny Policy"; he wanted such references done away with so that the mission would be referred to as the general delegation of the French government.

Despite his growing irritation, Sainteny valiantly tried to keep a French presence in the North, arguing that the French presence in Hanoi "was more effective than several divisions of the South Vietnamese army being trained by the Americans." His biggest concern remained the virulent American campaign against any French efforts to negotiate with the North, and that Paris's "allies rather than its adversaries would without hesitation crush any accord reached with Hanoi." Faure had reassured the Eisenhower administration that France would "not play a double game in Vietnam," following one policy in the South and another in the North, but most American officials doubted his sincerity.[16] What the Americans tended to forget was how many French interests existed in both North and South Vietnam.

Of course the French did not maintain their interests in the North. According to a mid-April 1955 CIA report, France considered its efforts to maintain installations in North Vietnam "a closed book." The Charbonnages du Tonkin had completed arrangements to sell its plant and equipment to the DRV, with all other French enterprises in North Vietnam expected to follow suit. In addition, in mid-May the last French soldier left North Vietnam. Militarily, France was gone. But, the French stepped up their efforts to ensure their cultural influence in North Vietnamese territory.[17] Culturally, according to Sainteny in an interview with Radio Lausanne, France still remained "present" in North Vietnam. As proof, Sainteny pointed to the Pasteur and Cancer Institutes, the Ecole Française d'Extrême Orient (EFEO), clinics, the 575 French students who still attended Albert Sarraut High School as well as 20 French professors and 1,800 Vietnamese students, and a Franco-Vietnamese hospital directed by a French professor who gave medical courses at the Hanoi School of Medicine. Still, Sainteny noted his unhappiness with the lack of instructions from the Quai, claiming he was "completely isolated" without "direction or information." For example, after waiting "in vain" for a debriefing of the talks with Dulles and British foreign minister Harold Macmillan in May, Sainteny went so far as to threaten to re-sign unless he received clear instructions. In response, French foreign min-ister Antoine Pinay informed him that the French, Americans, and British had agreed to a "common policy," which included complete support of Diem (especially since Congress would cut off aid if Diem was ousted), combating all antiwestern propaganda, and deciding at what level the FEC should be maintained.[18] Nothing in this common policy dealt with preserving French interests in the North or accommodating Hanoi.

After a series of Franco–North Vietnamese meetings in August 1955 to determine cultural affairs, especially the statute of the EFEO and the place of French language in Vietnamese establishments, Sainteny believed that France had succeeded in "safeguarding its cultural and economic presence" and "avoiding a total rupture" with the North; therefore, France had accom-plished its mission. But the more important long-term goal of maintaining a French presence in Southeast Asia and occupying a "favorable position at the moment when East-West détente is achieved," which was why Sainteny had accepted the mission to return to North Vietnam in the first place and had "made sacrifices and compromises despite the incomprehension of France's allies," seemed much more difficult to achieve. Sainteny feared that all the French sacrifices would come to naught unless France made a gesture of goodwill toward the DRV.

This gesture should be the installation in Paris of a diplomatic repre-sentation of the DRV. Sainteny's reasoning was that after Ho Chi Minh's "spectacular and productive voyage" to Beijing and Moscow, only a "mag-nanimous gesture" would "correct" the DRV's current leaning toward the communist bloc. Following such a move, France should conclude commer-cial and financial accords and arrange economic and cultural exchanges. Only if France took these actions would his return to Hanoi be justified, otherwise it would be "totally useless."[19] Sainteny had prepared a letter agree-ing to the appointment of a personal delegate by Ho Chi Minh in Paris in summer 1955, but Faure never signed the letter, fearing South Vietnamese and American reactions to the arrival of a DRV representative in France. Indeed, the Americans were busy cutting all ties with the North, including evacuating all staff and closing down the U.S. consulate and remaining buildings. Faure allowed only a commercial attaché instead, and Paris reminded the DRV that the French delegation in Hanoi and North Vietnamese commercial representation in Paris did not imply normal diplomatic relations.[20] North Vietnamese officials retaliated by refusing French entry visas, starting domestic help strikes, and attempting to bribe or coerce French military personnel for espionage purposes. This period represented the lowest point yet in Franco–North Vietnamese relations, as Hanoi was bitterly disappointed in the failure of official representation in Paris.

The North continued to press the issue, with the result that French foreign minister Christian Pineau and Sainteny in spring 1956 seriously considered how to bring about a reciprocal delegation. Subsequently, the French and North Vietnamese proceeded some way in negotiations before deadlocking. The North insisted on an official delegation with all attendant rights—such as diplomatic immunity, a twenty-person delegation, and the head designated as an official delegate general—whereas Pineau indicated that absolute reciprocity was unlikely and would only agree to a delegation with commercial and cultural affiliation. Hanoi tried to use cultural leverage, promising that French cultural institutions could stay in North Vietnam and that the DRV would work to resolve points of contention—such as reopening the Albert Sarraut High School, creating a closer association with the Cancer and Pasteur Institutes, allowing French films into the North, and opening a French library and news press. Sainteny tried to mediate by suggesting more informal missions to France and North Vietnam, but Hanoi wanted an official delegation.[21]

Another issue causing increased tensions between Paris and Hanoi was the FEC's disappearance. When Sainteny met with Ung Van Khiem (vice minister of foreign affairs), Pham Van Dong, and Ho Chi Minh, the three Vietnamese made it clear to Sainteny that even though the FEC was withdrawing and South Vietnam claimed it was not accountable to the accords, France was "not excused from its obligations to Geneva." Khiem also took the opportunity to insist again on a reciprocal North Vietnamese delegation in Paris. Hanoi clearly viewed the FEC's withdrawal as a betrayal and abdication of French responsibilities. In fact, Sainteny transmitted a letter to Paris in which Pham Van Dong reminded Pineau of article 27 of the cease-fire, which stated that "the signatories and their successors will be held accountable to the provisions of the accord." Hanoi demanded with increasing venom that France fulfill its obligations.[22]

Sainteny continued to deplore France's "missed chance" after Geneva. He fondly remembered when Indian prime minister Nehru had given a reception in October of 1954 and reserved the place of honor for the representative of France in Hanoi. He recognized that the realists in Hanoi had not gotten rid of France completely for fear of "economic asphyxiation," but he insisted that France "could and should have established normal relations with the North," especially in economic and cultural matters to safeguard French interests. About the only French success was the agreement to bring French films back to the North, providing they did not offend the "moralizing North Vietnamese regime."[23]

An interesting parallel can be drawn here—just as the United States replaced France in South Vietnam, the USSR, with some help from other communist powers, was busy replacing the Gallic nation in the North. For example, at the time of Sainteny's plaintive letter, the USSR had already given 40 million rubles for economic assistance and development and sent industrial equipment, 275 experts, goods, and food to North Vietnam. The Russians put into operation five industrial enterprises, including a tin mining and processing factory, a tea factory, a hydroelectric power station, and two lines of electricity transmission. They organized geological expeditions for wolfram, zinc, lead, uranium, and other deposits, modernized the port of Haiphong and North Vietnamese hospitals, arranged the production of cement and coal mining, and helped develop the army. And Moscow invited 249 Vietnamese specialists to the Soviet Union for further training.[24] Although the Americans were quick to criticize the heavy-handed communist presence in the North, accusing the DRV, and thus Moscow, of iron-fisted party control in every field including administration, justice, police, army, religion, schools, industry, and agriculture, the United States was attempting to assert its own form of control south of the seventeenth parallel.

According to Jacques Soustelle, the rupture with the North could have been justified if it had been "counterbalanced by a favorable French position in the South," which was not the case. Franco–North Vietnamese tension culminated with the French counselor at Hanoi and the economic, cultural, consular, and press attachés leaving in 1956. Even in late 1956 Sainteny was still convinced that a French presence was needed in the North; other officials also thought that France could still play an important role in both North and South Vietnam, especially as reunification moved forward, helping ensure a reunification without the "inhumane regime" of the North or the "dictatorial one" in the South.[25]

Paris, however, was unwilling to try any longer to maintain a serious presence in the North, a fact made clear by France's enthusiastic support of South Vietnam's attempt to enter the UN in 1957. The UN incident further soured Franco–North Vietnamese relations, with Ung Van Khiem violently protesting French support of South Vietnam's entry. The DRV was equally concerned about its major ally: in response to the resolution proposing the entries of South Vietnam and South Korea into the UN, the Soviet Union recommended South Vietnam, South Korea, North Vietnam, and North Korea all enter, which would mean de facto recognition of two Vietnamese states. Hanoi had not been consulted before Moscow made this move, and Pham Van Dong protested Moscow's actions, leading the Soviets to back down from their proposal. If South and North Vietnam had been accepted into the UN it would have been not only the consecration of Vietnam's division but also a blatant violation of the Geneva Accords. Moreover, the South Vietnamese government had agreed at the Bandung Conference final communiqué of April 24, 1955, that reunification would be a required condition for Vietnam to become a member of the UN. The DRV took French support of South Vietnam's entry as a clear indication of their turn toward Saigon.[26]

Indeed, as of April 1957 it was clear France had no hope left that North Vietnam would indemnify private French interests that had been appropriated after Geneva. Another problem was Hanoi's refusal to allow any more searches for French missing in action because the Saigon government would not allow the North to do searches in the South. The Albert Sarraut High School reopened its doors as a lay mission; the Cancer Institute was controlled entirely by the Vietnamese, as was the Pasteur Institute; and the Saint Paul Hospital functioned under one French doctor. The library and museum of the EFEO were under delicate negotiations since Saigon did not want to "see them pass under Hanoi's influence."[27] Sainteny left Hanoi in early April 1957, a sad and bitter man. His replacement, Jean-Baptiste Georges-Picot, was a diplomat of much lesser standing.

HANOI'S DIPLOMATIC AND PROPAGANDA CAMPAIGNS

As the French experienced the familiar sensation of being replaced, they, along with the Americans, had another concern vis-à-vis Hanoi: the DRV's ongoing diplomatic and propaganda campaigns. According to a CIA intelligence report, a discernable buildup of emphasis on "peaceful means" of uniting the DRV and the South and a downplaying of the threat of military force had been observed in communist propaganda since the summer of 1955, when literature signed by North Vietnam's "National United Front" was first distributed. The "peaceful unification" line was first announced by Chinese foreign minister Zhou Enlai in June, but it appeared to have taken a period of "selling" within the DRV before it was adopted in September.

Paris and Washington scrambled to respond to the North Vietnamese diplomatic campaign. The United States Information Agency (USIA) recognized that the DRV would continue to emphasize the need for a peaceful settlement of the Vietnam question as well as the need, in the meantime, for an exchange of political, economic, and cultural missions. Covertly, the DRV would concentrate on infiltrating key organizations in the South. The Vietnamese Fatherland Front was created in fall 1955 for the express purpose of rallying and holding public support; Soviet technicians assisted by installing broadcast relay systems in key provinces in the North. The DRV's most widely used media for propaganda purposes were radio, pamphlets, and postcards, in that order. In addition, since January 1956, Hanoi reported, the Motion Picture Service of North Vietnam had produced four newsreels per month and two instructional films every three months. The DRV also began its first mobile exhibition—interestingly enough on the Vietnamese Catholic Church, demonstrating freedom of worship in North Vietnam. Other innovations of 1956 included the introduction of recreation centers and libraries at key industrial and mining sites, the exchange of Catholic delegations with Soviet satellite countries, and the use of medical teams sent from the Soviet Union.[28]

North Vietnamese propaganda included claims that the South Vietnamese made "children's flesh into pie," that they had "nothing to eat during Tet" (traditional celebrations of the lunar new year), that Diem "lost the fight against the various sects and was forced to flee the country," and that South Vietnam had experienced "failures at the hands of a corrupt government" while North Vietnam had "many successes."[29] Both French and American officials worried about the negative effects of such propaganda in South Vietnam and feared that their own propaganda was not reaching the North. French and British newsmen and members of the ICC noted that the three main foreign stations in North Vietnam were Radio Saigon, Voice of America (VOA), and the British Broadcasting Corporation (BBC), and that the North Vietnamese favored the VOA and BBC over Radio Saigon.[30]

More subtle propaganda attempts included the DRV decision to allow a mild opposition press from 1956 to 1957 in accordance with the

"One Hundred Flowers Blooming" policy, which also existed in China. "One Hundred Flowers Blooming" referred to a statement by Karl Marx that many flowers had pleasant scents but no one flower had all of them—there were several roads to communism with no one system having a monopoly on it. The North continued its propaganda blitz in early 1958 with its "Spring is Triumphant, but Winter Will Surely Return" campaign, emphasizing that peace existed for the moment but that hard times would surely return given the nature of the Saigon regime. The DRV in 1958 maintained propaganda outlets in Rangoon, New Delhi, and Paris, which distributed literature in French and English throughout much of the western world and Asia.

The first "coming out" of North Vietnamese diplomacy had occurred at Geneva, but the delegation led by Pham Van Dong had looked more like an adjunct to the Chinese communist delegation than a nationalist one. During Bandung, the DRV made its second appearance, but again was completely overshadowed by the formidable presence of internationally known Asian figures such as Nehru, Zhou Enlai, and Filipino diplomat General Carlos Romulo. Moreover, the North Vietnamese were under a cloud because the Laotian government had accused them of aiding and abetting the activities of the Pathet Lao. Even more humiliating was that negotiations on this issue were carried out not between Laos and North Vietnam but between Laos, North Vietnam, and China. The agreement that emerged constituted the first international treaty outside the Geneva cease-fire signed by the DRV and a noncommunist nation. The DRV had hoped to be recognized as the sole legal government at least by neutralist countries as a result, but was bitterly disappointed on that score. Not a single Asian country outside the communist bloc granted it full recognition, and relations with non-Asian countries outside the Soviet bloc had declined. France continued to maintain a delegate general in Hanoi, but commercial exchange was very limited. The DRV thus remained isolated diplomatically. A Canadian observer remarked, "There never were as many white faces in Hanoi under French colonial rule as there are now under the Vietminh." The faces no longer belonged to the colonialists but to the Russian, East German, Czechoslovakian, Polish, and other "advisers."[31]

As early as February 1955 the DRV had proposed restoration of normal relations for post offices, roads, railways, and air and sea traffic between North and South Vietnam, thus launching the first volley in a series of propaganda and diplomatic initiatives aimed at implementing the Geneva Accords. Hanoi recommended in 1958 when Pham Van Dong sent a letter to Diem proposing the "organization of general elections, free circulation between zones, bilateral reduction of armed forces in the North and South, reestablishment of relations between North and South beginning with commercial exchanges, and a meeting of Northern and Southern officials" to discuss these issues. Dong also deplored SEATO and blamed the failure of peace and reunification on the "policy of intervention of American imperialism," which led to additional military personnel and war materials in South Vietnam, and transformed South Vietnam into "a military base of American aggression in Southeast Asia." He noted that the "American imperialists' policy of military support is linked with their economic and political control of South Vietnam," and that South Vietnam "cannot join a military alliance as per the Geneva Accords." Diem agreed to consider the proposal but had a list of six demands designed to be unacceptable to Hanoi. These were that the North (1) allow 92,319 people and 1,995 families who had asked to leave for the South to do so; (2) reduce the North Vietnamese military to the same level as that of the South; (3) renounce terrorism, assassination, and sabotage; (4) stop economic monopoly in the North and allow people to work freely; (5) allow free press; and (6) allow civil rights and better conditions. Even so, the dialogue between Hanoi and Saigon continued.

Hanoi's actions indicated its commitment to a last-ditch effort to start negotiations with the South before turning to subversion. Hanoi also sent the letter to Pineau, and North Vietnamese officials cherished the hope that the French would become more involved as a signatory to the Geneva Accords. The French found the letter interesting as it implied a weakening of the North Vietnamese position on French responsibilities to the accords. Moreover, the North had "backed away" from general elections or consultations but simply wanted a discussion to create the "necessary conditions" for elections. On April 1, Pineau decided he would have to do more than acknowledge receipt of the letter, but in his response he simply reminded Dong that France no longer had any obligations to the Geneva Accords, and that there was therefore nothing France could do. A month later, Dong sent another letter to Paris, but the French did not respond. And in late December, Dong, in a final attempt at negotiations, sent a letter to Saigon underscoring South Vietnam's economic, social, and political difficulties, the rearmament of South Vietnam, and American imperialism. He recommended trying to resolve these problems in face-to-face meetings, suggesting as an agenda discussions of no military alliances, reduction of personnel and military budgets, economic trade, no more propaganda, and normal circulation of cultural, scientific, economic, and sportive associations.[32]

North Vietnamese propaganda appeared to be playing well enough to concern French officials. For example, associations of doctors, rice planters, professors, and other groups in the North sent letters to the corresponding associations in the South to organize an exchange. When there was no response, the Northerners commented on the sad fact that the Southerners must be "under the oppression of the Americano-Diemish clique." French officials in the South suggested that perhaps the Diem regime should begin some propaganda of its own, inviting northern Boy Scouts, schoolchildren, artists, football players, and workers to the South.[33]

In general, Paris continued its status quo policy toward the North, much to Counselor Georges-Picot's despair. He argued that it was critical that France maintain direct intelligence on the North and that French officials in the South could not possibly know what was occurring in the DRV. Georges-Picot also continued to attempt a rapprochement with Hanoi, but was quickly crushed by the Foreign Ministry. When Georges-Picot queried the Quai d'Orsay about French participation in a parade for the "Vietnamese Union for Peace and Unity and for Friendship with France" in commemoration of Ho Chi Minh's birthday, Pineau quickly announced he was opposed because France did not have normal diplomatic relations with Vietnam.[34]

In 1959 the DRV increased its propaganda and diplomatic efforts. Demonstrations for unification of North and South became larger and more numerous. In a brilliant propaganda move, Hanoi asked the ICC to request that the Diem regime allow government contact between the North and South so people from both sides could see their families during Tet. The minister of national education suggested to his South Vietnamese counterpart "exchanges of cultural information for professors and students." A declaration of the Central Committee of the North Vietnam Communist Party in Hanoi signaled the need to "liberate" the South and reunify Vietnam. And on the fifth anniversary of the Geneva Accords, the DRV began a massive propaganda campaign. They launched the campaign at an African-Asian meeting in Cairo, where the permanent secretariat of the Council of Solidarity of African-Asian Peoples announced that July 19 would henceforth be considered the "Day of Vietnam" and would be celebrated in all countries that recognized North Vietnam as the only legitimate government of the entire country. French observers in Hanoi estimated a crowd of 150,000 people, but noted a decided lack of enthusiasm.

From this point forward, Hanoi emphasized the bad faith of the South Vietnamese government and its unquestioning obedience to the Americans. The North Vietnamese population was regularly mobilized for meetings and demonstrations, one of which ended up in front of the ICC's office. Hanoi even created a stamp depicting a peace column and dove stretching across the Ben Hai river, with a letter containing the words "Enslaved compatriots of the South" in the beak of the dove. The DRV produced a film entitled *Only One River*, which developed the story of two youths residing on separate sides of the Ben Hai river who could not marry because Diem refused to allow them to see each other. Hanoi, with strong Soviet and Chinese support, also called on twenty-one Afro-Asian countries to support the battle for reunification. It was clear that the DRV was trying to officially restart the problem of reunification in the diplomatic arena and that it only reluctantly gave up hope on political reunification as specified by the Geneva Accords.[35]

When all of these attempts came to naught, the DRV became much more aggressive in its attacks on Diem, the United States, and the ICC, but less aggressive in blaming France for the current situation. Pham Van Dong, in an interview with a British journalist in 1960, declared the United States "Public enemy number one," and deplored the fact that French influence in all domains was fading as American influence ascended. French minister to the North Albert Chambon also reported later in the year that the North Vietnamese realized the French appreciated Vietnamese civilization, and that the influence of French professors in the high schools as well as French missionaries, doctors, and businessmen would be felt much longer than the French currently believed. A May 26, 1960, article in *Le Figaro* ran in the Hanoi-controlled newspaper *Nhan Dan*, claiming that foreign observers residing in Saigon were unanimous in recognizing that Diem's prestige continued to "diminish day by day" and that Diem's army of 150,000 was "maintained entirely by American aid." Even though he had one of the best-equipped and best-trained armies in the world, it was "absolutely not up to the task in the face of popular opposition."[36]

In an insightful letter to his superiors at the Quai, Chambon reflected on the situation south and north of the seventeenth parallel. According to Chambon, France was poised to play a "cardinal role between the adversarial North and South" as Hanoi stepped up its campaign against the Diem regime and the increasing amounts of American personnel and arms arriving in Saigon. He argued that the disorder in the former French states was getting worse as U.S. credibility, which was never strong, was "frittered away by American awkwardness and incomprehension of Vietnamese psychology." France should thus think about how it should use its influence to preserve the situation. For example, Chambon favored taking advantage of the Sino-

Russian split that had become obvious by 1959. Chambon recognized that the Soviet faction had a tendency to conciliate and to achieve unification by peaceful means, but that the pro-Chinese faction saw "plentiful evidence of the failure of peaceful means" in the past six years and wanted action. It was this extremist wing that was in the ascendancy, evidenced by Truong Chinh's rise to power in the DRV. Regarding French policy, France could be doing useful work if it tried to "reinforce the more moderate faction." France therefore should work carefully "not to push North Vietnam into the arms of China." If France adopted a rigid position and refused to grant concessions, it would bring to power a group of men whose very clear purpose was "to chase the West from Southeast Asia." However, those who wanted a more moderate approach to South Vietnam would like a more liberal regime than the Diem one. If France tried to "push this avenue" it would end up with a less hostile regime but one that was more likely to be "evicted."[37]

Chambon saw France as the "only element" that could negotiate between the two parties because it was well placed on both sides to play this role and, as paradoxical as it seems, French credit was not "less grand in Hanoi than in Saigon." The "political failure of Diem" and the "moral failure of the socialist experience in the North" permitted France, six years after Geneva, to reestablish in the Indochinese peninsula a position that a few years before had been "much more compromised" than that of their allies. Chambon thus urged the Quai to ask the United States to help France avoid putting into place a pro-Chinese wing in the North. Chambon's thinking demonstrated French willingness to play a major role in negotiations between the two countries, and was perhaps even the precursor to the neutralization path French president Charles de Gaulle started to advocate a few years later.[38]

Chambon's letter had an impact on Foreign Ministry officials, who had clearly been thinking along similar lines and agreed that the confusion and instability currently reigning on the Indochinese peninsula appeared at a moment where American credibility was waning. This chaos created a favorable climate at the local level for "all sorts of intrigues," and, on the international level, "diverging positions were being taken on the part of the western allies as the communist powers benefited." In this general political context, it appeared that the military policy followed by the United States directly opposed French policy in the region. This state of affairs was "not new." Since 1955, the United States, in its attempt to assume "the leadership" of the three states of South Vietnam, Cambodia, and Laos, never consented except with great reluctance to share influence with its allies, most notably France.[39]

France had tried to preserve its influence in North Vietnam without imperiling more significant interests in South Vietnam or aggravating the United States, but such a policy was untenable. With their lack of interest in installing an official DRV mission in Paris and their inability to pressure the South Vietnamese to begin consultations for elections, French relations with the DRV quickly soured. The North Vietnamese themselves later saw as one of their major failings their lack of foresight that the *présence française* in Vietnam would diminish so quickly. At the time, they blamed the French for choosing Diem and the Americans.

The French did make tiny strides in rebuilding a diplomatic presence north of the seventeenth parallel at the end of the decade, and French observers continued to report on DRV activities. According to Chambon, by 1960 reunification of the country had become the North's biggest goal. Since peaceful means had not resulted in reunification, the DRV was ready to try more violent tactics. DRV representatives and elements in the South who were disgusted with the Diem regime formed the National Front for the Liberation of Southern Vietnam (NLF) on December 20, 1960. The NLF would resort to various forms of subversion in its attempt to bring down the Diem government. As a result, North Vietnamese cultural initiatives and propaganda began to decline. The propaganda that continued focused almost entirely on South Vietnam becoming an American "colony." Hanoi continued to send dozens of letters of protest to the ICC regarding U.S violations of the Geneva Accords, and in particular, the reinforcement of American personnel. Paris thus feared that the day of reckoning between North and South Vietnam was fast approaching.[40]

The amount of work the French put into keeping a presence in North Vietnam was astounding. Perhaps the Americans' biggest unintended victory against North Vietnam was forcing France to choose between the Atlantic alliance and its interests in North Vietnam. The Eisenhower administration thus eliminated what could have been a powerful French political presence in the North. Such a presence might have served as a successful counterweight to American influence in the South and helped create conditions for a much earlier reunification than the one that would finally occur in 1975. The French came quite close to forsaking the Diem regime and focusing their efforts on maintaining a presence in North Vietnam, which would have greatly complicated matters for the Eisenhower administration. If they had kept their economic and cultural interests in the North, French leaders would have been more interested in implementing the Geneva Accords. In addition, given France's difficulties with the Diem regime and diminishing presence in the South, a rapprochement with Ho Chi Minh, along the lines Sainteny envisioned, could have occurred. The result? Eisenhower officials would have faced less liberty of action vis-à-vis the two Vietnams and more difficulties in ignoring the Geneva Accords.

HOLDING ON IN SOUTH VIETNAM

But the French did not maintain a presence in the North. Instead, they gambled on maintaining at least some influence in South Vietnam and staked their last hope for control on the cultural front. At first, French attempts to retain cultural influence did not look any more promising than previous efforts to maintain political, military, and economic control. The French had lost their National School of Administration, English rather than French was becoming the most important foreign language, and South Vietnamese students were denied access to education in France. The French presence in South Vietnam had reached an all-time low by 1956, but Diem's foreign policy successes and improved internal security, along with major French concessions, eventually resulted in more amiable Franco–South Vietnamese diplomatic relations.

In June 1956, the arrival of Henri Hoppenot's replacement, Jean Payart, indicated the changeover from the French High Command to a normal diplomatic embassy. Whereas Ely and Hoppenot had presided over a period of "liquidation," the main goal of French policy had become the creation of a "constructive period." Ambassador Payart was therefore instructed "to try to build up economic and cultural domains," to reestablish a "climate of confidence" between France and Vietnam, and to "develop collaboration" between the two countries. Payart's appointment was thus an attempt to appease both the Americans and the South Vietnamese, and it marked an important transition for the French, Americans, and Vietnamese, as the French representative was untainted by colonial associations. In a meeting with the new French ambassador, Diem recognized that there were "valuable aspects" to the French mission in Vietnam. Diem, according to Payart, understood that "American aid always came with a price" and wanted to avoid American control of his country after he had "worked so hard to end French colonialism." Diem had thus begun to view France as "a counterweight to excessive American influence."[41]

Other small steps also eased tensions. In September, the French transferred responsibility for liaison with the ICC to the South Vietnamese. In addition, a French parliamentary mission to Vietnam, led by Edouard Frédéric-Dupont, was also favorably received. Following the mission, a

Franco-Vietnamese friendship society began. According to the departing Hoppenot, Diem no longer needed "a scapegoat for South Vietnamese problems" and could thus afford to be more cordial to the French, as evidenced by his warm reception of the Dupont mission.[42] A smoother Franco–South Vietnamese relationship had finally materialized. But many French officials continued to complain about the overpowering American presence that forestalled further Franco–South Vietnamese reconciliation.

Ultimately, a breakthrough occurred in Franco–South Vietnamese relations because of a single French political decision. The early 1957 hullabaloo over South Vietnam's attempt to join the UN began when Pham Van Dong at the end of January sent a note to the General Assembly and to the Security Council demanding that they reject South Vietnam's proposal. The French chose to support South Vietnam's claim, and this support went a long way toward improving Franco–South Vietnamese relations. Diem stated that "France had chosen between North and South Vietnam for the first time since the Geneva Conference."[43] Although South Vietnam's demand to join the UN was ultimately rejected, Franco–South Vietnamese relations continued to improve.

France hoped to capitalize on this improvement by using cultural diplomacy as a way of regaining prestige. The French would make every effort to maintain a presence—through the EFEO, the Alliance Française, the Société des Etudes Indochinoises, cultural centers in Saigon, Dalat, Nha Trang, Da Nang, and Hue, numerous confessional schools, the remaining 40 French professors, 20 university students sent each year in mission, 350 teachers, and 10,000 Vietnamese students. France also continued to operate, with Vietnamese collaboration, the Grall Hospital, the Pasteur Institute in Dalat, Nha Trang, and Saigon, and the Cancer Institute of Saigon. Jean-Pierre Dannaud and his successors were vital forces as the heads of the French Mission of Teaching and Cultural Cooperation.[44]

Still, the French continued to fight what appeared to be a losing battle between the English and French languages. From 1954 to 1956, the importation of French books to Vietnam dropped by more than 50 percent because the Americans decided that credits for importation of products would cover only technical and teaching books. As a result, in the first half of 1957, French books, journals, and magazines disappeared from bookstores in Saigon and the rest of the country. French officials responded by trying to set up a procedure to allow the financing through French credits of French imports—books and journals—that would complement the buying of books and journals with American aid credits. The South Vietnamese were amenable to renewed cultural exchanges, agreeing to the financing of classic, scientific, technical, and religious books but not modern novels.

According to French official Arnaud d'Andurain, there was no point in insisting on the fact that French literary and scientific production consti-tuted an "incomparable element in the maintenance of French intellectual influence," especially among the Vietnamese elite, whose experience with French literature "allowed them to know superior joy of spirit." If France did not "do something" an entire generation would be "ignorant of what French language can give," Andurain avowed, and the Quai should question whether it would be reasonable to continue to maintain French cultural machinery if the Vietnamese did not have recourse to the "personal and direct richness of France's intellectual patrimony."[45] Andurain went even further, stating to Vu Van Mau that if the Vietnamese people "renounced" their habit of looking to France for their intellectual formation and decided to "turn" toward the Unit-ed States, they would lose their "intelligence, subtlety of spirit, and dialectic," which only existed because of the French administration that "assumed the mission" of instructing those in the administration and government who formed the directing class of the country. He concluded that "nothing from this point forward would differentiate them from the Thai people."[46] Clearly, the civilizing mission was alive and well. Andurain's remarks were breathtak-ing in their arrogance but also insightful in demonstrating the importance the French attached to their cultural presence in Vietnam.

Payart worked hard to ensure this presence. During summer 1957, an-other DRV attempt at establishing economic and cultural representation in Paris had the South Vietnamese "up in arms" and prepared to "have a fit" if Paris agreed. Payart worried that the improved relations with the Diem government—established after the French delegation declarations at New York and Canberra convinced Diem that, between Ho Chi Minh and him-self, "France has chosen Diem"—would be lost. Knowing Diem and his "defiance toward France," Payart feared that "he would respond with retal-iatory measures against essential French political, commercial and cultural interests." Payart reminded the Quai that in 1956, French industry benefited from "23 billion francs of orders, France imported 10 billion francs worth of rubber, and from July 1956–57 French establishments repatriated 10 billion francs, not to mention the importance of France's cultural positions." Their maintenance was dependent on Diem's goodwill.[47] Pineau, after a meeting with various officials guiding Vietnamese policy, decided on August 2 that the status quo would be maintained with the North and that there would be no further discussion of the reciprocity requested by the DRV.[48]

THE FRENCH RESURGENCE

Of the fifteen thousand French remaining in South Vietnam in early 1958, three hundred teachers were still teaching, and five hundred French firms continued to operate in the plantation, industry, commerce, and banking sectors.[49] Relations between Paris and Saigon received an additional boost when Christian Pineau arrived in March, marking the first time a French foreign minister had set foot in South Vietnam. His visit raised South Vietnamese opinion of the French and cemented the political choice France had made in favor of Saigon and against Hanoi. Also pleasing to Diem was the move of the ICC headquarters from Hanoi to Saigon that same month. France thus began to lay the foundations for renewed political influence. French enterprises in South Vietnam were maintaining their position and French exports to Vietnam began to increase. Part of this success was due to the increasing amity toward the French and hostility toward the Americans of Diem's brother and chief political adviser Ngo Dinh Nhu. Although Paris applauded improved Franco-Vietnamese relations, French officials in Saigon cautioned the Quai d'Orsay that "France should not try too quickly to regain a larger political role," instead letting things take their own course while "trying to work quietly" for more French influence.[50]

The South Vietnamese, along with most of France, heralded General de Gaulle's return to power in 1958. De Gaulle had promised to resolve colonial issues, especially the problem of Algerian independence, which had led to a government crisis—just as Indochinese independence had four years earlier. Although de Gaulle had not favored independence for Vietnam prior to Geneva and had encouraged Edgar Faure to oust Diem during the sect crisis, he had apparently changed his tune: he emphasized the importance of South Vietnam as a noncommunist nation in a number of speeches. The South Vietnamese were also drawn to de Gaulle's idea of France as a third force in Europe that maintained its liberty of action toward the United States and the communist bloc. After a long talk with Diem in March 1959, Payart's replacement, Roger Lalouette, notified the Quai that Diem felt French policy had "turned around" and that, "just as de Gaulle advocated a third force between capitalism and communism in Europe, Diem hoped to create his own third force in Asia."[51]

Cultural issues remained a concern for Paris. Most Vietnamese wanted to learn English, since visitors to Vietnam were primarily American tourists and businessmen, and Diem refused to let South Vietnamese students study in France because they often failed to return after their studies. But Lalouette asserted that the French language and culture could still persevere—the Americans did not have the professors to replace the French ones and the Vietnamese desire to keep "French universities strong" worked in France's favor. Another example of French concern with preserving a cultural influence included their ensuring that French citizens were eligible for scholarships in France. For example, in 1958, three hundred requests were made by families residing in South Vietnam who wanted grants to send their children to French schools.[52]

The French were also trying to regain radio territory. According to Sainteny, since France had lost the right to broadcast through Radio France Asie two years ago it had become "practically impossible to find the French language spoken on Asian airwaves." The few hours designated for French language authorized by the Saigon government were insufficient, and the broadcast was inaudible from medium or long range. Moreover, the emissions from Radio Saigon barely made it past the seventeenth parallel. Sainteny thus advocated establishing a French radio post that could produce a much stronger signal.[53]

On the economic front, as early as 1956, the French wanted to implement their own agricultural and land reform programs as they discovered the lack of American success in this area; this was one domain where the French could "retake the initiative." In September 1958, a Franco-Vietnamese agreement was signed providing French aid for the Diem government's agrarian reform program. Here, then, was an example of the French actually starting to replace the Americans.[54]

The Americans were finally realizing the role that France could play in Vietnam, as South Vietnamese relations with France became disengaged from their colonial context and improved. France continued to buy 80 percent of South Vietnam's rubber, providing an economic incentive for Saigon to cooperate with Paris. France still had an important commercial role to play as American aid to South Vietnam was reduced, forcing the Diem government to expand purchases of goods on credit, especially from countries with which it had important commercial and cultural ties. French officials also urged their counterparts in Washington and London to undertake joint studies on trying to guarantee foreign investments, which the South Vietnamese appreciated. Thus, throughout 1959, Franco-Vietnamese relations steadily improved while Vietnamese-American ones declined. This was not a coincidence, according to Lalouette; the Vietnamese were feeling an "overpowering American presence."[55]

Three French organizations continued to provide technical and cultural

assistance in 1959—the French Cultural Mission, the Mission of Technical and Economic Assistance, and a group of about forty professors from
the University of Saigon. Fifty-three French-operated or French-subsidized
schools existed in Vietnam, with a total of twenty-four thousand pupils.
According to French officials at the University of Saigon, the cultural mission was flourishing—two high schools in Saigon, another at Dalat, colleges
at Nha Trang and Tourane, and an overflowing of students in the primary
schools in Saigon due in part to "Franco-Vietnamese affinity and superior
French teaching."[56] And in 1960, after a three-year suspension of the program, South Vietnamese students were finally allowed to return to France
to study.

The strongest French asset remained the cultural one. The Vietnamese
intellectual and ruling class was steeped in French culture, and Paris was
"Mecca" not only for the sophisticated and rich but also for all aspiring toward a higher education. Most educated Vietnamese spoke French well and
could quote Racine or Verlaine, and French influence in education was per-
vasive. Paris continued to spend a significant amount of its total overseas
expenditures for cultural purposes on activities in Vietnam. The French
stayed in control of primary education until 1960, with increasing numbers
of students attending Catholic schools. The Alliance Française helped with
films, expositions of artists, plays, concerts, and conferences. A successful
French-produced exposition on French books and journals held in Saigon
in December 1960 symbolized the significant progress the French had made
in maintaining a cultural foothold in Vietnamese affairs and demonstrated
to the French that they had not lost their cultural influence. The triumph of
the "Exposition of the French Book" was a shining moment for the French
presence in Vietnam.[57] It appeared the French cultural role would continue.

Looking back from the vantage point of December 1960, French ambassador to the United States Hervé Alphand noted that three essential elements
played against French interests in South Vietnam. First, Diem's animosity
undermined the French presence. Second, the American conception, so favored by CIA operative Edward Lansdale, that a country that achieves independence through the military defeat of a colonizing power should cut all
ties with that power even if that means potentially falling to communism,
had played a major role. Third, the psychological success of the United States
in Korea mitigated against keeping French military forces, perceived as colonial, in place in Vietnam. Etienne Manac'h, minister of Asian affairs at the
Quai, agreed with Alphand that, in the political domain, Diem's presence
and the influence of American advisers, especially Lansdale, "played against

France." Moreover, the fact that the Eisenhower administration left Lansdale to his own devices led France to assume that the United States wanted to "compromise France's military position and accelerate its withdrawal." For example, Washington had agreed to Ely's request to recall Lansdale, but a few months later Lansdale was back. Thus, during 1955 and 1956, American military policy was locally influenced by elements clearly hostile to France who had initialized the Vietnamese request that France withdraw its military mission. French official Claude Lebel also recognized that the maintenance in South Vietnam of French military personnel who were not "the best elements of the French army" had not helped the situation. But as early as 1957, and certainly by 1958, Washington recognized its errors in embracing anticolonialism, and Americans on the ground in Vietnam realized the importance of French influence.[58]

At the same time that the popularity of French cultural initiatives with both the Americans and the South Vietnamese grew, so too did North Vietnamese insurgency in the South. On October 22, 1957, U.S. personnel were injured in a bombing of MAAG and USIS installations in Saigon. On July 8, 1959, communist guerrillas who attacked a Vietnamese military base at Bien Hoa killed and wounded several MAAG personnel. As internal security became more difficult to achieve, French officials considered retaking political initiatives. According to French chargé d'affaires in Saigon René Fourier-Ruelle, "rebel activity had been increasing . . . Diem was completely isolated, and the creation of commandos and increases in MAAG personnel did not resolve the problem." The French Embassy believed a complete reorganization of command and employment of troops was necessary, contending that "the agrovilles were useless and the population was increasingly restless." Fourier-Ruelle argued that the time had come "to examine the situation with France's allies" but that France should have a policy regarding Vietnam before confronting the policies of others. "Close cooperation with the British and Americans, a serious examination of the situation, and permanent contacts with London and Washington" appeared to be the "best way of discreetly attaining France's goals." Fourier-Ruelle concluded that France should have a more pro-Diem stance and needed to do more to maintain South Vietnamese stability. In response to Fourier-Ruelle's letter, Manac'h agreed that France should become more involved, attempting an overall policy for South Vietnam, which the Americans had "failed to provide."[59]

French status in South Vietnam continued to rise with the Franco-Vietnamese accords of March 24, 1960, which transferred the last piece of French public property to the Diem government and allowed Paris and Saigon to move forward with economic exchanges. The political relationship between the two countries had also become more stable. France had once again become an important player in South Vietnamese affairs. According to Lalouette, what the United States had not yet accepted was that a "rebirth of amity" toward France existed among the South Vietnamese and that "increasing Franco-Vietnamese collaboration [was] paired with increasing anti-Americanism."[60] French observers in Saigon watched as the South Vietnamese and Americans failed to resolve divisive political, economic, and social problems in the South.

French officials in Saigon had become staunch advocates of reform in South Vietnam. In May 1960, Lalouette suggested to American ambassador Elbridge Durbrow that a tripartite meeting be held to discuss South Vietnamese domestic difficulties. Wary of moving too fast, Paris forbade Lalouette to take the initiative for holding a three-power consultation on the means to remedy the situation in South Vietnam since the French position "could be misunderstood or interpreted as a return to colonialism." Another attempt at political reform occurred as R. P. Lebret, director of a French research institute, sent a letter filled with suggestions on government reform to Ngo Dinh Nhu. Lebret had been invited by the National Bank of Vietnam to examine South Vietnamese problems, and French officials in Saigon hoped that Lebret's study would constitute the "psychological shock" needed to revitalize the regime.[61]

Before the reforms mentioned in Lebret's study could be discussed, on November 10 a military coup was attempted in Saigon. In a subsequent meeting with Lalouette, Nhu stated that the French had been "totally correct in their actions" during the coup attempt, but that he believed American agents had supported the rebels. Therefore, Nhu wanted "to work more closely with the French since he could not trust the Americans." A USIS report detailing the coup attempt against Diem noted that the Diem regime expressed its appreciation for "objective reporting of the coup especially by French and British correspondents," which caused much seething amongst the American correspondents. Diem subsequently promised a freer press and press relations as well as intensified and coordinated psychological warfare programs.[62] Among French circles the thought occurred that the American secret services aided the 1960 coup attempt, and that the coup failed because the majority of the army and navy supported Diem. "His sang froid and the timidity of insurgents worked for him." Any attempt to replace him by a coalition of parties and a parliamentary government would neither rally the army, "which is an essential element in the transition and the only entity actually capable of keeping order in the country," nor reorganize the state, which is "essential in reestablishing order." Such a regime would rapidly lead to "disorder, powerlessness, and division," with the end result that a neutralist government maneuvered by the communists could come to power.[63] In the end, the French actually advocated keeping Diem in power, and French officials in Saigon once again became political advisers to a South Vietnamese government.

Diem still complained about Paris, but his complaints had less venom than those of the 1954–1956 period. He felt that Paris favored other countries such as Cambodia and Laos, helping them fight the communists while preferring neutrality for Vietnam. And he believed that French secret services aided the opposition and that Paris listened to Hanoi too often, forgetting that there were "15,000 French privileged" in the South and "30 French tolerated" in the North. Diem also felt that the French economic group in South Vietnam was not sincere in providing reforms. Lalouette feared that Diem's bad humor would crystallize into action against French positions, which Lalouette was determined to avoid.

In fact, Diem and Nhu also seemed to be looking more and more toward the French for support in their battle against internal subversion and in their difficulties with the Americans. They were also worried about the youth of the country falling into the "Anglo-Saxon orbit." According to French officials in Saigon, all the Americans, British, Australians, Canadians, and New Zealanders multiplying their attention, gifts, aid, and invitations not only to officials but also to the intelligentsia, workers, towns, peasants, and montagnards were creating a current that could gently wash away French influence. Diem had finally decided that such an outcome, which the French certainly did not desire, might not be in his best interests either.[64]

According to a 1963 USIA report, the prime motivation of French cultural and information services was to preserve and, if possible, strengthen ties between new states with a French background and metropolitan France. A secondary motivation was the determination to "counteract non-French influences" in areas where French influence was still dominant. The report warrants further discussion, as this was one of the few times that American officials accurately identified French motivations. The authors of the report saw the traditional concept of the civilizing mission assuming "a new facet in recent years with the introduction of scientific and technical overseas training programs," which were considered of equal importance with cultural affairs. Another change in objectives had been to "integrate" French cultural activities, wherever possible, with existing national systems of education, rather than preserving and multiplying integral French institutions. Authorities realized the advisability of "adapting themselves" to given conditions by catering to the new states and their "sensitivities" in terms of equality and mutuality. The most pressing objective was to "maintain and where possible expand France's cultural position in the world." The preferred approach remained the "spreading of French education and above all the French language," even into areas of other linguistic dominance (i.e., English).[65]

Although French information and cultural services were global in scope, the countries of "French expression" (i.e., of former French affiliation) were the primary targets. For example, nearly three fifths of the 1962–1963 funds of the Direction Générale des Affaires Culturelles et Techniques (DGACT, formerly Services des Relations Culturelles) were earmarked for Morocco, Tunisia, and the former Indochinese states. The desire for a continued *présence française* in areas formerly French "provides the basic motivation for extensive efforts of the cultural services and technical aid." Part of this desire could be ascribed to the "expectation that cultural as well as economic ties may prove more durable than political association." The realization that, with few exceptions, the leaders and opinion-molding groups in these areas were French trained and that "French as a primary instrumentality of communications and education will prevail long after French political authority has been withdrawn" contributed much to the sustained effort toward preservation and extension of cultural influences.[66] American analysts finally had it correct; the French were determined to continue their cultural efforts in South Vietnam simply for the sake of preserving French culture.

CONCLUSIONS

At first glance, the evidence seems overwhelming that France had indeed lost all political, military, economic, and cultural influence in both South and North Vietnam in the two years following the Geneva Conference. Difficulties in coordinating Franco-American policy, Diem's determination to pursue his goals free from French influence, the South Vietnamese and American insistence on a French military withdrawal, French disengagement from the 1956 elections, an ever-smaller economic and cultural mission in South Vietnam, and increasing Franco–North Vietnamese tensions all indicated an end to the French presence. But this apparent withdrawal from Vietnam turned out to be temporary. Despite a diminishing French presence in the North, by 1960, Franco–South Vietnamese relations had undergone a dramatic improvement from their dismal state four years earlier.

France was once again making its voice heard as it continued its cultural and economic presence while reestablishing a political one. Although Hanoi continued to blame France for failing to uphold the 1956 elections, Saigon grew more receptive to French diplomats as well as French economic and cultural establishments. French support of South Vietnam's bid to enter the UN in 1957 went a long way toward easing remaining tensions between Saigon and Paris and caused Diem to view the French presence in Vietnam as a counterweight to the Americans. In the late 1950s, the French continued to make political progress with the Diem government and cultural progress with the South Vietnamese people.

By the early 1960s, then, France had made a miraculous comeback in South Vietnam. To the astonishment of most observers at the time, the French presence endured in Indochina as French officials worked behind the scenes to help reform the Diem government and maintain French cultural and economic institutions. In many ways, the French had come to be more respected by the South Vietnamese than the Americans were. The French did not overtly challenge the Americans in Vietnam, but they worked quietly to rebuild a moderate political presence as Vietnamese disenchantment with the Americans grew. French president Charles de Gaulle warned the United States as early as 1961 against deepening America's involvement in Vietnamese affairs. By 1963 he had begun to call for the neutralization of Vietnam, whereby the United States would withdraw and the Vietnamese themselves would settle their conflict without external influence. De Gaulle advocated a return to a Geneva-type conference or bilateral deal between Hanoi and Saigon to determine how neutralization would be implemented.[67] Paris was clearly trying to move toward a "Vietnamization" of the solution by claiming that the only way to resolve the problem was through the Vietnamese people themselves. Moreover, in a show of support for Diem, French officials announced that "to bring peace in South Vietnam, the government must regain control with the aid of the population." As a result of de Gaulle's actions, French officials played at least a partial role in the Diem government's willingness to reopen discussions with the DRV, until Diem and Nhu were assassinated in 1963.[68]

These French actions did not go unremarked. A *New York Times* article in September 1963 suggested that Paris was "pressuring the United States to stop attacking the Diem regime."[69] De Gaulle decided to keep Lalouette in Vietnam after his official tenure as a foil to the anti-French and increasingly anti-Diem American ambassador Henry Cabot Lodge. When Lalouette had met with Diem in early February 1962, Diem, for the first time, indicated he was willing to consider an exchange of views with Hanoi. Subsequently, Lalouette was perhaps too eager to work with Diem and Nhu, as he appeared to be helping Nhu contact the North and was cautioned by his superiors not to intervene in "domestic politics." According to French foreign minister Couve de Murville, even if reunification was the French goal, France should "not encourage contacts between Nhu and Northern emissaries."[70]

Thus the Franco-American competition for influence continued as Paris sought to keep Vietnam at least partially French while Washington insisted on making it American. Diem and Ho Chi Minh had their own plans, which did not include listening to the French or Americans. Still, as a new era unfolded in the early 1960s, the *présence française* endured in Vietnam despite the ever-growing *présence américaine*. Franco–South Vietnamese relations thus improved, while the American–South Vietnamese relationship became increasingly strained. Events appeared to have come almost full circle ten years after the Geneva Conference, except that France and the United States had switched roles. Now French officials warned their American counterparts about the risks of increasing involvement in Vietnam, unofficially advised leading South Vietnamese figures, argued for a political rather than a military solution, and advocated Diem's continued leadership while the Americans plotted to unseat him.

8

Building a Colony

BUILDING A NATION IS HARD WORK; it is much easier to construct a colony. As U.S. agencies attempted to modernize and westernize South Vietnam while imprinting American values and culture on the Vietnamese population, the Eisenhower administration replaced the French colonial presence in South Vietnam with an American neocolonial one. The United States did not directly colonize South Vietnamese territory, but it certainly exhibited neocolonial behavior in the sense that Americans and American institutions took over former French functions at all levels of South Vietnamese society. Americans trained, taught, guided, and controlled in their search for a stable, independent, and noncommunist South Vietnam.

Although at first Prime Minister Ngo Dinh Diem appeared to share the American vision of South Vietnam, thus ensuring increased U.S. aid and commitments to his regime, it became clear by the late 1950s that he would pursue his own course. The escalating clashes between South Vietnamese and American officials would eventually lead the Eisenhower administration to lose its anticolonial credentials as well as its ability to extricate itself from the ever more complicated situation in Vietnam. By the time Eisenhower left office, the United States was committed to a noncommunist, but not necessarily democratic, South Vietnam.

Eisenhower officials believed in the idea of an independent South Vietnam, but only if its leader followed an American model. Thus, while paying much lip service to Diem's nationalist credentials, Washington did not want an actual nationalist—the trappings would have sufficed. Unfortunately for those in the White House and U.S. Embassy in Saigon, Diem's nationalism only grew stronger as the tide of American advisers and agencies rose. As a result, American actions became more and more neocolonial in nature as they tried to persuade, and eventually coerce, Diem to follow American policy. Attempts to modify Diem's behavior began with cultural initiatives, but spread to the economic, political, and military realms as well. Neocolonialism under the Eisenhower administration would set the tone for future

American involvement in Vietnam, permanently marring its claims to be fighting for an independent South Vietnamese nation.

Although France and the United States shared a "colonial mentality" in that representatives of both countries operated on the assumption of their cultural superiority, the two differed in why they used cultural initiatives in South Vietnam. The French sought to preserve their civilizing mission; the Americans planned to stop the spread of communism. The French tried to separate cultural activities from propaganda whereas the Americans combined the two. It is perhaps fair to say that American cultural diplomacy in Vietnam began as propaganda in the war against communism, but propaganda eventually metamorphosed into cultural initiatives designed to build a nation. Although the Americans thought they would be able to avoid earlier French mistakes by replacing the civilizing mission with one of modernization, they too would come to be seen as imperialists rather than liberators.

American officials paid close attention to how institutions and characteristics of French origin "colored" the situation in Vietnam, recognizing that they "might" have been as important as native factors in determining South Vietnam's development and modernization. The Portuguese romanization of writing, which was imposed by the French, helped Vietnam gain "immeasurable ground" over those countries that succeeded in clinging to their ideographs in the race to make the entire population literate. Almost equally important was the secondary use of a European language, which gave a very influential portion of the population easy access to western knowledge and thought. French engineering "bestowed" on Vietnam a railway, several ports, an extensive canal system, roads reaching to every region, and a number of airports, as well as private plantations, a telephone system, and revenue-producing power companies. In the government structure the French had held almost all positions of responsibility, from administrators, technicians, and civil servants, down to very routine work. The rapid withdrawal of this vast responsible group after the independence of South Vietnam was a severe blow to the operation of the government.[1]

Americans, for the most part, quietly stepped into places the French had vacated as they attempted to build South Vietnam on an American rather than French model. Americans asserted their influence by "recovering the spot." They systematically replaced the French names for streets, buildings, institutions, roads, and just about every other French-designated object, with an American version. But Americans in Saigon did not create a more nationalist South Vietnam; they simply switched one authoritative western figure for another.

DEALING WITH DIEM

The first factor leading to an increased American commitment to nation-building in South Vietnam was Ngo Dinh Diem. Diem's supposedly pro-western, anticommunist, Catholic, and anticorruption credentials continued to appeal to American officials. And yet, Diem systematically thwarted American desires in South Vietnam by proclaiming himself not only an ardent anticommunist but also an independent Asian leader. From 1954 until his assassination in 1963, Diem welcomed American aid but resisted the Eisenhower administration's attempts to direct South Vietnamese policy. Diem thus succeeded in wagging the dog as he manipulated Washington into providing increasing amounts of aid while simultaneously distancing himself from American policies. A succession of American special representatives and ambassadors (Donald Heath, J. Lawton Collins, G. Frederick Reinhardt, and Elbridge Durbrow) failed to convince Diem of the value of American political, social, and economic advice.

In addition, Diem sought to gain the respect and cooperation of other Third World neutralist countries to escape being perceived as an American puppet. Diem dressed as a westerner because he realized the West was where the locus of power resided, but he was determined to follow his own path in Southeast Asia. Interestingly, by the late 1950s, the once passionately anti-French Diem had begun to work on repairing relations with Paris to demonstrate his independence from Washington. Despite Diem's actions, the Eisenhower administration continued to fund his government in order to achieve an independent, noncommunist nation. Diem thus succeeded in expanding, intensifying, and prolonging the American commitment to South Vietnam, as many other Third World leaders succeeded in "expanding, intensifying, and prolonging" the Cold War.[2]

The West consistently underestimated Diem. Most western accounts at the time and into the present assess Diem as an uncompromising and unskilled leader. But consider his accomplishments. This was the man who eliminated the Cao Dai, Hoa Hao, and Binh Xuyen sects, forced the FEC to leave South Vietnam, obtained considerable U.S. aid, and imposed on the international community not only the "end of the idea of the all Vietnamese 1956 elections" stipulated at the 1954 Geneva Conference, but also recognition that the country could not be reunified as long as the communists maintained power in the North. In addition, Diem created a constitution where the executive was all powerful, established a South Vietnamese National Assembly, and integrated at least eight hundred thousand North Vietnamese refugees.[3] Of course, Diem had his failings, as numerous critics past and present have demonstrated. Specifically, Diem's disastrous land reform policies, political repression, and refusal to listen to advisers other than family members all weakened his regime.

In the domestic arena, from 1955 to 1961 Diem began to consolidate his rule by promulgating the South Vietnamese constitution, reorganizing the government, and working on economic reform. American aid and advisers allowed him to carry out these tasks, but Diem tended to ignore American advice on their implementation and remained skeptical of American capabilities to understand the situation in South Vietnam. Guaranteed American aid and training of the ARVN ensured internal security, at least for the time being, allowing Diem to focus on foreign policy.

It was in the foreign arena that Diem experienced his greatest success. His first foreign policy goal was to raise South Vietnam's international standing by normalizing relations with other countries. Although Diem had a rocky start at the Bandung Conference in 1955 when he was snubbed by most African and Asian leaders, by October 1956, South Vietnam had diplomatic chiefs of mission in France, the United States, Britain, Spain, Italy, Japan, Thailand, the Philippines, Cambodia, Laos, Hong Kong, Djakarta, and Taipei, and had made greater strides than the North in being recognized internationally by more countries. Indeed, French fears that the Bandung Conference would increase Asian solidarity and further weaken ties between its former colony and the metropole were proven correct, as were American fears that Bandung would lead to greater neutralist sentiment in Saigon. Diem was increasingly concerned that Asian countries viewed him as a "western construction." Once he had ensured South Vietnam's political survival, and his own, by refusing to participate in consultations for the 1956 elections and ending the French military presence, he became less dependent on the Americans. Before the election deadline Diem disparaged noncommitted or "nonaligned" nations, but after the deadline he radically changed his policy by trying to improve relations with other Asian countries, moving away from a solely western, that is to say, American, focus. Diem's reliance on the United States made true nonalignment impossible, but the appearance of independence could benefit him domestically and throughout Asia. A more sovereign South Vietnam could also make excellent propaganda fodder for the United States, as the Eisenhower administration would be able to claim that it had built a truly independent nation. But American officials never grasped this subtlety and viewed each independent step Diem took with increasing suspicion. Washington was eager to proclaim South Vietnam's independence, as long as Diem followed American policy.[4]

In a series of articles in early January 1957, Georges Chaffard in *Le Monde* noted how Diem, through his energy and inflexible courage, his governmental team, and his army's loyalty, had "succeeded in erasing all traces of foreign domination, consolidating the South and assuring security," although there were complaints against Diem's "authoritarian paternalism." Moreover, American economic leadership, according to Chaffard, had not reduced Diem to a puppet. Diem reiterated this point in a meeting with French ambassador Jean Payart, stating that South Vietnam was looking for "its independence not only with respect to France but also vis-à-vis the United States." Diem argued that the fact that "Britain receives American aid doesn't mean it loses any of its sovereignty, which is how we envision our relationship with the U.S."[5] Diem thus sought to distance himself from the Eisenhower administration, although he was happy enough to bask in all the media attention during his trip to Washington on May 8, 1957. The trip raised Diem's prestige, since Eisenhower greeted him personally—only the second time Eisenhower had done so for another head of state. Still, Diem saw the dangers of too close a relationship with the Americans and attempted to shift his policy, which had been anti-French, toward autonomy from all other countries and cooperation with other Asian leaders.

Diem first went to work on improving relations with India, making a personal appearance in New Delhi in 1957. A major goal of his trip was to prove that he was not another Syngman Rhee or Jiang Jieshi, whom he considered vassals to the United States. Diem also began to travel to other countries and to receive a number of dignitaries, such as Burmese leader U Nu, in order to boost his international standing. He journeyed to Washington, Canberra, Seoul, Bangkok, Delhi, and Rangoon, and met with members from the Colombo Plan as well as the Japanese prime minister and the Moroccan and Iraqi missions.[6] Diem also secured an agreement with Australia, Korea, and Thailand on solidarity of action against the communists. He worked to develop relations with the neutralist bloc, establish contact with Arab countries, and negotiate with Japan on war reparations. And Diem attempted to join as many world organizations as possible to promote the South Vietnamese nation.

Diem's travels throughout Southeast Asia began to dispel Asian misgivings about the regime. At the beginning of 1958, Diem was more acceptable to hesitant neutrals than Jiang Jieshi or Syngman Rhee, and was recognized by more than forty nations. Considering where he had started three years ago, Diem's achievements in foreign relations were noteworthy.[7] As a result of American help, by late 1957, South Vietnam was represented in at least twenty UN special or affiliated agencies. South Vietnam became a member of the International Bank for Reconstruction and Development, the International Monetary Fund, and the Colombo Plan. South Vietnam even belonged to the World Meteorological Association. The South Vietnamese enjoyed the benefits of technical training under the Colombo Plan, and the ninth annual conference was hosted in Saigon, with twenty-one nations and observers from several international organizations participating.[8]

Domestically, South Vietnam did not fare so well. The Diem regime faced a host of economic, administrative, and security problems. Its dependency on American aid and fight to maintain internal security alienated much of the population. According to British observers, South Vietnam had made political improvements but long-term economic and administrative restructuring remained remote, and the population was becoming increasingly dissatisfied with Diem. Moreover, Diem had not successfully implemented land reform, with the result that less than 10 percent of the land had been redistributed. Despite the amount of aid the United States supplied, American power to influence Vietnamese policy in both domestic and foreign affairs was, as one British official noted, "remarkably incomplete"—a fact that frustrated American organizations in Vietnam. In particular, American officials despaired of Diem's unwillingness to encourage foreign investment and private enterprise. This American frustration would only grow more intense as Diem consistently disregarded American suggestions.[9]

Meanwhile, Diem continued his efforts to turn toward Asia. During his August 1957 visit to Bangkok, Diem emphasized the solidarity of Asian countries, the spiritual community that unified them and the need to keep close ties in the face of the communist menace. Diem applied these same values at home through his philosophy of personalism. The chief of state offered himself as a model to his people, exalting his exemplary private life, perfect familial education, profound piety, austerity, and his revolutionary activities and qualities as a man of action. More important, Diem rejected both liberal capitalism and communism as a means of modernizing South Vietnam. Rather, he intended to rally the South Vietnamese population to work together to build a socially engaged and economically secure state. Through "personalism, community development, and collective progress," South Vietnam would achieve political, social, and economic stability, according to Diem. Diem's plan ensured a difficult road ahead for South Vietnamese–American relations, as Ambassador Frederick Nolting and other American officials fretted over the term "personalism." They feared that it would be viewed as a concept of political leadership implying dictatorship.[10]

In assessing Diem's philosophy of personalism, Payart drew a parallel between Diem and Secretary of State John Foster Dulles, stating that "the essential vice of Marxist society, for Diem and Dulles, was the crushing of the individual and injury of human nature." Both men shared the same Manichean spirit, believing that this violence to the natural order could not last and that the people would reject it. Accordingly, the Vietnamese population would reject the communists. Diem envisioned "an Asian renaissance with himself as the leader of the Southeast Asia area."

Diem's "new look" policy for South Vietnamese politics became more pronounced as he tried to ingratiate himself with the rest of Asia while continuing his diplomatic shift away from U.S. influence.[11] American ambassador Elbridge Durbrow worried that the American tactic of encouraging Diem to assume a more important role as a free world leader in Asia had backfired to a certain extent, noting that Diem "has given indications that the real or organized enthusiasm shown him on his visits may have gone to his head. He is beginning to look upon himself a bit too pointedly as the great hope of Southeast Asia."[12]

This balancing act between Asia and the United States brought Diem to a major crossroads in his foreign policy by 1958. According to the leading western expert on Vietnam, Bernard Fall, South Vietnam could remain entirely in the American camp at the risk of being branded a satellite; or Saigon might find its way toward a middle path, but would then face political instability and economic problems without the large cushion of American support it now "enjoyed so well but not too wisely." Whichever the choice, "it would be agonizing—and it would have to be made by one man alone."[13] In the end, Diem and his brother Ngo Dinh Nhu, a figure of growing importance in the government, embraced the idea of maintaining South Vietnam's liberty of action vis-à-vis the United States. By 1960, fifty-five countries had extended formal recognition to South Vietnam, which compared favorably with the DRV's relative isolation in the international community. Continuing to proclaim his independence, Diem stated that "Vietnam neither accepts foreign military bases nor foreign troops on its territory," and that he had "no intention of joining SEATO." Diem also challenged the American conception of the army as an internal security force and wanted to exceed the hundred thousand men limit to meet external threats.[14] Notwithstanding Diem's moderately successful attempts to assert his independence in foreign policy during the mid-1950s, by the time John F. Kennedy was elected president, Diem was losing his grip in both the domestic and foreign arenas as a result of increasing American intervention and Diem's inability to address domestic problems.

American officials in South Vietnam faced an additional problem in convincing Diem to follow a U.S. model—themselves. Despite Eisenhower's assurance to Durbrow that he was indeed the top U.S. official in South Vietnam, Diem, with the support of other Americans, routinely ignored Durbrow's suggestions for reform. In theory, Durbrow was responsible for coordinating civilian agencies and had wide discretion to act, but Lieutenant General Samuel Williams, who had replaced John O'Daniel as the leader of MAAG, consistently undermined Durbrow and the U.S. Embassy in Saigon. Williams promised Diem that the Eisenhower administration would continue to support him whether he implemented political and economic reforms or not. Williams also had the support of the CIA. Diem trusted Williams, and Williams argued he had the right to consult with Diem about defense matters and bypass the embassy since Diem still served as his own defense minister. Williams was convinced that exposure to American training schools and methods would resolve ARVN's problems and establish internal security.

Durbrow had attempted to remove Williams a number of times, but Diem insisted he stay. In fact, Williams stayed until 1960, with the result that embassy officials and MAAG officers continued to battle inconclusively. It would not be until May 1960 that the issue of how to handle Diem would be brought up at a regular NSC meeting. American agencies also disagreed over whether to prioritize economic and political reform or military security. The embassy and USOM contended that the economic development of South Vietnam was at least as important as military training; MAAG and Diem argued that military considerations were paramount. Diem was thus able to play one American agency against another.[15]

The American effort in South Vietnam received another blow during the summer of 1959, when a series of articles by Albert Colgrove, a Scripps Howard reporter, exposed waste, fraud, and the general high living that American officials enjoyed in Saigon. Colgrove had been sent to South Vietnam to investigate U.S. assistance projects and returned home with a cynical view and a somewhat exaggerated account of the mismanagement actually occurring, as a later Congressional investigation confirmed. At the time, the articles infuriated Durbrow, Williams, and the AFV. Durbrow subsequently curtailed some of the more lavish American spending and he also stepped up his reform efforts toward the Diem regime, going so far as to give Diem a list of suggestions such as appointing a minister of defense, adding opposition figures to the government, and providing more government account-ability, transparency, and reorganization.

Another example of American divergences of opinion occurred over the issue of civic action. Director of the Foreign Operations Administration Leland Barrows feared that CIA operative Edward Lansdale's desire to link "civic action" with community development would duplicate or supersede aid from other American agencies. According to Barrows, civic action should not be used as an instrument of community development, as it seemed to be an "outgrowth of psychological warfare" rather than genuine assistance. Civic action sought to arm the government with a selected, trained, and disciplined body of agents who would move from village to village, seeking by the distribution of relief goods and by the organization of various propaganda efforts to counteract the infiltration of communist agents and to win the villagers' support of the Diem government while turning them against the communists and other "dissident" elements. Rather than stimulating local initiative and village self-development, the program sought to establish some measure of central government influence and control over village attitudes and activities, one of the Diem regime's goals.[16] Barrows's concerns went to the heart of the American dilemma in Vietnam—try to control South Vietnam through a psychological warfare program and military build up or try to develop Vietnam through economic and technical programs. In the end, hard power tactics would triumph.

These hard power tactics would be applied against Diem as well. As a result of Diem's attempts to distance himself from the Americans and his refusal to engage in political and economic reform, the Eisenhower administration finally appeared to be toughening its stance toward him. American officials in Washington and Saigon worried that the South Vietnamese population would begin to hold the United States responsible for Diem's failure to implement reforms. They also recognized that Diem would not adopt the necessary reforms unless the United States increased pressure to do so. Finally, a number of officials suggested that if Diem would not adopt what the United States considered "essential" reforms, Washington would have "no choice but to support some new leader who will." Such claims were somewhat premature as the opposition to Diem, the most active of whom were in France, was divided, and there was no one personality who could challenge him. Beginning in mid-1960, Durbrow indicated to Diem the strong American concern over corruption in his government, and that the United States was considering withholding military aid unless Diem agreed to political and economic reforms.[17]

Durbrow's observation of South Vietnamese affairs had led him to hold an increasingly unsympathetic stance toward Diem. Although Durbrow claimed that he "got along well" with Diem until he left and that he did "not want to get rid of Diem," he did feel obliged to consider "contingencies." Despite this attempt to place more pressure on Diem, additional bureaucratic battles among the various American agencies operating in Vietnam made such efforts difficult. For example, the MSUG wanted to suspend aid to the civil guard until Diem stopped using it as his own personal army, but MAAG refused to do so. Setting an early precedent that would become ever-more prevalent in the 1960s, military and economic aid to keep South Vietnam afloat would always trump political reform. Washington's support of Diem had increased the U.S. commitment to an independent, noncommunist South Vietnam and proved to be at least a temporary lifeline for Diem's government.

Increasing South Vietnamese difficulties can be attributed in part to the American failure to understand Third World nationalism and Diem's motivations. American officials in Saigon continued to express surprise that, despite substantial aid, Diem resisted American reforms. Diem, on the other hand, remained baffled as to why the Americans could not understand his determination to avoid both the democratic capitalist and the communist paths while pursuing his own. Even though American advisers had soured on the Diem regime, they still chose to work with it in the late 1950s and early 1960s. The way they did so, however, was almost guaranteed to subvert any chance of a genuinely independent South Vietnam.

AMERICAN NEOCOLONIALISM

The second factor leading to an increased U.S. commitment to South Vietnam was the nature of the Eisenhower administration's nation-building effort. Although American officials disdained the French colonial effort and civilizing mission, they too attempted to create an artificial edifice by building, naming, and teaching. Following in French footsteps, American agencies did not laud indigenous cultural achievements or the Vietnamese language; rather, they tried to impose American standards, culture, and language, teaching the Vietnamese about American institutions, history, consumer products, and democratic values. American officials insisted that their mission was generous, benevolent, and aimed at protection, just as the French had. Where the French had employed the civilizing mission, the Americans tried nation-building. As the Americans replaced the French militarily, politically, economically, and culturally, they assumed what George Allen has referred to as the "de facto mantle of colonial administration" in a country not yet capable of self-governance.[18] In other words, American efforts in South Vietnam represented a not-so-new form of colonialism and cultural imperialism that grated on South Vietnamese pride.

While American official and unofficial agencies proliferated, a number of small, yet significant, symbolic changes occurred, which highlighted the transition from the French to the American presence in South Vietnam and the increasingly neocolonialist behavior of the Americans. For example, Vietnamese military dress went from French to American. The insignia were now modeled on the American pattern, and in the armed forces, the helmet replaced the beret. Vietnamese money resembled American dollars; rue Catinat became known as Tu Do, or Freedom Street; and Lutece—a novelty store on the former rue Catinat—became "Chicago." After its official formation in October 1955, the new South Vietnamese government modeled itself after Washington. The ministers became secretaries, the Vietnamese constitution borrowed from the American one, and Diem, when he took office for his second term on April 29, 1961, modeled the ceremony after a U.S. presidential inauguration. From 1956, learning English became a major goal. The *Vietnam Press* published an English edition, *La Gazette de Saigon* became bilingual, and *The Times of Vietnam* became popular. More and more, whether in official publications or in simple invitations, Anglo-Vietnamese bilingualism replaced Franco-Vietnamese bilingualism.[19] These changes indicated an increasing American presence in all sectors of Vietnamese life.

As American cultural activities increased, OCB officials recognized the dangers of a "too noticeable" American presence in Vietnam. They feared alienating the local population, suggesting that American personnel should be limited to the absolute minimum required for effective operations and made fully aware of the necessity for discreet and circumspect personal behavior. One example of a too-noticeable American presence was the effort to switch to the longer American working hours in public administrations (7:00 a.m. to 3:00 p.m. with a half-hour break for lunch). The measure fell through in the face of determined resistance by all civil servants, but it remained in everyone's minds as an American attempt to make its presence felt.

American influence spread into all sectors of Vietnamese society. The American presence became very strong politically, exclusive in the military domain, predominant on the economic level, and increasing on the cultural level with the help of USIS, USOM, and MSUG. Whereas USIS focused primarily on the press, radio, and cinema, and USOM worked only in the cultural domain and provided technical assistance, MSUG acquired a number of functions. When it had first arrived in 1955, MSUG had planned to reorganize the police services. But it quickly moved into administrative reform and formation of functionaries, particularly for the NIA. MSUG also created libraries, reorganized the Ministry of National Education, and directed the instruction of fifteen hundred members of the Sureté Nationale (National Security force) and twenty-one thousand of the civil guard. With the help of USOM, MSUG put at South Vietnam's disposition arms, munitions, vehicles, and transmission machinery. In addition, a number of American experts worked with chiefs of service in different Vietnamese administrations. Perhaps one MSUG professor summed up the American presence best when he stated that "where it is proper for the French to fly a flag, it is equally so for the Americans." Although MSUG members purported to systematically replace French colonialism with American nation-building and modernization, they inadvertently imposed American cultural assumptions and used colonial methods to achieve their goals. Not one MSUG member spoke Vietnamese fluently.[20]

MSUG, along with the University of Southern Illinois and Ohio State University, reorganized primary and secondary teaching to the detriment of the French. As early as the end of 1956, several thousand Vietnamese in Saigon were capable of understanding English, and by the end of the 1960s, more than half the students in secondary education chose English as their second language. The AVA also had huge success with intensive English language courses (four hours a day, five days a week for three months)— English classes on the premises of the AVA at 55 Mac Dinh Street were filled to overflowing. In 1957 Charles Falk, head of the Education Division of USOM and professor at San Diego State College, noted that "one cannot help but observe that English now competes with French as the international language." According to one French journalist, the great majority of Americans in Saigon sincerely believed that in "transplanting" their institutions they would "immunize" South Vietnam against communism.[21]

This immunization continued as American methods of work organization and the English language spread. A structured workday was implemented, and brochures and films boasting of the advantages of productivity were distributed in the public services. *The Times of Vietnam* went from a weekly to a daily, new institutes to teach English continued to open, and the AVA inaugurated a new building with twenty rooms in which English was taught free of charge every day. The progress the English language had made could be seen at the ninth annual Colombo Conference held in South

Vietnam, at which English was decreed the official language. Ambassador Payart remarked that what was most "noticeable" about the American efforts to further their language was the sort of "crusading spirit" with which they acted.[22]

American officials at the time were enamored of the survey, and South Vietnam felt the full force of this American obsession. Surveys focused on what radio stations the Vietnamese listened to, how well they understood American movies, and how they perceived the United States. A constant assessment of every U.S. cultural effort took place in South Vietnam, with the expected outcome that all results were positive. For example, by 1959, American officials claimed there was more interest in English than French books.

Nhu also felt the weight of the American presence. According to Nhu, by mid-1958, "the honeymoon with the Americans was over." They were tolerated because they were rich and powerful and because South Vietnam had need of them. Other Vietnamese had also grown disillusioned with the American presence. Tran Van Do, former minister of foreign affairs, gave the following criticism of the Americans: "An Englishman who knows Vietnam and the Vietnamese well three years ago, when meeting a Vietnamese for the first time, would say I am not French. Today he says I am not American." According to Payart, "many Vietnamese [considered] the Americans rich and generous, but also clumsy people who could cause the Vietnamese people great unhappiness with the best intentions in the world."[23]

At least some American officials recognized the dangers an increasing American presence could bring. General John O'Daniel, former chief of MAAG and chairman of the AFV, visited South Vietnam in June 1958. Although O'Daniel felt South Vietnam was beginning to move "with more speed in the right direction," he also asserted that the U.S. approach had been "too regimented, and indifferent," and suggested that the American approach should be that "of a member of a team, not merely as a teacher or coach of the team," since being "too aloof and official" made Americans little different in approach from the French. He recommended that "U.S. personnel should play down American participation in projects and try to make it appear that the ideas had come from the Vietnamese themselves."[24] Of course, O'Daniel was more concerned that the Saigon regime *appeared* independent rather than that it actually was so. NSC officials also worried that the National Liberation Front propaganda campaign, in addition to its increased use of violence in the South, would succeed in alienating the masses by depicting Diem as a puppet of the "colonialist" Americans—successors of the hated French.[25]

O'Daniel's concerns were not shared by many. On April 4, 1959, Eisenhower called for more aid to Third World countries engaged in the battle against communism and heralded Vietnam as an example where progress and security there justified American aid. The number of projects the United States had undertaken during the 1954–1959 period was astounding. Americans helped build or rebuild hundreds of miles of roads and dozens of bridges, connecting all of South Vietnam to Saigon. Americans constructed an auto route from Saigon to Bien Hoa and National Routes 21 and 19. National Route 21 was the largest aid project since the settlement of North Vietnamese refugees in 1954–1955 and reflected the technological hubris of the Americans—it cost more than health, education, or any other service provided by the United States. Americans dredged hundreds of miles of canals to build navigable waterways and constructed a national railway system from Saigon to Dong Ha at the seventeenth parallel, as well as airports and deep-draft ports to receive economic and military aid. They increased water production in the countryside and towns, implemented a system of water adduction for Saigon, improved telecommunications, and developed electric energy, civil aviation, and food production. Americans also increased harvests, livestock, fishing, and training for farmers. Washington had established a national college of agriculture, credits for agricultural production, agricultural cooperatives, and rural development. Regarding education, the United States implemented teaching programs, American schoolbooks, and English language teaching. They also developed sanitary services, medical teaching, nursing, and disease control, not to mention industry, coal mining at Nong-Son, and cement and sugar industries. Americans organized industrial cooperatives, the Vietnam Textile Company, and the Vietnam Glass Corporation, and created a public administration and a national institute of statistics.[26] U.S. efforts extended to university formation, warehouses, civil police, paramilitary security forces, cinema, information centers, public finance, radio, and learning abroad for public service. The Americans were engaged in developing counterespionage, propaganda, an identity card program, and a Vietnamese bureau of investigation, modeled after the American Federal Bureau of Investigation. Washington was even making efforts to bring American tourists to Vietnam by appointing a tourist director. Here, then, was an enormous nation-building effort. These acts of creating and reforming placed a decidedly American imprint on the South Vietnamese landscape. And with good reason. The assumptions underlying all this aid were that South Vietnam would become like the United States, with a political, economic, and social structure along American lines, and that the United States had an obligation to help South Vietnam achieve this goal.

It is important to return to the point of where most American aid actually went. More than three quarters of all aid from the United States went directly to the military and security forces, and much of that went to pay inflated salaries. Of nonmilitary aid, agricultural improvement and land reform projects received 17 percent; health, education, and industrial development received 7 percent each; and social welfare and housing received 3 percent each. Much of the nonmilitary aid was devoted to two of Diem's pet projects—developing South Vietnamese settlements in the Central highlands and building a secondary road system to connect the highlands with coasts and cities. Once again, the Americans differed with Diem on where American aid should go, with USOM officials cynically referring to "Diem's roads into the bush." USOM, contrary to MAAG and Diem, viewed road building from an economic rather than military viewpoint and wanted to concentrate on rebuilding the main North-South coastal highway.[27]

The issue of aid was front and center during tripartite consultations in early February 1959. The *trois grands* discussed how to counter communist propaganda that they did not give aid to underdeveloped countries. Once again, South Vietnam served as a shining example of the results that could be obtained with American munificence. J. Graham Parsons, assistant undersecretary of state for Asian affairs, pointed out that the situation in Indochina represented a successful "equilibrium" that the West maintained in that area of the world. Parsons also discounted the attacks and subversion in the South as not "constituting any real danger."[28] At this point, South Vietnam appeared relatively stable as a result of American aid infusions and could thus be pushed to the back burner. But the situation was deteriorating, evidenced by the increase of MAAG advisers and the antigovernment subversion in the Tay Ninh province.

Despite the massive American nation-building effort, in 1960 French ambassador Roger Lalouette observed that five years of American experience in South Vietnam had not yielded great political results. The Americans had debarked in South Vietnam filled with "goodwill and assurance." After five years, they were bitterly disappointed. Their effort to import "democracy made in America," according to Lalouette, had not worked. In addition, Lalouette noted that the United States tended to operate on an "ad hoc basis" in South Vietnam and that, apart from the highest-ranking American officials in Saigon, most Americans were mediocre. He pointed out that MAAG, USOM, and USIS received their orders directly from Washington, counterbalancing if not upstaging the embassy, and that American agents working for the various agencies differed in their interests, practices, and methods, leading to different policies and "confusion in overall American policy." He concluded that these agencies tended to neglect "the political, psychological, and sociological aspects of South Vietnamese problems that North Vietnam was so good at exploiting." In the end, despite significant American aid, no real stability existed. The United States did create a national army, equip the country, cultivate the land, and aid Diem, but in Lalouette's words, "the American presence weighed too heavily on a newly emancipated country."[29] The United States had assumed a quasi-colonial position in South Vietnam.

EXPANSION AND ACTION

The American agencies that had set up shop in Saigon after Geneva—USIS Saigon, USOM, MSUG, AVA, and many others—had spread in different directions and taken on new activities in the late 1950s and early 1960s. The Eisenhower administration had made remarkable progress in replacing France, and the Kennedy administration was determined to follow the same path. After John F. Kennedy's inauguration, plans to expand already-large programs continued apace. In expanding these programs, the American officials demonstrated a greater *savoir-faire* than their predecessors in trying to make American projects look South Vietnamese initiated, but ultimately, few were fooled.

Americans in Saigon wanted to ensure that the South Vietnamese were exposed to every facet of the American way of life. One USIS report noted that traditionally there had been very little contact between the United States and Vietnam because of "geographic remoteness, colonial status with France, and economic ties with its mother" country. To the extent that the "educational and cultural horizons of the Vietnamese elite were broadened prior to 1954, their field of vision was limited largely to France and French culture." For this reason, South Vietnam, upon achieving independence, found itself in a state of almost complete ignorance toward the United States. Although a great deal had been done in the past seven years to change this, "French cultural if not political influence remains strong and the picture the Vietnamese have of the United States and of the West is still spotty." Therefore, the United States needed to "redouble" its efforts.[30]

As of 1961, the Americans had replaced the French as the largest western segment of the population. And because they differed markedly from the French in language, attitudes, habits, and social customs, officials on the ground felt an urgent need for establishing a rapport between the two peoples that would "obviate misunderstanding, prejudice, resentment and criticism and promote mutual esteem, confidence, appreciation, and friendship." USIS envisioned a three-fold mission for the future: to furnish maximum support to the U.S. military, economic, political, and psychological programs in the achievement of the primary U.S. objective—victory over the Viet Cong; to strengthen the Vietnamese people's understanding and appreciation of the United States—its government, people, and culture; and to promote effective personal relations between the large number of Americans currently on duty and the South Vietnamese people. USIS thus advocated a carefully developed operating plan. In particular, USIS long-range cultural objectives were emphasized, but psychological operations were also to be "sought out and promoted." USIS was also concerned about developing and maintaining effective working relationships with appropriate government departments and agencies, which involved the ability of USIS to "sell its plans and projects to appropriate officials" and to work "unobtrusively with the Vietnamese authorities so that all phases of the program appear to be government initiated, planned, and operated." USIS needed to "gain maximum operational support" from such groups as the army, Vietnamese Information Service, Civic Action cadres, Vietnamese youth, and labor unions. American officials thus wanted to build up information and exchange programs, which had been too "timid" in the past in the face of bold communist propaganda. Washington was determined to remain in South Vietnam for the duration, and the way to do so was to advertise more effectively the advantages of American democracy and capitalism.[31]

By 1961, the USIS information center occupied excellent roomy quarters in three floors of a prime street corner building in downtown Saigon, about a mile from the embassy. It was completely air-conditioned and included the Abraham Lincoln Library, a 150-seat auditorium, radio studios, and film and recording rooms. USIS also maintained branch posts at Hue and Can Tho, with sub-branches at Banmethuot and Nha Trang, and an additional sub-branch planned for Dalat. Libraries at each center taught English and conducted story hours. Thus the Americans sought not only to bring political, military, and economic aid on the American model, but also to transplant American technology, comforts, architecture, and organization to Vietnam. The development of the buildings alone indicated the American desire to construct in an American style.

USIS also had an extensive radio network, with plans to boost listening. The anticommunist programs included "Beyond the Benhai River," a daily

program analyzing events in North Vietnam, refuting stories and allegations put out by Hanoi, and showing weaknesses of the communist regime.
"Communism and Reality" was a weekly feature on communist practices
and theories. "Round Table Discussion" was a weekly multivoice program
on conditions in North Vietnam as contrasted with those in free Vietnam.
"Talking it Over" was a weekly two-voice discussion on what was happening
in the communist world in general. Other programs included "History in the
Making," a daily program on foreign aid and economic, social, and political
progress made in free Vietnam and the free world; "The World This Week,"
a weekly program on domestic and foreign news; "Friendly Nation," a daily
program on science, history, culture, education, and technology; "Questions
and Answers," a weekly program answering questions on various subjects
of interest except politics; "Science and Humanity," a weekly program on
scientific developments in the free world in general and in the United States
in particular; and two versions of "Chinese," a daily news program in Can-
tonese and a six-day one in Mandarin. In a nod to the French, "L'Amérique
Vous Parle" was a weekly program in French on subjects ranging from the
arts and education to industry and social developments in the United States.
Television was a new phenomenon, and one that had not been tried in Vietnam, but USIS officials believed it would become a critical medium in the
"psychological offensive" the government "must wage and win" against the
NLF.[32]

In terms of the press, there were fourteen Vietnamese- and ten Chinese-
language newspapers, as well as one English and one French in the Saigon
area. The English and French had a circulation of about 8,000 each. There
was only one Vietnamese newspaper published in the provinces. USIS distributed 90,000 copies of the Vietnamese edition of Free World to teachers,
students, government workers, businessmen, and the military. Young Citizen was a quarterly publication with 4,000 copies going to the Ministry of
Education and 3,000 copies going to the army. A total of 18,500 copies of
Informations et Documents, a French publication produced by USIS Paris,
were sent to upper-middle-class groups—government officials, businessmen, educators, and students. The periodical focused on various phases of
American life and culture. USIS was interested in stepping up its supply of
locally originated stories—picture stories of joint Vietnamese-American activities of all kinds and human interest stories that would help the Vietnamese understand Americans.

The International Cooperation Administration also publicized the U.S.
aid effort. Information officers "placed" an average of three stories a week

with photos in newspapers, and one to two stories per month were published in *Free World*. Special exhibits were produced for countrywide exploitation and an average of one story was included in every USIS-produced weekly newsreel, shown by most theaters throughout the country. About three news stories a week were broadcast by Radio Vietnam, a lengthy feature on some aspect of American aid was placed with the press an average of once a week, and three stories per month were placed with local correspondents for use by the U.S. press.

USIS newsreels and documentaries were apparently so successful in rural areas and so effective in picturing the benefits of the U.S. aid program to the Vietnamese people that, by late 1960, NLF members started sabotaging various aspects of the program and increased kidnappings and assassinations, making it impossible by the end of the year for USIS mobile units to show films outside city limits. A Catholic priest living in one of the "terrorist targeted areas" reported that people in his area accepted the stories in *Free World* "as fact" and that it was proving to be a "valuable tool" to refute oral and written communist propaganda.[33]

With respect to cinema, the film program sought to disseminate information about the United States, demonstrate the mutuality of American-Vietnamese interests, detail the communist threat, portray American support for and aid to Vietnam, and influence certain elite groups. Films produced in 1961, which included one of Kennedy's inauguration, *Highway for Friendship* (about USOM aid), and *X-15* and *Satellite Launching* (on space and rocket advances), attracted much favorable response from officials, teachers, and students. Unfortunately, motion pictures such as *Invasion of the Body Snatchers* and *Zombies of Mora Tau* were also included in agency lists of titles certified for support, which was "not the type of American culture the Vietnamese should be introduced to," according to USIS officials.

The American-Vietnamese Association (AVA), now renamed the Vietnamese-American Association (VAA) in an attempt to demonstrate South Vietnamese agency, remained the largest and oldest of the bi-national associations. The VAA in Saigon had an academic enrollment of 3,848 persons as of August 1961, and the VAA of Hue, founded in 1958, enrolled 269. The VAA's Board of Directors consisted of eleven members: six Vietnamese and five Americans. Student enrollment at the VAA had grown steadily, more than doubling since 1957. One hundred teachers were in place, largely MAAG officers and wives of MAAG, USOM, USIS, or embassy men. The bulk of enrollment was in ten basic English language courses; however, there were also students in English composition, American literature, shorthand,

and Vietnamese. The VAA had an expanding activities program, including forums and lectures; sponsorship of visiting artists and local music events and entertainment; recorded concerts; film and color slide showings; city tours; art, dance, and stamp-club activities; coffee hour; and various other social events. Total attendance at all of these in 1961 was almost 12,000, including South Vietnamese and members of the large American community in Saigon. Plans were also underway with the minister of education to have Peace Corps personnel teach English in Vietnamese schools.

The minister of education had notified USIS that in the early 1950s about 95 percent of the country's schoolchildren chose French for primary language study and about 5 percent chose English. By 1961, 45 percent selected English for primary study (they still took French courses but for shorter periods). These figures confirmed an enormous demand for English language instruction. Vietnamese youth sought higher education on an American model as well. Before the 1954 partition of the country, South Vietnam had only University of Hanoi branches; by 1961, it had three universities—two in Saigon and one in Hue—as well as a private Catholic institution in Dalat. The University of Saigon was formally established in 1955; it had an enrollment of almost 10,000 students in six faculties as of 1961, and a roster of 300 professors and instructors. The University of Hue was founded in 1957 and had an enrollment of 1,610 students in seven faculties and around 100 professors and instructors. The University at Dalat had about 250 students. The total university enrollment represented an increase of about 8,000 since 1955. Fields represented by visiting lecturers in the 1960–1961 academic year were American literature, political science, and botany; in 1961–1962 they would be American literature, political science, and English teaching; and for 1962–1963, American literature, political science, and western civilization. American literature had been taught by visiting lecturers at the University of Saigon since the 1957–1958 academic year, and 25 students had received certificates in American Literature and Civilization.

But even in 1961, American officials had trouble weaning the Vietnamese away from such texts as L'Anglais Vivant in order to teach English. Students preferred the obsolete French version because it was cheaper. American officials were thus working to persuade American textbook firms to lower sales prices of books for use in Vietnam. USIS also made simplified French versions of American books available in Vietnam. Although these books would not contribute to the more widespread use of English, they would be a "source of information" on American life and literature for the large French-speaking population of the country.[34]

USIS also sought to increase Exchange of Persons programs to "complement" the large-scale USOM and military training programs. By providing selected high-level opportunities for study and observation that were "so important to the nation's political, social and economic development," USIS officials could expose the South Vietnamese to American institutions as a means of "broadening Vietnam's window to the West," as virtually all of the country's western orientation in the past had been through France and French education. Exposure was also sought by bringing American lecturers, teachers, and specialists to Vietnam, particularly in areas where American scholarship could help fill specific Vietnamese academic and professional needs.

The Exchange of Persons program was "only an island in a sea of scholarship and training activity dominated by USOM and MAAG on the American side and by France as far as other efforts were concerned." USOM's 1961 allocation provided for 250 new grants, 250 extensions and renewals, and 126 third country grants. Although largely in technical training, these figures included 30 new and 62 extension grants in a Scholarship for Leadership program under which Vietnamese students received up to four years' support for undergraduate work at American universities. Grant coordination worked on an ad hoc basis with USIS, VAA, USOM, MAAG, the British Council, the Australian Embassy, the Colombo Plan, the Asia Foundation, and the University of Michigan's Southeast Asia Regional English project. Under MAAG's training program, 630 Vietnamese military personnel went to the U.S. in 1960. Possibilities for overlap existed with USOM on student and leader grants, but the State Department had one unique capability—that of bringing American professors to lecture at Vietnamese universities. USIS officials recognized that France still held a leading position among other foreign countries engaged in educational assistance and exchange activity because it maintained a large cultural mission, but this mission was concerned largely with the complete support and staffing of four secondary schools and the 40 professors who taught at the University of Saigon.[35]

The United States had long been consigned to second place vis-à-vis France in terms of cultural esteem in Vietnam. According to American officials, the President's Fund program had slowly begun to balance out the picture by providing exposure to American artists' performances, and a number of musical performances introducing American music had occurred in Vietnam by 1961. Other planned activities included having the Fulbright Program institute a program in Vietnam and continuing the very successful exhibit series already in place. American exhibits tended to focus on themes, developments, and customs deemed typical for American culture and society, including consumer products, high living standards, the advantages of a free market economy, and technology.[36]

The 1958 "Atoms for Peace" exhibit averaged 5,000 visitors per day. According to South Vietnamese officials, before the exhibit, the Vietnamese associated the atom with Hiroshima, but it "now meant many peaceful things as well." There was a buildup to the event through press stories and photos (prepared by the USIS press section), trailers on USIS newsreels, and spots on the radio. About 160,000 people attended. USIS felt that the impact and acceptability of the exhibit were helped tremendously by the publicized "co-sponsorship" of the exhibit by the Vietnamese Ministry of Information. USIS "consciously relegated" itself to a secondary role in the public view, making the exhibit a Vietnamese presentation and therefore adding to the credibility of what was said about U.S. accomplishments in the "Atoms for Peace" field. For instance, press materials, although prepared by USIS, were given to newspapers by the Ministry of Information, a device that resulted in excellent press coverage. Every available medium was brought into play—the press had produced and placed fourteen major stories, three photo features, and two advertisements; radio announcers had produced at least five hours of news commentary and other promotional material; and film officials placed a trailer. After the opening, publicity continued, some of it "natural" and some of it "generated." The exhibit's success led USIS officials to coordinate a subsequent exhibit on peoples' capitalism to tell the American story "dramatically and effectively."[37] "These Are Our People," an exhibit depicting the working activities, home lives, and community participation of U.S. steelworkers, was on display July 12–21, 1958. It featured the interiors of workers' homes, housewives making clothing on sewing machines, school buses transporting workers' children to and from school, union members planning recreation, and evidence of health and retirement benefit plans. "Sports in the USA" was also featured in 1958, as well as an exhibit on the Colombo Plan.

USIS proclaimed the 1959 "Abraham Lincoln and His America Today" exhibit another outstanding success. Just as Vietnamese students were "once exposed to Joan of Arc," they "now learned about Abraham Lincoln." "American Architecture," designed to emphasize the grandiose nature of American skyscrapers, was also a popular exhibit. According to USIS, South Vietnam was still recovering from colonialism. Its leaders were passionately engaged in building the country along lines "reflecting the best of modern Western civilization" without "casting off entirely lasting Asian and national characteristics." Thus, the display filled a need for Vietnamese students who would not have the opportunity to travel to the United States but recognized that it was where many architectural advances originated.[38] The "20th Century Highlights of American Painting" exhibit was yet another that USIS pronounced "most successful."

Other exhibits in 1959 included "Great Ideas of Western Man" and a series of posters on SEATO, which were displayed at various locations in Saigon. There was also an extensive exhibit on the Bien Hoa highway, which had been planned by Americans and constructed with American aid. Beginning on World Health Day, which in 1960 was dedicated to malaria eradication, USIS, USOM, the Administration for Malaria Eradication, the Ministry of Information, and the World Health Organization initiated a national, coordinated, all-media information campaign on the joint South Vietnamese–American aid project on malaria. The project, which already reached almost half the Vietnamese population, was identified in media output as a "free service for the people from the Government and American aid." Information services stressed the mutuality of South Vietnamese interests and President Eisenhower's statements on the worldwide campaign. For USIS, the campaign showed the South Vietnamese people that aid benefited them directly. A film on malaria was also produced and shown all day for two weeks at the USIS theater. A large exhibit on the joint Vietnamese-American aid effort toward malaria eradication was designed by USIS, produced by USOM, and displayed in the main Ministry of Information Exhibit Hall in downtown Saigon.[39]

These exhibits demonstrated a number of facts about the American effort in South Vietnam. The United States had achieved, through its various agencies, an impressive and coordinated propaganda machine, one that was devoted to political, psychological, and cultural methods of promoting American ideals and control. The perceived success of the exhibits in portraying the American way of life ensured that they would continue, and operations for 1960 and 1961 included the "American Pharmaceutical" exhibit, which enticed 5,000 viewers, the "U.S. Presidential Election" exhibit, which drew an audience of tens of thousands, and the "Highways to Progress" exhibit, which brought 20,000. Others on American labor and Hawaii and Alaska were popular as well. There were also innumerable exhibits on display in USIS library windows in Saigon. American officials carefully kept track of all attendance and tried to gauge how well the exhibits furthered understanding about American values and ideals.

Not all exhibits were an unqualified triumph for American cultural diplomacy. The exhibition of the hospital ship *HOPE* in Saigon turned out to be a mixed success because of its inability to meet the "fantastic clamoring" for treatment by the population, despite carefully worded publicity on the ship's mission and capabilities. The overall effect was judged to be positive. Other projects included distribution of donated magazines and books, and the visit of the U.S. Seventh Fleet's flagship—the USS *St. Paul*—to Saigon on South Vietnam's independence day, Oct 26, 1960. (Although, perhaps in a sign of times to come, when a squall broke out during an American–South Vietnamese event, the Americans went below while the South Vietnamese stayed on deck.[40]) Until 1961, the exhibits were used primarily to support USIS's second objective: "to strengthen understanding and appreciation of the U.S. and the American people." But in view of the increasing emphasis being placed on the first objective, a U.S. victory against northern-instigated subversion, USIS officials believed that exhibits should be used to a greater extent in a psychological offensive promoting the Diem regime and denigrating the DRV, particularly in the provinces. Thus, USIS efforts would shift from cultural diplomacy to outright propaganda and psychological warfare.

In September 1961, an exhibit titled "Forward March" opened in Saigon City Hall. The exhibit was sponsored by the Vietnamese secretary of state for defense, the secretary of state for civic action, the army psywar directorate, and the directorate general of information in close cooperation with USIS. The purpose of the exhibit was to portray "vividly" the "terrorism" of the NLF, comparing its destructive, negative actions with the constructive efforts of the Diem regime to improve the lot of the Vietnamese people, and to inspire their confidence in their government's viability and their armed forces' ability to cope with mounting NLF military campaigns. The exhibit also sought to raise the morale of the members of the South Vietnamese armed forces by developing a greater public recognition of the individual fighting man's efforts and sacrifices in the war against the NLF. The exhibit consisted of a display of captured weapons, such as light sidearms, rifles, semi-automatic and automatic weapons (many of them of Soviet or Chinese manufacture), NLF equipment and material (such as field radio receivers and transmitters), drugs and surgical tools of Eastern European origin, large photo panels of NLF atrocities, and examples of captured documents. A continuous newsreel proclaimed recent ARVN victories over NLF forces in the Mekong delta area. The highlights of the exhibit were two large sand tables portraying the battle of Kien Phong in the Plain de Joncs (fought and won by ARVN in late July). Thirty thousand Vietnamese attended the exhibit.[41]

The United States also employed more-traditional forms of "information" dissemination. A text and translations unit officer handled book translations, editing, research, propaganda analysis, and media assessment reporting. Translations worked on in 1961 included *Profiles in Courage* and *The Strategy of Peace*, by John F. Kennedy; *Deliver Us From Evil* and *The Edge of Tomorrow*, by Thomas Dooley; *My Several Worlds*, by Pearl S. Buck; *The American Republic*, by Raymond Bruckberger; and *The Economics of Freedom*, by Massimo Salvadori. USIS officials felt that the program was modestly successful, but because most Vietnamese intellectuals did their substantive reading in French, they planned to experiment with several French translations during the coming year. The program was projected to continue to grow as more students graduated from universities and studied abroad.

USIS considered that its presence on the local scene was "well accepted" and that it had avoided to "marked degree" the charges of "lavish American living" rendered by Albert Colgrove a couple of years earlier.[42] In fact, American officials were so confident of the progress they had made in South Vietnam that they began to actively encourage American tourism. Just as American tourists were encouraged to visit France after World War II, the Eisenhower administration also encouraged travel to Vietnam to spread a democratic model of middle-class leisure and consumerism and to try to promote private investment. According to administration officials, Americans had a leadership responsibility in the world that included vaunting the benefits of democracy and capitalism through mass tourism.[43] But all those Americans flying over to put their stamp on Vietnam, to promote democracy, and to modernize, made few attempts to understand Vietnamese culture. Vietnamese cultural and religious concerns, such as ancestor worship or Buddhism, were rarely mentioned in the increasing number of reports flowing back and forth between Saigon and Washington. The United States had exported a variety of cultures to South Vietnam—highbrow, middlebrow, even in some cases lowbrow—but interest in importing Vietnamese culture remained almost nonexistent. To be sure, none of the diplomats, businessmen, and other missionaries of modernization viewed themselves as cultural imperialists; and yet, it seems that is exactly what they were.

The U.S. aid program in South Vietnam by the late 1950s was second in size only to South Korea outside of Europe. Washington had spent $2 billion to $4 billion in 1950–1954 and another $1.5 billion to $2 billion dollars from 1955–1961, not including CIA or MAAG funds that were paid through the Defense Department. The focus from day one had been on a western model of development—but American, not French. In other words, South Vietnam needed to achieve rapid economic growth through industrial and technological progress, which would ultimately result in a western democratic state. In addition, South Vietnam was to be exposed to and eventually embrace American culture and way of life. But this was not the case in 1961. South Vietnam languished economically as the Diem regime remained fixed on military matters and ensuring internal security. Moreover, the South Vietnamese tended to be uninterested in adopting an American model of modernization or lifestyle, much to the surprise of the Americans in Saigon.

CONSTRUCTION CONTINUES

When the Kennedy administration took power in January 1961, the American nation-building effort in South Vietnam was securely in place; but the reality was that the United States had fostered the development of a colony, not a nation. Kennedy and his team would contribute to the work-in-progress as the South Vietnamese and American governments agreed to extend and build upon existing programs of military and economic aid. American aid and experts would be used to increase the regular armed forces, provide assistance for the entire Civil Guard, help South Vietnam's armed forces in health, welfare, and public works activities at the village level, and work out a financial plan as a basis for joint efforts.[44]

Kennedy thus continued the process of "modernization" that Eisenhower had begun in Vietnam. American officials hoped to transform Vietnam from a traditional and colonial society into a modern one, complete with new economic organization, political structure, and systems of social values built with the rational and analytical tools of social science. Americans in Washington and Saigon persisted in viewing the Vietnamese people as clay on a potter's wheel to be molded into free men by the United States. Contact through American institutions and culture was what would turn South Vietnam into a nation.

Modernization was not simply a social science but, as Michael Latham has argued, "an ideology, a conceptual framework that articulated a common collection of assumptions about the nature of American society and its ability to transform a world perceived as both materially and culturally deficient." Thus MSUG, USOM, and USIS bridged American ideas of modernization with projects on the ground in Vietnam. Certainly none of these modernizers viewed themselves as imperialists, but rather as progressive, enlightened, do-gooders who would lead backward Vietnamese culture into the liberal-democratic and capitalist orbit. Material assistance, rational organizations and structures, and the English language were the answer. Drawing on their belief in the unique nature of the United States and its advanced position in the world, Americans in South Vietnam believed success could only be achieved the American way. Like the French before them, the Americans were willing to transfer culture, but only in one direction.[45]

According to DRV foreign minister Ung Van Khiem, the Eisenhower and Kennedy administrations had "feverishly built" a series of military bases and strategic roads, airports, and military ports; "illegally introduced" into South Vietnam tens of thousands of tons of ammunition and war material; "raised" the MAAG military personnel to three thousand men; and "organized, trained, and often assumed the direct command" of the armed forces of the Diem administration. South Vietnam, according to Khiem, had in fact become "a colony of a new type, a military base serving the U.S. policy of intervention in Indochina and in Southeast Asia." He pointed out that eighty-seven delegations had visited Vietnam as high-ranking American civilian and military officials inspected and activated "America's plan for war." Vice President Lyndon Johnson and Diem had published a joint communiqué that was "tantamount to a bilateral military alliance."[46] Khiem had assessed the situation accurately. By 1961, it was undeniable that the Americans had made a major commitment to South Vietnam. Just what the Americans would do with this commitment remained to be seen.

Diem's success in manipulating the Eisenhower administration while distancing himself from American policies, and an increasingly neocolonialist American presence were vital factors in the American commitment to South Vietnam. But this commitment had not resulted in an independent nation. By 1961, American–South Vietnamese relations had become difficult, as Diem continued to make progress on the international front but refused to consider American suggestions for domestic problems. As a result, the Americans became increasingly disillusioned with Diem, and vice versa. In addition, convinced that the United States would succeed where France had failed, Washington's determination to replace the French created a full-fledged nation-building effort. Americans in Vietnam provided technical and military assistance, trained administrators and ministers, disbursed economic aid, and taught English. Each additional function U.S. agencies undertook increased not only the American presence, but also the imposition of U.S. culture and values in South Vietnam. Thus Diem's maneuverings and the incremental assumption of French duties by American organizations contributed decisively to the American presence. Presidential decisions, State Department diplomacy, and military imperatives all factored into increased American intervention, but so too did the many American missions in place that advocated a more forceful presence and an end to the French. Ultimately, replacing France would not help the United States achieve its goal of a noncommunist South Vietnam, but would bring disaster to Americans and Vietnamese alike.

Replacing France

CHARLES DE GAULLE FIRST CALLED for the "neutralization" of Vietnam, whereby South and North Vietnam would resolve their problems without external influence, in the summer of 1963. President Kennedy angrily responded by questioning de Gaulle's right to suggest such an action, noting that France had "neither armed forces, nor an economic aid program in Vietnam," and that the entire burden was being "shouldered by the United States."[1] True enough, but as the preceding chapters have shown, the reason France no longer had a military or economic presence was that Washington and Saigon had systematically pushed France out of Vietnam. The burden the United States "shouldered" was not imposed, but chosen.

A number of theories exist as to how and why early American involvement in Vietnam occurred. The "quagmire thesis" holds that successive U.S. presidents gradually became entangled in the war by small steps, each convinced that a limited commitment would eventually lead to victory. The "stalemate thesis" asserts that U.S. involvement was a series of deliberate acts by presidents who saw the quagmire for what it was, but could not bring themselves to accept defeat while in office. Other scholars claim that the United States "stumbled" into Vietnam.[2] For the period under examination here, none of these descriptions apply. The Truman, Eisenhower, and Kennedy administrations did not slip into Vietnam by inadvertence, nor did they deliberately use Vietnam as a holding action. Earlier interpretations have ignored the intra-alliance politics that were responsible, to a considerable degree, for increasing American intervention in Vietnam.

Intra-alliance conflict among France, Britain, and the United States hindered, rather than helped, western policy in Indochina. The three countries, while agreeing on common policies in theory—creating a coordinated Southeast Asian defense, building a national Vietnamese army, implementing the Navarre Plan, supporting South Vietnamese prime minister Ngo Dinh Diem, and encouraging consultations for the 1956 elections—never managed to carry through these policies in practice. The search for "common action" always appeared just out of reach. But in attempting to realize this goal, America increased its influence in Vietnam, with the result that by 1960 the Americans had replaced the French in almost all domains in South Vietnam and dissuaded them from maintaining a presence in North Vietnam. In the end, the western bloc as much as the communist one furthered the American commitment to a noncommunist South Vietnam, as the American entrance onto the scene went hand-in-hand with the French exit.

When exactly did this transfer occur? It is almost impossible to pinpoint an exact date or action. Certainly no French politician wanted to assume responsibility for the French loss of control. Witness Pierre Mendès France's defense that his administration could not be held accountable for the "*relève,*" or replacement of France by the United States. He argued that Americans were already installed in Saigon long before he came to power, and that the French "eviction" was a result of previous governments trying to obtain additional American economic and military aid. Regarding the U.S. assumption of French duties, he noted France had "systematically" initiated the Americans into first military and then civil and local affairs. According to Mendès France, the "fundamental French error" was "introducing" the Americans in the first place.[3]

This introduction, and the beginning of the transition from the French to the Americans, began in earnest in 1950. Chinese recognition of North Vietnam and French success in portraying their war effort as an anticommunist crusade led to the first tentative American steps toward intervention. During numerous tripartite meetings from 1950 to 1953, French officials slowly but surely persuaded Washington of Indochina's importance as an outpost for western defense. Thus, efforts to coax the United States into seeing the French cause in Indochina as an allied one were deliberate and longstanding. French success in convincing the United States not only to aid the French war effort but also to support a common Southeast Asian defense policy paved the way for future American involvement.

The portrayal of Indochina as an international affair by successive French governments did, to a certain degree, backfire. Paris found its liberty of action impeded as it coordinated with the Bao Dai government and the Americans in the fight against the DRV. To be sure, the French underappreciated the various American missions and dignitaries sent to observe and aid the war effort. But constant American claims that independence for the Associated States would magically resolve the situation also led to increased Franco-American tensions in Indochina. As Laurent Cesari has stated, "the Cold War, rather than leading the Americans to support colonial empires, forced them instead to denounce colonization." Since the United States could not support revolution as the Soviets did, "the Americans had to find other myths, such as national independence, that would mobilize Vietnamese opinion."[4]

By 1953, the American commitment to the French war effort had become linked to European defense issues. Because Paris claimed that it could not win the war in Indochina and build up the European Defense Community (EDC) simultaneously, the incoming Eisenhower administration agreed to supply additional aid for Indochina with the assumption that France would ratify the EDC—an American top priority. The French never ratified the EDC, but as a result of continued American aid for Indochina throughout 1953–1954, Washington found itself increasingly engaged there. In particular, Secretary of State Dulles's decision to informally link the EDC and Indochina and his refusal to consider alternatives to the EDC obliged Washington to acquiesce to French demands for more aid and accelerated the administration's financial and political commitment to prevent a communist takeover in Indochina.

The Indochina-EDC connection demonstrates the dangers of tying one policy goal to another. Both Paris and Washington thought they had linked policies in a way that would allow them maximum leverage against one another, but in the end, both became mired in their own cleverness. French leaders thought that by portraying their effort in Indochina as part of the greater battle against communism they would be assured American support. While the French did obtain this support, they also acquired increased American meddling in Indochina. The United States, in implicitly tying American aid to Indochina to the EDC's ratification, lost the EDC but ended up more committed to the Indochina effort. In addition, the United States could have insisted on Vietnamese independence prior to Geneva if it had been a little less concerned with the impact such insistence would have on the EDC's prospects for ratification by the French National Assembly.

The year 1954 was a critical one for American involvement in Vietnam. Dulles had agreed to a negotiated settlement of the Indochina conflict at the Berlin Conference, allowing France to place Indochina on the agenda for the forthcoming Geneva Conference. In addition, the Eisenhower administration came close to intervening militarily at Dien Bien Phu in the spring of 1954 through united action. The Americans did not intervene, and the

Franco-Vietminh agreement at the Geneva Conference to temporarily divide Vietnam at the seventeenth parallel ended military hostilities between
the French and the Vietminh. But the American refusal to sign the Geneva
agreements left the door open for future American involvement in Indochina.

Lloyd Gardner has described the American commitment to Vietnam
as being a "halfway" one until the Geneva Conference.[5] After Geneva, this
commitment would become full-blown as the United States became primarily responsible for South Vietnam's future. Because Eisenhower and Dulles
viewed the Geneva Accords as a setback for the noncommunist world, they
decided that the United States needed to play a larger role in South Vietnam to ensure that it too was not lost. Washington thus demanded more
control of military, strategic, economic, and administrative matters. Indeed,
Eisenhower administration officials relished reducing the French presence
in Indochina so that South Vietnam could be rebuilt from the foundation.
The Diem government offered the best chance for doing so, according to
Washington.

Following Geneva, Paris intended to maintain a significant amount of
influence in Vietnamese affairs, but American support of Diem created a
number of difficulties for the French. Franco-American conflict heightened
once again as the two countries disagreed over Diem's future as a viable South
Vietnamese leader. The French wanted to develop a joint Franco-American
policy toward South Vietnam to preserve western interests there. But the
Eisenhower administration resisted tying itself too closely to French policy.
In the end, Diem, with some help from the Americans, succeeded in keeping
himself in power, resulting in a reduced French presence in South Vietnam.

France continued to lose influence as the western bloc attempted to
resolve the 1956 elections issue. The elections failed, in part, because the
primary countries involved, with the exception of North Vietnam, placed
a low priority on elections. In addition, Diem's insistence that the French
withdraw the last of the FEC from Indochina, as well as his, and American,
efforts to reduce the French political and economic presence, caused Paris
to disengage from its commitment to holding the 1956 elections. Diem's refusal even to consider consultations, despite American pressure to do so,
indefinitely postponed the issue. The British, Soviets, and Chinese allowed
the election deadline to pass, having decided that maintaining the shaky
peace in Vietnam was more important than holding the elections. The non-
elections of 1956 ensured that the Americans would have time to shape
South Vietnam as they saw fit.

If it had been anyone but Diem in charge of South Vietnam, the French and American presence in that country could have played out very differently. In fact, if it had not been for Diem, there is a good chance that France would have persuaded a different South Vietnamese government to begin negotiations with the DRV, maintained a presence in the North, and perhaps even overseen the 1956 elections. Granted, this is mere speculation, but it is worth considering the path not taken.

By 1956, French influence in Indochina had greatly diminished as the United States superseded France politically, militarily, economically, and administratively. The final Franco-American battle for control occurred in the cultural realm. The French resisted American attempts to take over various French educational institutions in Indochina, but American agencies made significant gains. French observers noted that the "overwhelming" American presence in South Vietnam meant that the Americans were determined to forge ahead with their nation-building experiment.

French influence had not been completely eradicated. In an effort to counterbalance the United States, the Diem government slowly began to work toward better relations with France. But the American presence still pervaded almost every aspect of South Vietnamese life. The extent and ramifications of American investment and development assistance in Vietnam after Geneva were vast as the Eisenhower administration shifted from military defense assistance to programs oriented toward nation-building. During Eisenhower's second term, the administration understood more clearly the importance of using economic and cultural aid as weapons in the Cold War and furthered the efforts of American agencies engaged in nation-building work. Overall, the amount of aid to Vietnam actually went down from 1955 to 1961, but the numbers and activities of official and unofficial Americans in South Vietnam climbed steadily.

When examining the American nation-building effort in South Vietnam, the British observed in 1956 that the broad picture of American activities in South Vietnam was one of "gradual, unspectacular success."[6] This comment serves to underscore two key points. First, while Vietnam appeared relatively quiet on the surface after Geneva, the Americans were stealthily moving into the political, administrative, economic, and military domains. Second, observers at the time deemed American efforts in South Vietnam "successful." But successful at what? The various agencies at work built and modernized, to be sure, but had they ensured greater internal stability? Had they halted the communist-directed insurgency? Had they created a democratic and economically stable nation? The answers appear obvious today. But at the time most Eisenhower administration officials in Washington would have answered "yes" to all these questions.

If they had not created stability, stopped communist insurgency, and created a democratic nation, what exactly had the Americans achieved? They had completed the transition from French to American control in Vietnam, which represented a transition between two different types of imperialism— the old-fashioned French variety of formal, bureaucratic control and a new American neocolonial, or informal, one. Washington's determination to replace the French on every possible level in South Vietnam and its accelerated commitment to the Diem regime because it saw no other anticommunist and anticolonial alternative led to American activities in Vietnam that looked suspiciously like earlier French ones. Americans from 1954 until well into the 1960s claimed that the French effort failed because French leaders had sought to reestablish colonial rule and employ Bao Dai as a political façade to maintain control. The irony is difficult to miss, as these same Americans attempted to establish their own way of ruling South Vietnam and to use Ngo Dinh Diem as the front man for their efforts. After resisting all-out aid to the French effort for so long because of French colonial behavior, the Americans had become the colonialists. Neither western power ever delivered on its promise of an independent government in the South.

Imperialist activities were costly, not merely in terms of dollars or American anticolonial credentials, but also with respect to the Franco-American alliance. As French senator Michel Debré remarked, it was "not possible for France to be allies with the United States in Europe to be half abandoned by them in Africa and totally betrayed in the Far East. An alliance with the United States should not be limited geographically."[7] French foreign minister Christian Pineau went a step further in early 1956, declaring that "no common policy [existed] among the United States, United Kingdom, and France anywhere in the world."[8] Pineau believed that the United States had made a serious mistake in hoping to increase its strength in Indochina by eliminating the French. According to Pineau, the "loss of Western prestige" in the Far East was caused primarily by "divisions" in the Atlantic alliance.[9] Gaullist leader Jacques Soustelle also wrote in 1956 that the western alliance did "not prove favorable to France" in the Far East.[10] What troubled Debré, Pineau, Soustelle, and so many other leading French figures, was the American position of being allied when and where it was convenient.

Melvyn Leffler has written that Eisenhower and Dulles did seek solidarity with their allies and wrote guidelines into their national security strategy for the maintenance of "alliance cohesion." But they also emphasized that the United States should "act independently of its major allies" when the advantage of achieving U.S. objectives by such action clearly outweighed the danger of "lasting damage to its alliances." Therefore, American officials should consider the "likelihood" that unilateral action prior to allied acceptance might bring about subsequent allied support. Allied reluctance to act should not "inhibit the United States from taking action."[11] The administration wanted it both ways—it engaged in multilateralism on the diplomatic level but its methods and practice were unilateral. Clearly, the Eisenhower administration was not inhibited from pursuing an independent course of action toward Vietnam.

Looking back on the 1950s, Robert McNamara points out that there were a number of missed opportunities to settle the Indochina conflict long before major U.S. intervention occurred in the mid-1960s. In particular, McNamara notes that the Truman administration's decision to underwrite the French effort in Indochina in 1950 was an error, as was the American refusal to participate fully in the 1954 Geneva Conference and to sign the final agreement.[12] His focus on these two events indicates the importance of the Franco-American relationship in increasing the American presence in Vietnam. The Americans certainly did not learn the "lessons" that the French experience in Indochina had to offer; they, as the French had earlier, rejected diplomatic possibilities in order to reserve their independence of action.

In pursuing a transnational perspective—one that is neither American, nor French, nor Vietnamese—this study emphasizes a number of agencies and actors as well as specific conferences and events. Individuals and groups from one country within the alliance either cooperated, or more likely, did not cooperate, with other individuals and groups from another allied country. For example, chapter 1 looks at the sustained effort on the part of French military and political leaders to convince their counterparts in the United States and Britain to view Indochina as a Cold War battle and to create a Southeast Asian common defense, whereas chapter 2 looks at how Stalin's death persuaded France that peace in the Far East was possible while prompting the Americans to resist negotiations even more ferociously. Chapter 3 revolves around the alliance crisis before, during, and after the

Geneva Conference, and chapter 4 centers on Diem—perhaps the key player in determining Franco-American diplomacy toward Vietnam from 1954 to 1963. Chapter 5 tackles political centers—Washington, Paris, London, Hanoi, Saigon, Moscow, and Beijing—whereas chapter 6 focuses on specific military, economic, bureaucratic, and cultural entities. Chapter 7 addresses the dual nature of French policy as France struggled to maintain a presence in both North and South Vietnam, and chapter 8 details the role official and unofficial American agencies played in trying to build South Vietnam into a nation. The point is that individuals mattered, players on the ground in Saigon as well as in Washington and Paris, although the ones in Washington, with the possible exception of Diem, tended to matter most.

There are no heroes in this story. Still, a number of actors displayed thoughtful sensitivity to the myriad of problems that existed in Vietnam and the dangers of American intervention, and their advice warranted serious consideration. Unfortunately, most of them spoke French. Americans who painted a pessimistic picture, and in particular those who served as ambassador or special representative on the ground in Saigon, were also routinely ignored by Washington. Donald Heath, J. Lawton Collins, G. Frederick Reinhardt, and Elbridge Durbrow all sought to implement policy at a tactical level and all ultimately concluded that the American effort in South Vietnam was doomed. But the strategists in Washington always overrode them. Thus, the story becomes more than the difficulties the Franco-American relationship faced, or even the manner by which the United States replaced France in Vietnam to become the dominant player; this is the story of how the United States became committed to a noncommunist South Vietnam.

If there is a villain in the story, or at least someone to hold primarily responsible for this commitment, it might be John Foster Dulles. Dulles was undeniably fighting the good fight against communism. In fact, he no doubt enjoyed the opportunity to do battle with evil and supported Diem in part because the two men shared the same belief of one moral authority. For Dulles, neutralism was not an option, nor was the middle ground, which helps explain why Dulles and various French officials clashed so often. Dulles's villainy lies in his Manichean worldview, which precluded serious negotiations with his adversaries, and oftentimes with his allies. His failure to engage in diplomacy played a critical role in the breakdown of the Geneva Accords, making the resumption of hostilities much more likely.

The other villain, perhaps, is the pesky notion of American exceptionalism, which Dulles, among others, embraced wholeheartedly. While the Americans were happy to serve as a "shining example upon a hill" in

Vietnam, they often found this tactic a little slow in helping South Vietnam become like the United States. Americans on the ground favored a more active role, believing that additional resources and American methods, training, and values would create a stable, noncommunist South Vietnam. Thus, American cultural conceptions of themselves propagated an assertive foreign policy.[13]

And what of the enemy in the North? Hanoi's biggest mistake, and an ironic one at that, was relying on France to control the situation in the South after Geneva. The North Vietnamese leadership had also counted on the fact that the French, if they did not eliminate the Diem regime, would at least become so annoyed with it that they would turn their efforts to saving their considerable presence in the North. And indeed the French did weigh this option, as witnessed by the Sainteny mission. Hanoi had not foreseen how quickly Diem and the Americans would force France to withdraw, thus ending any possibility of negotiations. Nor had the DRV expected the lack of interest from the other Geneva conferees and neutralist countries, who preferred, as long as hostilities did not break out again, to bury the Vietnamese problem.

But Hanoi was not alone; all the signatories to the Geneva Accords had assumed that they would be sitting back down at the conference table at some point. No one anticipated that the United States and South Vietnam, who had not signed, would ensure a different outcome. Hanoi was caught by surprise and would spend a good part of the 1954–1960 period engaged in diplomatic and propaganda efforts designed to combat its relative isolation outside the communist orbit and to persuade the South Vietnamese that they were being oppressed by the Americans and Diem. Hanoi did not entirely close the door on negotiations with Saigon, but the North Vietnamese eventually began to embrace the idea of reunification by military rather than political means. As Philippe Devillers has noted, the Vietnamese people had always been caught between communism and a form of anticommunism that they could not accept. During the period of French control it was communism or colonialism. Once the Americans came onto the scene, it was communism or a dictatorship that, in the words of Devillers, was "Fascist and medieval."[14]

The East-West superpower clash presented both risks and opportunities to those in Vietnam during what they conceived as a crucial moment in North-South relations. Neither the Vietnamese nor the French frame of reference was dominated by Cold War politics the way the American one was. Because of its inability to see the situation without Cold War lenses, the

Eisenhower administration underestimated the forces of nationalism and decolonization.

Nation-building is a tricky business. For the United States, the reasons for its going awry are often similar. Nation-builders tend to focus on military buildup and internal security first and nation-building second. Moreover, the superimposition of American culture and values on a fundamentally different society is usually met with eventual hostility. Americans also have a tendency to operate on an ad hoc basis, with various organizations duplicating each other's efforts. And then there is always the seemingly unshakable twentieth and thus far twenty-first century American hubris that the United States can build better than anyone else. For example, in addition to the American military presence in 1950s Vietnam was the political, economic, administrative, and cultural structure the United States created. The Geneva Accords said nothing about nonmilitary personnel, which was why the Eisenhower administration came to embrace soft power tactics—economic aid, land and administrative reform, and cultural activities, to name a few. The catch was that eventually these tactics precipitated and facilitated hard power ones, at least in Vietnam.

One of the soft power tactics employed by Americans in Vietnam was the use of cultural initiatives. The United States initially disparaged the French cultural mission in Indochina and tended to associate France's civilizing mission with colonialism from 1950 to 1954. And yet, after Geneva, Washington soon began to export its own cultural mission and American agencies began to take on shades of neocolonialism. Returning to the theme of the United States as a neocolonial power and Vietnam as its, shall we say, neo-colony, this study has been most interested in attempted indirect rule (the American variety) as opposed to attempted direct rule (the French variety from the 1880s to World War II). Indirect rule is less visible and usually cheaper, but it still obliges its adherents to intervene in local society, and, in the case of Vietnam, to deal with political and military leaders, bureaucrats, teachers, religious-political sects, peasants, refugees, and others.

In reflecting whether the United States built a colony rather than a nation, it is worth considering this: the United States is founded on the practice of actual rather than virtual representation. In other words, the essential criterion of a successful democratic nation, according to American leaders, is voting—free, fair, and regularly occurring elections. The Eisenhower administration never reconciled its rhetoric of free elections with its attempts to subvert the 1956 elections in Vietnam. For Diem, there was no such dilemma—his concern was staying in power, not promoting democracy. And the United States went along with his flagrant abuses of power for a very long time. Although historians have duly noted that the 1956 elections were not held, that Diem's 1955 referendum was a mockery, and that Diem repeatedly engaged in political oppression and failed to ensure fair representation of political parties until his assassination, the deeper implications have not been fully articulated. If the United States supported a truly undemocratic leader, how could South Vietnam possibly be a nation? It had to be a colony, or at the very least a dependency. During his 1957 visit to the United States, Diem himself stated that "the frontier of the United States extends to the 17th parallel."[15] Frontier it certainly was. In 1950, the South Vietnamese had limited control over monetary and economic policy, could not participate in elections, experienced no freedom of press or assembly, and feared arbitrary arrest. What had changed by 1961? Very little.

Is there any way American nation-building in South Vietnam could have avoided becoming neocolonial in the existing Cold War circumstances? The answer, alas, is probably not. Mary Ann Heiss writes that "achieving both anticolonialism and Cold War foreign policy needs proved impossible." The nation "chose cold war over anticolonialism—informal rather than formal and defensive rather than offensive, but empire nonetheless."[16] Nowhere was the U.S. abandonment of anti-imperialism and reinvigoration of the idea of a U.S. mission more evident than in post-1954 Vietnam. In this case, the colonizer claimed it was not a colonizer, but American actions belied American rhetoric.

American sentiments might have been postcolonial in the idea of modernizing and nation-building, and of course they had no "territorial ambition," as they were fond of pointing out, but American methods did not differ significantly from French colonialist Albert Sarraut's 1920s policy of association. One of the amazing truths that emerges from evaluating U.S. policy during 1950–1960 is that the Americans constantly worried about appearing "colonial" in the first half of the decade, but in the second half they embraced the trappings and some of the substance of colonialism. Americans felt almost entitled to replace the French because they were sure their anticolonial methods had a better chance of preserving a noncommunist South Vietnam.

How deep did the change from the French to the Americans go? For the Vietnamese, there was little difference between the two western nations. If the South Vietnamese failed to distinguish between the French civilizing mission and the American modernization effort, then the two could not have been that different in practice. There is a reason colonialism ended up in the dustbin of history—it is unsustainable. The Americans, like the French, would learn this lesson the hard way.

The story contained within these pages has traced Washington's transition from a partner in the French war effort to *the* dominant western power in South Vietnam in the 1950s. It has also been a story of alliance failure. Challenging conventional interpretations of the origins of the Vietnam War—which generally emphasize the importance of decisions taken by the Kennedy and Johnson administrations—the focus here has been the critical role that the Franco-American alliance played in fostering the U.S. commitment to Vietnam in the 1950s and the importance of paying close attention to allied as well as adversarial motivations, behavior, and goals in times of crisis. It is a story that has relevance for current and future alliance members and one that policy makers might want to consider.

Of particular concern is the American tendency to equate allied dissent with disloyalty. U.S. leaders have been quick to criticize allies' motives and to penalize them for their lack of support. After Geneva, the French were punished when the United States, along with South Vietnamese prime minister Ngo Dinh Diem, forced them out of Vietnam. In return, the French washed their hands of the entire affair, including providing political or economic aid for the subsequent American war effort. After the Second Iraq War, the Bush administration carried out its threat of consequences by banning French firms from bidding on primary contracts for Iraq and barring French participation in long-planned military exercises. As a result, French cooperation in the Middle East, and elsewhere, has been difficult to attain. Thus, just as the United States replaced France in Vietnam and then ended up absorbing the costs of American intervention, Washington pushed away its allies in Iraq and continues to pay the political, economic, and physical price.

At first glance, the United States' overwhelming military superiority in the 1950s, and today, would seem to indicate its ability to go it alone—without need for an alliance. But the costs—economic, physical, and diplomatic—of this military superiority tend to undermine U.S. power, and, ultimately, American national interests, as witnessed in South Vietnam. Unilateralism should not be undertaken lightly as it often leads to accusations of imperialism. Vietnam was perhaps the one "real imperial nightmare" of the twentieth century for the United States.[17] While the Eisenhower administration's policies could be considered "imperialism lite," they set a tone and created a precedent upon which subsequent administrations would rely. The cumulative weight of ten years of direct American involvement from 1950 to 1960 created a momentum in South Vietnam that was not easily stopped. Even as Washington became more discouraged with the Diem regime, the American presence in Vietnam continued. The later American war effort was not inevitable, but the decisions and developments of the 1950s made it more difficult for future American leaders to disengage from Vietnam. At least one goal had been achieved—the process of replacing France was complete.

Notes

Introduction

1. With a few exceptions—most notably Aimaq, *For Europe or Empire?*; Cesari, "La France, Les Etats-Unis, et L'Indochine"; and Journoud, "Face-à-face"—scholarship providing a transnational emphasis on the 1950s is scarce.

2. Although *Indochina* refers to the three Associated States of Vietnam, Laos, and Cambodia, contemporaries, as do many scholars today, used the terms *Indochina* and *Vietnam* interchangeably until the 1954 Geneva Conference. I have continued this practice.

3. Decision making during the Kennedy and Johnson administrations has received the majority of academic and popular attention. For scholarship on this period, see Fredrik Logevall's excellent study *Choosing War*; Berman, *Planning a Tragedy*; Kahin, *Intervention*; McMaster, *Dereliction of Duty*; Herring, *LBJ and Vietnam*; Moise, *Tonkin Gulf*; and Kaiser, *American Tragedy*.

4. To assess how planning worked in Vietnam I spent a good deal of time examining French, American, and British Saigon embassy reports; official agency records that detail the effectiveness—and ineffectiveness—of French and American personnel in the political, military, economic, social, cultural, and educational spheres in Vietnam; French National Assembly and American Congressional records; newspapers; and documents from unofficial organizations. Specifically, I looked at records, memoranda, and letters from the United States Information Agency, the United States Operations Mission, the Michigan State University Group, the Military Assistance and Advisory Group, the American-Vietnamese Association, the International Rescue Committee, and the National Catholic Welfare Council. I also examined reports and letters from the French Cultural Mission, the French high command, the French Expeditionary Corps, the French Military Officer Training School, the Franco-American Training Relations Mission, and the French National School of Administration.

5. For an excellent assessment of Franco-American conflict in 2003 and the historical background of this conflict, see Wall, "The French-American War over Iraq."

6. The term "Axis of Weasels," a play on President George Bush's description of North Korea, Iran, and Iraq as an "axis of evil," became a popular way to refer to France and Germany when they refused to support U.S. plans for military intervention in Iraq.

7. Eisenhower to Gruenther, June 8, 1954, EL, Alfred Gruenther Papers, 1941–1983, Eisenhower Correspondence series, box 1, Eisenhower 1954 (1); John Foster Dulles telephone conversation, July 21, 1954, microfilm, 1953–1954, *Minutes of Telephone Conversations of John Foster Dulles and Christian Herter, 1953–1961*, ed. Kesaris and Gibson.

8. See Jervis, *Perception and Misperception* and Matthews, Rubinoff, and Gross Stein (eds.), *International Conflict and Conflict Management*.

9. See Cogan, *French Negotiating Behavior* for a discussion of differences in French and American negotiating tactics. See also Dallek, *American Style of Foreign Policy*. Record, *Making War, Thinking History* and Khong, *Analogies at War* have also demonstrated the American aversion to making concessions to the communist bloc, which they attribute to the Munich analogy's powerful sway over presidential decision making in Vietnam. Both authors focus primarily on the Kennedy and Johnson administrations rather than the Eisenhower administration.

10. Kuisel, *Seducing the French*, 36.

11. For first-rate work on the U.S. role during the 1940–1950 period, see Marr, *Vietnam 1945;* Tonnesson, *The Vietnamese Revolution of 1945;* Lawrence, *Assuming the Burden* and "Transnational Coalition-Building"; Bradley, *Imagining Vietnam and America;* and Hess, *The United States' Emergence as a Southeast Asian Power.* For comprehensive studies of the entire period of American involvement, see Herring, *America's Longest War;* Kattenburg, *The Vietnam Trauma;* Young, *The Vietnam Wars;* Hess, *Vietnam and the United States;* Mann, *A Grand Delusion;* Karnow, *Vietnam;* Smith, *An International History of the Vietnam War;* and Schulzinger, *A Time for War.*

12. See, for example, Duiker, *U.S. Containment Policy;* Rotter, *The Path to Vietnam;* and Lee, *Outposts of Empire.*

13. For literature on the Franco-American relationship during the First Indochina War, see Hammer, *The Struggle for Indochina;* Spector, *Advice and Support;* Irving, *The First Indochina War;* Gardner, *Approaching Vietnam;* Devillers and Lacouture, *End of a War;* and Dommen, *The Indochinese Experience.*

14. See, for example, Jacobs, "Our System Demands the Supreme Being" and Kahin, *Intervention*, 66.

15. In this case, Carl von Clausewitz's famous dictum that "War is merely a continuation of politics by other means" was inverted, as the Geneva conferees moved from a military strategy to a political one. Carlyle Thayer has explored this theme with respect to the formation of the National Liberation Front in *War by Other Means.*

16. Akira Iriye defines the cultural approach to foreign relations as one that examines the "sharing and transmitting of consciousness within and across national boundaries . . . the creation and communication of memory, ideology, emotions, life styles, scholarly and artistic works, and other symbols such as religion, law, customs, and literature." Iriye, "Culture and International History," 215. See also Arndt, *The*

First Resort of Kings for an in-depth discussion of how the United States government has attempted to achieve foreign policy goals through planned cultural programs.

17. See Gienow-Hecht, "Shame on U.S.?" 472–73, 486, for her discussion of Williams's interpretation and American cultural imperialism, and Kuisel, *Seducing the French*, xi, xii, on how American cultural inroads in post–World War II France exacerbated French anxieties and sense of self-identity. Other studies on American cultural imperialism include Pells, *Not Like Us*; Wagnleitner, *Coca-Colonization and the Cold War*; and Poigner, "Beyond 'Modernization' and 'Colonization.'" All of these works focus primarily on Europe.

18. See Cooper, *France in Indochina*, chapters 1–3, for a detailed analysis of the establishment of French colonialism in Indochina.

19. Although Michael Latham focuses on the Kennedy administration's attempts to "modernize" Vietnam, his conception of modernization as "a means to promote a liberal world in which the development of 'emerging' nations would protect the security of the United States" is equally applicable to the Eisenhower administration's policies in South Vietnam. Latham, *Modernization as Ideology*, 209.

20. Robert McMahon posits that the United States looked a lot like an empire in Southeast Asia in the 1950s but avoids referring to Vietnam as a colony. McMahon, *The Limits of Empire*.

21. In contrast to "hard power" tactics—coercion based on military and economic might—"soft power" tactics are used to achieve a country's goals through persuasion by cultivating relations with allies, providing economic assistance, and promoting cultural exchanges with other countries to demonstrate the attractiveness of a country's culture, political ideas, and policies. See Nye, *Soft Power* for the most up-to-date account of soft power.

1. Decolonization and Cold War

1. After negotiators failed to reach a compromise between Vietnamese nationalist demands and French determination to preserve the empire, hostilities broke out between Vietminh and French forces in late 1946. For the origins and course of the First Indochina War, see Shipway, *Road to War*; Dalloz, *The War in Indochina*; Ruscio, *La Guerre française d'Indochine*; Devillers, *Histoire du Vietnam*; and Fall, *Street without Joy*.

2. For a firsthand account of the negotiations regarding the March 1949 accords, see Bao Dai, *Le Dragon d'Annam*, 217–19. See also Dommen, *The Indochinese Experience*, 187–91.

3. American bureaucratic infighting with respect to Vietnamese independence is discussed in Spector, *Advice and Support*, 93–95; Blum, *Drawing the Line*, 115–17; and Dommen, *The Indochinese Experience*, 188–89. See also Rotter, *The Path to Vietnam*, 84–102, for an account of American policy toward Vietnam in 1949.

4. Conclusions of Chief of General Staff General George Revers, top secret

memorandum, May 11–June 21, 1949, Archives Nationales, Paris, France (hereafter cited as AN), 560AP/40.

5. Lee, *Outposts of Empire*, 43–44.

6. Pignon to Jean Letourneau, French minister of overseas France, top secret, November 7, 1949; Letourneau to Pignon, November 1949, and Pignon to Letourneau, December 1, 1949, AN, Conseil des Ministres, F60 3036.

7. By 1949, France's two most prominent political parties had split on the Indochina issue. The socialists (SFIO) wanted a more liberal policy in Indochina and felt that contacts should be made with Ho Chi Minh. The Christian democrats (MRP) insisted Bao Dai was the only acceptable representative in Vietnam.

8. Duiker, *U.S. Containment Policy*, 87.

9. The MDAP came into being in 1949 as part of the Mutual Defense Assistance Act to provide economic aid to the noncommunist world. Section 303 authorized $75 million to be used in the general area of China. Spector, *Advice and Support*, 98. For details on the Congressional process of approving section 303 funds, see Blum, *Drawing the Line*, 200–220. There was very little Congressional debate in deciding to provide initial funds for the French war effort in Indochina.

10. Problem Paper prepared by DOS working group, February 1, 1950, *Foreign Relations of the United States* (hereafter cited as FRUS) *1950* 6:711–15, 945–54; Spector, *Advice and Support*, 103. Blum, *Drawing the Line* and Hays (ed.), *The Beginning of American Aid to Southeast Asia* assess the U.S. decision to provide aid for Vietnam within the context of the Cold War and the need for Southeast Asian defense.

11. Deputy Director of the Office of European Regional Affairs Douglas MacArthur, memorandum, February 20, 1950, *FRUS 1950* 3:1360–62.

12. Cesari, "La France, Les Etats-Unis, et L'Indochine," 389; Bonnet to Ministère des Affaires Etrangères (MAE), February 10, 1950, Ministère des Affaires Etrangères, Paris, France (hereafter cited as MAE), Papiers d'Agents, Archives Privés, Henri Bonnet, vol. 1.

13. Spector, *Advice and Support*, 11.

14. Lee, *Outposts of Empire*, 51–52.

15. Foreign Office, minute, January 6, 1950, Public Record Office, Kew, Britain (hereafter cited as PRO), Foreign Office (FO) 371/83606.

16. Aimaq, *For Europe or Empire?* 171–76.

17. See Hays (ed.), *The Beginning of American Aid to Southeast Asia* for more on the Griffin mission. The mission was led by Economic Cooperation Administration (ECA) official and former deputy chief of the China mission Allen Robert Griffin.

18. Note, April 13, 1950, MAE, Secrétariat Général, vol. 20; note on American aid, March 18, 1950, AN, Conseil des Ministres, F60 3037.

19. MAE to Saigon, top secret, March 10, 1950, Centre des Archives d'Outre Mer, Aix-en-Provence, France (hereafter cited as CAOM), Haut Commissariat, Indochine, Conseiller Politique, vol. 61.

20. Memorandum, n.d., CAOM, Conseiller Politique, vol. 61; Schuman-Bevin conversation, March 7, 1950, MAE, Secrétariat Général, vol. 23.

21. Adjunct director of political affairs, note for the minister, April 5, 1950; Bonnet to MAE, top secret, April 13, 1950, MAE, Secrétariat Général, vol. 21; American minister in the French Embassy Charles Bohlen to Voorhees Group, April 3, 1950, *FRUS 1950* 3:1369–72.

22. Note regarding Indochina, n.d.; note, April 22, 1950, MAE, Secrétariat Général, vol. 20.

23. Note regarding Indochina, n.d.; note, April 22, 1950; note for the minister, April 26, 1950, MAE, Secrétariat Général, vol. 20.

24. Secretary of defense to secretary of state, April 14, 1950, *FRUS 1950* 6:780–85; Duiker, *U.S. Containment Policy*, 94.

25. Defense Ministry to Quai, top secret, May 4, 1950, AN, 560AP/40.

26. Massigli to MAE, May 7, 1950, MAE, Secrétariat Général, vol. 21.

27. Spector, *Advice and Support*, 106–7.

28. Memorandum in preparation for tripartite talks, April 24, 1950, PRO, FO 371/83609; and secretary of state to acting secretary of state, May 8, 1950, *FRUS 1950* 3:1007–13.

29. Secretary of state to acting secretary, May 14, 1950, *FRUS 1950* 3:1061–67.

30. Tripartite meetings, top secret, May 6, 1950, MAE, Cabinet du Ministre, Cabinet Schuman, vol. 8; and tripartite meetings, top secret, May 8, 1950, MAE, Cabinet du Ministre, Cabinet Schuman, vol. 7.

31. Note, May 1950, CAOM, Conseiller Politique, vol. 208.

32. Duiker, *U.S. Containment Policy*, 97.

33. Internal memorandum, L'Aide Économique Américaine aux Etats Associés d'Indochine, n.d., MAE, Cambodge, Laos, Vietnam (CLV), Aide Militaire, Généralités, carton 3. (The cartons in this series have not been declassified and are only available upon special request.)

34. Auriol, Schuman, Letourneau, Pignon, Prime Minister and President of the Council Georges Bidault, Vice President of the Council Henri Quenille, and Superior Commander of Armed Forces in the Far East General Marcel Carpentier attended the meeting. Meeting of National Defense Committee (NDC), top secret, June 22, 1950, AN, 560AP/40.

35. Aimaq, *For Europe or Empire?* 179. See Rotter, *The Path to Vietnam*, 209–13, for the impact of the Korean War on Indochina. Although some scholarship has compared military strategies in the Korean and Indochinese conflicts or assessed the Korean War's influence on future American decisions in Vietnam, historians have not detailed how the Korean War altered American views of the conflict in Indochina at the time. See Lee, *Outposts of Empire* for a comparison of strategies and Khong, *Analogies at War* for an analysis of how the "lessons" of Korea influenced American decision making in Vietnam in the 1960s. Others, such as Spector, *Advice and Support* (123) dismiss the outbreak of war in Korea as having a significant impact in

shaping American policy, claiming that basic decisions related to American policy toward Indochina had already been made. This study draws different conclusions.

36. Lee, *Outposts of Empire*, 114–16; Blum, *Drawing the Line*, 213; Bernard Fall report, "The International Position of South Vietnam 1954–1958," MAE, CLV, Sud-Vietnam (SV), vol. 68.

37. Hitchcock, *France Restored*, 4, 134.

38. Duiker, *U.S. Containment Policy*, 100.

39. Gibbons, *The U.S. Government and the Vietnam War*, 80.

40. See Spector, *Advice and Support*, 115–20, for more detail on MAAG's establishment and growth.

41. Massigli to Auriol and Schuman, August 1, 1951, MAE, Cabinet du Ministre, Cabinet Schuman, vol. 50.

42. NDC meeting, top secret, August 18, 1950, AN, 560AP/42; French counsel general in Los Angeles Raoul Bertrand to MAE, February 1, 1951, MAE, Cabinet du Ministre, Cabinet Schuman, vol. 106; note, November 20, 1950, MAE, Cabinet du Ministre, Cabinet Schuman, vol. 14.

43. Secretary of state to Saigon, September 1, 1950, *FRUS 1950* 6:868–70; David Bruce to Assistant Secretary of State for Far Eastern Affairs Dean Rusk, September 5, 1950, *FRUS 1950* 6:875–76. The idea of building up Vietnamese forces, or "Vietnamizing" the conflict—usually associated with the American war effort under the Nixon administration—in fact had been an issue of Franco-American debate since 1950.

44. Bruce to secretary of state, August 17, 1950, *FRUS 1950* 6:860–61. Georges Bidault had served as prime minister from October 28, 1949, to July 2, 1950. After a very short interim government, Pleven took over on July 12.

45. Bruce to secretary of state, July 28, 1950, *FRUS 1950* 3:54; Director of PPS Paul Nitze, memorandum of conversation, October 5, 1950, *FRUS 1950* 3:358–61.

46. Rusk to secretary, top secret, September 8, 1950, National Archives Records Administration, College Park, Maryland (hereafter cited NA), Record Group (RG) 59, Executive Secretariat, Conference files, box 5.

47. U.S. delegation minutes, fourth meeting of the foreign ministers, secret, September 14, 1950, *FRUS 1950* 3:1224–28.

48. Note for the president, September 27, 1950, AN, Conseil des Ministres, F60 3037.

49. Southeast Asia Aid Policy Committee to DOS and DOD, memorandum, October 11, 1950; and annex *FRUS 1950* 6:886–90. The committee was a joint State/Defense/ECA group formed in April.

50. Aimaq, *For Europe or Empire?* 192; Spector, *Advice and Support*, 125.

51. NSC 64/1, December 21, 1950, *FRUS 1950* 6:945–53.

52. See Aimaq, *For Europe or Empire?* 193–203, for more on the French perspective in the second half of 1950, and Spector, *Advice and Support*, 123–34, for the American perspective during this period.

53. Gibbons, *The U.S. Government and the Vietnam War,* 84.

54. Pleven to Letourneau, October 22, 1950, AN, 560AP/42; Duiker, *Sacred War,* 72–73; Hammer, *The Struggle for Indochina,* 287; Dommen, *The Indochinese Experience,* 195.

55. Note on the government mission of Letourneau and Juin, October 1950, AN, 560AP/42.

56. Pignon to MAE, April 27, 1950; Pignon to Pleven, top secret, November 24, 1950; Pignon to Letourneau, top secret, November 21, 1950; Pignon to Letourneau, top secret, November 21, 1950; and Pignon to Council President Bidault, top secret, November 30, 1950, AN, 560AP/42.

57. Note, November 7, 1950, PRO, FO 371/83630; FO to Head of the Southeast Asia Department Robert H. Scott, November 14, 1950, PRO, FO 371/83630.

58. Atlee-Pleven meetings, December 2, 1950; and Massigli to MAE, top secret, December 4, 1950, MAE, Secrétariat Général, vol. 23; Spector, *Advice and Support,* 134.

59. Mélandri, "France and the Atlantic Alliance," 275; top secret memorandum, December 4, 1950, AN, 560AP/42; NDC notes, January 1, 1951, AN, 74AP/43; Letourneau to Pleven, January 27, 1951, AN, Conseil des Ministres, FO60 3037.

60. Pleven to MAE, top secret, January 29, 1951, AN, 560AP/46; negotiating papers for Truman-Pleven talks, January 25, 1951, NA, RG 59, Executive Secretariat, Conference files, box 7.

61. Meeting in Secretary's Office, top secret, January 29, 1951, NA, RG 59, Executive Secretariat, Conference files, box 7; Bonnet to MAE, top secret, January 28 and 29, 1951, MAE, Secrétariat Général, vol. 23; U.S. minutes of the second meeting between Truman and Pleven, top secret, January 30, 1951, *FRUS 1950* 4:315–28. Top secret conversations, January 30, 1951, MAE, Secrétariat Général, vol. 23; Bonnet to MAE, January 31, 1951, MAE, Secrétariat Général, vol. 23.

62. Meeting in Secretary's Office, top secret, January 29, 1951, NA, RG 59, Executive Secretariat, Conference files, box 7; Gibbs to FO, February 14, 1951, PRO, FO 371/92412; Gibbs to FO, July 11, 1951, PRO, FO 371/92422; NA, RG 59, Executive Secretariat, Meetings of Foreign Dignitaries, box 34. See also Truman-Pleven talks, January 29, 1951, *FRUS 1951* 4:305–13; January 30, 1951, *FRUS 1951* 3:120; and background memorandum prepared in DOS, March 1951, *FRUS 1951* 4:349–62.

63. Bonnet to MAE, secret, April 2, 1951, MAE, Secrétariat Général, vol. 24.

64. Assistant Secretary of State Lucius D. Battle, top secret memorandum of conversation; top secret minutes of a private conference among the French, British, and U.S. foreign ministers, September 12 and 14, 1950, *FRUS 1950* 3:285–88, 293–301; secretary of state to acting secretary of state, top secret memorandum, September 17, 1950; and memorandum of conversation, October 16, 1950, *FRUS 1950* 3:1412–16.

65. This study does not provide details of the EDC proposal, protocols, and process. The mechanics of the EDC, its possibilities as an alternative to West Ger-

many's entry into NATO, and its use to further European integration have been ably discussed by Fursdon, *The European Defense Community;* Aimaq, *For Europe or Empire?;* Trachtenberg, *A Constructed Peace,* 110–25; Monnet, *Mémoirs,* 345–49; Melandri, "France and the Atlantic Alliance"; and Leffler, *A Preponderance of Power,* 453–63. This study focuses on the EDC only as it applies to Franco-American policy in Indochina and intra-alliance politics.

66. Ambrose, *Eisenhower,* 302.

67. Juin, *Memoirs, II,* 261–63, 276.

68. Note, July 27, 1951, MAE, Asie Océanie 1944–1955, Indochine, vol. 270; Bruce to Acheson, August 25, 1951, *FRUS 1951* 3:1184–88; and Schuman to Acheson, August 26, 1951, *FRUS 1951* 3:1191.

69. General Director of the Associated States Tezenas de Montecel to MAE, note, August 28, 1951, MAE, Cabinet du Ministre, Cabinet Schuman, vol. 90.

70. Bonnet to Bidault, top secret, September 9, 1951, MAE, Cabinet du Ministre, Cabinet Schuman, vol. 12; Bonnet to MAE, secret, September 12, 1951, MAE, Asie Océanie 1944–1955, Indochine, vol. 270; Bonnet to Schuman, secret, September 12, 1951, MAE, Cabinet du Ministre, Cabinet Schuman, vol. 12.

71. Bonnet to MAE, September 18, 1951, MAE, Asie Océanie 1944–1955, Indochine, vol. 270; Bonnet to Schuman, September 28, 1951, MAE, Cabinet du Ministre, Cabinet Schuman, vol. 90; secret memorandum of conversation, September 20, 1951, NA, RG 59, Director Office of Philippine and Southeast Asian Affairs, International Conferences, Talks, and Meetings, box 1. See Spector, *Advice and Support,* 141–44, for more on de Lattre's visit to the United States.

72. Duiker, *U.S. Containment Policy,* 116; top secret note on meeting, October 4, 1951, MAE, Asie Océanie 1944–1955, Indochine, vol. 270. The concern by some American officials was that France would cut commitments in Europe before those in Asia. Bruce to DOS, November 1, 1951, *FRUS 1951* 3:908–9.

73. NDC meeting, top secret, October 15, 1951, AN, F60 3037. The committee also considered implementing an obligatory two-year service in order to ensure enough troops for both theaters, but eventually decided against this idea for fear of alienating the general population.

74. NDC meeting, December 4, 1951, AN, 560AP/42.

75. Christie, "The Sentimental American," 152–53.

76. Saigon to Paris, secret note on American economic aid, June 17, 1950, Interministerial Committee for European Economic Cooperation Affairs, CAOM, Conseiller Politique, vol. 208; Duiker, *U.S. Containment Policy,* 114.

77. Robert Blum, American Economic Aid Mission memorandum, June 30, 1951, NA, RG 469, Mission to Vietnam, Program and Support Division, Well Program, box 7; internal memorandum, L'Aide Economique Américaine aux Etats Associés d'Indochine, n.d., MAE, CLV, Aide Militaire, Généralités, carton 3.

78. NA, RG 469, Mission to Vietnam, Program and Support Division, Subject files, 1950–1956, 1950–1954, correspondence and films, box 2.

79. Spector, *Advice and Support,* 121.

80. Gibbons, *The U.S. Government and the Vietnam War,* 91; Cesari, "La France, Les Etats-Unis, et L'Indochine," 495; British ambassador Gibbs to FO, April 28, 1951, PRO, FO 371/92420.

81. Pignon to Letourneau, top secret, March 21, 1950, AN, Conseil des Ministres, F60 3037.

82. Notes, 1951, CAOM, Conseiller Politique, vol. 208.

83. Gautier to Haut-Commissaire en mission, secretary general for the expedition of cultural affairs, n.d., CAOM, Conseiller Politique, vol. 208.

84. Heath, cable, June 29, 1951, *FRUS 1951* 6:432–38; Gibbons, *The U.S. Government and the Vietnam War,* 92, 98.

85. Prados, "Central Intelligence Agency," 7–8.

86. Lee, *Outposts of Empire,* 122; note, August 31, 1951, CAOM, Conseiller Politique, vol. 208; Bonnet to MAE, top secret, January 9, 1952, MAE, Secrétariat Général, vol. 26; Bonnet to MAE, February 10, 1952, MAE, Secrétariat Général, vol. 27.

87. Bonnet to Schuman, January 25, 1952, MAE, Cabinet du Ministre, Cabinet Schuman, vol. 107.

88. Allison to Acheson, February 11, 1952, *FRUS 1952–1954* 13:28–34.

89. American minister in the Paris Embassy Charles Bohlen to DOS, February 7, 1952, *FRUS 1952–1954* 5:610–11.

90. *FRUS 1952–1954* 13:39, 61–62 ed. notes.

91. Bonsal to the director of the Office of Philippine and Southeast Asian Affairs (William Lacy), March 31, 1952, *FRUS 1952–1954* 13:93–98.

92. Note, April 22, 1952, MAE, Asie Océanie 1944–1955, Indochine, vol. 282; Ely, notes, November 28, 1952, Service Historique de l'Armée de la Terre, Château de Vincennes, France (hereafter cited as SHAT), Fonds Paul Ely, vol. 37.

93. Bonnet to MAE, January 18, 1952, MAE, Asie Océanie 1944–1955, vol. 281; and Eden-Schuman conversations, February 1, 1952, MAE, Secrétariat Général, vol. 27.

94. Note, April 22, 1952, MAE, Cabinet du Ministre, Cabinet Schuman, vol. 90; Spector, *Advice and Support,* 152.

95. Top secret memorandum for the files, May 19, 1952, Dwight D. Eisenhower Presidential Library, Abilene, Kansas (hereafter cited as EL), White House Office, NSC Staff Papers 1948–1961, Executive Secretary's Subject File series, box 17, special file #1 (9).

96. Meeting notes, secret, May 28, 1952, MAE, Cabinet du Ministre, Cabinet Schuman, vol. 81.

97. U.S. minutes of tripartite foreign ministers meeting, May 28, 1952, *FRUS 1952–1954* 13:157–66.

98. Acheson-Schuman discussion, London, June 28, 1952, MAE, Cabinet du Ministre, Cabinet Schuman, vol. 81.

99. Bonnet to Auriol, top secret, October 20, 1952, MAE, Asie Océanie 1944–1955, Indochine, vol. 285.

100. Bonnet to Auriol, top secret, October 20, 1952, MAE, Asie Océanie 1944–1955, Indochine, vol. 285.

101. See Spector, *Advice and Support,* 157–61, for details on the operation.

102. Top secret note, December 1, 1952, MAE, Papiers d'Agents, Henri Bonnet, vol. 1.

103. Head of Southeast Asia Department in the Foreign Office John Tahourdin, minutes, January 6 and 15, 1953; FO, note, January 2, 1953, PRO, FO 371/106765.

104. Note for the president, December 12, 1952, MAE, Cabinet du Ministre, Cabinet Schuman, vol. 153; Melandri, "France and the Atlantic Alliance," 273.

2. A Death in March

1. Chronology, EL, Dulles Papers, Chronological, box 8, July 1954 (2).

2. Although a link between the EDC and Indochina is often noted in the literature, scholars tend to spend little time examining how such a link occurred or how it furthered American intervention in Vietnam. Most scholars end their analysis with claims that American concerns about a Soviet-dominated communist state in Vietnam left the Eisenhower administration a hostage to French policy as the French indefinitely delayed the EDC's ratification in order to extract additional support for Indochina. For example, see Herring, *America's Longest War,* 22, 82; Hess, *Vietnam and the United States,* 37, 39; Kahin, *Intervention;* Patti, *Why Vietnam?* 404–5; Kattenburg, *The Vietnam Trauma,* 23; and Billings-Yun, *Decision against War,* 7. For more detailed analysis on the EDC's importance in Franco-American relations regarding Indochina, see Wall, *The United States and the Making of Postwar France,* 233–96; Artaud, "France between the Indochina War and the European Defense Community"; and Aimaq, *For Europe or Empire?* Aimaq provides a more multifaceted analysis of the relationship between the EDC and Indochina than other scholars but concludes that successive French governments chose empire over the EDC. Although this argument makes some sense in the 1950–1952 period, when the French still thought they could defeat the Vietminh, by 1953 the French had begun seeking a negotiated settlement.

3. Unlike Truman, Eisenhower came into office well versed in international relations and well prepared to lead the nation in foreign policy. Contrary to first accounts of Eisenhower's foreign policy, additional scholarship has demonstrated that Eisenhower took an active interest in foreign affairs. The debate over whether Eisenhower was in charge of the presidency no longer exists—it is clear he was. More recent accounts of Eisenhower focus on his understanding of Third World nationalism. See, for example, Foot, *The Wrong War* and McMahon, "Eisenhower and Third World Nationalism."

4. Director of the Office of Philippine and Southeast Asian Affairs Philip Bonsal to Dulles and Assistant Secretary of State for Far Eastern Affairs John Allison, January 29, 1953, NA, RG 59, Director Office of Philippine and Southeast Asian Affairs, International Conferences, Talks, and Meetings, box 3.

5. Much scholarly debate exists on whether Dulles was an uncompromising idealistic cold warrior or a realist. Early accounts of Dulles, such as Hoopes, *The Devil and John Foster Dulles,* portray him as an ideologue who advocated policies of brinksmanship, massive retaliation, and rollback against the communists. Revisionist accounts, such as Holsti, "Will the Real John Foster Dulles Please Stand Up?" argue that Dulles was flexible and realistic in dealing with international crises. Since the mid-1980s, post-revisionists have sought a middle ground, recognizing that Dulles's idealistic rhetoric was often at odds with his pragmatic decisions regarding American foreign policy. Post-revisionists provide a more complex picture of Dulles but tend to support revisionist claims that Dulles was not as ideologically driven as Hoopes suggests. This study contends that if Dulles did at times support a more pragmatic policy toward the communist bloc than his rhetoric suggested, it was usually because of French and British pressure. Moreover, with respect to Indochina, I concur with former American intelligence official George Allen's claim that regardless of what his staff felt or what world opinion was, if Dulles "thought he was doing right—and there was a certain mysticism in his feeling of right being handed down from on high—he did it." George Allen, oral history, EL, Oral Histories (OH) 280, 1 of 2, 1967.

6. See, for example, MAE, Asie Océanie 1944–1955, Indochine, vols. 179, 261, 291.

7. At the beginning of 1953, France's third ministerial crisis in a year occurred with Antoine Pinay resigning and René Mayer, a radical socialist, replacing him.

8. Livingston Merchant, oral history, EL, OH 117, 1–2, 1967. Dulles's and Merchant's observations suggest that the foreign policy of the Fourth Republic was stronger and more stable than has generally been acknowledged by historians, French or American. Contrary to earlier scholarship on the Fourth Republic, more recent accounts such as Hitchcock, *France Restored* and Aimaq, *For Europe or Empire?* have rehabilitated French foreign policy during this period.

9. Memorandum, n.d., MAE, Secrétariat Général, vol. 179; Bonsal to Dulles and Allison, top secret, January 29, 1953, NA, RG 59, Director Office of Philippine and Southeast Asian Affairs, International Conferences, Talks, and Meetings, box 3.

10. Irving, *The First Indochina War,* 104, and Hammer, *The Struggle for Indochina,* 292–93.

11. Interministerial meeting, January 31, 1953, AN, 457AP/52; Bidault to Cabinet du Ministre, February 11, 1953, AN, 457AP/44.

12. *FRUS 1952–1954* 13:660; Bonnet to MAE, memorandum, March 10, 1954, MAE, Secrétariat Général, vol. 179.

13. Memoranda, January 30 and February 2, 1953, MAE, Asie Océanie 1944–1955, Indochine, vol. 261.

14. Minutes of Bidault-Dulles discussion, February 2, 1953, MAE, Asie Océanie 1944–1955, vol. 261; note, January 22, 1953, MAE, Cabinet du Ministre, vol. 178.

15. Notes, January 30 and February 2, 1953, MAE, Asie Océanie 1944–1955, Indochine, vol. 261.

16. Memorandum on psychological impact of U.S. policies in France, February 17, 1953, EL, White House Office, NSC Staff Papers 1953–1961, PSB Central File series, box 12, PSB 091 France (20).

17. Bonnet to MAE, telegram, March 16, 1953, MAE, Asie Océanie 1944–1955, Indochine, vol. 261; top secret telegram, January 13, memorandum, January 21, 1953, internal memorandum, n.d., MAE, Secrétariat Général, vol. 179; Massigli to MAE, telegram, January 5, 1953, MAE, Asie Océanie 1944–1955, Indochine, vol. 261.

18. An article by Stewart Alsop entitled "Between France and the United States on Indochina and the European Army" that ran in the major American newspapers made this point. Bonnet, memorandum, March 27, 1953, MAE, Asie Océanie 1944–1955, Indochine, vol. 329; Bonnet, memorandum, August 19, 1953, MAE, Asie Océanie 1944–1955, Indochine, vol. 384.

19. *Cleveland Plain Dealer,* November 27, 1953; article in *Detroit Free Press,* November 27, 1953.

20. Dulles to Eisenhower, top secret luncheon discussion, March 24, 1953, Dulles Papers, Dulles-Herter Correspondence, 1953–1961, microfilm, reel 4.

21. Chronology, EL, Dulles Papers, Chronological, box 8, July 1954 (2); and Hitchcock, *France Restored,* 181.

22. See Gibbons, *The U.S. Government and the Vietnam War,* 130–35, for a discussion of the amendment.

23. Duchin, "The Agonizing Reappraisal," 207; Louis de Guiringaud, consul general of France at San Francisco, to Bonnet, telegram, August 13, 1953, MAE, Asie Océanie 1944–1955, Indochine, vol. 265.

24. Note, March 11, 1953, AN, 457AP/44; top secret memorandum, January 13, 1953, MAE, Cabinet du Ministre, vol. 179.

25. For more detailed discussion of Senate and House views on the EDC and its connection to Indochina, see Senate Foreign Relations Committee Meetings, 83rd Congress, vol. 149, May, 1953, 194–200, vol. 152, June, 1954, 1–10, 18, 29–34, 127–28, 145–54; and House Foreign Affairs Committee Meetings, 83rd Congress, vol. 55, March–May, 1953, 148, 164–65, vol. 57, April–June, 1954, 658–85.

26. Senate Foreign Relations Committee, 83rd Congress, Senate Library, May 11, 1953, vol. 1051, card 12. Members in the House appeared equally aware of French difficulties. House Committee on Foreign Affairs, 83rd Congress, Senate Library, March 25, 1953, vol. 1404, card 6.

27. Fish, "After Stalin's Death," 333.

28. Jackson to Robert Cutler, March 4, 1953, EL, Ann Whitman file, Administration series, box 29; Jackson to Dulles, March 3, 1953, EL, C. D. Jackson Papers, box 104, Stalin's death speech (3). Undersecretary Walter Bedell Smith to Acting Director of the Psychological Strategy Board George Morgan, memorandum, March 10, 1953, *FRUS 1952–1954* 8:1111–12.

29. See Bowie and Immerman, *Waging Peace,* 110–14; Osgood, "Form before

Substance," 418–19, 424; and Garthoff, *Assessing the Adversary*, 5–10, for more detail on the Eisenhower administration's debate over the use of psychological warfare following Stalin's death.

30. CIA Special Estimate, Probable Consequences of the Death of Stalin and of the Elevation of Malenkov to Leadership in the USSR, March 12, 1953, NA, RG 263, CIA, National Intelligence Estimates, box 1; Intelligence report, "Implications of Stalin's Demise," March 4, 1953, NA, RG 59, Miscellaneous lot files, Intelligence Bureau, Office of the Director, 1950–1959, lot 58D528, box 65, file IE 50.

31. Memorandum for the president, June 2, 1953, NA, RG 59, Executive Secretariat, Conference files, box 28; Charles Taquey, memorandum, "Support Program for Rolling Back Communist Influence in Vietnam, Cambodia, and Laos," May 18, 1953, NA, White House Office, NSC Staff Papers 1953–1961, PSB Central File series, box 12, PSB 091 Indochina 1.

32. Bonsal to Allison, top secret, March 9, 1953, NA, RG 59, Director Office of Philippine and Southeast Asian Affairs, International Conferences, box 3.

33. "Recommendation for the President to Begin Talks with Mayer," March 21, 1953, NA, RG 59, Executive Secretariat, Conference files, box 21.

34. Note regarding American aid, March 19, 1953, MAE, Asie Océanie 1944–1955, Indochine, vol. 272.

35. Soffer, *General Matthew B. Ridgway*, 196; memorandum of conversation, May 4, 1953, EL, White House Office, NSC Staff Papers 1953–1961, PSB Central File series, box 12, PSB 091 Indochina 1.

36. Charles Taquey, secret memorandum, March 26, 1953; secret memorandum for the record, April 8, 1953, EL, White House Office, NSC Staff Papers 1953–1961, PSB Central File series, box 12.

37. U.S. Psychological Strategy with Respect to the Peoples of Southeast Asia, top secret, July 2, 1953, EL, White House Office, NSC Staff Papers 1953–1961, PSB Central File series, box 16.

38. "Use of American Influences in Support of U.S. Objectives in Vietnam, Cambodia, and Laos," June 15, 1953, EL, White House Office, NSC Staff Papers 1953–1961, PSB Central File series, box 12.

39. See Arthur Cox, memorandum, June 16, 1953; memorandum, June 9, 1953, EL, White House Office, NSC Staff Papers 1953–1961, PSB Central File series, box 12, PSB 091 Indochina 1.

40. Draft, June 15, 1953, memorandum, July 22, 1953, memorandum, August 25, 1953, EL, White House Office, NSC Staff Papers 1953–1961, PSB Central File series, box 12, PSB 091 Indochina 3.

41. Taquey, memorandum, May 18, 1953, EL, White House Office, NSC Staff Papers 1953–1961, PSB Central File series, box 12, PSB 091 Indochina 1.

42. Ely to Pleven, top secret, July 1953, AN, 457AP/44.

43. Memorandum, June 1953, AN, Conseil des Ministres, F60 3037.

44. Note on common strategy in Southeast Asia, April 23, 1953, MAE, Cabinet

du Ministre, Cabinet Pinay, vol. 23; Dillon to Dulles, top secret, conversation with Mayer, April 9, 1953, EL, Papers as President, Ann Whitman file, International series, box 12, France 1953 (2); Merchant to Robertson, top secret, May 5, 1953; and Robertson to Merchant, top secret, May 8, 1953, NA, RG 59, Director Office of Philippine and Southeast Asian Affairs, International Conferences, Talks, and Meetings, box 4.

45. Memorandum, June 1953, AN, Conseil des Ministres, F60 3037.

46. Dillon to Eisenhower, secret, May 15, 1953, EL, Papers as President, Ann Whitman file, International series, box 12, France 1953 (20).

47. Taquey to acting director, secret, August 10, 1953, EL, White House Office, NSC Staff Papers 1953–1961, PSB Central File series, box 12.

48. Duiker, *U.S. Containment Policy*, 146. See Richter, *Khrushchev's Double Bind*, 30–52, for the Soviet perspective of the consequences of Stalin's death and subsequent decision-making process in the Kremlin.

49. Robert Bowie, oral history, EL, OH 102, 1967. See also Fish, "After Stalin's Death," 333–55.

50. Memorandum, n.d., MAE, Secrétariat Général, vol. 179; Bonnet to MAE, telegram, June 5, 1953, MAE, Asie Océanie 1944–1955, Indochine, vol. 384.

51. Note, July 3, 1953, MAE, Asie Océanie 1944–1955, vol. 273.

52. Bidault-Dillon conversation, September 1953, MAE, Asie Océanie 1944–1955, Indochine, vol. 273.

53. Bidault-Dillon conversation, September 1953, MAE, Asie Océanie 1944–1955, Indochine, vol. 273; Daridan and Smith meeting, August 17, 1953, AN, 457AP/45.

54. Secret memorandum, September 11, 1953, EL, White House Office, NSC Staff Papers 1953–1961, PSB Central File series, box 12; Harold Callender, *New York Times,* September 11, 1953.

55. Steininger, "John Foster Dulles, the European Defense Community, and the German Question," 82; Herring, *America's Longest War,* 23.

56. Dillon to DOS, top secret, September 7, and Dillon to DOS, secret, September 8, 1953, *FRUS 1952–1954* 13:758–59.

57. Bonnet, memorandum, June 5, 1953, MAE, Asie Océanie 1944–1955, Indochine, vol. 384.

58. Daridan and Smith meeting, August 14, 1953, MAE, Asie Océanie 1944–1955, Indochine, vol. 292; Duchin, "The Agonizing Reappraisal," 212.

59. Intelligence report, "Prospects for the Continuation of the French Military Effort in Indochina," December 2, 1953, NA, RG 59, Miscellaneous lot files, Intelligence Bureau, Office of Director, lot 58D528, box 65.

60. Political note on Indochina, June 15, 1953, MAE, Cabinet du Ministre, Cabinet Pinay, vol. 21.

61. Ely to Defense Minister René Pleven, July 1953, AN, 457AP/44; Bonnet to Bidault, July 13, 1953, MAE, Asie Océanie 1944–1955, Indochine, vol. 291; political

note on Indochina, June 15, 1953, MAE, Cabinet du Ministre, Cabinet Pinay, vol. 21.

62. Bidault to French representative to the United Nations Jean Chauvel, July 1, 1953, AN, 457AP/44.

63. Intelligence report, "Prospects for the Continuation of the French Military Effort in Indochina," December 2, 1953, NA, RG 59, Miscellaneous lot files, Intelligence Bureau, Office of Director, lot 58D528, box 65; Bonnet to Bidault, July 13, 1953, MAE, Asie Océanie 1944-1955, Indochine, vol. 291.

64. Minute, August 10, 1953, PRO, FO 371/106769. Western officials feared that the PRC would move aggressively toward the nationalist government established in Formosa and hoped to defuse the situation there.

65. Bidault to Jean Chauvel, personal, July 1, 1953, AN, 457AP/44.

66. Minute, August 10, 1953, PRO, FO 371/106769; interview with Albert Sarraut, July 10, 1953, MAE, Cabinet du Ministre, Cabinet Pinay, vol. 21.

67. Bonnet to MAE for Bidault, July 12, 1953, top secret, AN, 457AP/45; memorandum of conversation, August 11, 1953, NA, RG 59, Director Office of Philippine and Southeast Asian Affairs, International Conferences, Talks, and Meetings, box 4; Quai official Maurice Schumann to MAE, August 28, 1953, MAE, Asie Océanie 1944-1955, Indochine, vol. 292.

68. Daridan to MAE, September 1 and 3, 1953; and Henri Hoppenot to MAE, September 23, 1953, MAE, Asie Océanie 1944-1955, Indochine, vol. 292.

69. Joxe to Bidault, September 2, 1953, MAE, Asie Océanie 1944-1955, Indochine, vol. 292; Joxe to MAE, September 9, 1953, MAE, Asie Océanie 1944-1955, Indochine, vol. 292.

70. National Defense Committee meeting, top secret, July 24, 1953, AN, 560AP/50.

71. Memorandum, October 7, 1953, EL, White House Office, NSC Staff Papers 1953-1961, PSB Central File series, box 12, PSB 091 Indochina 3. See Hammer, *The Struggle for Indochina*, 313-14, and Spector, *Advice and Support*, 179-81, for more on American internal debate on the Navarre Plan.

72. Navarre to Ely, strictly personal, November 3, 1953, SHAT, Fonds Paul Ely, vol. 137.

73. October 28, 1953, debate, NA, RG 59, Executive Secretariat, Meetings of Foreign Dignitaries, box 23.

74. Devillers and Lacouture, *End of a War*, 45; top secret memorandum for the record, December 10, 1953, EL, White House Office, NSC Staff Papers 1948-1961, Executive Secretary's Subject File series, box 17, special file #1 (9), SA Cutler memoranda 1953 (8).

75. Jackson to Eisenhower, top secret, June 3, 1953, EL, Papers as President, Ann Whitman file, Administration series, box 21, Jackson 1953 (2).

76. Bermuda Conference summary, December 10, 1953, EL, Papers as President, Ann Whitman file, Administration series, box 16. See Young, "Churchill, the

Russians and the Western Alliance," 889–912, for more detail on western differences at Bermuda.

77. Dulles and Smith to MAE, telegram, December 18, 1953, MAE, Asie Océanie 1944–1955, Indochine, vol. 290. See also telegram, December 14, 1953, MAE, Asie Océanie 1944–1955, Indochine, vol. 297; telegram, December 12, 1953, MAE, Asie Océanie 1944–1955, Indochine, vol. 290.

78. Memorandum of conversation, January 18, 1954, EL, Dulles Papers, Personnel series, Chiefs of Mission, subject file, box 3, strictly confidential (1).

79. Special Study Mission to Southeast Asia and Pacific Report by Walter Judd, January 29, 1954, Committee of Foreign Affairs, AN, 74AP/37.

80. Ely, note on American action in Indochina, February 26, 1954, SHAT, Fonds Paul Ely, vol. 46.

81. See Larres, *Churchill's Cold War* and Young, *Winston Churchill's Last Campaign* for more details on Churchill's visions of détente. For a detailed discussion of the Anglo-American perspective at Berlin, see Rather, "The Geneva Conference of 1954," 80–96, and Devillers and Lacouture, *End of a War*, 54–59.

82. Bidault to MAE, top secret, January 25, 1954, AN, 457AP/50; Duiker, *U.S. Containment Policy*, 153.

83. Top secret memorandum for the record, January 28, 1954, NA, RG 59, Executive Secretary and Undersecretary's memoranda of conversation, box 18; Dulles to Eisenhower, January 20, 1954, points #3 and #4, Dulles Papers, Dulles-Herter Correspondence, 1953–1961, microfilm, reel 4; C. D. Jackson, memorandum, January 29, 1954, NA, RG 59, Executive Secretariat, Conference files, box 32.

84. February 1954, MAE, Asie Océanie 1944–1955, Indochine, vol. 308; Rather, "The Geneva Conference of 1954," 92–93.

85. Maurice Schumann to MAE, February 20, 1954, AN, 457AP/501; note, February 18, 1954, AN, 457AP/50.

86. Jackson to Luce, February 25, 1954, EL, C. D. Jackson Papers, box 68; Duiker, *U.S. Containment Policy*, 153.

87. Bonnet to MAE, telegram, February 20, 1954, MAE, Asie Océanie 1944–1955, Indochine, vol. 74; February 1954, MAE, Asie Océanie 1944–1955, Indochine, vol. 308. A *New York Times* article on February 15, 1954, entitled "Can We Exchange the EDC for Peace in Indochina?" stated that elements in France were willing to do so. See also Dulles to Smith, February 25, 1954; Dulles to Eisenhower, February 26, 1954; and Dulles to Merchant and MacArthur, March 30, 1954, Dulles Papers, Dulles-Herter Correspondence, 1953–1961, microfilm, reel 4; Dulles to Eisenhower, top secret, February 9, 1954, *FRUS 1952–1954* 13:1025.

88. Top secret memorandum of 184th NSC meeting, February 11, 1954, EL, Ann Whitman file, NSC series, box 5, 184th, February 11, 1954; Evaluation of Chiefs of Mission, EL, Dulles Papers, Personnel series, Chiefs of Mission, box 1.

89. Taquey, memorandum, March 26, 1953, and Taquey, memorandum, "Support Program for Rolling Back Communist Influence in Vietnam, Cambodia, and

Laos," May 18, 1953, EL, White House Office, NSC Staff Papers 1953–1961, PSB
Central File series, box 12, PSB 091 Indochina 1.

3. Negotiating toward Geneva

1. A number of works have addressed the Geneva Conference—Cable, *The
Geneva Conference of 1954;* Immerman, "The United States and the Geneva Conference of 1954"; Randle, *Geneva 1954;* and Joyaux, *La Chine et le règlement du premier
conflit d'Indochine*—but most focus on the relationship between the communist and
noncommunist blocs rather than on the problems within the Western alliance or
were written without the benefit of many documents declassified in the 1990s. For a
dated but lively narrative of the negotiations at Geneva, see Devillers and Lacouture,
End of a War. Rather, "The Geneva Conference of 1954" concentrates primarily on
the Anglo-American relationship.

2. Quoted in Jian, "China and the First Indochina War," 102.

3. Rather, "The Geneva Conference of 1954," 218–19.

4. Note, March 2, 1954, AN, 457AP/55; Reynaud to Laniel, March 18, 1954,
AN, 74AP/37.

5. Pleven report, top secret, February 28, 1954, AN, 560AP/50.

6. Top secret OCB memorandum, March 10, 1954, EL, White House Office,
NSC Staff Papers 1953–1961, OCB Central File series, box 37, Indochina file #1 (2)
November 1953–July 1954.

7. Top secret memorandum for special committee, March 17, 1954, EL, White
House Office, NSC Staff Papers 1953–1961, OCB Central File series, box 37, Indochina file #1 (3) November 1953–July 1954.

8. This study does not provide a detailed history of Dien Bien Phu; it is concerned only with how the events at Dien Bien Phu affected intra-alliance politics and
increased American involvement in Vietnam. For detailed accounts of Dien Bien
Phu, see Fall, *Hell in a Very Small Place,* 293–326, and Roy, *The Battle of Dien Bien
Phu.* For the North Vietnamese perspective, see Vo, *Dien Bien Phu.*

9. Although the internationalization of the war in Vietnam and the concept of
"united action" are usually associated with Dulles's strategy in the months just before
and during the Geneva Conference, in fact their roots lie in the comparatively ne-
glected early period of the war and the inter-allied debate about the most efficacious
means of defending the region from communism. See, for example, Lee, *Outposts of
Empire,* 142, and chapters 1 and 2 of this study.

10. For a detailed account of Operation Vulture, see Prados, *The Sky Would
Fall.*

11. Duiker, *U.S. Containment Policy,* 156–57; secret note on March 27 meeting,
SHAT, Fonds Paul Ely, vol. 37.

12. Top secret conversation between Eisenhower and Dulles, March 24, 1954,
Dulles Papers, Dulles-Herter Correspondence, 1953–1961, microfilm, reel 4.

13. Duiker, *U.S. Containment Policy*, 158; 190th NSC meeting, March 25, 1954, *FRUS 1952–1954* 13:1164–68; secretary of state to DOS, April 13, 1954, *FRUS 1952–1954* 5:930.

14. Historians remain divided over the nature of united action and whether Eisenhower and Dulles saw it as a viable option. Robert Randle, Melanie Billings-Yun, and John Burke and Fred Greenstein have argued that Eisenhower and Dulles followed a prudent course, deciding against united action by early April. Randle, *Geneva 1954*; Billings-Yun, *Decision against War*; and Burke and Greenstein, *How Presidents Test Reality*. Richard Immerman and George Herring viewed the Eisenhower administration's actions to bring about united action as risky. See Herring, "Franco-American Conflict in Indochina," 40–41, and Herring and Immerman, "Eisenhower, Dulles, and Dien Bien Phu," 82–83. Given the available documentation, this study concurs with Herring and Immerman.

15. Cabinet du Ministre, memorandum, March 10, 1954, MAE, Secrétariat Général, vol. 179.

16. Dulles to Churchill, top secret, April 4, 1954, EL, Dulles Papers, Post Presidential Papers 1961–69, Augusta Walter Reed series, box 1, Goodpaster briefings (2) August 4–20, 1965.

17. Dulles meeting with members of Congress, April 5, 1954, Dulles Papers, Dulles-Herter Correspondence, 1953–1961, microfilm, reel 4; Rather, "The Geneva Conference of 1954," 119–48.

18. James Hagerty, diary, April 29, 1954, EL, James Hagerty Papers, 1952–1974, box 1.

19. Eisenhower to Gruenther, personal and confidential, April 26, 1954, EL, Personal Diary January–November 1954, Papers as President, Ann Whitman file, Diary series, box 4. Also quoted in Ambrose, *Eisenhower*, 361–62.

20. Gruenther to Eisenhower, April 27, 1954, EL, Papers as President, Ann Whitman file, Administration series, box 16.

21. James Gavin, "Outline Plan for Conducting Military Operations in Indochina with U.S. and French Union Forces," top secret, April 5, 1954, NA, RG 319, G-3 DCSOPS 1954 1400020 opi Indochina.

22. Top secret memorandum of Eisenhower-Dulles conversation, May 19, 1954, Dulles Papers, Dulles-Herter Correspondence, 1953–1961, microfilm, reel 5; Cable, *The Geneva Conference*, 53–60; Bonnet to Bidault, secret memorandum, April 25, 1954, AN 457AP/52.

23. See Gibbons, *The U.S. Government and the Vietnam War*, 189–95, for a detailed account of the April 3 meeting. Duiker, *U.S. Containment Policy*, 168–71; luncheon conversation between Dulles and Eisenhower, May 11, 1954, Dulles Papers, Dulles-Herter Correspondence, 1953–1961, microfilm, reel 5.

24. See Joint Resolution Draft, April 2, 1954, EL, Dulles Papers, Subject series, box 8; and Draft of the Congressional Resolution, May 17, 1954, Dulles Papers, Dulles-Herter Correspondence, 1953–1961, microfilm, reel 5. Congress had no in-

tention of granting this "discretionary authority," as members were more concerned with limiting the president's power. This issue arose again during the 1964 Tonkin Gulf crisis, when Lyndon B. Johnson got his resolution. See Johns, "Opening Pandora's Box," 1-32, for more on the 1964 resolution. Interestingly, the 1964 resolution differed from its predecessor in that it did not contain the word "authorize," as the Johnson administration wanted to avoid the issue of needing Congressional authorization.

25. William Knowland, oral history, EL, OH 233, 2 of 3, 1967; top secret report, April 23, 1954, AN, 74AP/38.

26. April 7, 1954, MAE, Asie Océanie 1944-1955, Indochine, vol. 290; top secret memorandum of Dulles-Eisenhower conversation, May 19, 1954, Dulles Papers, Dulles-Herter Correspondence, 1953-1961, microfilm, reel 5.

27. Scholars still debate whether Dulles did indeed make the offer. From the documents available, it seems unlikely. Still, one wonders about excised parts of telegrams such as the one sent by Dulles to Dillon and Walter Bedell Smith in which Dulles discusses possible U.S. intervention and bitterness on Bidault's part that such intervention could no longer take place. See Dulles to Dillon and Smith, top secret, June 14, 1954, EL, Dulles Papers, Subject series, box 9, Indochina June 1954-April 1956 (4).

28. Dulles to Dillon and Smith, top secret memorandum, May 11, 1954, Dulles Papers, Dulles-Herter Correspondence, 1953-1961, microfilm, reel 5.

29. Bonnet to MAE, top secret telegram, June 6, 1954, and Bonnet to MAE, memoranda, June 8 and 9, 1954, MAE, Asie Océanie 1944-1955, Indochine, vol. 76.

30. Hazlett, *Ike's Letters to a Friend*, 11.

31. Eisenhower to Gruenther, June 8, 1954, EL, Alfred Gruenther Papers, 1941-1983, Eisenhower Correspondence series, box 1, Eisenhower 1954 (1).

32. Duiker, *U.S. Containment Policy*, 172, 191.

33. Lee, *Outposts of Empire*, 233; Devillers and Lacouture, *End of a War*, 186. Billings-Yun has argued that Eisenhower purposely made conditions for intervention impossible in order to ensure against united action and keep clear of the Indochina War, but the evidence suggests otherwise. Billings-Yun, *Decision against War*. This study concurs with David Anderson's argument in *Trapped by Success* that Eisenhower seriously considered intervention but chose to define very specific criteria to ensure domestic and international support.

34. Bidault to Schumann, May 10, 1954, AN, 457AP/55; top secret note, June 7, 1954, SHAT, Fonds Paul Ely, vol. 45.

35. Secretary of state, memorandum of conversation, March 30, 1954, *FRUS 1952-1954* 16:487.

36. Bidault to Maurice Schumann, May 3, 1954, AN, 457AP/55; Dulles to Dillon, top secret memorandum, May 15, 1954, Dulles Papers, Dulles-Herter Correspondence, 1953-1961, microfilm, reel 5. French negotiators at Geneva included Jean Chauvel, Adjunct Director of Political Affairs Roland Jacquin de Margerie,

Raymond Offroy, Jean Laloy, Jacques Roux, and Chief Adjunct of the ministerial cabinet for foreign affairs Claude Cheysson. Both Offroy and Cheysson were familiar with Indochina. For the Indochina phase of the conference the Americans set up a working committee, which included Douglas MacArthur, Robert Bowie, Everett Drumright, and Paul Sturm.

37. The roles of the communist nations involved with the Indochina phase of the Geneva Conference have received some scholarly attention. The best full-length study on China's role in Geneva remains Joyaux's *La Chine et le règlement du premier conflit d'Indochine*. According to recent scholarship on the Chinese perspective, China exerted a tremendous amount of influence over the DRV throughout the early 1950s and at the Geneva Conference. See Jian, "China and the First Indochina War"; Zhai, "China and the Geneva Conference of 1954"; and Zhai, *China and the Vietnam Wars*, 43–64. For a recent and very well documented account of the Soviet role at Geneva, see Gaiduk, *Confronting Vietnam*, 28–53. For details on the North Vietnamese position, see Dommen, *The Indochinese Experience*, 230–54.

38. Bidault, note, March 25, 1954, AN, 457AP/52. Bidault had made a similar declaration to the French press on April 25. MAE, Papiers d'Agents, Maurice De-Jean, vol. 143.

39. MAE, top secret memorandum, March 31, 1954, AN, 457AP/52.

40. Buttinger, *Vietnam*, vol. 2, 821; Lee, *Outposts of Empire*, 148. For a firsthand account from a British official who participated at Geneva, see Cable, *The Geneva Conference*. Cable provides a laudatory view of British diplomacy, concluding that "without British efforts, the Geneva Conference would never have been held, allowed to continue or permitted to end in even the limited measure of agreement achieved" (126). Devillers and Lacouture concur with Cable's assessment of Eden but also emphasize the importance of Zhou Enlai's diplomacy in arriving at a negotiated agreement. Devillers and Lacouture, *End of a War*, 128.

41. Ely to MAE, secret, May 14, 1954, SHAT, Fonds Paul Ely, vol. 37.

42. DeJean to MAE, May 13, 1954; Washington Embassy to MAE, May 24, 1954; Bonnet to MAE, May 24, 1954; MAE, memorandum, n.d.; Hoppenot to MAE, May 25, 1954, AN, 457AP/55.

43. Top secret memorandum of 201st NSC meeting, eyes only, June 10, 1954, EL, Ann Whitman file, NSC series, box 5.

44. DeJean to MAE, May 14, 1954, AN, 457AP/55.

45. State to U.S. delegation, May 13, 1954, *FRUS 1952–1954* 16:790–91; Rather, "The Geneva Conference of 1954," 292–302; Bidault to MAE, top secret, May 10, 1954, AN, 457AP/52; Bonnet to MAE, top secret, May 23, 1954, AN 457AP/55; note for Bidault, top secret, May 31, 1954, AN, 457AP/52; Bidault to Schumann, top secret, June 5, 1954, AN, 457AP/52. The seven conditions were: (1) France and the three Associated States asked the United States for help; (2) France also asked the Philippines, Thailand, Australia, New Zealand, and Great Britain, although the United States would be satisfied if only the Philippines and Thailand joined and the

others agreed in principle; (3) the UN gave cover for the undertaking; (4) the French government declared that the three states were entirely independent; (5) France did not pull out its troops; (6) the three states and France worked out the training of the Vietnamese army; and (7) the French demand was approved by the French parliament (requested because of the uncertain tenure of French governments).

46. DeJean to Bidault, May 24, 1954; Bidault to MAE, secret, May 27, 1954, AN, 457AP/55.

47. Smith to Dulles, secret, May 27, 1954, NA, RG 59, Executive Secretariat, Conference files, box 49.

48. Quoted in Spector, *Advice and Support,* 220–21; Mendès France to National Assembly deputy Edouard Frédéric-Dupont, January 15, 1955, Institut Pierre Mendès France, Paris (hereafter cited as IPMF), DPMF, Indochine, IV; Devillers and Lacouture, *End of a War,* 114; Dommen, *The Indochinese Experience,* 240–43.

49. Quoted in Gibbons, *The U.S. Government and the Vietnam War,* 230.

50. Top secret summary of talks, June 8 and 16, 1954, AN, 457AP/52; Mendès France to Frédéric-Dupont, note, January 15, 1955, IPMF, DPMF, Indochine, IV; DeJean to Brebisson, June 8, 1954, AN, 457AP/55.

51. Jean Sainteny, note, May 1954, Archives d'histoire contemporaine, Centre d'histoire de l'Europe du vingtième siècle, Paris (hereafter cited as CHEVS), 1 SA 13. See also McNamara, *Argument without End* for confirmation that the Vietminh were sincere in their negotiations.

52. Edward Lilly to Elmer Staats, "Informal Report on Delays and Inhibitions Traceable to EDC Policy," top secret, May 26 and June 9, 1954, EL, White House Office, NSC Staff Papers 1953–1961, OCB Central File series, box 32, OCB 091 France file #1 (2).

53. Dillon to DOS, top secret, May 19, 1954, *FRUS 1952–1954* 5:956–59.

54. Dillon to DOS, top secret, May 19, 1954; Dulles to American Embassy in France, secret, May 18 and 20, 1954, *FRUS 1952–1954* 5:956–59.

55. Laniel, *Jours de gloire et jours cruels,* 285.

56. Commenting on the fall of the Laniel government, René Massigli mentioned that the British press believed the immediate consequence would be a political solution at Geneva and an end to the EDC. Massigli to MAE, telegram, June 13, 1954, MAE, Asie Océanie 1944–1955, Indochine, vol. 388. The British press was also highly critical of Prime Minister Eden's actions at Geneva, claiming that he had followed a policy of an "Asian Munich." Embassy in Britain to Laniel, telegram, MAE, Etats-Associés 1945–1957, vol. 368B. According to William Hitchcock, Mendès France did not differ significantly from his predecessors in foreign policy and in fact capitalized on the progress that Bidault had already made at Geneva to bring the conference to a successful conclusion. Hitchcock, *France Restored,* 190.

57. Chauvel to MAE, top secret, June 14 and 15, 1954, AN, 457AP/52; Smith-Chauvel meeting, June 16, 1954, AN, 457AP/52. Chauvel had served as director for Asian affairs at the Quai and was the current French ambassador to Switzerland.

58. Republican leader Henry Cabot Lodge, after visiting with Laniel, stated that there appeared to be no discipline at the Quai. It was common knowledge that the undersecretary of the Quai, Alexandre Parodi, openly disagreed with Bidault's actions at Geneva, and that high-level agreements were sabotaged at the working level through all sorts of interference. Lodge concluded that Bidault had very few supporters left. Lodge to Dulles, top secret, eyes only, June 11, 1954, EL, Dulles Papers, General Correspondence and Memoranda series, box 2, strictly confidential L (2).

59. Top secret memorandum of 205th NSC meeting, July 1, 1954, EL, Ann Whitman file, NSC series, box 5; Cable, *The Geneva Conference*, 111–12.

60. Meeting in the Secretary's Office, NSC member Robert Bowie and Dulles exchange, top secret, July 1, 1954, NA, RG 59, Executive Secretary and Undersecretary's memoranda of conversation, box 18.

61. Dulles to Dillon, top secret memorandum, July 1954, Dulles Papers, Dulles-Herter Correspondence, 1953–1961, microfilm, reel 5.

62. Mendès France to Bonnet, telegram, July 9, 1954, MAE, Etats-Associés 1945–1957, vol. 290; internal memorandum, July 9, 1954, MAE, Cabinet du Ministre, Cabinet Mendès France, vol. 169.

63. John Foster Dulles telephone conversation, July 21, 1954, microfilm, 1953–1954, *Minutes of Telephone Conversations of John Foster Dulles and Christian Herter, 1953–1961*, ed. Kesaris and Gibson.

64. Telegram to Bonnet, July 25, 1954, MAE, Cabinet du Ministre, Cabinet Mendès France, vol. 169; telegram to Washington, D.C., London, and Bonn, July 26, 1954, MAE, Cabinet du Ministre, Cabinet Mendès France, vol. 169. Denise Artaud asserts that even though the Indochina War could be considered to have directly slowed the ratification of the EDC treaty, French military leaders never proposed that their government sacrifice its obligations in Europe in order to save its position in the Far East. Artaud, "France between the Indochina War and the European Defense Community," 254; note, July 5, 1954, IPMF, DPMF, Indochine, IV. See Gaiduk, *Confronting Vietnam,* 50–51, for further confirmation from the Soviet side that no deal was struck.

65. John Foster Dulles Oral History project, Princeton, Mendès France interview, Paris, France, June 17, 1964, IPMF, DPMF, Indochine, IV. "La Question Indochinoise de 1945 à 1955," Exposé de Jean Marie Merillon à Ecole National d'Administration, February 9, 1955, MAE, Asie Océanie 1944–1955, Conflit Vietnam, vol. 308.

66. Bonnet to Mendès France, top secret memorandum, July 4, 1954, MAE, Cabinet du Ministre, Cabinet Mendès France, vol. 179.

67. Kaplan, "The United States, NATO, and French Indochina," 239; Massigli to MAE, top secret memorandum, July 1, 1954, MAE, Cabinet du Ministre, Cabinet Mendès France, vol. 176.

68. Bonnet to MAE, telegram, June 30, 1954, MAE, Asie Océanie 1944–1955, Indochine, vol. 76; U.S. delegation to state, July 18, 1954, *FRUS 1952–1954* 16:1405–

7; U.S. delegation to state, July 18, 1954, *FRUS 1952–1954* 16:1431–34; and Bonnet to MAE, top secret telegram, June 30, 1954, MAE, Asie Océanie 1944–1955, Indochine, vol. 76; Bonnet to MAE, telegram, August 27, 1954, MAE, Cabinet du Ministre, Cabinet Mendès France, vol. 179.

69. Bonnet to MAE, top secret telegram, June 30, 1954, MAE, Asie Océanie 1944–1955, Indochine, vol. 76; and Rather, "The Geneva Conference of 1954," 461.

70. Both Laos and Cambodia gained full independence and joined the UN shortly after the conference. See Dommen, *The Indochinese Experience*, 256–60, for a detailed breakdown of the accords for all three countries.

71. Smith on the situation in Indochina, as quoted in Herring, "A Good Stout Effort," 225.

72. Crosswell, *The Chief of Staff*, 336–37; Lacouture, *Vietnam*, 10–11; DOS Research memorandum, "Summary of Principal Events in the History of Vietnam," January 10, 1962, MAE, Asie Océanie 1944–1955, Conflit Vietnam, vol. 308.

73. Dulles to American Embassy in France, secret, June 28, 1954, *FRUS 1952–1954* 13:1758 n5.

74. National Intelligence Estimate, Communist Course of Action in Asia through 1957, October 7, 1954, NA, RG 263, CIA, National Intelligence Estimates, box 2.

75. National Intelligence Estimate, Communist Course of Action in Asia through 1957, October 7, 1954, NA, RG 263, CIA, National Intelligence Estimates, box 2; Cesari, "La France, Les Etats-Unis, et L'Indochine," 868.

76. Bonnet to MAE, March 27, 1954, MAE, Asie Océanie 1944–1955, Indochine, vol. 179; Mendès France to Bonnet, telegram, August 13, 1954, *Documents diplomatiques français* (hereafter cited as *DDF*) *1954*, 244.

77. September 27, 1954, Action Report, NA, RG 306, USIA, Office of Research, Special Reports, 1953–1956, box 6.

78. Bonnet to Mendès France, September 1, 1954, *DDF 1954*, 244.

79. French foreign minister to French ambassador to the United States, December 1955, MAE, Asie Océanie 1944–1955, Indochine, vol. 188.

80. Lee, *Outposts of Empire*, 219.

81. Top secret NSC briefing, July 21, 1954, NA, CREST.

82. Lee, *Outposts of Empire*, 242–43.

83. Mendès France to Chief of the French delegation Chauvel, telegram, July 13, 1954; memorandum, July 16, 1954, IPMF, DPMF, Indochine, IV.

84. Top secret note on relations with Vietnam, n.d., MAE, Asie Océanie 1944–1955, Conflit Vietnam, 311.

85. Jackson to Henry Luce, July 27, 1954, EL, Jackson Papers, box 68, log 1954 (3).

86. Jackson to Henry Luce, July 27, 1954, EL, Jackson Papers, box 68, log 1954 (3).

87. Mendès France to Cheysson, December 6, 1956, IPMF, DPMF, Inventaire Analytique Correspondance avec Claude Cheysson, dossier Cheysson; Mendès France to Frédéric-Dupont, note, January 15, 1955, IPMF, DPMF, Indochine, IV.

See also Navarre, *Agonie de l'Indochine*. The National Assembly had not been aware of the secret negotiations between the French and the Vietminh. Once it was clear Mendès France would succeed Laniel, he was quickly informed that negotiations were on track. Such information could have played a role in his dramatic declaration that he would achieve peace in thirty days or resign. Mendès France has been both highly praised for his actions at Geneva, and condemned. See Devillers and Lacouture, *End of a War* and Dommen, *The Indochinese Experience*, respectively. This study attempts to strike a balance by carefully assessing the opportunities and constraints surrounding Mendès France. I do not agree with Dommen's statement that the breakdown of the Geneva agreements "was due primarily to the short-term nature of the arrangements made by Mendès France, not by any other party or individual" (245–46), as the rest of this study makes clear.

88. Lee, *Outposts of Empire*, 250.

89. Gaiduk, *Confronting Vietnam*, 61–62; Mendès France to Guy La Chambre, February 4, 1955, IPMF, DPMF, Relations Internationales, chemise R 1/3. A Protocol to the Manila Pact (or Southeast Asia Collective Defense Treaty) stipulated that Article IV applied to South Vietnam. Article IV stated that in the event of an armed attack "against any of the Parties or against any State or territory which the Parties by unanimous agreement may hereafter designate" the Pact members would "act to meet the common danger in accordance with its constitutional processes." Southeast Asia Collective Defense Treaty, September 8, 1954.

90. National Intelligence Estimate, Communist Course of Action in Asia through 1957, October 7, 1954, NA, RG 263, CIA, National Intelligence Estimates, box 2.

4. The Diem Experiment

1. High commissioner of France in Indochina to Saigon, political report, November 6, 1950, CAOM, Conseiller Politique, vol. 208; note, February 1953, AN, Conseil des Ministres, F60 3037; Saigon to MAE, telegram, July 27, 1953; secret telegram to MAE, August 17, 1953, AN, Reynaud Papers, 74AP, vol. 35.

2. Note on Tran Chan Thanh meeting with Maurice DeJean, March 25, 1954; Jean Daridan to Bidault, April 1, 1954, MAE, Asie Océanie 1944–1955, Indochine, vol. 82; memorandum, July 10, 1954, SHAT, Fonds Paul Ely, vol. 40. Former French high commissioner to Vietnam Georges Gautier, Director General of the Associated States Ministry Robert Tezenas de Montecel, and French official Paul Devinat thought that Diem's bellicosity fit well with the tone the French wanted to achieve at Geneva. Cesari, "La France, Les Etats-Unis, et L'Indochine," 812. Just as contemporary American officials did, a number of American scholars have lumped all French officials together as anti-Diemists. See, for example, Spector, *Advice and Support*, 224; Buttinger, *Vietnam*, vol. 2, 849; Warner, *The Last Confucian*, 65–66; Shaplen, *The Lost Revolution*, 101; and Kattenburg, *The Vietnam Trauma*, 53.

3. Top secret memorandum of conversation between Ngo Dinh Luyen, Smith, and Bonsal, May 18, 1954, NA, RG 59, Executive Secretary and Undersecretary's memoranda of conversation, box 18; McClintock to DOS, secret, June 14, 1954, NA, RG 59, lot files, conference files, 1949–1972, entry 3051B, box 52.

4. Some scholars claim that the United States pressured Bao Dai to appoint Diem and then forced France to accept Diem's appointment. See Hoopes, *The Devil and John Foster Dulles*, 251; Kolko, *Anatomy of a War*, 82–83; and Cesari, "La France, Les Etats-Unis, et L'Indochine," 812, for this view. Others argue that Diem was not the American candidate and that he was a logical choice in Vietnamese circles. See, for example, Warner, *The Last Confucian*, 66; Olson, "Eisenhower and the Indochina Problem," 118; Anderson, *Trapped by Success*, 52–55; and Duiker, *U.S. Containment Policy*, 197. Bao Dai supports the latter interpretation in his memoir, stating that he first consulted with numerous Vietnamese leaders and then notified Dulles of his plans to replace Buu Loc with Diem. Bao Dai, *Le Dragon d'Annam*, 328. Contrary to the other two schools of thought, Paul Kattenburg claims that the French, hoping to save at least a vestige of noncommunist Vietnam, persuaded Bao Dai to appoint Diem. Kattenburg, *The Vietnam Trauma*, 51–53. The extent to which the United States precipitated Diem's rise to power will probably not be established until CIA documents from the period are fully declassified.

5. At the time, various French and British officials were under the impression that Diem owed his success to the CIA. See Foreign Office official J. C. Cloake, minute, October 7, 1954, PRO, FO 371/112122.

6. Duiker, *U.S. Containment Policy*, 245.

7. Numerous scholarly works have examined the American perspective of Diem's rise to power and leadership in South Vietnam. See Scigliano, *South Vietnam*, 12–25, 130–35, 190–216, and Fitzgerald, *Fire in the Lake*, 96–184, for details on Diem's rise to power, leadership, organization of South Vietnam, and Vietnamese rapport with the United States. The most comprehensive account of the American nation-building effort before and after the Geneva Conference is David Anderson's excellent study *Trapped by Success*. See also Anderson's article "J. Lawton Collins, John Foster Dulles, and the Eisenhower Administration's 'Point of No Return' in Vietnam," 127–47, and George Herring, Gary Hess, and Richard Immerman's "Passage of Empire." Although no single French work provides an in-depth analysis of the months following Geneva, some works that discuss the French perspective of events include Dalloz, *The War in Indochina* and Ruscio, *La Guerre française d'Indochine*. See also Ely, *Mémoires*, 286–325. For the British perspective, Anthony Eden's *Full Circle* provides a firsthand account of events after Geneva. See also Combs, "Path Not Taken" for an analysis of the British outlook on American efforts in South Vietnam. Finally, Warner provides an in-depth look at Diem's reasoning during the 1954–1955 period in *The Last Confucian* (65–86), as does Anthony Bouscaren in *The Last of the Mandarins*. For the most recent scholarship on Diem's policies, see Catton, *Diem's Final Failure* and Jacobs, *America's Miracle Man in Vietnam*. No updated biography

of Diem exists, and his character remains difficult to capture even if his motivations are clear. This study concentrates on the French perspective of Diem's possibilities for success and his foreign policy rather than domestic decisions.

8. Hammer, *The Struggle for Indochina*, 355; Heath to DOS, November 7, 1954, *FRUS 1952–1954* 13:2222.

9. Dillon to DOS, August 12, 1954, *FRUS 1952–1954* 13:1935, 751G.00/8-1254. Ruscio, *La Guerre française d'Indochine*, 229. DeJean to MAE, September 10, 1954, *DDF 1954*, 320–21.

10. Duiker, *U.S. Containment Policy*, 198.

11. Dulles to Embassy in France, August 18, 1954, *FRUS 1952–1954* 13:1957.

12. For example, John Cloake, an officer at the Foreign Office's Southeast Asia Department, commented in summer 1954 that the Diem government was "about the best one we can get." Combs, "Path Not Taken," 40. For internal debate in the Foreign Office on whether Diem should stay in power, see Combs, "Path Not Taken," 33–57.

13. The Cao Dai and Hoa Hao were political-religious groups with their own private armies. The Binh Xuyen was a criminal gang engaged in various illegal activities.

14. McClintock to DOS, June 27, 1954; article by Ton That Thien in *Gazette de Lausanne*, reprinted from *Vietnam Press*, June 27, 1954, NA, RG 59, lot files, conference files, 1949–1972, entry 3051B, box 52.

15. Robert McClintock to undersecretary, August 12, 1954, NA, RG 59, Director Office of Philippine and Southeast Asian Affairs, International Conferences, Talks, and Meetings, box 2.

16. Smith to Robert Anderson, deputy secretary of defense, September 7, 1954, NA, RG 59, Director Office of Philippine and Southeast Asian Affairs, International Conferences, Talks, and Meetings, box 2.

17. Ely to MAE, September 8, 1954, MAE, Asie Océanie 1944–1955, Indochine, vol. 339.

18. Spector, *Advice and Support*, 236; CIA report, August 23, 1954, *FRUS 1952–1954* 13:1979–80; Mendès France to Saigon, August 30, 1954, MAE, CLV, Aide Militaire, Généralités, carton 3.

19. *Pentagon Papers*, 210–11.

20. *Pentagon Papers*, 204, 213–14; Hoopes, *The Devil and John Foster Dulles*, 251, 254; and Prados, *The Sky Would Fall*, 194.

21. Anderson, *Trapped by Success*, 63. See Herring, Hess, and Immerman, "Passage of Empire" for an analysis of Dulles's thinking.

22. Top secret OCB minutes, August 4, 1954, EL, White House Office, NSC Staff Papers 1953–1961, OCB Central File series, box 38.

23. Major General Arthur Trudeau, Report of Visit to Pacific Areas, top secret, August 31, 1954, EL, Collins Papers, J. Lawton Collins file, box 24.

24. MAE, note, July 29, 1954, MAE, Cabinet du Ministre, Cabinet Pineau, vol. 18.

25. Ely to MAE, August 2, 1954; meetings, August 21 and 24, 1954; memorandum of meeting in Paris, n.d., SHAT, Fonds Paul Ely, vol. 37; French official Philippe Baudet to MAE, telegram, August 13, 1954, MAE, Asie Océanie 1944–1955, Indochine, vol. 157.

26. Anderson, *Trapped by Success*, 79; Heath to DOS, September 18, 1954, *FRUS 1952–1954* 13:2035.

27. DeJean to MAE, confidential, September 10, 1954, MAE, Cabinet du Ministre, Cabinet Pinay, vol. 21.

28. Minute of understanding agreed to during conversations between Undersecretary of State Walter Bedell Smith, Acting Minister of the Associated States Guy La Chambre, and Finance Minister Edgar Faure, September 27–29, 1954, paragraph 4; Smith to the Embassy in Vietnam, top secret telegram, September 28, 1954, *FRUS 1952–1954* 13:2080–81.

29. Top secret NSC briefing, October 6, 1954, NA, CREST; La Chambre to Mendès France, October 13, 1954, IPMF, DPMF, Indochine, VII.

30. Kidder to acting secretary, top secret, September 21, 1954, NA, RG 59, Director Office of Philippine and Southeast Asian Affairs, International Conferences, Talks, and Meetings, box 4; top secret NSC briefings, October 21 and 28, 1954, NA, CREST.

31. Hammer, *The Struggle for Indochina*, 357.

32. Hoopes, *The Devil and John Foster Dulles*, 253.

33. Gibbons, *The U.S. Government and the Vietnam War*, 244; Bonnet to Mendès France, October 15, 1954, *DDF 1954*, 559–61.

34. Quoted in Costigliola, *France and the United States*, 109. See also *Pentagon Papers*, 223; Duiker, *U.S. Containment Policy*, 204; and Spector, *Advice and Support*, 235. Also, see La Chambre to MAE, October 23, 1954, MAE, Asie Océanie 1944–1955, Indochine, vol. 194.

35. Acting secretary of state to Dulles, top secret telegram, October 22, 1954, *FRUS 1952–1954* 13:2159. See also Olson, "Eisenhower and the Indochina Problem," 120–21; Dalloz, *The War in Indochina*, 195; Anderson, *Trapped by Success*, 85–87; DeJean to MAE, confidential, October 25, 1954, MAE, Cabinet du Ministre, Cabinet Pinay, vol. 21.

36. Saigon Embassy to Dulles, secret, October 28, 1954, EL, Collins Papers, box 25.

37. Top secret memorandum for the record, October 19, 1954, EL, White House Office, Office of the Special Assistant, NSC series, Briefing Notes subseries, box 11, Indochina 1954.

38. Top secret memorandum of conversation between Mendès France, Anthony Eden, and Dulles, October 23, 1954, MAE, Asie Océanie 1944–1955, Indochine, vol. 194; October 26, 1954, *FRUS 1952–1954* 13:2187. See also secret internal memorandum, November 12, 1954, MAE, Asie Océanie 1944–1955, Indochine, vol. 85; Dillon to DOS, telegram, October 25, 1954, *FRUS 1952–1954* 13:2176; and Dillon to Mendès France, top secret, October 30, 1954, MAE, Asie Océanie 1944–1955, vol. 194.

39. Memorandum of 219th NSC meeting, October 26, 1954, *FRUS 1952–1954*
13:2184; Costigliola, *France and the United States,* 109. Gibson to DOS, November
30, 1954, *FRUS 1952–1954* 13:2330; summary of Dulles–Mendès France meetings,
November 18, 1954, MAE, Asie Océanie 1944–1955, Indochine, vol. 195; note, October 25, 1954, IPMF, DPMF, Indochine, VII; Bonnet to Saigon, telegram, October
26, 1954, MAE, Asie Océanie 1944–1955, Indochine, vol. 194.

40. Heath to DOS, November 7, 1954, *FRUS 1952–1954* 13:2222.

41. Top secret memorandum of conversation, October 30, 1954, EL, Dulles Papers, White House Memoranda series, box 1, Meetings with the president 1954 (1).

42. Collins, *Lightning Joe,* 386; note for the president, November 13, 1954, MAE,
Asie Océanie 1944–1955, Indochine, vol. 195; Allen, minute, November 22, 1955,
PRO, FO 371/112041.

43. *Pentagon Papers,* 220–25; secret summary of the political situation in South
Vietnam, November 12, 1954, MAE, Asie Océanie 1944–1955, Indochine, vol. 85.

44. Top secret NSC briefings, October 21, 25, and 28, 1954, NA, CREST.

45. Top secret NSC briefings, October 21 and 28, November 8, 1954, NA,
CREST.

46. See Heath to DOS, telegram, September 11, 1954, *FRUS 1952–1954* 13:2020;
215th NSC meeting, September 24, 1954, *FRUS 1952–1954* 13:2058; Guy La Chambre to Bonnet, telegram, October 23, 1954, MAE, Asie Océanie 1944–1955, Indochine, vol. 194; Duiker, *U.S. Containment Policy,* 206; and *Pentagon Papers,* 219, for
more on the Hinh crisis.

47. Memorandum of conversation, December 7, 1954, NA, RG 59, Director Office of Philippine and Southeast Asian Affairs, International Conferences, Talks, and
Meetings, box 2.

48. 1955 aid program for Indochina, NA, RG 59, Director Office of Philippine
and Southeast Asian Affairs, International Conferences, Talks, and Meetings, box 2;
Daridan to Claude Cheysson, December 3, 1954, IPMF, DPMF, Indochine, VII.

49. "Alternative to Diem Solution," Turner Cameron to Kidder and Collins, secret, December 18, 1954, EL, Collins Papers, J. Lawton Collins file, box 27.

50. Hoopes, *The Devil and John Foster Dulles,* 255; *Pentagon Papers,* 214, 228–29;
and see Dillon to DOS, top secret telegram, December 30, 1954, *FRUS 1952–1954*
13:2437.

51. Dillon to DOS, top secret, December 26, 1954, EL, Collins Papers, J. Lawton
Collins file, box 25, monthly papers, December 1954 (3).

52. Young to Collins, secret, December 15, 1954, EL, Collins Papers, J. Lawton
Collins file, box 31; Young to Robertson, December 10, 1954, NA, RG 59, Director
Office of Philippine and Southeast Asian Affairs, International Conferences, Talks,
and Meetings, box 2

53. Collins to state, secret, December 10, 1954, EL, Collins Papers, J. Lawton
Collins file, box 31.

54. MacDonald to Eden, December 12, 1954, PRO, PREM 11/1310.

55. Top secret NSC briefing, December 20, 1954, NA, CREST.

56. Top secret NSC briefing, November 8, 1954, NA, CREST.

57. Daridan to Cheysson, December 3, 1954, IPMF, DPMF, Indochine, VII.

58. Foreign Office official James Cable, minute, January 18, 1955, PRO, FO 371/117176; Ely to MAE, telegram, December 1, 1954, meeting with British official Malcolm MacDonald, MAE, Asie Océanie 1944–1955, Indochine, vol. 85; Cheysson to Mendès France, December 28, 1954, IPMF, DPMF, Indochine, VII.

59. Gullion draft, "What Next in Indochina?" secret, February 15, 1955, EL, Collins Papers, J. Lawton Collins file, box 27.

60. French ambassador to the United States Maurice Couve de Murville to MAE, January 31, 1955, MAE, Asie Océanie 1944–1955, Indochine, vol. 86; Ely, note, spring 1955, SHAT, Fonds Paul Ely, vol. 37; Stephenson to Anthony Eden, Annual Review of Events in South Vietnam, March 7, 1955, PRO, FO 371/117093.

61. Stephenson to FO, March 2 and 15, 1955, PRO, FO 371/117097.

62. Director of the Office of Philippine and Southeast Asian Affairs Kenneth Young to DOS, secret telegram, March 25, 1955, FRUS 1955–1957 1:147.

63. USIS official Edward Stansbury to Collins, March 12 and 17, 1955, EL, Collins Papers, J. Lawton Collins file, box 30.

64. See Bator, Vietnam, 191–205. See also Anderson, "J. Lawton Collins," 131.

65. For more information on the exact chronology of the spring crisis, see Artaud, "Spring 1955." For a firsthand account of the sect crisis, see Shaplen, The Lost Revolution, 119–24. Although the Binh Xuyen created the immediate crisis, the Cao Dai and Hoa Hao also represented a significant threat to Diem.

66. Scigliano, South Vietnam, 22; Karnow, Vietnam, 222. See also Fisher Howe to Dulles, secret memorandum, May 6, 1955, NA, RG 59, Subject files of the Bureau of Intelligence and Research, lot 58D776, box 11; Olson, "Eisenhower and the Indochina Problem," 123.

67. Dulles to French Embassy, secret telegram, April 3, 1955, FRUS 1955–1957 1:193.

68. See Stephenson to FO, secret telegram, April 5, 1955, PRO, FO 371/117097.

69. Secretary of State of the Associated States Robert LaForest to Ely, March 31, 1955, DDF 1955, 373–74.

70. Ely to LaForest, March 31, 1955, DDF 1955, 374–77; discussion, n.d., SHAT, Fonds Paul Ely, vol. 37; French ambassador to Britain René Massigli to DOS, telegram, April 2, 1955; Jacques Roux to Washington and London Embassies, telegram, April 6, 1955; and Couve de Murville to MAE, telegram, April 4, 1955, MAE, Asie Océanie 1944–1955, Indochine, vol. 87.

71. Collins to Dulles, top secret telegram, March 31, 1955, NA, RG 59, Central Decimal files, Indochina, Internal and Foreign Affairs, 1955–1959, 751G.00/3-3155. American internal divisions over whether to abandon Diem are discussed in Anderson, Trapped by Success, 101–19. See also Dulles to Dillon, top secret telegram, 12 April; Dillon to Dulles, top secret telegram, 13 April, FRUS 1955–1957 1:244–45.

72. LaForest to Ely, April 2, 1955, *DDF 1955*, 386-88.

73. Couve de Murville to Minister of the MAE Pinay, April 4, 1955, *DDF 1955*, 396-97.

74. Ely to LaForest, April 2, 1955, *DDF 1955*, 389-93. See also Couve de Murville to MAE, telegram, April 1, 1955, Asie Océanie 1944-1955, Indochine, vol. 87; Roux to MAE, telegram, May 4, 1955, MAE, Asie Océanie 1944-1955, Indochine, vol. 88.

75. Cable, minutes, April 5, 1955, PRO, FO 371/117117.

76. Cable, minutes, April 6, 1955, PRO, FO 371/117117.

77. Ely to LaForest, telegram, April 6, 1955, *DDF 1955*, 412-13.

78. Dulles to French Embassy, top secret telegram, April 18, 1955, *FRUS 1955-1957* 1:258.

79. Dulles to Collins, top secret telegram, April 20, 1955, *FRUS 1955-1957* 1:270; Dulles to Dillon, top secret telegram, April 27, 1955, *FRUS 1955-1957* 1:294-95.

80. According to Cesari, this letter was a stalling tactic to give Diem time to reorganize. Cesari, "La France, Les Etats-Unis, et L'Indochine," 1042. But American documentation suggests that top officials were at last ready to consider alternatives. David Anderson concurs in "J. Lawton Collins," 136-38.

81. Couve de Murville to MAE, telegram, April 11, MAE, Asie Océanie 1944-1955, Indochine, vol. 87; Couve de Murville to Pinay, April 18, 1955, *DDF 1955*, 466-71.

82. Top secret questions from the United States to France, Gibson to Roux, April 13, 1955, MAE, Asie Océanie 1944-1955, Indochine, vol. 196; Dillon to DOS, April 13, 1955, NA, RG 59, microfilm, C0008, reel 2; Roux to MAE, telegram, April 14, 1955, MAE, Asie Océanie 1944-1955, Indochine, vol. 87; LaForest to Ely, telegram, April 13, *DDF 1955*, 437-39; Dulles to Saigon, top secret telegram, NA, RG 59, microfilm, LM071, reel 15; and Antoine Pinay to Couve de Murville, April 21, 1955, *DDF 1955*, 484-86.

83. Top secret memorandum for the record, April 22, 1955, EL, White House Office, Office of the Special Assistant for NSA Records 1952-1961, Special Assistant series, Chronological subseries, box 1, April 1955 (6).

84. Paris to state, top secret telegram, April 21, 1955, EL, Collins Papers, J. Lawton Collins file, box 26.

85. Couve de Murville to MAE, top secret, April 28, 1955, *DDF 1955*, 523-24. See also Dulles to Dillon, top secret telegram, April 28, 1955, *FRUS 1955-1957* 1:313. Dulles stated that Dillon should make the following points to the French orally, but not in writing: "In our judgment, even with full support of the U.S., no government in Vietnam will succeed unless it enjoys—1. Nationalist Vietnamese support; 2. Unambiguous French support; and 3. Full support by Bao Dai."

86. In an April 29 meeting, Dillon told Pinay and LaForest that the United States had three conditions for continued American support: total French support of any government; guarantees by Bao Dai that the government had complete authority of

the police as well as the national army; and reintegration of the sects into society. Pinay to Couve de Murville, April 29, 1955, *DDF 1955*, 541–43.

87. Couve de Murville to Faure, Pinay, and LaForest, top secret, April 27, 1955; Couve de Murville to Quai, telegrams, April 29 and 30, 1955, MAE, Amérique 1952–63, Etats-Unis, vol. 372.

88. Ely to MAE, top secret, April 21, 1954, SHAT, Fonds Paul Ely, vol. 39.

89. See Anderson, *Trapped by Success*, 110–13, for more detail on the sect crisis. See Lansdale, *In the Midst of Wars*, 244–312, for a firsthand account. Covert U.S. support in Vietnam also included the CIA-controlled airline Civil Air Transport (CAT), which began transporting people and supplies in the spring of 1953.

90. Programs for the Implementation of U.S. Policy Towards South Vietnam, top secret, April 25, 1955, EL, Collins Papers, J. Lawton Collins file, box 31, USIA.

91. See Anderson, "J. Lawton Collins," 146–47.

92. Ely to MAE, May 2, 1955; Couve de Murville to MAE, May 3, 1955; Ely to MAE, May 4, 1955, MAE, Asie Océanie 1944–1955, Indochine, vol. 88; Ely to LaForest, May 6, 1955, *DDF 1955*, 588–93; and Hoppenot to minister, top secret, August 13, 1956, MAE, CLV, SV, vol. 73.

93. Anderson, *Trapped by Success*, 121; Special National Intelligence Estimate, May 2, 1955, *FRUS 1955–1957* 1:348; Stephenson to FO, May 4, 1955, PRO, PREM 11/1310; Stephenson to FO, May 21, 1955, PRO, FO 371/117097; Cable, minute, May 6, 1955, PRO, FO 371/117119.

94. Gibbons, *The U.S. Government and the Vietnam War*, 299.

95. Greene, "John Foster Dulles and the End of the Franco-American Entente in Indochina," 551.

96. Hoover to Dulles, top secret telegram, May 9, 1955, *FRUS 1955–1957* 1:385–86; Dulles to DOS, top secret telegrams, May 8 and 9, 1955, *FRUS 1955–1957* 1:372–80.

97. Summary of tripartite talks, PRO, FO 371/117119; Dulles to DOS, top secret telegram, May 8, 1955, *FRUS 1955–1957* 1:375.

98. Spector, *Advice and Support*, 251.

99. For a firsthand account of Collins's views on Diem's future, see Collins, *Lightning Joe*, 408.

100. Stephenson to FO, telegram, May 21, 1955, PRO, FO 371/117097; Ely to MAE, top secret, May 6, 1954, SHAT, Fonds Paul Ely, vol. 39; Ely to MAE, May 15, 1955, SHAT, Fonds Paul Ely, vol. 40.

101. Top secret internal report on French policy in Vietnam, author unknown, June 22, 1955, MAE, Asie Océanie 1944–1955, Indochine, vol. 88.

102. Bonnet to Quai, August 4, 1954, MAE, Asie Océanie 1944–1955, Indochine, vol. 188; Guy La Chambre to Roux, August 26, 1954, MAE, Asie Océanie 1944–1955, Indochine, vol. 188. Spellman had started a campaign in the United States asking American Catholics for their help, and he demanded a similar campaign in France. Guy La Chambre reassured Dulles that as soon as the South Vietnamese

brought up the refugee issue, France would offer transportation from the North to the South.

103. Quoted in Spector, *Advice and Support*, 225–26. This provision had been one of the seven Anglo-American conditions for a negotiated settlement at Geneva (see chapter 3, page 103).

104. Quoted in Wiesner, *Victims and Survivors*, 3.

105. Note for Mendès France regarding transplantation of certain Vietnamese, December 13, 1954, MAE, CLV, Aide Militaire, Guerre d'Indochine et Contentieux Franco-Indochinois, Conséquences de la Conférence de Genève, Transports Militaires, Evacuation du Nord.

106. D. C. Lavergne, notes, August 17, 1954, NA, RG 469, Mission to Vietnam, Resettlement and Rehabilitation, subject files, 1953–1958, 1953–1955 Mission Program, refugee letters, box 2; Report of the Refugee Coordinating Committee, August 27, 1954, NA, RG 469, Mission to Vietnam, Resettlement and Rehabilitation, subject files, 1953–58, 1953–55 Mission Program, refugee letters, box 2.

107. Spector, *Advice and Support*, 226–27.

108. D. C. Lavergne, Acting Special Deputy report, August 19, 1954, NA, RG 469, Mission to Vietnam, Resettlement and Rehabilitation, subject files, 1953–1958, 1953–1955 Mission Program, refugee letters, box 2.

109. Status Report on the Evacuation of Refugees from North and South Vietnam, September 18, 1954, NA, RG 469, Mission to Vietnam, box 5.

110. Quarterly Report, October–December 1954, NA, RG 469, Mission to Vietnam, Resettlement and Rehabilitation, subject files 1953–1958, 1953–1955, Mission Program, refugee letters, box 2; confidential letter, March 1955, NA, RG 469, USOM Vietnam, Resettlement and Rehabilitation, box 3.

111. Memorandum on the refugee problem, January 20, 1955, MAE, CLV, Aide Militaire, Guerre d'Indochine et Contentieux Franco-Indochinois, Conséquences de la Conférence de Genève, Transports Militaires, Evacuation du Nord, 1954–56.

112. Bonnet to Mendès France, December 30, 1954, MAE, Asie Océanie 1944–1955, Indochine, vol. 188; Mike Adler, chief, Field Service, to D. C. Lavergne, memorandum, December 20, 1954, NA, RG 469, Mission to Vietnam, Resettlement and Rehabilitation, subject files, 1953–1958, 1953–1955 Mission Program, refugee letters, box 2.

113. Dooley, *Deliver Us from Evil*, 45, 143. In particular, Dooley recognized Captain Gerald Cauvin, chief of the Deuxième Bureau (French Intelligence) for his efforts in the North.

114. Saigon to Etats-Associés, February 11, 1955, MAE, Asie Océanie 1944–1955, Indochine, vol. 188.

115. Richard Brown to Paul Everett, acting director of mission, September 2, 1954, NA, RG 469, NND 877731, box 5.

116. Lavergne to Everett, September 2, 1954, NA, RG 286, Mission to Vietnam, Resettlement and Rehabilitation, classified subject files, 1954–1958, box 2.

117. Wiesner, *Victims and Survivors*, 9.

118. Vietminh leaflet, n.d., NA, RG 469, Mission to Vietnam, Program and Support, subject files 1950-1956, 1950-1954, Technical School personnel-Well Program, box 7; *Observateur*, October 14, November 13, 1954, January 20, 1955.

119. Ormesson to Mendès France, November 19, 1954, MAE, Asie Océanie 1944-1955, Indochine, vol. 188; Ely to Etats Associés, secret, April 7, 1955, MAE, CLV, Aide Militaire, Guerre d'Indochine et Contentieux Franco-Indochinois, Conséquences de la Conférence de Genève, Transports Militaires, Evacuation du Nord, 1954-1956.

120. Dulles remark to Agence France-Presse, March 1955, MAE, Asie Océanie 1944-1955, Indochine, vol. 188.

121. James Roper, "Vietnam Refugee Flood Becomes United States Problem," *Washington Star*, April 18, 1955; Geographic Intelligence Review, January 1957, NA, CIA Office of Research and Reports, CREST.

122. MAE to Hoppenot, August 2, 1955, MAE, Papiers d'Agents, Henri Hoppenot, vol. 15.

123. MAE memorandum, September 24, 1956, MAE, CLV, SV, vol. 7. See Spector, *Advice and Support*, 251; Greene, "John Foster Dulles," 551-57; *Pentagon Papers*, 211; and Hoopes, *The Devil and John Foster Dulles*, 261, for the perspective that the sect crisis and May talks effectively ended the French presence in Vietnam.

5. The Non-elections of 1956

1. A proposal to hold general elections was first made by North Vietnamese foreign minister Pham Van Dong on May 10, 1954. Dong brought up the point again on June 16, after military matters had been settled. The majority of negotiations on this point were carried out secretly by the Vietminh and the French.

2. Final Declaration of the Geneva Conference on Indochina, July 21, 1954. Precisely how these elections would be conducted remained unspecified. Although the cease-fire agreement was considered a valid document under international law, the final declaration was more ambiguous as the United States and South Vietnam refused to attach their names to the document and issued separate statements. Considerable debate exists over what legal obligations the United States and South Vietnam incurred under the Geneva agreements. A fall 2000 discussion posted on the online discussion list H-Diplo (http://www.h-net.org/~diplo/), prompted by reviews of Robert McNamara's book *Argument without End*, led to spirited debate over whether nationwide elections, as noted in the final declaration, were binding for the United States. Interestingly, no one in the discussion raised the point that no matter the American obligations, the cease-fire agreement made the elections compulsory for the French, North Vietnamese, British, and Soviets. Randle, *Geneva 1954* and Falk (ed.), *The Vietnam War and International Law*, 543-73, also address this issue. The legal implications of the Geneva Accords are not discussed in this study, but it

is worth noting that the United States, in an effort to justify its own policies, consistently claimed that the legal basis of the accords was ambiguous at best. See, for example, William Sebald to Dulles, memorandum, June 14, 1955, *FRUS 1955–1957* 1:452.

3. Scholars who address the 1956 elections issue typically do so in a fairly cursory manner and, for the most part, focus on American policy and American support of Diem's refusal to begin consultations with North Vietnam as the primary reasons for the elections' failure. See, for example, Herring, *America's Longest War,* 55–56; Scigliano, *South Vietnam,* 134; Levy, *The Debate over Vietnam,* 32, 48; Kahin, *Intervention,* 89; and Karnow, *Vietnam,* 24. Laurent Cesari goes further when he asserts that the non-elections of 1956 were a "triumph of American policy," and that South Vietnam was a "loyal instrument of U.S. policy." He also suggests that American policy in Vietnam was "fixed early on"—the Americans were committed to keeping the DRV and China in complete isolation and to sabotaging the 1956 elections, which was why they kept Diem in power. No other South Vietnamese leader would be "so hostile" to the elections. Cesari, "La France, Les Etats-Unis, et L'Indochine," 891–92, 913, 968, 1074–75. See also Porter, *Perils of Dominance,* chp. 3. All of these scholars have one point in common—they focus on American agency in supporting Diem's refusal to go through with the 1956 elections, implying that American policy toward the 1956 elections was organized and steadfast.

4. Some scholars have recognized that considerations beyond the borders of Vietnam influenced the Geneva participants' policy toward elections, but their discussions are brief. See, for example, Duiker, *U.S. Containment Policy,* 217; Devillers, "The Struggle for the Unification of Vietnam," 3; Weinstein, *Vietnam's Unheld Elections;* Greene, "John Foster Dulles,"; and Anderson, *Trapped by Success.* Anderson concludes that Saigon and Washington had sought to sabotage the 1956 elections, "but they had accomplices in London, Paris, Moscow, and Beijing who were not eager to risk involvement in a rekindled conflict for the sake of Hanoi" (123–24, 127).

5. The unilateral declaration of the United States read by Undersecretary of State Walter Bedell Smith, July 21, 1954, Final Session, is as follows: "In the case of nations, now divided against their will, we shall continue to seek to achieve unity through free elections, supervised by the United Nations to insure that they are conducted fairly. With respect to the statement made by the representative of the State of Vietnam, the United States reiterates its traditional position that peoples are entitled to determine their own future and that it will not join in an arrangement which would hinder this. Nothing in its declaration just made is intended to or does indicate any departure from this traditional position."

6. Herring, *America's Longest War,* 55–56. In a note attached to a February 1, 1955, paper, "Considerations Bearing on the Problem of 1956 Elections in Vietnam," Paul Kattenburg asserts that the State Department was trying "to figure out a way around the elections but had done some planning in case the elections were held."

NA, RG 59, Director Office of Philippine and Southeast Asian Affairs, International Conferences, Talks, and Meetings, box 2.

7. Kenneth Young to Walter Robertson, top secret, December 10, 1954, NA, RG 59, Director Office of Philippine and Southeast Asian Affairs, International Conferences, Talks, and Meetings, box 1.

8. "The Question of Nationwide Elections in Vietnam, 1954-1960," top secret, November 1966, NA, RG 59, Research Projects, Executive Secretariat, Historical Office Research Projects, 1969-1974, research project 833, box 3.

9. Report on Vietnam for the NSC, top secret, January 27, 1955, EL, White House Office, Office of the Special Assistant for NSA Records 1952-1961, Special Assistant series, Chronological subseries, box 1, April 1955 (6).

10. Considerations Bearing on the Problem of the 1956 Elections in Vietnam, secret intelligence report, February 1, 1955, EL, Collins Papers, J. Lawton Collins file, box 30; Edmund Gullion draft, "What Next in Indochina?" secret, February 15, 1955, EL, Collins Papers, J. Lawton Collins file, box 27.

11. Secret meeting between South Vietnamese foreign minister Tran Van Do and Dulles, March 1, 1955, NA, RG 59, Director Office of Philippine and Southeast Asian Affairs, International Conferences, Talks, and Meetings, box 2.

12. "The Question of Nationwide Elections in Vietnam, 1954-1960," top secret, November 1966, NA, RG 59, Research Projects, Executive Secretariat, Historical Office Research Projects, 1969-1974, research project 833, box 3.

13. U.S. Policy on All Vietnam Elections, top secret statement, March 28, 1955, NA, RG 59, Director Office of Philippine and Southeast Asian Affairs, International Conferences, Talks, and Meetings, box 2.

14. The ICC was headed by India and composed of members from India, Poland, and Canada. Some scholars have addressed the ICC's ineffectiveness in ensuring the 1956 elections. See, for example, Thakur, *Peacekeeping in Vietnam;* Hannon, "The International Control Commission Experience"; and Weinstein, *Vietnam's Unheld Elections.* Laurent Cesari claims that the ICC evolved from an instrument for applying the Geneva Accords to a means of maintaining the status quo. Cesari, "La France, Les Etats Unis, et L'Indochine," 1075. The ICC was hindered by a number of factors. Among these was the fact that it was seldom included in tripartite talks among the French, Americans, and British concerning the 1956 elections. Moreover, Diem's government essentially ignored the ICC, accusing it on occasion of spying for the North. Finally, the amount of power the ICC had in ensuring the 1956 elections was never clearly established. The ICC eventually acknowledged that it was unable to perform its functions because of both South and North Vietnam's intransigence. ICC members asked the co-chairs to ensure the Geneva Accords since the ICC could not. The ICC did agree to continue its supervisory role after the 1956 deadline, but both South and North Vietnam continued to ignore ICC claims of Geneva violations.

15. U.S. Policy on All-Vietnam Elections, top secret statement, March 28, 1955;

Walter Robertson to Dulles, U.S. Position Regarding Elections in Vietnam, top se-
cret, April 5, 1955, NA, RG 59, Director Office of Philippine and Southeast Asian
Affairs, International Conferences, Talks, and Meetings, box 2; Tactics for Talks with
British and French on All-Vietnam Elections, secret, April 21, 1955, EL, Collins Pa-
pers, J. Lawton Collins file, box 27, election file (1). Douglas MacArthur to Dulles,
April 1, 1955, NA, RG 59, Director Office of Philippine and Southeast Asian Affairs,
International Conferences, Talks, and Meetings, box 2; U.S. Policy on All-Vietnam
Elections, top secret NSC report, May 17, 1955, *FRUS 1955–1957* 1:410–12.

16. Robert Hoey to William Leonhart, April 18, 1955, NA, RG 59, Director
Office of Philippine and Southeast Asian Affairs, International Conferences, Talks,
and Meetings, box 2. See also Statler, "The Diem Experiment." U.S. Policy on All-
Vietnam Elections, top secret NSC report, May 17, 1955, EL, White House Office,
Office of the Special Assistant for NSA Records, NSC series, Policy Papers subseries,
box 16, NSC 5519, Vietnam Elections.

17. Dulles to Saigon Embassy, secret, May 27, 1955; Young to American ambassador in Saigon G. Frederick Reinhardt, June 2, 1955, *FRUS 1955–1957* 1:421,
428–29.

18. 251st NSC meeting, top secret discussion on NSC 5519, June 9, 1955, EL,
Ann Whitman file, NSC series, box 7; Duiker, *U.S. Containment Policy*, 214; Young
to Reinhardt, June 10, 1955; Sebald to Dulles, secret, June 14, 1955, *FRUS 1955–
1957* 1:444–45, 450. Daniel O'C. Greene points out that Diem's refusal to consult
preempted NSC 5519 before it was ever seriously discussed. Greene, "John Foster
Dulles," 570.

19. Reinhardt to Young, top secret, July 1, 1955, NA, RG 59, Director Office of
Philippine and Southeast Asian Affairs, box 4; top secret briefing note, June 9, 1955,
EL, White House Office, Office of the Special Assistant for NSA Records 1952–1961,
Special Assistant series, Chronological subseries, box 1, June 1955 (2).

20. Memorandum, July 13, 1955, NA, RG 59, Director Office of Philippine and
Southeast Asian Affairs, International Conferences, Talks, and Meetings, box 2;
Dulles to Saigon Embassy, secret, July 15, 1955, *FRUS 1955–1957* 1:486. The heads
of state of the United States, Soviet Union, Britain, and France met at Geneva to
discuss questions of German reunification, European security, and nuclear disarmament. For full coverage of the Geneva summit, see Bischof and Dockrill (eds.), *Cold
War Respite*.

21. U.S. Policy on All-Vietnam Elections, top secret NSC report, May 17, 1955,
FRUS 1955–1957 1:410–12.

22. Duiker, *U.S. Containment Policy*, 217. See Dacy, *Foreign Aid, War, and Economic Development*; Kaufman, *Trade and Aid*; and Adamson, "Delusions of Development."

23. George Kahin notes that senior American officials were not disposed to
pressure Diem to participate even in preliminary consultations, and by the time the
meetings were scheduled, official U.S. policy had swung behind him in his refusal

to do so. Kahin, *Intervention*, 90. More recently, Qiang Zhai has written that after the July 20, 1955, deadline passed, "the Diem government, pressured by the United States, was displaying not the slightest intention to hold the meetings." Zhai, *China and the Vietnam Wars*, 77.

24. Chargé d'Affairs in Vietnam Dillon Anderson to DOS, secret, September 20, 1955, *FRUS 1955–1957* 1:540–42.

25. U.S. stance on elections, attached to letter from French Embassy in United States to Antoine Pinay, December 9, 1955, MAE, CLV, SV, vol. 73. In a top secret telegram from Ely to Mendès France, Ely stated that his recent meeting with Collins confirmed French fears about American plans for the 1956 elections. November 16, 1954, Asie Océanie 1944–1955, Indochina, vol. 85. Duiker, *U.S. Containment Policy*, 213; *Pentagon Papers*, 239.

26. Dillon to DOS, secret telegram, *FRUS 1955–1957* 1:420; Chronologie, MAE, Asie Océanie 1944–1955, Conflit Vietnam, vol. 1.

27. Henri Hoppenot to French foreign minister Antoine Pinay, January 18 and 26, 1956; and Asie Océanie, note, February 11, 1956, *DDF 1956*, vol. I, 55–56, 78–79, 190–91.

28. Chronologie, MAE, Asie Océanie 1944–1955, Conflit Vietnam, vol. 1; Pineau to Anthony Eden and Vyacheslav Molotov, note, May 14, 1956, MAE, CLV, SV, vol. 69; Hoppenot to Pineau, secret, July 14, 1956, MAE, CLV, SV, vol. 73.

29. Hoppenot to Pineau, top secret, August 13, 1956, MAE, CLV, SV, vol. 73.

30. Pineau to Jean Payart, August 29, 1956, *DDF 1956*, vol. II, 316–24.

31. Kahin, *Intervention*, 91; Jacobs, "Our System Demands the Supreme Being," 596.

32. See Combs, "Path Not Taken" for the British perspective on Anglo-American conflict over Vietnam following Geneva.

33. Frank Tomlinson to FO, February 4, 1955, PRO, FO 371/117097; British Embassy memoranda, April 16 and 18, 1955, EL, Collins Papers, J. Lawton Collins file, box 27, Election file (1).

34. Roger Makins to FO, June 18, 1955, and Eden, minute, June 27, 1955, PRO, PREM 11/1310.

35. "The Question of Nationwide Elections in Vietnam, 1954–1960," top secret, November 1966, NA, RG 59, Research Projects, Executive Secretariat, Historical Office Research Projects, 1969–1974, research project 833, box 3; memorandum of conversation, June 18, 1955, *FRUS 1955–1957* 1:460.

36. "The Question of Nationwide Elections in Vietnam, 1954–1960," top secret, November 1966, NA, RG 59, Research Projects, Executive Secretariat, Historical Office Research Projects, 1969–1974, research project 833, box 3; Chronologie, MAE, Asie Océanie 1944–1955, Conflit Vietnam, vol. 1.

37. James Cable, minute, September 21, 1955, PRO, FO 371/117146; memorandum, October 17, 1955, PRO, FO 371/117147.

38. Eden, minutes, September 1 and 3, 1955, PRO, FO 371/117145; note, Sep-

tember 26, 1955, PRO, FO 371/117146; Stephenson to FO, September 24, 1955, PRO, FO 371/117146.

39. "The Question of Nationwide Elections in Vietnam, 1954–1960," top secret, November 1966, NA, RG 59, Research Projects, Executive Secretariat, Historical Office Research Projects, 1969–1974, research project 833, box 3; Chronologie, MAE, Asie Océanie 1944–1955, Conflit Vietnam, vol. 1.

40. Note, January 1956; Cable, comment, March 5, 1956, PRO, FO 371/123444. See also Stephenson's annual review to Lloyd, February 1, 1957, PRO, FO 371/129701.

41. Sebald to Dulles, secret, May 10, 1956, *FRUS 1955–1957* 1:680–82; co-chair meeting notes, April 1956, PRO, FO 371/123452; and memorandum, April 19, 1956, PRO, FO 371/123450.

42. Graves to F. S. Tomlinson, June 4, 1956, PRO, FO 371/123429. See also Gibbons, *The U.S. Government and the Vietnam War*, 304.

43. FO, memorandum, March 27, 1956, PRO, FO 371/123447; Cable, minute, September 19, 1955, PRO, FO 371/117146. See also Landymore, note, November 9, 1955, PRO, FO 371/117147.

44. Tomlinson, note, July 24, 1956, PRO, FO 371/123457; FO, minute, July 26, 1956, PRO, FO 371/123457.

45. Cesari, "La France, Les Etats Unis, et L'Indochine," 1075; top secret note, February 10, 1956, MAE, CLV, SV, vol. 24; Sebald to Dulles, June 14, 1955, *FRUS 1955–1957* 1:449–55.

46. Considerations Bearing on the Problem of the 1956 Elections in Vietnam, NA, RG 59, Director Office of Philippine and Southeast Asian Affairs, International Conferences, Talks, and Meetings, box 2.

47. See Dulles to Saigon Embassy, July 26, 1955, *FRUS 1955–1957* 1:497–98; Anderson, *Trapped by Success*, 127; Zubok, "Soviet Policy Aims at the Geneva Conference," 65, 72, for more detail on Soviet policy aims at the 1955 conference. See Gaiduk, *Confronting Vietnam* for an in-depth account of post-Geneva Soviet policy toward Vietnam. See Richter, *Khrushchev's Double Bind*, 64–73, for the impact of domestic politics on Soviet foreign policy.

48. Briefing paper for non-agenda item, NA, RG 59, Director Office of Philippine and Southeast Asian Affairs, International Conferences, Talks, and Meetings, box 2.

49. Eden, *Toward Peace in Indochina*, 10–11.

50. Chronologie, MAE, Asie Océanie 1944–1955, Conflit Vietnam, vol. 1.

51. Bilateral foreign ministers meeting, January 31, 1956, *FRUS 1955–1957* 1:628–30; Office of Intelligence Research, intelligence brief on the general situation in South Vietnam, February 7, 1956, *FRUS 1955–1957* 1:637–39.

52. Karnow, *Vietnam*, 224; Young to Reinhardt, October 5, 1955, *FRUS 1955–1957* 1:551–54.

53. Note, May 1956, PRO, FO 371/123454.

54. Bernard Fall report, "The International Position of South Vietnam 1954–1958," February 1958, MAE, CLV, SV, vol. 68.

55. Gaiduk, *Confronting Vietnam*, 80–88.

56. Sainteny, *Histoire*, 153.

57. Berman, *No Peace, No Honor*, 18.

58. Historians disagree about the extent of North Vietnamese sincerity in pursuing elections. P. J. Honey in "North Vietnam's Party Congress" asserts that the North Vietnamese did not expect the elections to take place. Jeffrey Race in *War Comes to Long An* (34) seconds this assertion, suggesting that the North Vietnamese recognized early on that the elections would probably not take place, as does Gaiduk in *Confronting Vietnam*. Scigliano in *South Vietnam* (133) and Thayer in *War by Other Means* (6–7) make the argument that because of the vociferous campaign waged by DRV authorities to hold elections, it seems probable that the DRV favored elections as a means of unifying the country. Moreover, Robert Brigham in *Guerrilla Diplomacy* (3) notes that after the elections failed, Hanoi and anti-Diemists in the South began to form the National Liberation Front. Lloyd Gardner reaffirmed this point in his review of *Argument without End* (H-Diplo, fall 2000), by noting that, for North Vietnam, "the status quo was the defeat of the French in 1954, and the failure of the expected process of reunification represented a deterioration in normal expectations." William Duiker in *Sacred War* (99–100) suggests that Ho Chi Minh, along with numerous other North Vietnamese leaders, believed that the elections would occur, although they were well aware that they might not.

59. Sebald to Dulles, June 14, 1955, *FRUS 1955–1957* 1:449–55; note, n.d., MAE, CLV, SV, vol. 124.

60. Note of political information, February 10, 1956, MAE, CLV, SV, vol. 124.

61. Hoppenot to MAE, top secret, March 1, 1956, MAE, CLV, SV, vol. 23.

62. Acting Special Assistant for Intelligence Howe to acting secretary of state, U.S. Estimates memorandum, October 26, 1955, *FRUS 1955–1957* 1:564; Hoppenot to MAE, July 2, 1956, MAE, CLV, SV, vol. 125.

63. "The Question of Nationwide Elections in Vietnam, 1954–1960," top secret, November 1966, NA, RG 59, Research Projects, Executive Secretariat, Historical Office Research Projects, 1969–1974, research project 833, box 3. See also Dommen, *The Indochinese Experience*, 344.

64. Considerations Bearing on the Problem of the 1956 Elections in Vietnam, NA, RG 59, Director Office of Philippine and Southeast Asian Affairs, International Conferences, Talks, and Meetings, box 2; Reinhardt to DOS, June 4, 1955, *FRUS 1955–1957* 1:434–35; and OCB, secret memorandum, June 23, 1955, EL, White House Office, NSC Staff Papers, 1948–1961, OCB Central File series, box 39, 091 Indochina April–September 1955, file #4 (6).

65. Deputy assistant secretary of state for Far Eastern affairs to Dulles, memorandum, June 8, 1955; and memorandum of top secret State Department conversation, June 8, 1955, *FRUS 1955–1957* 1:436–41.

66. Chronologie, MAE, Asie Océanie 1944–1955, Conflit Vietnam, vol. 1; OCB, secret daily intelligence abstracts, July 19, 20, 1955, EL, White House Office, NSC Staff Papers, OCB Central File series, box 11, OCB 350.05 file #2 (3), December 1954–February 1956.

67. Dulles to DOS, telegram, July 22, FRUS 1955–1957 1:494; "The Question of Nationwide Elections in Vietnam, 1954–1960," top secret, November 1966, NA, RG 59, Research Projects, Executive Secretariat, Historical Office Research Projects, 1969–1974, research project 833, box 3.

68. Chronologie, MAE, Asie Océanie 1944–1955, Conflit Vietnam, vol. 1.

69. Hoppenot to MAE, February 10, 1956, MAE, CLV, SV, vol. 124; Anderson, Trapped by Success, 130.

70. Reinhardt to DOS, secret telegram, March 15, 1956; and Anderson to DOS, secret, March 17, 1956, FRUS 1955–1957 1:660–62; Hoppenot to MAE, top secret, April 25, 1956, MAE, CLV, SV, vol. 124.

71. Political Situation in Vietnam as of 31 May 1956, Hoppenot to MAE, top secret, June 1, 1956, MAE, CLV, SV, vol. 125.

72. Hoppenot to MAE, top secret, July 2, 1956, MAE, CLV, SV, vol. 125.

73. Anderson, Trapped by Success, 122–27.

74. See Jean Filliol to MAE, top secret telegram, August 22, 1956, MAE, CLV, SV, vol. 73; and note of information, January 9, 1957, MAE, CLV, SV, vol. 8.

75. Smith on the situation in Indochina, quoted in Herring, "A Good Stout Effort," 225.

6. From the French to the Americans

1. Chauvel, note, July 30, 1954, CHEVS, 1 SA 13 Jean Sainteny.

2. Commissariat Générale de France, September 1954, MAE, CLV, Aide Militaire, Généralités, carton 2.

3. Dommen, The Indochinese Experience, 258–62.

4. Young to American ambassador G. Frederick Reinhardt, June 2, 1954, NA, RG 59, Director Office of Philippine and Southeast Asian Affairs, International Conferences, Talks, and Meetings, box 4.

5. Bonnet to Saigon, August 30, 1954, MAE, CLV, Aide Militaire, Généralités, carton 3; T. E. de Shazo, major general, U.S. Army, chief of MAAG, to chief of French liaison group, memorandum, August 30, 1954, MAE, CLV, Aide Militaire, Guerre d'Indochine et Contentieux Franco-Indochinois, Conséquences de la Conférence de Genève, Transports Militaires, Evacuation du Nord, 1954–56.

6. Mendès France to Saigon, November 20, 1954, and Ely to MAE, December 14, 1954, MAE, CLV, Aide Militaire, Généralités, carton 3; note on Indochine, n.d., IPMF, DPMF, Relations Internationales, chemise R1/4, Compte rendu voyage du president en Amerique, 17–23 November 1954. Years later, Mendès France would insist that if subsequent French governments had held the Americans accountable

to the December 1954 agreements, all the "drama" of the next years could have been avoided. He argued that the Second Indochina War did not find its origin in the actions he took, but in a series of events that occurred after he left power. Mendès France to reporter André Fontaine, January 12, February 4, May 25 1966, June 1, 1967, June 5, 1972, and Fontaine to Mendès France, June 28, 1972, IPMF, DPMF, Dossier André Fontaine, Pierre Mendès France Papers.

7. Bonnet to MAE, top secret, November 25, 1954, MAE, CLV, Aide Militaire, Généralités, carton 3; *Pentagon Papers*, 217; Spector, *Advice and Support*, 238; Mendès France to Guy La Chambre, November 28, 1954, IPMF, DPMF, Indochine, VI.

8. Daridan to Cheysson, December 3, 1954, IPMF, DPMF, Indochine, VII; top secret note, December 23, 1954, MAE, CLV, Asie Océanie 1944–1955, Guerre d'Indochine et Contentieux Franco-Indochinois, Conséquences de la Conférence de Genève, Réorganisation CEFEO, 1954–56 (hereafter cited as MAE, CLV, Asie, CEFEO).

9. Top secret memorandum, May 20, 1955, MAE, CLV, Asie, CEFEO; Spector, *Advice and Support*, 253.

10. Jacquot to minister, top secret, October 17, 1955, and memorandum, n.d., MAE, CLV, Asie, CEFEO.

11. Hoppenot to MAE, secret, October 24, 1955; memorandum for the minister, October 25, 1955; top secret note, October 14, 1955, MAE, CLV, Asie, CEFEO; Ely to Mendès France, top secret telegram, and Mendès France to Ely, top secret telegram, November 16, 1954, MAE, Asie Océanie 1944–1955, Indochine, vol. 195.

12. Jacquot to Quai d'Orsay, December 8, 1955, Hoppenot to minister, December 10, 1955, and top secret note, December 30, 1955, MAE, CLV, Asie, CEFEO.

13. Hoppenot to French foreign minister Antoine Pinay, January 18, 1956, *DDF 1956*, vol. I, 55–56; and Hoppenot to minister, January 26 and 28, 1956, MAE, CLV, Asie, CEFEO.

14. Hoppenot to Pinay, January 18, 1956, *DDF 1956*, vol. I, 55–56; and Hoppenot to Quai, January 30, 1956, MAE, CLV, Asie, CEFEO.

15. Mendès France to Guy La Chambre, January 6, 1955, CHEVS, 1 SA 13.

16. Hoppenot to MAE, telegram, March 15, 1956, MAE, CLV, SV, vol. 73; and Hoppenot to MAE, April 6, 1956, MAE, CLV, SV, vol. 42.

17. Note, July 1955, and meeting, October 25, 1955, MAE, CLV, Asie, CEFEO.

18. See note for the minister, February 29, 1956, MAE, CLV, SV, vol. 44; and memorandum of conversation between French ambassador to the United States Maurice Couve de Murville and Dulles, February 28, 1956, *FRUS 1955–1957* 1:648.

19. Paris to Eden and Molotov, note, May 14, 1956, MAE, CLV, SV, vol. 69; *DDF 1956*, vol. I, 1016–17, 1026–29.

20. La Mission Militaire Française Près le Gouvernement Vietnamien, March 14, 1957, MAE, Aide Militaire, Rapport 1957, e. 420 (unclassified series); Dulles to Mendès France, top secret, January 24, 1955, IPMF, DPMF, Indochine, VII. According to Spector, in March 1955 there were 68 American officers and 209 French ones

in TRIM, but by March 1956 there were 189 Americans and not a single Frenchman. Spector, *Advice and Support,* 252.

21. Hoppenot to MAE, April 25, 1956, MAE, CLV, SV, vol. 42; Christian Pineau to minister of national defense, top secret, February 17, 1956, MAE, CLV, SV, vol. 40.

22. Hoppenot to MAE, March 23, 1956, MAE, CLV, SV, vol. 41; Ely to MAE, May 27, 1955, SHAT, Fonds Paul Ely, vol. 39; Lansdale, *In the Midst of Wars,* 182, 326; Lansdale to Collins, secret, January 3, 1955, EL, Collins Papers, J. Lawton Collins File, box 28 (2).

23. Hoppenot to MAE, March 6, 1956; notes, July 12 and 13, 1956, MAE, CLV, SV, vol. 38; Jacquot to minister of Quai and defense, top secret, n.d., MAE, CLV, SV, vol. 40.

24. Quai to Washington, August 14, 1956, MAE, CLV, SV, vol. 43.

25. Allen, *None So Blind,* 98; American ambassador to France Douglas Dillon to DOS, Dulles to Paris and Saigon, August 15, 1956, NA, RG 59, 651.00/3-24-55 to 651.51G9/1-12-55, box 2618.

26. Durbrow to DOS, April 29, 1957, *FRUS 1955–1957* 1:791.

27. Houghton to DOS, May 28, 1957, *FRUS 1955–1957* 1:824. Houghton replaced Dillon in 1957.

28. Hoppenot to MAE, memoranda, March 2, 6 and 19, June 15, July 1956, MAE, CLV, SV, vol. 38; Hoppenot to minister, top secret, August 13, 1956, MAE, CLV, SV, vol. 73. Hoppenot claimed he had in his possession a letter from General Williams dated March 16 that proved the idea of closing the EMS was an American initiative. See also Couve de Murville to MAE, July 9, 1956, MAE, CLV, SV, vol. 38.

29. Chauvel, note, July 30, 1954, CHEVS, 1 SA 13 Jean Sainteny; Mendès France to Saigon, telegrams, November 20, 1954, MAE, CLV, Aide Militaire, Généralités, carton 3. The French had suspected that the United States would try to take over VNA training; in a secret annex to a treaty project between France and Vietnam in February 1954, the French stipulated that the Vietnamese government guarantee it would put no facilities at the disposition of armed forces of another state without first getting the accord of the French government and, in addition, would not address the demands of foreign governments for personnel and materials necessary for the formation, instruction, and equipment of the VNA without first consulting France. Secret annex, February 1954, MAE, Asie Océanie 1944–1955, Indochine, vol. 83.

30. "U.S. Inherits Another Headache: France Turns Over Indochina Job to America," *U.S. News and World Report,* December 10, 1954, IPMF, DPMF, Indochine, VII.

31. Mendès France to Saigon, January 7, 1955, MAE, CLV, Aide Militaire, Généralités, carton 3; top secret minutes of OCB meeting, January 10, 1955, EL, White House Office, Office of the Special Assistant for NSA Records, OCB series, Administrative subseries, box 3, OCB minutes of meetings, 1955 (1); top secret memoran-

dum for the record, December 29, 1954, NA, RG 59, Director Office of Philippine and Southeast Asian Affairs, International Conferences, Talks, and Meetings, box 2. Robert McClintock and Chief of Staff Matthew Ridgway also opposed taking over the training of the VNA, whereas O'Daniel wanted to proceed.

32. For more detail on the American decision to take over training, see Spector, *Advice and Support*, 228–30, 255.

33. Mendès France to Guy La Chambre, January 6, 1955, CHEVS, 1 SA 13.

34. Spector, *Advice and Support*, 285.

35. Spector, *Advice and Support*, 257.

36. Couve de Murville to MAE, secret, February 25, 1956, MAE, CLV, SV, vol. 44. According to French sources, the State Department had a difficult time convincing the Pentagon to put forth the TERM proposal because MAAG was afraid it would have to make known how many people and how much material it had at its disposal. Couve de Murville to Quai, April 5, 1956, Affaires Exterieures, CLV, Aide Militaire, Généralités, carton 2, Aide américaine en Indochine. Couve de Murville to MAE, secret, February 25, 1956, MAE, CLV, SV, vol. 44.

37. Hoppenot to MAE, February 28, 1956; note for the minister, February 27, 1956; Roux to Saigon, February 28, 1956; and note for the minister, February 29, 1956, MAE, CLV, SV, vol. 44.

38. The ICC agreed in 1958 to allow the United States to replace military equipment that the French and TERM had removed. Couve de Murville to Pineau, note, February 29, 1956, MAE, Cabinet du Ministre, Cabinet Couve de Murville, vol. 30. See also U.S. Embassy in Saigon to DOS, "Present and Future Political Situation in South Vietnam," December 7, 1960, NA, RG 84, box 6, Chief Executive; and deputy assistant secretary of state for Far Eastern affairs to deputy undersecretary of state for political affairs, memorandum, July 26, 1957, *FRUS 1955–1957* 1:827.

39. Interviews between Dulles, Lloyd, and Pineau, March 1956, Karachi, MAE, Cabinet du Ministre, Cabinet Pinay, 21; MAE, Secrétariat Général, vols. 1, 2, 3, Entretiens et messages, Cabinet Guy Mollet; Scigliano, *South Vietnam*, 192; Spector, *Advice and Support*, 239.

40. Position paper for Mendès France talks, secret, November 1954, EL, White House Office, NSC Staff Papers, OCB Central File series, box 32; secret minutes of first Plenary meeting, November 18, 1954, NA, RG 59, Executive Secretariat, Conference files, box 61.

41. Top secret memorandum of conversation between Mendès France, Anthony Eden, and Dulles, October 23, 1954, MAE, Asie Océanie 1944–1955, Indochine, vol. 194; Rioux, *The Fourth Republic*, 232; note for the minister, MAE, CLV, Asie, CEFEO; February 18, 1956, aid mission to Vietnam, MAE, CLV, SV, vol. 87; Papp, *Vietnam*, 14; Dacy, *Foreign Aid*, 3.

42. NSC 5525, "Status of National Security Programs on June 30, 1955," *FRUS 1955–1957* 10:15–25. R. E. L. Counts, deputy chief, TCPI&M Division, to Captain Nyland, chief, TCPI&M Division, August 17, 1954, NA, RG 469, Mission to Viet-

nam, Transportation, Communications, and Power Division, subject files, 1951–1956, box 11; Gibbons, *The U.S. Government and the Vietnam War*, 315. See Dacy, *Foreign Aid*, 25–29, 34–37, 192–97, 206–9, and Adamson, "Delusions of Development" for greater detail on U.S. economic assistance. Economic aid as a tool of containment had first come into use with the Truman administration's Point Four program.

43. Saigon Embassy and USOM Saigon to DOS, dispatch, September 19, 1955, NA, RG 59, DOS central files, Indochina, Internal and Foreign Affairs, 1955–1959, C0008, reel 40.

44. Gardner Palmer to DOS, September 19, 1955, NA, RG 59, DOC central files, Indochina, Internal and Foreign Affairs, 1955–1959, C0008, microfilm, reel 40.

45. Saigon Embassy to MAE, April 24, 1956, from Agence Vietnamienne d'information Bac-Bo, Nord Vietnam, April 13, 1956, MAE, CLV, SV, vol. 55. See Kolko, *Anatomy of a War* for a discussion of the importance of American economic interests in determining U.S. policy in Vietnam. See also Saigon Embassy to MAE, April 24, 1956, from Agence Vietnamienne d'information Bac-Bo, Nord Vietnam, April 13, 1956, MAE, CLV, SV, vol. 55.

46. William Baze to Faure, Dec 6, 1955, CHEVS, 1 SA 14 Jean Sainteny; February 18, 1956, aid mission to Vietnam, MAE, CLV, SV, vol. 87.

47. Wesley Haraldson, deputy director, to H. Robert Slusser, chief, Research and Statistics section, November 28, 1956, NA, RG 469, Mission to Vietnam, Program and Requirements Division, Research and Statistics section, subject files, 1956, trade-Vietnam, box 7.

48. Saigon Embassy and USOM Saigon to DOS, dispatch, September 19, 1955, NA, RG 59, DOS central files, Indochina, Internal and Foreign Affairs, 1955–1959, C0008, microfilm, reel 40.

49. Morgan, *The Vietnam Lobby*, 59–60.

50. Journoud, "Face-à-face," 149; *Journal Officiel*, December 15, 1954, 2114.

51. Extract from OCB minutes, top secret, July 28, 1954, EL, White House Office, NSC Staff Papers, OCB Central File series, box 38; Hoppenot to Pineau, top secret, August 13, 1956, MAE, CLV, SV, vol. 73; Internal memorandum, November 16, 1954, PRO, FO 371/112133.

52. Hoppenot to minister, top secret, August 13, 1956, MAE, CLV, SV, vol. 73. Fitzgerald, *Fire in the Lake*, 114.

53. Dr. Paul Peterson, chief of the Health and Sanitation Division, to Leland Barrows, December 6, 1954, NA, RG 469, Mission to Vietnam, Program and Requirements Division, subject files 195057.

54. USIA in Indochina since Geneva, January 27, 1955, EL, Collins Papers, J. Lawton Collins file, box 31, USIA.

55. Secret memorandum, December 9, 1954, EL, Collins Papers, J. Lawton Collins file, box 29, militant liberty; USIA in Indochina since Geneva, January 27, 1955, EL, Collins Papers, J. Lawton Collins file, box 31, USIA.

56. USIS Inspection Report, Vietnam, March 8–31, 1956, NA, RG 306, Inspection Staff, Inspection Reports and Related Records, 1954–1962, box 10.

57. See Morgan, *The Vietnam Lobby* for a detailed account of the AFV's efforts to strengthen Diem's government.

58. Elliot Newcomb and Harold Oram had a contract with Diem's government before joining the AFV. Diem paid Newcomb and Oram $3,000 a month, and one third of that amount was earmarked for a full-time campaign director, who happened to be Gilbert Jonas. Gibbons, *The U.S. Government and the Vietnam War*, 302.

59. Morgan, *The Vietnam Lobby*, 47.

60. Gibbons, *The U.S. Government and the Vietnam War*, 304.

61. USIS Inspection Report, Vietnam, March 8–31, 1956, NA, RG 306, Inspection Staff, Inspection Reports and Related Records, 1954–1962, box 10.

62. See Ernst, *Forging a Fateful Alliance* for more on MSUG activities. For an earlier firsthand account that focuses on the technical aspects of the MSUG and its ambiguous relationship with other American agencies, see Scigliano and Fox, *Technical Assistance in Vietnam*, 43–49. See Fitzgerald, *Fire in the Lake*, 118–20, for a critical account of Fishel's attempts to promote Diem as an advocate of democracy.

63. Note for the general direction of cultural relations, September 13, 1957, and Payart to minister, August 20, 1957, MAE, CLV, SV, vol. 51.

64. IRC, memorandum, n.d., NA, RG 469, Mission to Vietnam, Resettlement and Rehabilitation Division, subject files 1953–1958, 1953–1955, Mission Program, Refugee Letters, box 2.

65. Franco-American working group, December 15, 1954, MAE, CLV, SV, vol. 47.

66. Note on Franco-Indochinese cultural problems, July 3, 1953, AN, 457AP/52; note, 1954, MAE, Asie Océanie 1944–1955, Indochine, vol. 83; memorandum of French working group discussion in Saigon, December 3, 1954, SHAT, Fonds Paul Ely, vol. 37; and Franco-American working group meeting, December 15, 1954, MAE, CLV, SV, vol. 47.

67. June 9, 1955, MAE, CLV, SV, vol. 47; note to MAE, September 10, 1955, MAE, CLV, SV, vol. 47; and note to MAE, September 28, 1955, MAE, CLV, SV, vol. 47. See Ernst, *Forging a Fateful Alliance*, 41–57, for a detailed look at the formation of the NIA.

68. Couve de Murville to Quai, October 15, 1955, MAE, Asie Océanie 1944–1955, Indochine, vol. 339.

69. Quoted in Journoud, "Face-à-face," 152–53.

70. See Reinhardt to Kenneth Young, November 26, 1955; Weidner to Leland Barrows, director of USOM, November 9, 1956, NA, RG 59, Director Office of Philippine and Southeast Asian Affairs, International Conferences, Talks, and Meetings, box 4; and Weidner to Barrows, November 9, 1955, MAE, CLV, SV, vol. 47. See also note, January 25, 1956, MAE, CLV, SV, vol. 47; Hoppenot to minister, February 21, March 12, 1956, CLV, SV, vol. 47; Inspector of Academy A. Debuissy to French Embassy, note, November 18, 1957, MAE, CLV, SV, vol. 47.

71. Hoppenot to Pinay, February 11, 1956, MAE, CLV, SV, vol. 51; Inspector

General of Public Instruction and Chief of the French Mission of Teaching and Cultural Cooperation in Vietnam Jean-Pierre Dannaud to the commissariat of the republic, March 24, 1956, MAE, CLV, SV, vol. 48. Dannaud had served as a cultural attaché to Saigon from 1948 to 1950 and then as director of the French Information Services until 1954. In 1954, he was named chief of the French Cultural Mission in South Vietnam until 1956 and as cultural counselor to the French Embassy.

72. NA, RG 469, USOM Vietnam, Resettlement and Rehabilitation, subject file, 1954–1958, box 3.

73. Journoud, "Face-à-face," 158, 162. Journoud and I differ in our interpretations of Franco-American cultural cooperation in the 1954–1956 period: Journoud argues that not all Americans wanted France out and that what was true of USOM and CIA personnel in Saigon was not necessarily true in Washington. Although there were rare instances of cooperation, conflict was the order of the day between the French and Americans at all levels in all locales.

74. Chargé d'Affaires Arnaud d'Andurain de Maytie to MAE, May 9, 1957, MAE, Cabinet du Ministre, Cabinet Pineau, vol. 17; August 12, 1958, MAE, CLV, SV, vol. 33; Dannaud to French foreign minister and minister of education, September 4, 1956, MAE, Etats-Associés 1945–1957, section IV, vol. 191.

75. As one French official noted, the Americans went so far as to avoid social and professional contact with the French in South Vietnam. Hoppenot to MAE, January 6, 1956, MAE, CLV, SV, vol. 73. See also Asie Océanie, note, "French Policy in Vietnam," February 11, 1956, DDF 1956, vol. I, 190–92; Question Orale Avec Debat Inscrite a l'Ordre du Jour de la Seance 21 February 1956 du Conseil de la Republique, MAE, CLV, SV, vol. 87; and Hoppenot to Pineau, secret, July 14, 1956, DDF 1956, vol. II, 99–107.

76. Pineau comments at Anglo-American Press Association, March 2, 1956, MAE, CLV, SV, vol. 41; secret note, n.d., MAE, Aide Militaire, 12–17.

77. Michael Crozier, quoted in Hoffmann, Huntington, May, and Neustadt, "Vietnam Reappraised," 13.

78. Hoppenot to minister, top secret, August 13, 1956, MAE, CLV, SV, vol. 73.

79. Quoted in Hughes, The Ordeal of Power, 208.

80. Soustelle, "France Looks at Her Alliances," 118, 126.

7. Maintaining a Presence

1. Deputy Director General of Political Affairs Jacques Roux to Washington, August 20, 1954, MAE, Asie Océanie 1944–1955, Indochine, vol. 84.

2. Anderson, Trapped by Success, 68, 95. Jacques Dalloz argues that, despite American suspicions, Paris never chose Hanoi in preference to Saigon. Dalloz, The War in Indochina, 195. See also Duiker, U.S. Containment Policy, 226, and FRUS 1952–1954 13:2246–49, for more on French relations with South and North Vietnam.

3. See Roux to Washington, August 20, 1954, MAE, Asie Océanie 1944–1955,

Indochine, vol. 84; Ely to MAE, September 8, 1954, MAE, Asie Océanie 1944–1955, Indochine, vol. 339.

4. Dillon to DOS, top secret, December 30, 1954, EL, Collins Papers, J. Lawton Collins file, box 25, monthly papers, January 1955 (3).

5. Sainteny, note to minister, September 16, 1954, CHEVS, 1 SA 13. For more detail on Hanoi's attempts to pursue a middle course between Moscow and Beijing after Geneva, see Gaiduk, *Confronting Vietnam*, 54–121.

6. Bonnet and Massigli to MAE, August 17, 1954; note for the president, September 16, 1954; note, September 18, 1954; Saigon to MAE, September 23, 1954, MAE, CLV, Aide Militaire, Généralités, carton 3.

7. Evolution of the Vietminh Situation since the Cease Fire, note, September 18, 1954, MAE, CLV, Aide Militaire, Généralités, carton 3; Sainteny to Quai, November 25, 1954, CHEVS, 1 SA 18; note on Indochine, n.d., IPMF, DPMF, Relations Internationales, chemise R1/4, Compte rendu voyage du president en Amérique, November 17–23, 1954; top secret NSC briefing, December 20, 1954, NA, CREST.

8. Ely to Minister in Charge of Relations with the Associated States Guy La Chambre, telegram, November 30, 1954, *DDF 1955*, vol I, 823–24; note on the situation in Indochina, January 1, 1955, IPMF, DPMF, Indochine, VII.

9. *Newsweek*, February 28, 1955, XLV (9), 36, 40.

10. Hanoi to Quai, telegram, February 23, 1955, CLV, Aide Militaire, Guerre d'Indochine et Contentieux Franco-Indochinois, Conséquences de la Conférence de Genève, Transports Militaires, Evacuation du Nord, 1954–56; top secret NSC briefing, January 25, 1955, Vietnam Notes, NA, CREST; chief, Industry and Mining Division, to director of mission, February 7, 1955, NA, RG 286, Mission to Vietnam, Resettlement and Rehabilitation Division, Field Services, classified subject files, 1954–1958, box 2.

11. See J. Lawton Collins to Dulles, top secret memorandum, January 20, 1955, *FRUS 1955–1957* 1:54; Stephenson to FO, secret letter, December 23, 1954, PRO, FO 371/117097; and Stephenson to Anthony Eden, annual review of events, March 7, 1955, PRO, FO 371/117093; Mendès France to Faure, February 19, 1955, CHEVS, 1 SA 13.

12. Couve de Murville to Etats Associés, telegram, February 19, 1955, CHEVS, 1 SA 16 JS.

13. Massigli to Quai, February 22, 1955, CHEVS, 1 SA 16.

14. Massigli to Washington and Paris, February 17, 1955, CHEVS, 1 SA 16 JS; Couve de Murville to Etats-Associés, February 22, 1955; Massigli to Hanoi, February 18, 1955; Couve de Murville to Saigon and Hanoi, February 7, 1955, MAE, CLV, Aide Militaire, Guerre d'Indochine et Contentieux Franco-Indochinois, Conséquences de la Conférence de Genève, Transports Militiaires, Evacuation du Nord, 1954–1956; Dalloz, *The War in Indochina*, 195–96; Fall, "Indochina since Geneva," 20; and Sainteny, *Ho Chi Minh and His Vietnam*, 108.

15. Ely to Guy La Chambre, February 3, 1955, IPMF, DPMF, Indochine, VII.

338   Notes to Pages 225–232

16. Sainteny to Faure, March 1, 1955, CHEVS, 1 SA 13; Kenneth Young to DOS, secret telegram, March 25, 1955, *FRUS 1955–1957* 1:147.

17. Top secret Current Intelligence Bulletin, April 14, 1955, NA, CREST.

18. Sainteny, May 1955, CHEVS, 1 SA 14; Sainteny to minister, May 23, 1955, minister to Sainteny, May 27, 1955, CHEVS, 1 SA 18.

19. Sainteny to La Chambre, August 6, 1955, CHEVS, 1 SA 16.

20. J. Aurillac, chief of Political and Cultural Affairs Services, to director of Asie Océanie and chief of Economic and Financing Affairs Services, top secret, February 7, 1956, MAE, CLV, République du Vietnam du Nord (RDVN), vol. 44; and note for the president of the council, June 7, 1958, MAE, CLV, RDVN, vol. 35.

21. Sainteny to Pineau, top secret, May 20, 1956; Pineau to Sainteny, top secret, May 26, 1956; Sainteny to Quai, top secret, July 4, 1956, CHEVS, 1 SA 18.

22. Sainteny to Quai, April 13, 1956; Sainteny to Hoppenot, April 26, 1956; Sainteny to Pineau, top secret, July 16, 1954, CHEVS, 1 SA 18.

23. Sainteny to Jacques Doniol-Valcroze, July 6, 1956, CHEVS, 1 SA 14.

24. Sainteny to minister, July 24, 1956, CHEVS, 1 SA 14; Gaiduk, *Confronting Vietnam*, 98.

25. Soustelle, "France Looks at Her Alliances," 118, 126; Sainteny to Pineau, November 26, 1956, CHEVS, 1 SA 16; Director of EFEO Durand to minister, December 27, 1956, MAE, Cabinet du Ministre, Cabinet Pineau, 1956–1958, Chine à V, Asie Généralités, vol. 17.

26. Sainteny to Quai, top secret telegram, January 26, 1957, CHEVS, 1 SA 14; Gaiduk, *Confronting Vietnam*, 85–86.

27. "Intérêts Français au Nord Vietnam fin Juin 1957," MAE, Cabinet du Ministre, Cabinet Pineau, 1956–1958, CLV, Direction des Etats Associés. The EFEO closed in 1958.

28. "The International Communist Line: Current Patterns," March 1956, NA, CREST; USIA report, "An Evaluation of the Communist Psychological Effort in Southeast Asia during 1956," October 29, 1956, NA, RG 306, Office of Research, Production Division Research reports, 1956–1959, 1956 P-127 through 1957 P-1.1, box 1.

29. USIA report, November 29, 1956, NA, RG 306, Office of Research, Production Division Research reports, 1956–1959, box 1.

30. Robert Speer, country public affairs officer, to USIA, December 4, 1956, NA, RG 306, Research reports, 1953–1993, box 22.

31. USIA report, "Spring is Triumphant, but Winter Will Surely Return: 1954–1957. Three Years of Viet-Minh Rule in North Vietnam," February 5, 1958, NA, RG 306, Office of Research, Production Division Research reports, 1956–1959, 1957 P-65 through 1958 P-1.6, box 4.

32. Pham Van Dong to Diem and Pineau, March 7, 1958, and Payart to Quai, top secret, April 30, 1958, MAE, Asie Océanie 1944–1955, Conflit Vietnam, 312; Notre Problème de la réunification du Vietnam, summary memorandum, Septem-

ber 19, 1960, MAE, Asie Océanie 1944–1955, Conflit Vietnam, 311; Chronologie, MAE, Asie Océanie 1944–1955, Conflit Vietnam, vol. 1.

33. Summary of elections, n.d., MAE, Asie Océanie 1944–1955, Conflit Vietnam, vol. 1.

34. J. B. Georges-Picot to Roux, plenipotentiary minister, adjunct director general for political affairs, March 17, 1958; Pineau to prefect of the police, May 1958, MAE, Cabinet du Ministre, Cabinet Pineau, 1956–1958, Chine à Vietnam, Asie, Généralités, vol. 17.

35. Délégué général in Hanoi to minister, August 10, 1959, Asie Océanie 1944–1955, Conflit Vietnam, vol. 298; Notre Problème de la réunification du Vietnam, summary memorandum, September 19, 1960, MAE, Asie Océanie 1944–1955, Conflit Vietnam, vol. 311.

36. Chambon to Quai, April 26, 1960, Chambon to minister, November 7, 1960, MAE, Asie Océanie 1944–1955, Conflit Vietnam, vol. 299; article in Le Figaro, May 26, 1960, MAE, Asie Océanie 1944–1955, Conflit Vietnam, vol. 299.

37. Chambon to Quai, October 17, 1960, MAE, Asie Océanie 1944–1955, Conflit Vietnam, vol. 44; Chambon to Quai, November 7, 1960, MAE, Asie Océanie 1944–1955, Conflit Vietnam, vol. 299.

38. Chambon to Quai, October 17, 1960, MAE, Asie Océanie 1944–1955, Conflit Vietnam, vol. 44; Chambon to Quai, November 7, 1960, MAE, Asie Océanie 1944–1955, Conflit Vietnam, vol. 299.

39. French official Claude Lebel to Chargé d'Affaires of the Asian Department at the Quai Etienne Manac'h, internal memorandum, December 7, 1960; Manac'h to French ambassador to the United States Hervé Alphand, memorandum, MAE, CLV, Militaire, Généralitiés, carton 2.

40. MAE to Chambon, December 22, 1959, MAE, CLV, RDVN, vol. 12. Only about one hundred French nationals still lived in the North at this point. See also Chambon to MAE, May 16, 1960, MAE, CLV, RDVN, vol. 37, and note, October 1960, MAE, CLV, RDVN, vol. 45; J. F. de La Bossière, délégué général of North Vietnam, to Couve de Murville, telegram, July 6, 1961, Asie Océanie 1944–1955, Conflit Vietnam, vol. 44.

41. June 18, 1956, MAE, CLV, SV, vol. 87; Pineau to Payart, August 29, 1956, DDF 1956, vol. II, 316–24; Payart to minister, secret, October 3, 1956, and Payart to minister, November 21, 1956, MAE, CLV, SV, vol. 87.

42. Hoppenot to minister, top secret, August 3, 1956, MAE, CLV, SV, vol. 125.

43. Sainteny to MAE, January 29, 1957, MAE, CLV, RDVN, vol. 32; French consulate in New York to MAE, January 30, 1957, CLV, SV, vol. 71.

44. Journoud, "Face-à-face," 142.

45. Nguyen Huu Chau, secretary of state charged with the expedition of current affairs, to Payart, March 9, 1957, MAE, Cabinet du Ministre, Cabinet Pineau, 1956–1958, Chine à Vietnam, Asie, Généralités, vol. 17; Arnaud d'Andurain to minister, May 9, 1957, MAE, Cabinet du Ministre, Cabinet Pineau, 1956–1958, Chine à Vietnam, Asie, Généralités, vol. 17.

46. Arnaud d'Andurain to minister, May 9, 1957, MAE, Cabinet du Ministre, Cabinet Pineau, 1956–1958, Chine à Vietnam, Asie, Généralités, vol. 17.

47. Payart to C. H. Bauchard, director of the cabinet, July 4, 1957, MAE, Cabinet du Ministre, Cabinet Pineau, 1956–1958, Chine à Vietnam, Asie, Généralités, vol. 17.

48. Payart to Bauchard, July 4, 1957, Bauchard to Payart, August 6, 1957, MAE, Cabinet du Ministre, Cabinet Pineau, 1956–1958, Chine à Vietnam, Asie, Généralités, vol. 17.

49. Dalloz, *The War in Indochina*, 109.

50. Note, January 14, 1958, MAE, CLV, SV, vol. 9; Payart to minister, top secret, June 30, 1958, MAE, CLV, SV, vol. 129.

51. Lalouette to Couve de Murville, top secret, March 31, 1959, MAE, CLV, SV, vol. 131.

52. Lalouette to Couve de Murville, May 15, 1959, MAE, CLV, SV, vol. 48.

53. Sainteny to Pineau, note, January 22, 1958, Cabinet du Ministre, Cabinet Pineau, 1956–1958, Chine à Vietnam, Asie, Généralités, 17.

54. Note Introductive Pour Une Action Agronomique Française au Vietnam, February 22, 1956, MAE, Cabinet du Ministre, Cabinet Pineau, 1956–1958, CLV, Direction des Etats Associés.

55. Note, December 22, 1958, Direction d'Asie, MAE, Asie Océanie 1944–1955, Conflit Vietnam, vol. 308; February 1959, MAE, Secrétariat Général, entretiens et messages Cabinet Guy Mollet, microfilm, vol. 6b; Arthur Gardiner, counselor of embassy for economic affairs, to DOS, November 13, 1959, NA, RG 59, DOS central files, Indochina, Internal and Foreign Affairs, 1955–1959, C0008, microfilm, reel 41; Lalouette to Couve de Murville, top secret, September 30, 1959, MAE, CLV, SV, vol. 133.

56. R. Benoit, professor at University of Sciences of Saigon, note, 1959, MAE, CLV, SV, vol. 47.

57. Lalouette to Couve de Murville, December 31, 1960, MAE, CLV, SV, vol. 136.

58. Lebel to Manac'h, internal memorandum, December 7, 1960; Manac'h to Alphand, Alphand to Manac'h, memoranda, December 21, 1960, MAE, CLV, Aide Militaire, Généralités, carton 2, Aide américaine en Indochine, 1954–61.

59. Fourier-Ruelle to Manac'h, April 11, 1960, *DDF 1960*, vol. I, 455–62; Manac'h response to Fourier-Ruelle letter, April 12, 1960, MAE, CLV, SV, vol. 87. Also in *DDF 1960*, vol. I, 462.

60. Note, May 28, 1960, MAE, CLV, SV, vol. 71; Lalouette to Couve de Murville, September 17, 1960, MAE, CLV, SV, vol. 75.

61. Lalouette to MAE, October 1, 1960, Chauvel to MAE, telegram, October 11, 1960, MAE, CLV, SV, vol. 69. See also Manac'h to Lalouette, October 15, 1960, Lalouette to Couve de Murville, October 24, 1960, MAE, CLV, SV, vol. 11.

62. Lalouette to MAE, extremely urgent, November 18, 1960, MAE, CLV, SV, vol. 136; John M. Anspacher, country public affairs officer, to USIA, November, 30, 1960, NA, RG 306, Office of Research, Correspondence, 1952–1963, U-Y, box 21.

63. Note, n.d., MAE, Asie Océanie 1944–1955, Conflit Vietnam, 308.
64. Lalouette to Couve de Murville, November 12, 1962, *DDF 1962*, vol. II, no. 148.
65. USIA French External Cultural and Informational Services Report, May 7, 1963, NA, RG 306, Office of Research, R Reports, 1960–1963, box 15.
66. USIA French External Cultural and Informational Services Report, May 7, 1963, NA, RG 306, Office of Research, R Reports, 1960–1963, box 15. See Journoud, "Face-à-face," 158–66, for a discussion of the continued French cultural presence in South Vietnam from 1961 to 1975.
67. See Logevall, "De Gaulle, Neutralization and American Involvement in Vietnam," and Logevall, *Choosing War*, 13–15, 68, 129–33, 187–88, for a discussion of the neutralization option.
68. Statement to the diplomatic press, November 15, 1961, Asie Océanie 1944–1955, Conflit Vietnam, vol. 162; Lalouette to Couve de Murville, February 1, 1962, *DDF 1962*, vol. I, no. 33.
69. "The News of the Week in Review, Vietnam Dilemma: What Course for U.S.?" *New York Times*, September 1, 1963.
70. Couve de Murville to Lalouette, September 5, 1963, *DDF 1963*, vol. I, 226.

8. Building a Colony

1. Wesley Haraldson, deputy director, to H. Robert Slusser, chief, Research and Statistics Section, November 28, 1956, NA, RG 469, Mission to Vietnam, Program and Requirements Division, Research and Statistics section, subject files 1956, trade-Vietnam, box 7.
2. My research findings tend to corroborate recent studies focusing on the ability of Third World leaders to shape their own destinies, to take advantage of western leaders to fulfill their own domestic and foreign policy goals, and even to guide the diplomacy of greater powers. See, for example, Tony Smith, "New Bottles for New Wine" and Karabell, *Architects of Intervention*, 226–27. I also make use of the alliance politics theory that weaker members in an alliance, in this case Diem, were able to dictate U.S. foreign policy to a greater extent than their size warranted. See, for example, Keohane, "The Big Influence of Small Allies"; Snyder, *Alliance Politics*; and Walt, *The Origins of Alliances*.
3. Hoppenot to MAE, top secret note, July 2, 1956, MAE, CLV, SV, vol. 125; and Jean Filliol to MAE, top secret telegram, May 18, 1956, MAE, CLV, SV, vol. 124.
4. French ambassador to Saigon Jean Payart to MAE, n.d., Bernard Fall report, February 1958, MAE, CLV, SV, vol. 68; note, March 31, 1955, MAE, Cabinet du Ministre, Cabinet Pinay, 1955–1956, Asie, Généralités, vol. 18.
5. Payart to minister, January 9, 1957, MAE, Etats Associés, 1945–1957, section IV, 261.
6. The Colombo Plan was an economic self-help organization of the Commonwealth members in Asia and the Pacific formed in 1950, which had grown

to include practically every nation in the Far East as well as the United States and Canada.

7. Bernard Fall report, February 1958, MAE, CLV, SV, vol. 68.

8. Bernard Fall report, February 1958, MAE, CLV, SV, vol. 68.

9. Duiker, *Sacred War*, 109; Stephenson to Lloyd, 1956 annual report, PRO, FO 371/129701; Counselor of Saigon Embassy Gardner Palmer to DOS, September 29, 1955, NA, RG 59, DOS central files, Indochina, Internal and Foreign Affairs, 1955–1959, C0008, microfilm, reel 40. According to Michael Adamson, the crucial factor in determining South Vietnamese reform was not what American officials did but what Diem and his officials decided to do. Adamson, "Delusions of Development," 157–82.

10. Diem Address to the Republic of Vietnam, March 15, 1961, NA, RG 84, Saigon Embassy files, General Records, 1956–1963, box 5, Internal Political Affairs, Elections, 1959–1961; Nolting to USOM official Eugene Stanley, July 8, 1961, NA, RG 84, Saigon Embassy files, General Records, box 6, Chief Executive, 1959–1961. See Catton, *Diem's Final Failure*, 41–50, for an excellent in-depth analysis of Diem's philosophy of personalism.

11. Payart to minister, August 31, 1957, MAE, CLV, SV, vol. 68. See Jacobs, "Our System Demands the Supreme Being," as well as Jacobs, *America's Miracle Man in Vietnam* for a critical appraisal of Dulles's religious convictions and missionary zeal to spread Christian values to South Vietnam. See also note, January 14, 1958, MAE, CLV, SV, vol. 9. See Catton, *Diem's Final Failure*, 3, 23, for a cogent analysis of conflicting U.S.–South Vietnamese views on nation-building and modernizing South Vietnam. Catton points out that Diem was extremely sensitive about being viewed as a collaborator or stooge of the United States. Taking issue with customary views of Diem as a traditional mandarin, Catton notes that he was a modern nationalist, determined to push ahead with his own nation-building agenda, which, in turn, created a major source of tension in U.S.–South Vietnamese relations.

12. Durbrow to DOS, December 5, 1957, *FRUS, 1955–1957* 1:882.

13. Bernard Fall report, February 1958, MAE, CLV, SV, vol. 68.

14. Dommen, *The Indochinese Experience*, 299; Spector, *Advice and Support*, 228.

15. Durbrow, Oral History, Interview 4, June 23, 1981, by John T. Mason Jr., Hoover Institution Archives, Elbridge Durbrow Papers, box 45, 230–37. See also Durbrow to DOS, December 5, 1957, *FRUS 1955–1957* 1:871; David W. Mabon, "1958–1960: Divided Counsels amid Growing Insurgency," Remarks delivered at the Society for Historians of American Foreign Relations (SHAFR) session on Vietnam, Georgetown, June 26, 1986, Hoover Institution Archives, Leland Barrows Papers, box 3–4; Spector, *Advice and Support*, 282; Adamson, "Ambassadorial Roles and Foreign Policy," 236.

16. Barrows to Louis Miniclier, chief of the Community Development Division of the ICA, December 12, 1955, NA, RG 286, Mission to Vietnam, box 1.

17. Secret note, April 23, 1960, MAE, CLV, SV, vol. 10; "Present and Future

Political Situation in South Vietnam," Saigon Embassy to DOS, secret, December 7, 1960, and Deputy Coordinator for Mutual Security R. B. Peterson to Director of the Office of Southwest Pacific Affairs James D. Bell, secret memorandum, January 9, 1961, NA, RG 59, General Records DOS, General Decimal file, 1960–1963, box 1780; special report, Possible Actions to Improve the Situation in Vietnam, secret, June 15, 1960, EL, White House Office, NSC Staff Papers, OCB Secretariat series, box 7, Southeast Asia NSC 6012 (3). David Mabon, memorandum of an interview with Elbridge Durbrow, Office of the Historian, DOS, April 2, 1984, Hoover Institution Archives, Elbridge Durbrow Papers, box 51, 12–14.

18. Allen, *None So Blind*, 76.

19. Hoppenot to MAE, February 10, 1956, MAE, CLV, SV, vol. 35.

20. Payart to minister, August 31, 1957, MAE, CLV, SV, vol. 68; Hervé Alphand to Couve de Murville, March 17, 1959, excerpt from Dr. Adrian Jaffe, Michigan State University in Saigon 1957–1958, MAE, CLV, SV, vol. 48. See Latham, *Modernization as Ideology*, 150–207, for a case study of modernization in practice through the Strategic Hamlet Program in South Vietnam.

21. Journoud, "Face-à-face," 149–50; Spector, *Advice and Support*, 282.

22. Payart to minister, October 12, 1957, MAE, CLV, SV, vols. 51 and 74.

23. Payart to minister, top secret, May 31, 1958, MAE, CLV, SV, vol. 129.

24. Summary of General John O'Daniel's Report on His Visit to Vietnam, July 27, 1958, NA, RG 59, DOS central files, Indochina, Internal and Foreign Affairs, 1955–1959, C0008, microfilm, reel 10.

25. NSC briefing, September 30, 1958, NA, CREST.

26. See James Carter, "Nation Building, Private Contractors, and War Profiteering from Iraq to Vietnam," SHAFR paper, June 2005, NA, for more on private investment in South Vietnam.

27. Spector, *Advice and Support*, 307.

28. February 1959, MAE, Secrétariat Général, entretiens et messages Cabinet Guy Mollet, microfilm, vol. 6b.

29. Lalouette to Couve de Murville, September 17, 1960, MAE, CLV, SV, vol. 75; Lalouette to Couve de Murville, top secret, September 30, 1959, MAE, CLV, SV, vol. 133.

30. Inspection report, August 31, 1961, USIA, NA, RG 306, Inspection Staff, Inspection Reports and Related Records, 1954–1962, Uruguay through USIA, Inspection manual, box 10 (hereafter Inspection report, August 31, 1961, USIA).

31. Gienow-Hecht, "Shame on U.S.?" 472–73; Inspection report, August 31, 1961, USIA.

32. Inspection report, August 31, 1961, USIA.

33. Inspection report, August 31, 1961, USIA.

34. John Anspacher, country public affairs officer, to USIA, August 28, 1961, NA, RG 306, Research Reports, 1953–1993, box 22.

35. Inspection report, August 31, 1961, USIA.

36. Gienow-Hecht, "Shame on U.S.?" 472–73.

37. Darrell Price, acting country public affairs officer, April 18, 1958, NA, RG 306, USIA, Exhibits in Foreign Countries, 1955–1967, box 35, Uruguay to Vietnam, Mobile Unit Display panels, 1959 (hereafter Exhibits, 1959).

38. Chester Opal to USIA, June 11, 1959, NA, RG 306, USIA, Exhibits, 1959.

39. Anspacher to USIA, April 26, 1960, NA, RG 306, USIA, Exhibits, 1959.

40. Inspection report, August 31, 1961, USIA.

41. Anspacher to USIA, October 6, 1961, NA, RG 306, USIA, Exhibits, 1959.

42. One USIS house listed on the Mansfield Committee among examples of residences exceeding government ceilings had been disposed of. Inspection report, August 31, 1961, USIA.

43. See Endy, *Cold War Holidays* for details on tourism as a diplomatic tool.

44. DOS research memorandum, "Summary of Principal Events in the History of Vietnam," January 10, 1962, MAE, Asie Océanie 1944–1955, Conflit Vietnam, vol. 308.

45. Latham, *Modernization*, 5–6.

46. Ung Van Khiem to co-chairs Soviet foreign minister Andrei Gromyko and British minister for foreign affairs Alexander Home, July 3, 1961, MAE, Asie Océanie 1944–1955, Conflit Vietnam, vol. 44. Khiem also complained that the ICC was furthering U.S. imperialism by "sanctioning its competence to examine and investigate so-called subversive activities in South Vietnam."

Conclusion

1. Note, n.d., MAE, Asie Océanie 1944–1955, Conflit Vietnam, vol. 162.

2. For examples of the quagmire thesis, see Schlesinger, *Bitter Heritage;* Halberstam, *The Best and the Brightest;* and Halberstam, *The Making of a Quagmire.* For examples of the stalemate thesis, see Gelb and Betts, *The Irony of Vietnam* and Ellsberg, *Papers on the War.* A recent H-diplo thread developed over the idea of the United States "stumbling" into Vietnam.

3. Mendès France to reporter André Fontaine, January 12, 1966, February 4, 1966, May 25, 1966, June 1, 1967, and June 5, 1972; and Fontaine to Mendès France, June 28, 1972, IPMF, DPMF, Dossier André Fontaine, Pierre Mendès France Papers.

4. Cesari, "La France, Les Etats-Unis, et L'Indochine," 1110.

5. Gardner, keynote address, November 1, 2002, Lyndon Baines Johnson Library, First Indochina War Symposium.

6. Etherington Smith to F. S. Tomlinson, November 12, 1956, PRO, FO 371/123429.

7. *Journal Officiel* Débats Parlementaires Assemblée Nationale, October 21, 1955, séance 20, 2406.

8. Quoted in Cesari, "La France, Les Etats-Unis, et L'Indochine," 1116.

9. Pineau speech in front of the Council of the Republic, February 23, 1956, PRO, FO 371/123425.

10. Soustelle, "France Looks at Her Alliances," 126.

11. Quoted in Leffler, "9/11 and American Foreign Policy," 399.

12. McNamara, *Argument without End*, 95–96.

13. For more on the connections between American foreign policy and domestic culture, see Walter Hixson's provocative SHAFR 2005 paper, "Diplomatic Historians and the Usable Past," NA.

14. Devillers, "The Struggle for the Unification of Vietnam," 8, 9, 21.

15. Quoted in Dalloz, *The War in Indochina*, 197–98.

16. Heiss, "The Evolution of the Imperial Idea and U.S. National Identity."

17. See Stephanson, "Imperial Pursuits," 586.

Bibliography

Primary Sources (Archives)

Abilene, Kansas, Dwight D. Eisenhower Presidential Library (EL)

Ann Whitman File, DDE Papers as President: Administration Series, Ann Whitman Diary Series, Cabinet Series, Dwight D. Eisenhower Diary Series, International Series, International Meetings Series, Legislative Leaders Meeting Series, NSC Series

J. Lawton Collins File

White House Central Files: Confidential File, General File

Dulles Papers: General Correspondence and Memoranda Series, JFD Chronological Series, Personnel Series, Subject Series, White House Memoranda Series

Alfred Gruenther Papers

James Hagerty Papers

C. D. Jackson Papers

Post Presidential Papers: Augusta Walter Reed Series

White House Office, NSC Staff Papers: Executive Secretary's Subject File Series, Operations Coordinating Board Central File Series, PSB Central File Series

White House Office, Office of the Special Assistant for National Security Affairs Records: NSC Series, Briefing Notes Subseries, Policy Papers Subseries; Special Assistant Series, Chronological Subseries, Presidential Subseries

Oral Histories (OH): George Allen, Robert Bowie, William Knowland, Livingston Merchant

College Park, Maryland, National Archives Records Administration (NA)

CIA Records Search Tool (CREST) [CD Rom]

National Intelligence Estimates (NIE)

Record Group 273, National Security Council

Record Group 218, Joint Chiefs of Staff

Record Group 59, General Records of the Department of State, 1910–1963, Central File

Record Group 59, General Records of the Department of State, Bureau of Far Eastern Affairs, 1910–1963, Central Files, LM 171, C0014, C0008, LM071, LM170 [microfilm]

Record Group 59, Lot Files (Conference Files, Director Office of Philippine and Southeast Asian Affairs, Executive Secretariat, Intelligence Bureau, Miscellaneous, Southeast Asia)

Record Group 263, Records of the Central Intelligence Agency (CIA)
Record Group 286, Records of the Agency for International Development and Pre-
    decessor Agencies
Record Group 306, Records of the United States Information Agency (USIA)
Record Group 319, Records of the Army Staff
Record Group 330, Records of the Department of Defense
Record Group 349, Records of the Joint Commands
Record Group 469, Records of U.S. Foreign Assistance Agencies
Records of Bureau and Intelligence (INR) 1945–1960

Washington, D.C., National Security Archive (NSA)

George McT. Kahin Papers

Aix-en-Provence, Centre des Archives d'Outre Mer (CAOM)

Conseiller Politique
Haut Commissariat, Indochine
Nouveaux Fonds

Château de Vincennes, Service Historique de l'Armée de la Terre (SHAT)

Fonds Cabinet du Ministre
Fonds Paul Ely
Fonds Indochine

Paris, Archives d'histoire contemporaine, Centre d'histoire de l'Europe du vingtième siècle (CHEVS)

Fonds Maurice Couve de Murville
Fonds Jean Sainteny

Paris, Archives Nationales (AN)

74AP Paul Reynaud Papers
457AP Georges Bidault Papers
552AP Vincent Auriol Papers
560AP René Pleven Papers
F60 Conseil des Ministres

Paris, Institut Pierre Mendès France (IPMF)

Fonds Pierre Mendès France Cabinet I et II, Dossiers Thèmatiques
DPMF, Indochine
DPMF, Relations Internationales, Fezzan, Extreme Orient, USA
Claude Cheysson
André Fontaine

Paris, Ministère des Affaires Etrangères (MAE)

Série Asie Océanie 1944–1955, sous-série Conflit Vietnam, sous-série Dossiers Généraux, sous-série Indochine
Série Cabinet du Ministre, sous-série Cabinets Georges Bidault, Maurice Couve de Murville, Pierre Mendès France, Antoine Pinay, Christian Pineau, Robert Schuman
Série Cambodge, Laos, Vietnam (CLV), sous-série Aide Militaire, Généralités, sous-série Laos, sous-série Sud-Vietnam (SV), sous-série République du Vietnam du Nord (RDVN)
Série Etats Associés 1945–1957, section IV
Série Papiers d'Agents, Archives Privés, sous-série Henri Bonnet, sous-série Maurice DeJean, sous-série Henri Hoppenot, sous-série René Massigli
Série Secrétariat Général

Kew, England, Public Record Office (PRO)

Record Class Foreign Office (FO) 371
Cabinet Series (CAB) Indexes 128–29
Prime Minister's Office (PREM) 11 (Correspondence and Papers 1951–1964)

Primary Sources (Published)

Documents diplomatiques français, 1954–1963. Paris: Imprimerie Nationale, 1987–2002.
Dulles Papers, Dulles-Herter Correspondence, 1953–1961. Microfilm. Reels 1–7.
Foreign Relations of the United States: 1950, vol. 3, *Western Europe.* Washington, D.C., 1977.
Foreign Relations of the United States: 1950, vol. 6, *East Asia and the Pacific.* Washington, D.C., 1976.
Foreign Relations of the United States: 1951, vol. 3, *European Security and the German Question.* Washington, D.C., 1982.
Foreign Relations of the United States:1951, vol. 6, *Asia and the Pacific.* Washington, D.C., 1978.
Foreign Relations of the United States: 1952–1954, vol. 5, *Western European Security.* Washington, D.C., 1983.
Foreign Relations of the United States: 1952–1954, vol. 12, *East Asia and the Pacific.* Washington, D.C., 1984.
Foreign Relations of the United States: 1952–1954, vol. 13, *Indochina,* part 1. Washington, D.C., 1982.
Foreign Relations of the United States: 1952–1954, vol. 16, *The Geneva Conference: Korea and Indochina.* Washington, D.C., 1981.
Foreign Relations of the United States: 1955–1957, vol. 1, *Vietnam.* Washington, D.C., 1985.

Foreign Relations of the United States: 1958–1960, vol. 1, *Vietnam.* Washington, D.C., 1986.

Journal Officiel. Débats parlementaires. (Assemblée Nationale.)

Minutes of Telephone Conversations of John Foster Dulles and Christian Herter,1953–1961. Ed. Paul Kesaris and Joan Gibson. Washington, D.C.: University Publications of America, 1980. Microfilm.

Smith, Walter. Department of State Bulletin, "Europe as a Bulwark of Peace." European and British Commonwealth Series no. 10, 1949.

The Pentagon Papers: The Defense Department History of United States Decisionmaking on Vietnam. vol. 1. Gravel Edition. Boston: Beacon Press, 1971.

United States Congress. House Committee Hearings 83rd Congress, Senate Library vol. 1404, 1953.

United States Congress. Senate Committee Hearings 83rd Congress, Senate Library vol. 1051, 1953.

United States Congress. Senate Appropriations Committee on Foreign Aid Program in Europe, July 1953.

Senate Foreign Relations Committee Meetings, 83rd Congress, vol. 149, May, 1953, vol. 152, June, 1954.

House Foreign Affairs Committee Meetings, 83rd Congress, vol. 55, March–May, 1953, vol. 57, April–June, 1954.

Senate Foreign Relations Committee, 83rd Congress, Senate Library, May 11, 1953, vol. 1051, March 25, 1953.

House Committee on Foreign Affairs, 83rd Congress, Senate Library, 1953, vol. 1404.

Secondary Sources

Acheson, Dean. *Present at the Creation: My Years in the State Department.* New York: W.W. Norton, 1969.

Adamson, Michael. "Ambassadorial Roles and Foreign Policy: Elbridge Durbrow, Frederick Nolting, and the U.S. Commitment to Diem's Vietnam, 1957–61." *Presidential Studies Quarterly* 32 (June 2002): 229–55.

———. "Delusions of Development: The Eisenhower Administration and the Foreign Aid Program in Vietnam, 1955–1960." *Journal of American–East Asian Relations* 5 (summer 1996): 157–82.

Ageron, Charles-Robert. *La décolonisation française.* Paris: Armand Colin, 1991.

Aimaq, Jasmine. *For Europe or Empire? French Colonial Ambitions and the European Army Plan.* Lund: Lund University Press, 1996.

Allen, George. *None So Blind: A Personal Account of Intelligence Failure in Vietnam.* Chicago: Ivan R. Dee, 2001.

Ambrose, Stephen. *Eisenhower: Soldier and President.* New York: Touchstone, 1990.

Anderson, David. "Eisenhower, Dien Bien Phu, and the Origins of U.S. Military Intervention in Vietnam." *Mid-America* 71 (April–July 1989): 101–17.

————. "J. Lawton Collins, John Foster Dulles, and the Eisenhower Administration's 'Point of No Return' in Vietnam." *Diplomatic History* 12 (spring 1988): 127–47.

————. *Shadow on the White House: Presidents and the Vietnam War, 1945–1975.* Lawrence: University Press of Kansas, 1993.

————. *Trapped by Success: The Eisenhower Administration and Vietnam, 1953–1961.* New York: Columbia University Press, 1991.

Andrew, Christopher, and A. S. Kanya-Forstner. *The Climax of French Imperial Expansion: 1914–1924.* Stanford, Calif.: Stanford University Press, 1981.

Ang, Cheng Guan. *Vietnamese Communists' Relations with China and the Second Indochina Conflict, 1956–62.* Jefferson, N.C.: McFarland, 1992.

Arndt, Richard. *The First Resort of Kings: American Cultural Diplomacy in the Twentieth Century.* Dulles, Va.: Potomac Books, 2005.

Aron, Raymond, and Daniel Lerner. *La Querelle de la CED: Essais d'analyse sociologique.* Paris: Armand Colin, 1956.

Artaud, Denise. "France between the Indochina War and the European Defense Community." In *Dien Bien Phu and the Crisis of Franco-American Relations.* Ed. Kaplan, Artaud, and Rubin: 251–68.

————. "Spring 1955: Crisis in Saigon." In *Dien Bien Phu and the Crisis of Franco-American Relations.* Ed. Kaplan, Artaud, and Rubin: 211–25.

Auriol, Vincent. *Mon Septennat, 1947–1954.* Paris: Gallimard, 1970.

Bao Dai, *Le Dragon d'Annam.* Paris: Plon, 1980.

Baritz, Loren. *Backfire: A History of How American Culture Led Us Into Vietnam and Made Us Fight the Way We Did.* New York: William Morrow, 1985.

Barnett, Richard. *The Alliance.* New York: Simon and Schuster, 1983.

Bartlett, C. J. *The Global Conflict, 1880–1970: The International Rivalry of the Great Powers.* London: Longman, 1984.

————. *The Special Relationship: A Political History of Anglo-American Relations since 1945.* London: Longman, 1992.

Bator, Victor. *Vietnam: A Diplomatic Tragedy: The Origins of U.S. Involvement.* New York: Oceana Publications, 1965.

Bell, Philip W. "Colonialism as a Problem in American Foreign Policy." *World Politics* 5 (October 1952): 86–109.

Beresford, Melanie. *National Unification and Economic Development in Vietnam.* London: Macmillan, 1989.

Berman, Larry. *No Peace, No Honor: Nixon, Kissinger, and Betrayal in Vietnam.* New York: Free Press, 2002.

————. *Planning a Tragedy: The Americanization of the War in Vietnam.* New York: Norton, 1982.

Betts, Raymond. *France and Decolonization, 1900–1960.* New York: Macmillan, 1991.

————. *Tricouleur: The French Overseas Empire.* New York: Gordon and Cremonesi, 1978.

Bidault, Georges. *Resistance: The Political Autobiography of Georges Bidault.* Trans. Marianne Sinclair. New York: Praeger, 1967.

Billings-Yun, Melanie. *Decision against War: Eisenhower and Dien Bien Phu, 1954.* New York: Columbia University Press, 1988.

Bischof, Günter, and Saki Dockrill, eds. *Cold War Respite: The Geneva Summit of 1955.* Baton Rouge: Louisiana State University Press, 2000.

Blum, Robert. *Drawing the Line: The Origin of American Containment Policy in East Asia.* New York: Norton, 1982.

Bossuat, Gerard. *Pierre Mendès France et le role de la France dans le monde.* Ed. Claude Cheysson. Grenoble: Presses universitaires de Grenoble, 1991.

Boulding, Kenneth. "National Images and International Systems." *Journal of Conflict Resolution* 3 (June 1959): 120–31.

Bouscaren, Anthony. *The Last of the Mandarins: Diem of Vietnam.* Pittsburgh: Duquesne University Press, 1965.

Bowie, Robert, and Richard Immerman. *Waging Peace: How Eisenhower Shaped an Enduring Cold War Strategy.* New York: Oxford, 1998.

Bradley, Mark. *Imagining Vietnam and America: The Making of Postcolonial Vietnam, 1919–1950.* Chapel Hill: University of North Carolina Press, 2000.

Brands, H. W. "The Dwight D. Eisenhower Administration, Syngman Rhee, and the 'Other' Geneva Conference of 1954." *Pacific Historical Review* 56 (February 1987): 59–86.

———. *What America Owes the World: The Struggle for the Soul of Foreign Policy.* Cambridge: Cambridge University Press, 1998.

Brigham, Robert. *Guerrilla Diplomacy: The NLF's Foreign Relations and the Vietnam War.* Ithaca, N.Y.: Cornell University Press, 1999.

Brogi, Alessandro. *A Question of Self-Esteem: The United States and the Cold War Choices in France and Italy.* Westport, Conn.: Praeger, 2002.

Brunschwig, Henri. *French Colonialism, 1871–1914: Myths and Realities.* New York: Praeger, 1966.

Burke, John, and Fred Greenstein, in collaboration with Larry Berman and Richard Immerman. *How Presidents Test Reality: Decisions on Vietnam 1954 and 1965.* New York: Russell Sage Foundation, 1989.

Burrows, Matthew. "Mission Civilisatrice: French Cultural Policy in the Middle East 1860–1914." *Historical Journal* 29/1 (1986).

Buttinger, Joseph. *Vietnam: A Dragon Embattled.* 2 vols. New York: Praeger, 1967.

Buzzanco, Robert. *Informed Dissent: Three Generals and The Vietnam War.* Chevy Chase, Md.: Burning Cities Press, 1992.

Cable, James. *The Geneva Conference of 1954 on Indochina.* New York: St. Martins, 1986.

Cady, John. *The Roots of French Imperialism in Eastern Asia.* Ithaca, N.Y.: Cornell University Press, 1967.

Cameron, A. *Vietnam Crisis: A Documentary History, vol. 1, 1940–1956.* Ithaca, N.Y.: Cornell University Press, 1971.

Catton, Philip. *Diem's Final Failure: Prelude to America's War in Vietnam*. Lawrence: University Press of Kansas, 2003.

Cesari, Laurent. "La France, Les Etats-Unis, et L'Indochine 1945–1957." Ph.D. diss., Université de Nanterre, 1991.

Chafer, Tony, and Amanda Sackur, eds. *Promoting the Colonial Idea: Propaganda and Visions of Empire in France*. New York: Palgrave Macmillan, 2002.

Chaffard, Georges. *Indochine: Dix Ans d'Indépendence*. Paris: Calmann-Lévy, 1964.

———. *Les Deux Guerres du Vietnam: De Valluy à Westmoreland*. Paris: La Table Ronde, 1969.

Chamberlain, Muriel. *Decolonization: The Fall of European Empires*. Oxford: Basil Blackwell, 1985.

Chauvel, Jean. *Commentaire*, vol 2. Paris: Fayard, 1973.

Chi, Hoang Van. *From Colonialism to Communism: A Case Study of North Vietnam*. New York: Praeger, 1964.

Christie, Clive. "The Sentimental American: American Literature on Indochina in an Era of Transition, 1950–1960." In *America, France, and Vietnam: Cultural History and Ideas of Conflict*. Ed. Phil Melling and Jon Roper. Aldershot: Gower, 1991: 152–53.

Clesse, Armand. *Le Projet de CED du Plan Pleven au "crime du 30 aout": histoire d'un malentendu européen*. Baden Baden: Nomos, 1989.

Cogan, Charles. *French Negotiating Behavior: Dealing with La Grande Nation*. Washington, D.C.: U.S. Institute of Peace Press, 2003.

———. *Oldest Allies, Guarded Friends: The United States and France since 1940*. Westport, Conn.: Praeger, 1994.

Cole, Allan. *Conflict in Indochina and International Repercussions: A Documentary History*. Ithaca, N.Y.: Cornell University Press, 1956.

Collins, J. Lawton. *Allied Participation in Vietnam: The Development and Training of the South Vietnamese Army, 1950–1972*. Washington, D.C.: Department of the Army, 1975.

———. *Lightning Joe: An Autobiography*. Baton Rouge: Louisiana State University Press, 1979.

Combs, Arthur. "The Path Not Taken: The British Alternative to U.S. Policy in Vietnam, 1954–1956." *Diplomatic History* 19 (winter 1995): 33–57.

Connelly, Matthew. *A Diplomatic Revolution: Algeria's Fight for Independence and the Origins of the Post–Cold War Era*. Oxford: Oxford University Press, 2000.

———. "Taking off the Cold War Lens: Visions of North-South Conflict during the Algerian War for Independence." *American Historical Review* 105 (June 2000): 739–69.

Cooper, Chester. *The Lost Crusade: The Full Story of U.S. Involvement in Vietnam*. New York: Dodd, Mead, 1971.

Cooper, Nicola. *France in Indochina: Colonial Encounters*. Oxford: Berg, 2001.

Costigliola, Frank. *France and the United States: The Cold Alliance 1940–1990*. New York: Twayne, 1992.

Cottrell, Alvin, and James Dougherty. *The Politics of the Atlantic Alliance*. New York: Praeger, 1964.

Craig, Gordon. *Force and Statecraft: The Diplomatic Problems of Our Time*. 3rd ed. New York: Oxford University Press, 1995.

Crosswell, D. K. R. *The Chief of Staff: The Military Career of General Walter Bedell Smith*. New York: Greenwood Press, 1991.

Currey, Cecil. *Edward Lansdale: The Unquiet American*. Boston: Houghton Mifflin, 1988.

Dacy, Douglas. *Foreign Aid, War, and Economic Development: South Vietnam, 1955–1975*. Cambridge: Cambridge University Press, 1986.

Dallek, Robert. *The American Style of Foreign Policy: Cultural Politics and Foreign Affairs*. Oxford: Oxford University Press, 1990.

Dalloz, Jacques. *The War in Indochina, 1945–54*. Dublin: Gill and Macmillan, 1990.

Daridan, Jean. "Prelude à l'enlisement américain en Indochine, 1954–1955." *Defense Nationale* 41 (August–September 1985): 85–97.

Davidson, Philip. *Vietnam At War: The History 1946–1975*. London: Sidgwick and Jackson, 1988.

de La Gorce, Paul-Marie. *Apogée et Mort de la IVè République, 1952–1958*. Paris: Bernard Grasset, 1979.

Devillers, Philippe. *Histoire du Vietnam de 1940 à 1952*. Paris: Editions Seuil, 1953.

———. "The Struggle for the Unification of Vietnam." *China Quarterly* 9 (January–March 1962): 2–23.

Devillers, Philippe, and Jean Lacouture. *End of a War: Indochina, 1954*. New York: Praeger, 1969.

Dingman, Roger. "John Foster Dulles and the Creation of SEATO in 1954." *International History Review* 11 (August 1989): 457–77.

Divine, Robert. *Eisenhower and the Cold War*. New York: Oxford University Press, 1981.

Dommen, Arthur. *The Indochinese Experience of the French and Americans: Nationalism and Communism in Cambodia, Laos, and Vietnam*. Bloomington: Indiana University Press, 2001.

Dooley, Thomas. *Deliver Us from Evil: The Story of Vietnam's Flight to Freedom*. New York: Farrar, Straus, and Cudahy, 1956.

Drake, David. "Les Temps Modernes and the French War in Indochina." *Journal of European Studies* 28 (March–June 1998): 25–41.

Dreifort, John. *Myopic Grandeur: The Ambivalence of French Foreign Policy toward the Far East*. Kent, Ohio: Kent State University Press, 1991.

Duchin, Brian. "'The Agonizing Reappraisal': Eisenhower, Dulles, and the European Defense Community." *Diplomatic History* 16 (spring 1992): 201–21.

Duiker, William. *Ho Chi Minh*. New York: Theia, 2000.

———. *Sacred War: Nationalism and Revolution in a Divided Vietnam*. Boston: McGraw Hill, 1995.

————. *U.S. Containment Policy and the Conflict in Indochina.* Stanford, Calif.: Stanford University Press, 1994.

Dunn, Peter. *The First Vietnam War.* London: Hurst, 1985.

Eden, Anthony. *Full Circle: The Memoirs of Anthony Eden.* Boston: Houghton Mifflin, 1960.

————. *Toward Peace in Indochina.* Boston: Houghton Mifflin, 1966.

Eisenhower, Dwight D. *Mandate for Change, 1953–1956.* Garden City, N.Y.: Doubleday, 1963.

————. *Waging Peace, 1956–1961.* Garden City, N.Y.: Doubleday, 1965.

Elgey, Georgette. *Histoire de la Quatrième République.* Paris: Fayard, 1968.

Ellsberg, Daniel. *Papers on the War.* New York: Simon and Schuster, 1972.

Ely, Paul. *Mémoires: L'Indochine dans la Tourmente.* Paris: Plon, 1964.

Endy, Christopher. *Cold War Holidays: American Tourism in France.* Chapel Hill: University of North Carolina Press, 2004.

Ernst, John. *Forging a Fateful Alliance: Michigan State University and the Vietnam War.* East Lansing: Michigan State University Press, 1998.

Falk, Richard, ed. *The Vietnam War and International Law.* Princeton, N.J.: Princeton University Press, 1968.

Fall, Bernard. *Hell in a Very Small Place.* Philadelphia: Lippincott, 1967.

————. "Indochina since Geneva." *Pacific Affairs* 28 (March 1955): 3–25.

————. *Street without Joy.* Harrisburg, Pa.: Stackpole, 1967.

————. "Tribulations of a Party Line: The French Communists and Indochina." *Foreign Affairs* 33 (April 1955): 499–510.

Faure, Edgar. *Mémoires: Avoir toujours raison, c'est un grand tort.* Paris: Plon, 1982.

Fauvet, Jacques. *La IVe République.* Paris: Fayard, 1958.

Ferrell, Robert, ed. *The Diary of James Hagerty: Eisenhower in Mid-Course, 1954–1955.* Bloomington: Indiana University Press, 1983.

Fish, Steven. "After Stalin's Death: The Anglo-American Debate over a New Cold War." *Diplomatic History* 10 (fall 1986): 333–55.

Fitzgerald, Frances. *Fire in the Lake: The Vietnamese and the Americans in Vietnam.* New York: Vintage Books, 1972.

Foot, Rosemary. *The Wrong War: American Policy and the Dimensions of the Korean Conflict, 1950–1953.* Ithaca, N.Y.: Cornell University Press, 1985.

Franchini, Philippe. *Les Guerres d'Indochine,* vols. I and II. Paris: Pygmalion, 1988.

Furniss, Edward. *France: Troubled Ally: De Gaulle Heritage and Prospects.* New York: Praeger, 1960.

Fursdon, Edward. *The European Defense Community: A History.* New York: St. Martin's, 1980.

Gaddis, John Lewis. "The Emerging Post-revisionist Synthesis on the Origins of the Cold War." *Diplomatic History* 7 (summer 1983): 171–204.

————. *The Long Peace: Inquiries into the History of the Cold War.* New York: Oxford University Press, 1987.

————. *Strategies of Containment: A Critical Appraisal of Postwar American National Security Policy*. New York: Oxford University Press, 1982.

————. "The Unexpected John Foster Dulles: Nuclear Weapons, Communism, and the Russians." In *John Foster Dulles and the Diplomacy of the Cold War*. Ed. Richard Immerman. Princeton, N.J.: Princeton University Press, 1990: 79–81.

————. *The United States and the End of the Cold War: Implications, Reconsiderations, Provocations*. New York: Oxford University Press, 1992.

Gaiduk, Ilya. *Confronting Vietnam: Soviet Policy toward the Indochina Conflict, 1954–1963*. Washington D.C.: Woodrow Wilson Center Press, 2003.

Gardner, Lloyd. *Approaching Vietnam: From World War II through Dienbienphu*. New York: Norton, 1988.

Garthoff, Raymond. *Assessing the Adversary: Estimates by the Eisenhower Administration of Soviet Intentions and Capabilities*. Washington, D.C.: Brookings Institution, 1991.

Gelb, Leslie, and Richard Betts. *The Irony of Vietnam: The System Worked*. Washington, D.C.: Brookings Institution, 1979.

Genty, Robert. *Ultimes Secours pour Dien Bien Phu, 1953–1954*. Paris: L'Harmattan, 1991.

Giauque, Jeffrey. *Grand Designs and Visions of Unity: The Atlantic Alliance Powers and the Reorganization of Western Europe, 1955–1963*. Chapel Hill: University of North Carolina Press, 2002.

Gibbons, William. *The U.S. Government and the Vietnam War: Executive and Legislative Roles and Relationships, Part I: 1945–1960*. Princeton, N.J.: Princeton University Press, 1986.

Gienow-Hecht, Jessica C. E. "Shame on U.S.? Academics, Cultural Transfer, and the Cold War: A Critical Review." *Diplomatic History* 23 (summer 2000): 465–94.

Gienow-Hecht, Jessica C. E., and Frank Schumacher. *Culture and International History*. New York: Berghahn Books, 2003.

Gilpin, Robert. *The Political Economy of International Relations*. Princeton, N.J.: Princeton University Press, 1987.

Girardet, R. *L'Idée coloniale en France, 1871–1962*. Paris: La Table Rond, 1972.

Goscha, Chris. "Le Contexte Asiatique de la guerre franco-vietnamienne: Relations, reseaux, et économie, 1945–1954." Ph.D. diss., Ecole Pratique des Hautes Etudes Sorbonne, Paris, 2000.

Gras, Yves. *Histoire de la guerre d'Indochine*. Paris: Plon, 1979.

Greene, Daniel O'C. "John Foster Dulles and the End of the Franco-American Entente in Indochina." *Diplomatic History* 16 (fall 1992): 511–49.

Greene, Graham. *The Quiet American*. London: William Heinemann, 1955.

Greene, John. "Bibliographic Essay. Eisenhower Revisionism, 1952–1992: A Reappraisal." In *Reexamining the Eisenhower Presidency*. Ed. Shirley Anne Warshaw. Westport, Conn.: Greenwood Press, 1993.

Greenstein, Fred. *Hidden-Hand Presidency: Eisenhower as Leader*. Baltimore, Md.: Johns Hopkins University Press, 1982.

Grimal, Henri. *La décolonisation de 1919 à nos jours*. Paris: Editions Complexe, 1985.

Grosser, Alfred. *Affaires Extèrieures: la politique de la France, 1944-1984*. Paris: Flammarion, 1984.

Halberstam, David. *The Best and the Brightest*. New York: Random House, 1972.

———. *Ho*. New York: Random House, 1971.

———. *The Making of a Quagmire*. New York: Random House, 1965.

Hammer, Ellen. *The Struggle for Indochina 1940-1955*. Stanford, Calif.: Stanford University Press, 1966.

Hannon, J. S. "The International Control Commission Experience and the Role of an Improved International Supervisory Body in the Vietnam Settlement." *Virginia Journal of International Law* 9 (December 1968): 20-65.

Harrison, Michael. *The Reluctant Ally: France and Atlantic Security*. Baltimore, Md.: Johns Hopkins University Press, 1991.

Hays, Samuel, ed. *The Beginning of American Aid to Southeast Asia: The Griffin Mission of 1950*. Lexington, Mass.: Heath Lexington, 1971.

Hazlett, Everett. *Ike's Letters to a Friend*. Lawrence: University Press of Kansas, 1984.

Heiss, Mary Ann. "The Evolution of the Imperial Idea and U.S. National Identity." *Diplomatic History* 26 (fall 2002): 537-39.

Herring, George. "'A Good Stout Effort': John Foster Dulles and the Indochina Crisis, 1954-1955." In *John Foster Dulles and the Diplomacy of the Cold War*. Ed. Richard Immerman. Princeton, N.J.: Princeton University Press, 1990: 213-33.

———. *America's Longest War: The United States and Vietnam, 1950-1975*. New York: Knopf, 1986.

———. "Franco-American Conflict in Indochina, 1950-1954." In *Dien Bien Phu and the Crisis of Franco-American Relations*. Ed. Kaplan, Artaud, and Rubin: 29-48.

———. *LBJ and Vietnam: A Different Kind of War*. Austin: University of Texas Press, 1994.

———. "The Truman Administration and the Restoration of French Sovereignty in Indochina." *Diplomatic History* 1 (spring 1977): 97-117.

Herring, George, and Richard Immerman. "Eisenhower, Dulles, and Dien Bien Phu: 'The Day We Didn't Go to War' Revisited." In *Dien Bien Phu and the Crisis of Franco-American Relations*. Ed. Kaplan, Artaud, and Rubin: 81-103.

Herring, George, Gary Hess, and Richard Immerman. "Passage of Empire: The United States, France, and South Vietnam, 1954-1955." In *Dien Bien Phu and the Crisis of Franco-American Relations*. Ed. Kaplan, Artaud, and Rubin: 171-95.

Hershberg, James. "'Explosion in the Offing': German Rearmament and American Diplomacy, 1953-1955." *Diplomatic History* 16 (fall 1992): 511-49.

Hess, Gary. "The First American Commitment to Indochina: The Acceptance of the Bao Dai Solution, 1950." *Diplomatic History* 2 (fall 1978): 331-50.

———. "Franklin Roosevelt and Indochina." *Journal of American History* 69 (September 1972): 353–68.

———. *The United States' Emergence as a Southeast Asian Power 1940–1950.* New York: Columbia University Press, 1987.

———. *Vietnam and the United States: Origins and Legacy of War.* Boston: Twayne, 1990.

Hitchcock, William. *France Restored: Cold War Diplomacy and the Quest for Leadership in Europe, 1944–1954.* Chapel Hill: University of North Carolina Press, 1998.

Hixson, Walter. *Parting the Curtain: Propaganda, Culture, and the Cold War, 1945–1961.* New York: Palgrave Macmillan, 1997.

Ho Chi Minh. *Action et Revolution.* Paris: Union Generale d'Editions, 1968.

Ho Chi Minh (Nguyen Ai Quoc). *Le Procès de la Colonisation Française.* Hanoi: Vietnam Quoc Gia An Thu Cuc, 1925.

Hobsbawm, E. J. *Nations and Nationalism since 1780.* Cambridge: Cambridge University Press, 1990.

Hoffman, Stanley. "French Perceptions and American Policy." In *Image and Reality in World Politics.* Ed. J. C. Farrel and A. P. Smith. New York: Columbia University Press, 1968.

Hoffmann, Stanley, Samuel Huntington, Ernest May, and Richard Neustadt. "Vietnam Reappraised." *International Security* 6 (summer 1981): 13.

Holsti, Ole. "Models of International Relations and Foreign Policy." *Diplomatic History* 13 (winter 1989): 15–44.

———. "Will the Real John Foster Dulles Please Stand Up?" *International Journal* 30 (1974–1975): 34–44.

Honey, P. J. *Communism in North Vietnam: Its Role in the Sino-Soviet Dispute.* Westport, Conn.: Greenwood, 1973.

———. "North Vietnam's Party Congress." *China Quarterly* 70 (October–December 1960): 66–75.

Hoopes, Townsend. *The Devil and John Foster Dulles.* Boston: Little, Brown, 1973.

Hostetter, John. "John Foster Dulles and the French Defeat in Indochina." Ph.D. diss., Rutgers University, 1972.

Hughes, Emmet John. *The Ordeal of Power: A Political Memoir of the Eisenhower Years.* New York: Atheneum, 1963.

Immerman, Richard. "Confessions of an Eisenhower Revisionist. An Agonizing Reappraisal." *Diplomatic History* 14 (summer 1990): 319–42.

———. *John Foster Dulles and the Diplomacy of the Cold War.* Princeton, N.J.: Princeton University Press, 1990.

———. "The United States and the Geneva Conference of 1954: A New Look." *Diplomatic History* 14 (winter 1990): 43–66.

Ireland, Timothy. *Creating the Entangling Alliance: The Origins of NATO.* Westport, Conn.: Greenwood Press, 1981.

Iriye, Akira. *Cultural Internationalism and World Order.* Baltimore, Md.: Johns Hopkins University Press, 1997.

————. "Culture and International History." In *Explaining the History of American Foreign Relations.* Ed. Michael Hoganson and Thomas Paterson. Cambridge: Cambridge University Press, 1994.

Irving, Ronald. *The First Indochina War: French and American Policy, 1945-1954.* London: Croom-Helm, 1975.

————. "The MRP and French Policy in Indochina 1945-1954 with Special Reference to the Influence of Catholicism." *France-Asie/Asia* 23/3 (1969): 257-69.

Isoart, Paul. "Le Control et la surveillance de la cessation des hostilités en Indochine." In *L'Inspection International: quinze études de la pratique des Etats et désorganisations internationales.* Ed. Georges Fischer and Daniel Vignes. Brussels: Bruylant, 1976: 169-222.

Jacobs, Seth. *America's Miracle Man in Vietnam: Ngo Dinh Diem, Religion, Race, and U.S. Intervention in Southeast Asia, 1950-1957.* Durham, N.C.: Duke University Press, 2004.

————. "'Our System Demands the Supreme Being': America's Religious Revival and the 'Diem Experiment,' 1954-1955." *Diplomatic History* 25 (fall 2001): 589-624.

Jennings, Eric. *Vichy in the Tropics: Pétain's National Revolution in Madagascar, Guadeloupe, and Indochina, 1940-1944.* Stanford, Calif.: Stanford University Press, 2004.

Jervis, Robert. *Perception and Misperception in International Politics.* Princeton, N.J.: Princeton University, 1976.

Jian, Chen. "China and the First Indochina War, 1950-1954." *China Quarterly* no. 133 (March 1993): 85-111.

Johns, Andrew. "A Voice from the Wilderness: Richard Nixon and the Vietnam War, 1964-1966." *Presidential Studies Quarterly* 29 (spring 1999): 317-35.

————. "Opening Pandora's Box: The Genesis and Evolution of the 1964 Congressional Resolution on Vietnam." *Journal of American-East Asian Relations* 6 (summer-fall 1997): 1-32.

Johnson, U. Alexis. *The Right Hand of Power.* Englewood Cliffs, N.J.: Prentice Hall, 1984.

Journoud, Pierre. "Face-à-face culturel au Sud-Vietnam, 1954-1965." In *Entre rayonnement et réciprocité: Contributions à l'histoire de la diplomatie culturelle.* Ed. Pierre Journoud. Paris: Publications de la Sorbonne, 2002: 139-66.

Joyaux, François. *La Chine et le règlement du premier conflit d'Indochine, Genève 1954.* Paris: Publications de la Sorbonne, 1979.

Juin, Alphonse. *Memoirs, II: 1944-1958.* Paris: Artheme Fayard, 1960.

Julliard, Jacques. *La IVe République 1947-1958.* Paris: Calmann-Lévy, 1958.

Just, Ward. *A Dangerous Friend.* Boston: Houghton Mifflin, 1999.

Kahin, George McT. *Intervention: How America Became Involved in Vietnam.* New York: Anchor, 1986.

Kahler, Miles. *Decolonization in Britain and France: The Domestic Consequences of International Relations*. Princeton, N.J.: Princeton University Press, 1984.

Kaiser, David. *American Tragedy: Kennedy, Johnson, and the Origins of the Vietnam War*. Cambridge, Mass.: Belknap Press, 2002.

Kane, Thomas. "The Missionary Theme in the Rhetoric of John Foster Dulles." Ph.D. diss., University of Pittsburgh, 1968.

Kaplan, Amy. *The Anarchy of Empire in the Making of U.S. Culture*. Cambridge: Harvard University Press, 2002.

Kaplan, Amy, and Donald Pease. *Cultures of United States Imperialism*. Durham, N.C.: Duke University Press, 1994.

Kaplan, Lawrence. "The United States, NATO, and French Indochina." In *Dien Bien Phu and the Crisis of Franco-American Relations*. Ed. Kaplan, Artaud, and Rubin: 229–50.

Kaplan, Lawrence, Denise Artaud, and Mark Rubin, eds. *Dien Bien Phu and the Crisis of Franco-American Relations, 1954–1955*. Wilmington, Del.: SR Books, 1990.

Karabell, Zachary. *Architects of Intervention: The United States, the Third World, and the Cold War, 1946–1962*. Baton Rouge: Louisiana State University Press, 1999.

Karnow, Stanley. *Vietnam: A History*. New York: Viking, 1983.

Kattenburg, Paul. *The Vietnam Trauma: American Foreign Policy, 1945–1975*. New Brunswick, N.J.: Transaction Books, 1980.

Kaufman, Burton. *Trade and Aid: Eisenhower's Foreign Economic Policy, 1953–1961*. Baltimore, Md.: Johns Hopkins University Press, 1982.

Keohane, Robert. "The Big Influence of Small Allies." *Foreign Policy* 2 (spring 1997): 161–82.

———. "The United States and the Postwar Order: Empire or Hegemony." *Journal of Peace Research* 28/4 (1991): 435–39.

Khong, Yuen Foong. *Analogies at War: Korea, Munich, Dien Bien Phu, and the Vietnam Decisions of 1965*. Princeton, N.J.: Princeton University Press, 1992.

Kiem, Nguyen. *Le Sud-Vietnam depuis Dien Bien Phu*. Paris: Maspero, 1963.

Kimball, Jeffrey. *To Reason Why: The Debate about the Causes of U.S. Involvement in the Vietnam War*. New York: McGraw Hill, 1990.

Kolko, Gabriel. *Anatomy of a War: Vietnam, the United States, and the Modern Historical Experience*. New York: Pantheon Books, 1985.

Kuisel, Richard. "Coca-Cola and the Cold War: The French Face Americanization 1948–1953." *French Historical Studies* 17 (spring 1991): 96.

———. *Seducing the French—The Dilemma of Americanization*. Berkeley: University of California Press, 1993.

Kutler, Stanley. *The Encyclopedia of the Vietnam War*. New York: Simon and Schuster, 1995.

Lacouture, Jean. *Ho Chi Minh*. Paris: Le Seuil, 1977.

———. *Pierre Mendès France*. New York: Holmes and Meier, 1984.

————. *Vietnam: Between Two Truces*. New York: Random House, 1966.

LaFeber, Walter. "Roosevelt, Churchill, and Indochina 1942–1945." *American Historical Review* 80 (December 1975): 1277–95.

Laffrey, John. "French Far Eastern Policy." *Modern Asian Studies* 23 (February 1989): 117–39.

Lafon, Monique, ed. *Le Parti Communiste Français dans la Lutte Contre le Colonialisme*. Paris: Editions Sociales, 1962.

Lancaster, Donald. *The Emancipation of French Indochina*. London: Oxford University Press, 1966.

Langguth, Jack. *Our Vietnam: The War, 1954–1975*. New York: Simon and Schuster, 2002.

Laniel, Joseph. *Jours de gloire et jours cruels, 1908–1958*. Paris: Presses de la cité, 1971.

————. *Le drame indochinois de Dien Bien Phu au pari de Genève*. Paris: Plon, 1957.

Lansdale, Edward. *In the Midst of Wars: An American's Mission to Southeast Asia*. New York: Harper and Row, 1972.

Larkin, Maurice. *France since the Popular Front: Government and People 1936–1986*. Oxford: Clarendon, 1988.

Larres, Klaus. *Churchill's Cold War: The Politics of Personal Diplomacy*. New Haven, Conn.: Yale University Press, 2002.

Larson, Arthur. *Eisenhower: The President Nobody Knew*. New York: Scribner, 1968.

Latham, Michael. *Modernization as Ideology: American Social Science and "Nation-Building" in the Kennedy Era*. Chapel Hill: University of North Carolina Press, 2000.

Lawrence, Mark. *Assuming the Burden: Europe and the American Commitment to War in Vietnam*. Berkeley: University of California Press, 2005.

————. "Transnational Coalition-Building and the Making of the Cold War in Indochina, 1947–1949." *Diplomatic History* 26 (summer 2002): 453–80.

Lebovics, Herman. *True France: The Wars over Cultural Identity, 1900–1945*. Ithaca, N.Y.: Cornell University Press, 1992.

Lee, Steven Hugh. *Outposts of Empire: Korea, Vietnam, and the Origins of the Cold War in Asia, 1949–1954*. Montreal: McGill-Queen's University Press, 1995.

Leffler, Melvyn. *A Preponderance of Power: National Security, the Truman Administration, and the Cold War*. Stanford, Calif.: Stanford University Press, 1992.

————. "9/11 and American Foreign Policy." *Diplomatic History* 29 (summer 2005): 395–413.

Lester, Robert. *Vietnam Documents and Research Notes Series: Translation and Analysis of Significant VietCong/North Vietnamese Documents—A Guide to the Microfilm Edition of Vietnam War Research Collections*. Bethesda, Md.: University Publications of America, 1992.

Levy, David. *The Debate over Vietnam*. Baltimore, Md.: Johns Hopkins University Press, 1995.

Logevall, Fredrik. *Choosing War: The Lost Chance for Peace and the Escalation of War in Vietnam.* Berkeley: University of California Press, 1999.

———. "De Gaulle, Neutralization, and American Involvement in Vietnam, 1963–1964." *Pacific Historical Review* 61 (February 1992): 69–102.

———. *The Origins of the Vietnam War.* Harlow: Pearson Educated Limited, 2001.

Lundestad, Geir. "'Empire by Invitation' in the American Century." *Diplomatic History* 23 (spring 1999): 189–217.

———. "Empire by Invitation? The United States and Western Europe, 1945–1952," *SHAFR Newsletter* (September 1984): 1–21.

Lundestad, Geir, ed. *The American "Empire" and Other Studies of U.S. Foreign Policy in a Comparative Perspective.* Oxford: Oxford University Press, 1990.

———. *"Empire" by Integration: The United States and European Integration, 1945–1997.* Oxford: Oxford University Press, 1998.

———. *No End to Alliance: The United States and Western Europe: Past, Present, and Future.* New York: St. Martin's, 1998.

Mann, Robert. *A Grand Delusion: America's Descent into Vietnam.* New York: Basic Books, 2001.

Marks, Frederick. "The Real Hawk at Dien Bien Phu, Dulles or Eisenhower?" *Pacific Historical Review* 59/4 (1990): 297–322.

Marquis, Jefferson. "The Other Warriors: American Social Science and Nationbuilding in Vietnam." *Diplomatic History* 24 (winter 2000): 79–105.

Marr, David. *Vietnam 1945: The Quest for Power.* Berkeley: University of California Press, 1995.

Marshall, Bruce. *The French Colonial Myth and Constitution-Making in the Fourth Republic.* New Haven: Yale University Press, 1973.

Massigli, René. *Une Comedie des erreurs, 1943–1956.* Paris: Plon, 1978.

Matthews, Robert, Arthur Rubinoff, and Janice Gross Stein. *International Conflict and Conflict Management: Readings in World Politics.* Scarborough, Ont.: Prentice-Hall, 1984.

McMahon, Robert. "Eisenhower and Third World Nationalism: A Critique of the Revisionists." *Political Science Quarterly* 101 (fall 1986): 453–73.

———. *The Limits of Empire: The United States and Southeast Asia since World War II.* New York: Columbia University Press, 1999.

McMaster, H. R. *Dereliction of Duty: Lyndon Johnson, Robert McNamara, the Joint Chiefs of Staff, and the Lies that Led to Vietnam.* New York: HarperCollins, 1997.

McNamara, Robert. *Argument without End: In Search of Answers to the Vietnam Tragedy.* New York: Public Affairs, 1999.

Mélandri, Pierre. *L'Alliance Atlantique.* Paris: Gallimard, 1979.

———. "France and the Atlantic Alliance 1950–1953: Between Great Power Policy and European Integration." In *Western Security, the Formative Years: European and Atlantic Defense 1947–1953*. Ed. Olav Riste. Oslo: Norwegian University Press, 1985.

Melby, John. "Vietnam-1950." *Diplomatic History* 6 (winter 1982): 97–109.

Melling, Phil, and Jon Roper, eds. *America, France, and Vietnam: Cultural History and Ideas of Conflict*. Aldershot: Gower, 1991.

Mendès France, Pierre. *Gouverner C'est Choisir 1954–1955*. Paris: Gallimard, 1986.

Michel, Marc. "De Lattre et les debuts de l'américainisation de la guerre d'Indochine." *Revue Française d'Histoire d'Outre Mer.* 72/268 (1985): 321–34.

Moise, Edwin. *Tonkin Gulf and the Escalation of the Vietnam War*. Chapel Hill: University of North Carolina Press, 1996.

Monnet, Jean. *Mémoires*. Paris: Fayard, 1976.

Montague, Lee. *General Walter Bedell Smith as Director of Central Intelligence, October 1950–February 1953*. University Park: Pennsylvania State University Press, 1992.

Morgan, Joseph. *The Vietnam Lobby: The American Friends of Vietnam, 1955–1975*. Chapel Hill: University of North Carolina Press, 1997.

Navarre, Henri. *Agonie de l'Indochine, 1953–1954*. Paris: Plon, 1956.

Nelson, Anna Kasten. "John Foster Dulles and the Bipartisan Congress." *Political Science Quarterly* 102 (spring 1987): 43–64.

Neustadt, Richard. *Alliance Politics*. New York: Columbia University Press, 1970.

Nguyen Khac Vien. *Vietnam: A Long History*. Hanoi: Foreign Languages Pub. House, 1987.

Nye, Joseph S. Jr. *Soft Power: The Means to Success in World Politics*. New York: Public Affairs, 2004.

O'Ballance, Edgar. *The Indochina War, 1945–1954: A Study in Guerilla Warfare*. London: Faber and Faber, 1964.

Olson, Gregory A. "Eisenhower and the Indochina Problem." In *Eisenhower's War of Words: Rhetoric and Leadership*. Ed. Martin J. Medhurst. East Lansing: Michigan State University Press, 1994: 97–135.

Olson, Marie. *Solidarity and National Revolution: The South Vietnamese and the Vietnamese Communists 1954–60*. Oslo: IPS, 1997.

Osgood, Kenneth. "Form before Substance: Eisenhower's Commitment to Psychological Warfare and Negotiations with the Enemy." *Diplomatic History* 24 (summer 2000): 405–33.

Ovendale, Ritchie. "Britain, the United States, and the Cold War in Southeast Asia, 1950–1954." *International Affairs* 58 (summer 1982): 447–64.

Pach, Chester, and Elmo Richardson. *The Presidency of Dwight D. Eisenhower*. Lawrence: University Press of Kansas, 1991.

Papp, Daniel. *Vietnam: The View from Moscow, Washington, and Peking*. Jefferson, N.C.: McFarland, 1981.

Parmet, Herbert. "The Making and Unmaking of Ngo Dinh Diem." In *The Second Indochina War*. Ed. John Schlight. Washington, D.C.: U.S. Army, 1986.

Patti, Archimedes. *Why Vietnam? Prelude to America's Albatross.* Berkeley: University of California Press, 1980.

Pells, Richard. *Not Like Us: How Europeans Have Loved, Hated, and Transformed American Culture since World War II.* New York: Basic Books, 1997.

Pemberton, James. "Australia, the United States, and the Indochina Crisis of 1954." *Diplomatic History* 13 (winter 1989): 45–66.

Penniman, Howard. *Elections in South Vietnam.* Washington, D.C.: American Enterprise Institute, 1972.

Pike, Douglas. *Vietnam and the Soviet Union: Anatomy of an Alliance.* Boulder, Colo.: Westview Press, 1987.

Pinto, Roger. "La France et les Etats d'Indochine devant les accords de Genève." *Revue Française de Science Politique* 5 (January–March 1955): 63–91.

Poiger, Uta. "Beyond 'Modernization' and 'Colonization.'" *Diplomatic History* 23 (winter 1999): 45–56.

Porter, Gareth. *Perils of Dominance: Imbalance of Power and the Road to War in Vietnam.* Berkeley: University of California Press, 2005.

Prados, John. *The Hidden History of the Vietnam War.* Chicago: I.R. Dee, 1995.

———. "The Central Intelligence Agency and the Face of Decolonization under the Eisenhower Administration." In *The Eisenhower Administration, the Third World, and the Globalization of the Cold War.* Ed. Kathryn Statler and Andrew Johns. New York: Rowman and Littlefield, 2006: 27–46.

———. *The Sky Would Fall: Operation Vulture: The U.S. Bombing Mission in Indochina, 1954.* New York: Dial, 1983.

Pruessen, Ronald. *John Foster Dulles: The Road to Power.* New York: The Free Press, 1982.

Rabe, Stephen. "Eisenhower Revisionism: A Decade of Scholarship." *Diplomatic History* 17 (winter 1993): 97–115.

Race, Jeffrey. *War Comes to Long An: Revolutionary Conflict in a Vietnam Province.* Berkeley: University of California Press, 1972.

Radford, Arthur. *From Pearl Harbor to Vietnam: The Memoirs of Admiral Arthur Radford.* Ed. Stephen Jurika Jr. Stanford, Calif.: Hoover Institution Press, 1980.

Randle, Robert. *Geneva 1954: The Settlement of the Indochinese War.* Princeton, N.J.: Princeton University Press, 1969.

Rather, Lucia. "The Geneva Conference of 1954: Problems in Allied Unity." Ph.D. diss., George Washington University, 1994.

Record, Jeffrey. *Making War, Thinking History: Munich, Vietnam, and Presidential Uses of Force from Korea to Kosovo.* Annapolis, Md.: Naval Institute Press, 2002.

Rémond, René. *The Right Wing in France: From 1815 to De Gaulle.* Philadelphia: University of Pennsylvania Press, 1966.

Rice-Maximin, Edward. *Accommodation and Resistance: The French Left, Indochina, and the Cold War, 1944–1955.* New York: Greenwood, 1986.

Richter, James. *Khrushchev's Double Bind: International Pressures and Domestic Coalition Politics.* Baltimore, Md.: Johns Hopkins University Press, 1994.

Rioux, Jean-Pierre. *The Fourth Republic, 1944-1958.* Cambridge: Cambridge University Press, 1987.

Roberts, Chalmers. "The Day We Didn't Go to War." *Reporter* 2 (September 14, 1954): 31-35.

Roger, Philippe. *Rêves et cauchemars américains: L'Amérique au miroir de l'opinion publique française, 1945-1953.* Villeneuve d'Ascq: Presses universitaires du Septentrion, 1996.

Rosenberg, Emily. *Spreading the American Dream: American Economic and Cultural Expansion, 1890-1945.* New York: Hill and Wang, 1982.

Rostow, Walt. *Eisenhower, Kennedy, and Foreign Aid.* Austin: University of Texas Press, 1985.

Rotter, Andrew. *The Path to Vietnam: Origins of the American Commitment to Southeast Asia.* Ithaca, N.Y., and London: Cornell University Press, 1987.

Rousso, Henry. *The Vichy Syndrome: History and Memory in France since 1944.* Cambridge: Harvard University Press, 1991.

Roy, Jules. *The Battle of Dien Bien Phu.* New York: Harper and Row, 1965.

Ruscio, Alain. *Dien Bien Phu: La Fin d'une Illusion.* Paris: L'Harmattan, 1986.

———. *La Guerre française d'Indochine.* Brussels: Editions Complexe, 1992.

———. "L'Opinion française et la guerre d'Indochine 1945-1954 Sondages et temoignanges." *Vingtième Siècle* 29 (January–March 1991): 35-45.

Sainteny, Jean. *Face à Ho Chi Minh.* Paris: Seghers, 1970.

———. *Histoire d'une paix manquée.* Paris: Amiot-Dumont, 1953.

———. *Ho Chi Minh and His Vietnam: A Personal Memoir.* Chicago: Cowles Book Co., 1972.

Sarraut, Albert. *Grandeur et Servitude Coloniales.* Paris: Editions du Sagittaire, 1931.

———. *La Mise en Valeur des Colonies Françaises.* Paris: Payot et Cie, 1923.

Schlesinger, Arthur. *The Bitter Heritage: Vietnam and American Democracy 1941-1968.* New York: Fawcett, 1968.

———. *Robert Kennedy and His Times.* New York: Ballantine, 1978.

———. *A Thousand Days: John F. Kennedy in the Whitehouse.* New York: Fawcett, 1965.

Schulzinger, Robert. *A Time for War: The United States and Vietnam, 1941-1975.* Oxford: Oxford University Press, 1997.

Scigliano, Robert. *South Vietnam: Nation under Stress.* Boston: Houghton Mifflin, 1964.

Scigliano, Robert, and Guy Fox. *Technical Assistance in Vietnam: The Michigan State University Experience.* New York: Praeger, 1965.

Shao, Kuo-kang. "Zhou Enlai's Diplomacy and the Neutralization of Indochina 1954-1955." *China Quarterly* 107 (September 1986): 483-504.

Shaplen, Robert. *The Lost Revolution.* New York: Harper and Row, 1965.

Shepley, James. "How Dulles Averted War." *Life* (January 16, 1956): 70-80.

Shipway, Martin. *The Road to War: France and Vietnam, 1944-1947.* Providence, R.I.: Berghahn, 1996.

Short, Anthony. *The Origins of the Vietnam War.* New York: Longman, 1989.

Siracusa, Joseph. "FDR, Truman, and Indochina: The Forgotten Years." In *The Impact of the Cold War: Reconsideration.* Ed. Glen St. John Barclay. Port Washington, N.Y.: Kennikat Press, 1977.

Smith, Ralph B. *An International History of the Vietnam War, Vol. I: Revolution Versus Containment, 1955-61.* London: Macmillan, 1983.

————. *Vietnam and the West.* London: Heinemann, 1968.

Smith, Tony. "New Bottles for New Wine: A Pericentric Framework for the Study of the Cold War." *Diplomatic History* 24 (fall 2000): 567–91.

————. "The French Colonial Consensus and the People's War, 1946-1958." *Journal of Contemporary History* 9 (October 1974): 221–47.

Smith, Walter. *My Three Years in Moscow.* Philadelphia, Pa.: Lippincott, 1950.

Snyder, Glenn. *Alliance Politics.* Ithaca, N.Y.: Cornell University Press, 1997.

Soffer, Jonathan. *General Matthew B. Ridgway: From Progressivism to Reaganism, 1895-1993.* Westport, Conn.: Praeger, 1998.

Sorum, Paul Caly. *Intellectuals and Decolonization in France.* Chapel Hill: University of North Carolina Press, 1977.

Soustelle, Jacques. "France Looks at Her Alliances." *Foreign Affairs* 35 (October 1956): 116–30.

————. "Indochina and Korea: One Front." *Foreign Affairs* 39 (October 1950): 56–66.

Spector, Ronald. *Advice and Support: The Early Years of the United States Army in Vietnam, 1941-1960.* New York: Free Press, 1985.

Statler, Kathryn C. "After Geneva: The French Presence in Vietnam, 1954-1963." In *The First Vietnam War: Colonial Conflict and Cold War Crisis.* Ed. Fredrik Logevall and Mark Lawrence. Cambridge: Harvard University Press, 2007: 263–81.

————. "Alliance Politics After Stalin's Death: Franco-American Conflict in Europe and in Asia, 1953-1954." In *The Cold War After Stalin's Death: A Missed Opportunity for Peace?* Ed. Klaus Larres and Kenneth Osgood. New York: Rowman and Littlefield, 2006: 157–75.

————. "Building a Colony: The Eisenhower Administration and South Vietnam, 1953-1961." In *The Eisenhower Administration, the Third World, and the Globalization of the Cold War.* Ed. Kathryn C. Statler and Andrew Johns. New York: Rowman and Littlefield, 2006: 101–23.

————. "The Diem Experiment: Franco-American Conflict over South Vietnam, July 1954-May 1955." *Journal of American-East Asian Relations* 6 (summer–fall 1997): 145–73.

Steininger, Rolf. "John Foster Dulles, the European Defense Community, and the German Question." In *John Foster Dulles and the Diplomacy of the Cold War.* Ed. Richard Immerman. Princeton, N.J.: Princeton University Press, 1990: 79–108.

Stephanson, Anders. "Imperial Pursuits." *Diplomatic History* 28 (fall 2004): 581–86.

Stoker, Ann. "Sexual Affronts and Racial Frontiers: European Identities and the Cultural Politics of Exclusion in Colonial Southeast Asia." *Comparative Studies in Society and History* 34 (July 1992): 514–51.

Stora, Benjamin. *Imaginaires de guerre: Algerie, Vietnam, en France et aux Etats-Unis.* Paris: Editions La Decouverte, 1997.

Tananbaum, Duane. *The Bricker Amendment Controversy: A Test of Eisenhower's Political Leadership.* Ithaca, N.Y.: Cornell University Press, 1988.

Tang, Truong Nhu. *A Vietcong Memoir.* San Diego, Calif.: Harcourt, 1985.

Tertrais, Huges. "La piastre et le fusil: Le cout de la guerre d'Indochine, 1945–1954." Paris: Comité pour l'histoire économique et fiancière de la France, 2002.

Thakur, Ramesh. *Peacekeeping in Vietnam: Canada, India, Poland, and the International Commission.* Edmonton: University of Alberta Press, 1984.

———. "Tacit Deception Reexamined: The Geneva Conference of 1954." *International Studies Quarterly* 21 (March 1982): 127–39.

Thayer, Carlyle. *War by Other Means: National Liberation and Revolution in Vietnam.* Sydney: Allen and Unwin, 1989.

Thomas, Martin. *The French Empire at War, 1940–1945.* Manchester: Manchester University Press, 1998.

———. *The French Empire between the Wars: Imperialism, Politics, and Society.* Manchester: Manchester University Press, 2005.

Thorne, Christopher. *Allies of a Kind: The United States, Britain, and the War Against Japan, 1941–1945.* New York: Oxford University Press, 1978.

Tonnesson, Stein. *Déclenchement de la guerre d'Indochine.* Paris: L'Harmattan, 1987.

———. *The Vietnamese Revolution of 1945: Roosevelt, Ho Chi Minh, and De Gaulle in a World at War.* Oslo: Sage, 1991.

Trachtenberg, Marc. *A Constructed Peace: The Making of the European Settlement, 1945–1963.* Princeton, N.J.: Princeton University Press, 1999.

Tran Van Do. *Les Guerres du Vietnam.* Paris: Vertiges Publications, 1985.

Turnball, Mary. "Britain and Vietnam 1948–1955." *War and Society* 6 (September 1988): 104–24.

Vaisse, Maurice. *La Grandeur: politique étrangère du General de Gaulle, 1958–1969.* Paris: Fayard, 1998.

Vo Nguyen Giap. *Dien Bien Phu.* Hanoi: Quan Doi Nhan Dan, 1979.

Wagnleitner, Rheinhold. *Coca-Colonization and the Cold War: The Cultural Mission of the United States after World War II.* Chapel Hill: University of North Carolina Press, 1994.

Wall, Irwin. "The French-American War over Iraq." *Brown Journal of World Affairs* 10 (winter–spring 2004): 123–39.

———. *The United States and the Making of Postwar France, 1945–1954.* Cambridge: Cambridge University Press, 1991.

Walt, Stephen. *The Origins of Alliances,* Ithaca, N.Y.: Cornell University Press, 1984.

Warner, Denis. *The Last Confucian.* New York: Macmillan, 1963.

Warner, Geoffrey. "The United States and Vietnam 1945–65: Part I: 1945–54." *International Affairs* 48 (July 1972): 379–94.

Weinstein, Franklin. *Vietnam's Unheld Elections: The Failure to Carry Out the 1956 Reunification Elections and the Effect on Hanoi's Present Outlook.* Ithaca: Cornell University Press, 1966.

Werner, Jayne, and Luu Doan Huynh, eds. *The Vietnam War: Vietnamese and American Perspectives.* New York: M. E. Sharpe, 1993.

West, Richard. *War and Peace in Vietnam.* London: Sinclair-Stevenson, 1995.

Wiesner, Louis. *Victims and Survivors: Displaced Persons and Other War Victims in Vietnam, 1954–1975.* New York: Greenwood Press, 1988.

———. "Vietnam Exodus from the North and Movement to the North, 1954–1955." *Vietnam Forum* 11 (winter–spring 1988): 214–43.

Williams, J. E. "The Colombo Conference and Communist Insurgency in South and Southeast Asia." *International Relations* 4 (May 1972): 94–107.

Williams, Philip. *French Politicians and Elections, 1951–1969.* London: Cambridge University Press, 1970.

Williams, William Appleman. *The Tragedy of American Diplomacy.* New York: Delta Books, 1962.

Woodis, Jack, ed. *Ho Chi Minh Selected Articles and Speeches, 1920–1967.* London: Lawrence and Wishart, 1969.

Young, John. "Churchill's Bid for Peace with Moscow, 1954." *History* 73 (October 1988): 425–48.

———. "Churchill, the Russians, and the Western Alliance: The Three Powers Conference at Bermuda, December 1953." *English Historical Review* 101 (October 1986): 889–912.

———. *Winston Churchill's Last Campaign: Britain and the Cold War 1951–55.* Oxford: Clarendon Press, 1996.

Young, Marilyn. *The Vietnam Wars, 1945–1990.* New York: Harper Perennial, 1991.

Zagare, Frank. "The Geneva Conference of 1954: A Case Study of Tactic Deception." *International Studies Quarterly* 23/3 (1979): 390–411.

Zagoria, Donald. *Vietnam Triangle: Moscow, Hanoi, Peking.* New York: Pegasus, 1967.

Zahniser, Marvin. *Uncertain Friendship: American-French Diplomatic Relations through the Cold War.* New York: John Wiley and Sons, 1975.

Zhai, Qiang. "China and the Geneva Conference of 1954." *China Quarterly* 129 (March 1992): 103–23.

———. *China and the Vietnam Wars, 1950–1975.* Chapel Hill: University of North Carolina Press, 2000.

Zubok, Vladislav. "Soviet Policy Aims at the Geneva Conference, 1955." In *Cold War Respite: The Geneva Summit of 1955.* Ed. Günter Bischof and Saki Dockrill. Baton Rouge: Louisiana State University Press, 2000: 55–74.

Index

Lightning Source UK Ltd.
Milton Keynes UK
UKOW02f1815170516

274450UK00001B/171/P